T0313824

SUNSHINE WAS NEVER ENOUGH

John H. M. Laslett · SUNSHINE WAS
NEVER ENOUGH

Los Angeles Workers, 1880–2010

University of California Press

Berkeley   Los Angeles   London

University of California Press, one of the most distinguished university presses in the United States,
enriches lives around the world by advancing scholar-
ship in the humanities, social sciences, and natural
sciences. Its activities are supported by the UC Press
Foundation and by philanthropic contributions from
individuals and institutions. For more information,
visit www.ucpress.edu.

University of California Press
Berkeley and Los Angeles, California

University of California Press, Ltd.
London, England

The epigraph on page vi is from the Carey
McWilliams Papers (Collection 1319), Box 85,
Folder 6 (Department of Special Collections,
Charles E. Young Research Library, University
of California, Los Angeles).

Library of Congress Cataloging-in-Publication Data

Laslett, John H. M.
    Sunshine was never enough : Los Angeles workers,
1880–2010 / John H. M. Laslett.
        p.   cm.
    Includes bibliographical references and index.
    ISBN 978-0-520-27345-0 (cloth : alk. paper) —
ISBN 978-0-520-95387-1 (ebook)
    1. Working class—California—Los Angeles—
History.   2. Labor—California—Los Angeles—
History.   3. Labor movement—California—Los
Angeles—History.   I. Title.
    HD8083.C2L37   2012
    331.09794' 940904—dc23   2012021914

Manufactured in the United States of America

22 21 20 19 18 17 16 15 14 13
10 9 8 7 6 5 4 3 2 1

In keeping with a commitment to support environ-
mentally responsible and sustainable printing practices, UC Press has printed this book on Rolland
Enviro100, a 100% post-consumer fiber paper that is
FSC certified, deinked, processed chlorine-free, and
manufactured with renewable biogas energy. It is
acid-free and EcoLogo certified.

For Lenny Potash

He who writes about Hollywood, bougainvilleas, and
the Mediterranean climate tells but half the story.

CAREY MCWILLIAMS

CONTENTS

ILLUSTRATIONS

PREFACE AND
ACKNOWLEDGMENTS

This is the first history of Southern California that links the experience of L.A.'s working men and women to the city's political history, to the occupations and lifestyles of its working-class neighborhoods, and to the complex social, economic, and cultural relationships that developed between the business community and the working class. By including catchment areas to the north, south, and east of the metropolis, it also casts its net more widely than most previous histories of the region.

The book begins in 1880, when Los Angeles was a tiny frontier town and its labor movement was insignificant. It ends in 2010, when the unions in the (now huge) city were doing quite well, but when the future of organized labor in the rest of the country was in doubt. In the 1990s and early 2000s Southern California's immigrant-based unions, such as SEIU, with its organizing campaigns among service workers, appeared to have halted the decline of the local labor movement—a development that ran counter to labor's ongoing decline in the rest of the country. But the long-term consequences of these organizing campaigns remain unclear. Will they bring the hope of a recovering labor movement to workers in Los Angeles—and perhaps to workers elsewhere in the nation? Or do they merely represent a temporary reprieve in a period of terminal decline?

As of this writing, the latter outcome seems to be more likely than the former. Until recently, the AFL-CIO's dramatic loss of support in the private sector of the economy was to some extent counterbalanced by its success among teachers, health care workers, and other government employees. But the recent recession and attacks on public sector unions have made the preservation and expansion of these successes less certain.

No one can predict the future. But even if the future of unionism in the United States looks dubious, the story that follows should nonetheless appeal to readers with a general interest in American social and economic history. This is because the narrative deals not only with unions but also with the present (and perhaps the future) problems facing the California working class as a whole. Los Angeles occupies an important niche on the Pacific Rim of the global economy. It is the biggest recipient of immigrant workers, and it remains on the cutting edge of technological change. Hence the fortunes of its workers—blue-collar and white-collar, male and female, immigrant and native-born—are intimately connected to the fortunes of workers elsewhere in the country.

The chapters that follow discuss labor politics, immigrant and nativist movements, race and gender issues, and the reactions of L.A.'s working-class families to periods of prosperity and recession as well as war and peace. Despite important differences, most of the issues are similar to those faced by workers throughout the country.

The narrative also assesses some of the historical advantages and disadvantages of migrating to the "Great Metropolis of the West." This book does not deny the many advantages of living in Southern California. But it offers a counter narrative, based on new research, to those who too easily accept the dominant interpretation of Southern California's past as an unending story of prosperity, leisure, and material success.

·   ·   ·

I first considered writing this book in the 1980s, when I served on the board of the Southern California Library, a small private repository on Vermont Avenue in South Los Angeles, which specializes in labor and radical history. My thanks go first to my old friends Sarah Cooper, Mary Tyler, and others at SCL who introduced me to its holdings. My writing was also encouraged by discussions with students in my history seminars at UCLA, and especially by my conversations with Jeff Stansbury, a talented labor organizer and journalist, who completed an excellent doctoral dissertation on L.A. labor history in 2008 but died—sadly and prematurely—soon after.

I am grateful, too, to the UCLA Institute for Research on Labor and Employment for two grants that enabled me to conduct research, and to my research assistants David Struthers and Anton Cheremukhin for their fieldwork. Numerous other colleagues and friends in the academic community, as well as inside and outside the labor movement, led me to new sources, made valuable suggestions, and read early drafts of the text. I should particularly like to thank the following individuals for their advice and assistance: Lenny Potash, Peter Olney, Goetz Wolff, Devra Weber, Mike Davis, Phil Ethington, Nelson Lichtenstein, Harold Meyerson, Michael Laslett, Sarah Laslett, Allen J. Scott, Edward Soja, Roger Waldinger, Ruth Milkman, Kent Wong, Becky Nicolaides, Steve Ross, Jan Reiff, and Eric Avila.

Thanks are also owed to the participants in the Los Angeles History Seminars, held at the Autry National Center of the American West and at the Huntington Library, for suggestions they made when I presented papers there. The same goes for my friends in the Los Angeles Study Group on Social History, who read and improved several chapters of this book. I am grateful, too, for help from the staff at various libraries and research repositories, including those at Berkeley, Stanford, Claremont Graduate School, the California State University campuses at Northridge and at Long Beach, San Francisco State University, the Huntington Library, and the Walter P. Reuther Library in Detroit. Denis Deriev was extremely helpful in preparing the manuscript for publication.

I benefited greatly from the advice of Niels Hooper, history editor at the University of California Press, and from the editing skills of Kim Hogeland, Rose Vekony, and Mary Renaud. I also would like to thank the staff at the Charles E. Young Research Library for their help and the employees of the History Department's Computer Center for their unfailing kindness and assistance.

Last, but far from least, my thanks go to my wife and fellow historian, Lois Banner, with whom I have shared many tricks of the trade.

John H. M. Laslett
Los Angeles
March 2012

Introduction

Scope and Purpose

In the summer of 2011, the *Los Angeles Times* published several letters commenting on the fading role of labor unions in American society. One critic, annoyed that local grocery workers might strike, suggested that unions were no longer relevant in the modern United States: "History has passed the unions by." A Latina correspondent disagreed, saying that her immigrant father would never have gotten his job in a metalworking shop had it not been for his trade union. Let the grocery workers strike, she said; "I will not cross a picket line."[1]

As it turned out, L.A.'s grocery workers did not strike in 2011. But this exchange illustrates the current debate over the status of organized labor in the United States. In recent years many excellent studies have been published about the rich contribution working men and women—including African Americans, Mexican Americans, and other minorities—have made to the development of Southern California.[2] But little attention has been paid to the institutions that have been their most reliable defense against unscrupulous employers—namely, their trade unions. The wages and benefits unions secure have helped U.S. workers to attain a middle-class standard of living, though that standard has declined significantly in recent decades. This book provides a historical narrative that illuminates the problems currently facing workers in the United States generally as well as in Los Angeles.

The history of the Los Angeles labor movement has been neglected partly because it is not as "sexy"—even though it has been just as essential to the city's development—as the story of Hollywood or the tales of popular sports icons, and partly because the power of the anti-union lobby before and after World War I rendered the city's unions weaker than most of those in the East and the Midwest. The history of workers and their unions has also been slighted because the AFL-CIO and other national labor organizations are currently in decline and thus command less public attention than they once did. Moreover, despite their major role as guarantors of decent wages and working conditions, unions today are viewed by much of the public as corrupt and obstructionist or as out-of-date vestiges of the 1930s New Deal.[3]

An exception to this neglect is the work of labor specialists such as Ruth Milkman, whose *L.A. Story* (2006) describes the revival of immigrant-based unionism in Los Angeles in the last two decades.[4] That revival began with the Justice for Janitors march in West L.A. in June 1990, which blossomed into a full-fledged social movement. The immigrant workers who marched demanded recognition, respect, and union contracts for the thousands of predominantly African American, Asian, and Latino employees—especially women—who worked in the city's hotels, restaurants, hospitals, and nursing homes. That social movement is still with us today, as evidenced by recent campaigns to organize Southern California's much-abused car wash workers.[5]

The 1990s union revival in Los Angeles also deserves attention because it ran counter to the decline of the AFL-CIO in other parts of the United States. Has the militancy of Southern California's embattled public employees and service workers been merely a flash in the pan? Was it simply a spin-off from nationwide immigrant demands for social justice? Or will it presage something more?

This book, which is designed for the general reader, for students, and for those with a special interest in the region's workers, answers some of these questions. It takes the reader to events and places as varied as the *Los Angeles Times* downtown office in 1890; the San Pedro waterfront in 1934; the home of Communist leader Dorothy Healey in 1952; Donald Douglas's aircraft factory in Santa Monica during World War II; and a labor demonstration in Century City in June 1990. It also incorporates much new archival research.

Modern historians have argued among themselves about the best way to write Southern California history. Some observers, pointing to the relative absence of major class conflict in L.A.'s past, suggest that the lens of race relations and racial conflict, rather than that of class, offers a clearer view of the city's development.[6] Others, pointing to the previous neglect of women's role, emphasize the important part women have played in recent labor struggles. My own approach is to suggest that the distinction between these three approaches (or analytic tools) is to some extent an artificial one, and that the social conflicts to which class, race, and gender struggles give rise should be seen not as separate spheres of activity but as inter-related sources of protest. In the Justice for Janitors campaign, for example, class and gender interests clearly played a mutually reinforcing role in the efforts of poor, female office cleaners to secure union recognition. If, in addition, the service workers happened to be Latina—as most of them were—then resentment over racial discrimination is present as an added (not a separate) source of discontent.

The book ends with some comparative reflections on the reasons for the relative weakness of the labor movement in Los Angeles during much of its history, compared to the greater strength of the movement in America's other large industrial cities.

.   .   .

Present-day Los Angeles has grown rapidly to an enormous size. Its diverse industries, sprawling neighborhoods, and complex mixture of white and minority populations present a major challenge to the social historian. The five-county megalopolis is now so large that it necessitates a selective approach to the areas, industries, and groups of workers chosen for study. A one-volume history like this book cannot claim to cover them all. But it does deal with most of the important industrial conflicts, political changes, and ethno-cultural tensions with which Southern California's employers and workers have struggled, in both the public and private sectors, between 1880 and 2010, suggesting some new interpretations along the way.[7]

The geographical framework chosen for this book, on the other hand, is broadly based. Given the extent of cross-border migration and the interdependence of labor and product markets in Mexico, Los Angeles, and Pacific Rim countries, previous historians of Southern California have defined L.A.'s catchment area too narrowly. This book examines the history of the working class in a wider context. For example, the success or failure of organizing campaigns undertaken by labor activists in L.A.'s large garment manufacturing industry were, and still are, influenced by the movement of cheap migrant labor across the Mexican border, by the level of demand for clothing in other parts of the United States, and by the ability of L.A.'s garment manufacturers to transfer their factories to Third World countries if they cannot make a profit at home.[8]

To introduce the areas, industries, and groups of workers—both native-born and immigrant—included in this study, map 1 draws a "Sixty-Mile Circle" around the city of Los Angeles, radiating out sixty miles in all directions from the downtown area. To the north, the arc of the Sixty-Mile Circle lies just south of the San Joaquin Valley, where a number of the oil fields that helped to spur the 1920s oil boom were located. In the western area of the circle is Santa Monica, where the Douglas aircraft factory employed many "Rosie the Riveters" during World War II.[9] The circle also extends east into the citrus ranches of the San Gabriel Mountains and the Pomona Valley, north of Fontana in San Bernardino County. In the south it ends just above San Diego County, which adjoins the Mexican border. In recent years some of L.A.'s electronics employees have gone back and forth between high-tech plants in the metropolis and the low-wage manufacturing facilities known as *maquiladoras* inside Mexico itself.[10]

Map 1 is also subdivided into three concentric circles—each one increasing in size—to help elucidate the development of the Southern California economy. Zone A refers to the central manufacturing district, the oldest and smallest industrial zone in downtown Los Angeles, which controlled the city's commerce from approximately 1870 through 1920. This district was dominated by the artisanal mode of production—in other words, its workers, a mixed group of native-born whites, Mexicans, Italians, and Eastern Europeans, which grew from about five thousand to twenty-five thousand over the years, used mostly hand skills at their daily tasks in the small metal foundries, tortilla bakeries, brick yards, warehouses, and garment and furniture shops that flourished on both sides of the Los Angeles River. The Hollywood movie industry, on the northern edge of this inner circle, employed more white-collar workers and skilled craft workers in a setting that was technologically more advanced than the central manufacturing district.[11]

Given the high rate of in-migration and the need for housing in Los Angeles and its outlying communities, the largest group of workers in this first period, and in several subsequent periods, were employed in the city's large construction industry, most of them under the open shop regime. Under the open shop system, which dominated the labor scene between 1890 and the mid-1930s, organized labor was too weak to make union membership a condition of employment. When the unions became stronger during and after World War II, they were able in some industries to enforce a "closed," or "union," shop, in which all workers had to belong to a union in order to get a job with a given employer or at a given workplace.

Zone B in map 1 covers the so-called old industrial suburbs. They started in the Alameda corridor (which ran south from Huntington Park to Long Beach), leapfrogged across downtown, and ended up in the eastern part of the San Fernando Valley. This manufacturing zone, which flourished between 1920 and 1980, was based on the industrial—sometimes called smokestack—mode of production.

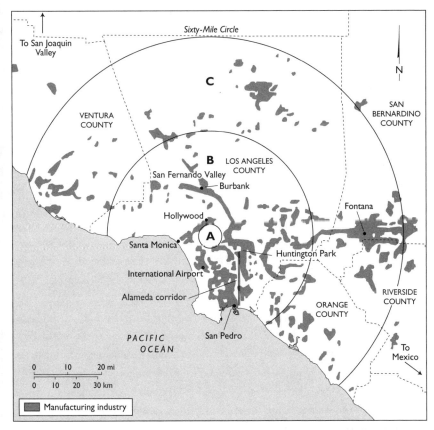

MAP 1. Visualizing the Greater Los Angeles area: The Sixty-Mile Circle. Courtesy of *The California Geographer*. Richard E. Preston, "The Changing Form and Structure of the Southern California Metropolis," *The Californian Geographer* 12 (1971): 8.

Its large-scale factories, which often enrolled more than one hundred workers under a single roof, introduced assembly-line methods of production and a more extensive division of labor. Most of L.A.'s unionized workers in this period were white, blue-collar employees who refined oil, loaded ships in San Pedro Harbor, built houses in the suburbs, assembled automobiles in Burbank or South Gate, and worked in machine shops and warehouses near the airport (later LAX) or in some other industrial community. During and after World War II, they were joined by thousands of skilled mechanics and technicians employed in the city's giant aircraft factories, and later in the aerospace and weapons production plants located farther out in the San Fernando Valley and in Orange County.[12]

In the 1930s and 1940s, the Los Angeles working class, energized by mass organizing campaigns from below and the New Deal's labor reforms from above, ended the rule of the open shop. By World War II, these workers had built an independent labor movement, which, like labor in America's other big industrial cities, benefited from the nationwide growth of both the American Federation of Labor (AFL) and the Congress of Industrial Organizations (CIO). In 1950, Los Angeles unions were strong enough in most occupations to level the playing field with the employers.

Zone C, the area in map 1 farthest from downtown, has played three separate roles in the region's history. For several generations after the Mexican-American War of 1846–1848, it was a sparsely settled hinterland inhabited by landless Indians, indigenous Mexicans, and pioneering white farmers. Its second role, which developed between 1890 and 1960, was as a mass producer of citrus and other agricultural products. After World War II, Zone C took on its third role as a mixed landscape of dormitory suburbs, autonomous cities, and industrial parks hosting electronics factories, aerospace firms, and weapons manufacturing plants.[13]

·   ·   ·

Why is this study entitled *Sunshine Was Never Enough?* The point of the title is relatively simple. It juxtaposes the popular image of Los Angeles as a new frontier of leisure, moviemaking, and—in the early days—white middle-class suburbs with the cultural and material reality many working-class families encountered when they stepped off the train at one of the city's railroad stations in the early years, or the plane at LAX in more recent decades. For years, newcomers to the city, especially those who had arrived from the plains states of the Midwest during an icy winter, were delighted by the warm sunshine, the snow-capped mountains, and the inviting beaches. (Some new arrivals still are.)

Until World War II, L.A.'s population growth continued to be dominated by white migrants from the Midwest and the border South. Many of them were able to replace their dilapidated Chicago apartments or the farm buildings they left behind in Iowa or Oklahoma with modern, two-bedroom homes. When they got jobs, however, the majority of working men and women found that their work lives in Los Angeles differed very little from the work lives they had left behind. Those who worked downtown also found that the central manufacturing district contained a higher proportion of Mexicans and other foreign-born immigrants than they had been led to believe.

The newspapers and booster pamphlets many of them had read before coming to Los Angeles promised the newcomers high wages, pleasant working conditions, and accommodating employers. But, although conditions varied, Southern California workers discovered that wages were sometimes lower than in other industrial cities, that rates of homeownership were not as high as claimed, and that many of the city's employees were—either directly or indirectly—under the thumb of the powerful and virulently anti-union Merchants and Manufacturers Association. Until World War II, in fact, Los Angeles was known as the open shop capital of the United States. In other words, many newcomers found that, contrary to myth, they had to struggle just as hard to make a living in Southern California as workers did in the East and the Midwest—and sometimes even harder.

The propaganda machine of the Los Angeles Chamber of Commerce, which distributed booster literature through railroads, shipping companies, and newspapers all over the country, was highly successful. Partly as a result of that propaganda, the city grew from a population of ten thousand in 1890 to well over two million in the 1930s, and it has continued to grow ever since. But today it is obvious to even the most casual observer that the increasingly severe racial, budgetary, environmental, and housing problems of recent years have diminished many of the city's initial advantages.

These changes have not necessarily undermined the faith of those who still believe in the Southern California way of life. Among cultural critics, however, these paradoxical elements in L.A.'s history have led to two strikingly different interpretations of its past: one dominated by "sunshine," the other by "noir."

The "sunshine" view, zealously upheld in earlier years by L.A. boosters and currently espoused by Kevin Starr in his *Americans and the California Dream* series, asserts that despite race riots, smog, crime, and irreversible sprawl, Los Angeles still retains some of its original magic. Otherwise, Starr asks, why do so many people still want to move here?[14] The "noir" view is epitomized by Mike Davis's analysis in his *City of Quartz* and *Ecology of Fear*.[15] For Davis, Los Angeles long ago lost all genuine sense of community. Instead, it has become a city of violent and repressive extremes, a Nietzschean monolith dominated by a sinister elite that flouts ecological reality, manipulates the masses, and privatizes everything in sight.

I subscribe to neither of these two schools of thought. Nor am I entirely persuaded by the "Los Angeles exceptionalism" thesis espoused earlier by Carey McWilliams and more recently by the "L.A. school" of urban historians.[16] The "sunshine" (or utopian) school is misleading because Los Angeles has now palpably lost so many of its earlier advantages. The "noir" (or dystopian) view is unconvincing because it is overdrawn and because much of what ails Los Angeles today also afflicts other large industrial cities.

Sunshine Was Never Enough acknowledges the many advantages that Southern California's climate, open spaces, and bucolic character offered to generations of newcomers. But it argues—contrary to the myth of leisure and ease—that in terms of wages, hours, and conditions on the job, the workaday world in Los Angeles differed very little historically from the workaday world in America's other industrial cities. Indeed, in some respects it has been worse. Nevertheless, L.A.'s labor movement, despite recent signs of growth, for many years lacked the strength of labor organizations in San Francisco or in industrial cities such as Chicago, Pittsburgh, or Detroit. Why?

In part, the difference was the result of specific historical circumstances like the pre–World War I open shop movement, which targeted the unions in Los Angeles more successfully than it did elsewhere. But the weakness of the labor movement in L.A. can also be attributed to a number of special (but not unique) cultural, demographic, and economic characteristics that have distinguished the region's history from that of America's other great industrial cities. These include the fragmented nature of the city's geography; the late arrival of manufacturing industry, compared to the Midwest; and the markedly different ethno-racial characteristics of the Southern California labor force. The concluding section of this book provides a more extensive analysis of these special characteristics, in light of the developments that took place in the intervening years.

· · ·

The following chapters provide a narrative history of L.A. workers from 1880 to 2010. They discuss not only the development of unions but also cultural and political questions involving race, gender, immigration, conservative politics, left-wing movements, and political economy. Part One describes the position of the city's working class between 1880 and 1929, in the heyday of the open shop. Part Two covers the period from the Great Depression to 1945, when women entered the labor force on a large scale for the first time and the unions acquired sufficient political and economic strength to defeat the open shop.

Part Three describes the impact of the Cold War and of technological and cultural change on L.A. workers as the region transitioned from an industrial to a postindustrial economy in the years following the Second World War. It also discusses the waning of the AFL-CIO and the new burst of organizing that occurred among the city's immigrant service workers in the 1990s. The book ends with a retrospective look at some of the features of Southern California society that inhibited the growth of the labor movement and points up their significance by comparing labor's fortunes in Los Angeles and in a number of other cities.

.   .   .

At no point in the history of Los Angeles was "sunshine's paradox"—the disjunction between hope and reality, between propaganda and myth, and between the interests of workers and those of their employers—more fully on display than in the evidence presented to the U.S. Commission on Industrial Relations, whose report was published in 1915. It is with the evidence of that report that Chapter One begins.

ONE · Myth versus Reality in
the Making of the Southern
California Working Class,
1880–1903

DIVERGENT OPINIONS, OR SOMETHING MORE?

In its final report in 1915, the federally appointed U.S. Commission on Industrial Relations portrayed a nation torn by industrial violence, unemployment, and social discontent. Everywhere the commissioners looked, from the New York sweatshops to the Pennsylvania steel mills, and from the southern textile towns to the western metal mines, class lines were hardening. Even the Socialists were gaining political support. Unless something was done, America seemed poised for a social revolution.[1]

Yet the commission largely exempted Los Angeles from its criticisms. Except for the October 1910 bombing of the *Los Angeles Times* building, L.A. had never experienced industrial violence of the kind that exploded in April 1914 in Ludlow, Colorado, when the Colorado National Guard, acting on behalf of coal mining companies, massacred striking coal miners and some members of their families. Los Angeles civic leaders believed that the city's Mediterranean climate, its lack of heavy industry, and its location in the middle of a seemingly endless fertile plain enabled it to avoid the pitfalls of poverty, unemployment, and class conflict.[2] Many of these beliefs still linger in people's minds today. Most residents of the city will acknowledge that Los Angeles has experienced major conflicts over race, urban sprawl, and public education. But if you tell them that it once had a strong socialist movement and experienced several episodes of serious class conflict, they will express surprise. Such ideas do not fit with the popular image of Southern California as the home of Hollywood, orange groves, plentiful opportunity, and perpetual sunshine.

The idea of Los Angeles as a consumers' paradise is attractive, and in some ways it reflects the reality of lived experience. But it is only part of the city's story. Many Angelenos today think that the city's white residents have always been middle class and that poverty has largely been confined to Mexicans and other immigrants. Yet until World War II the majority of the city's workers were native-born whites, not immigrants, and they were frequently forced to undertake strikes and other forms of protest to protect themselves against wage cuts and mistreatment by their employers.[3]

These beliefs about Los Angeles are not just the result of historical amnesia. They were deliberately cultivated by a wide array of L.A. boosters who, from the 1880s to the 1920s and beyond, promoted Southern California as a paradise for settlers from the East.[4] Members of the city's business elite continued to trumpet this belief to the U.S. Commission on Industrial Relations when its representatives visited the city in 1914. For example, General Harrison Gray Otis, the belligerent and powerful publisher and editor of the *Los Angeles Times*, began his presentation of evidence before the commission by asserting confidently that most L.A. workers were "prosperous and contented."[5]

The reason for this, said Otis, was that land in the area was cheap and readily available and that most of the white midwesterners then flooding into Southern California had brought enough savings with them to buy homes of their own.[6] In addition, Otis added, the prevalence of the open shop (meaning that L.A.'s workers were not compelled to join labor organizations as a condition of employment) limited the formation of unions, organizations that Otis believed stifled employee initiative and interfered with the employers' right to hire and fire anyone they chose.[7]

Otis's testimony before the commission was followed by that of Owen T. Rice, another L.A. booster who also hailed the virtues of the open shop. The weakness of the city's unions, Rice said, meant that any competent man could secure "a wage commensurate with his ability without the assistance of a union card."[8] Realtor Edwin Janss took the open shop argument even further. He said that the absence of unions kept labor costs down, guaranteed the profits of the real estate industry, and enabled it to build single-family homes throughout the Southland.[9]

At a time when unions are again in disrepute, some readers may find these arguments plausible. Do not unions, especially unions that enforce the closed (union) shop, raise wages to artificially high levels? Are they not often bureaucratic and corrupt? Do they not force workers to pay dues against their will? The debate about trade unionism is, of course, legitimate. But, in 1914, Southern California's open shop champions failed to mention that there was then—as there still is today—a price to be paid for the absence of unions. In that year, wages in Los Angeles were lower than in several other industrial cities; most workers lacked insurance and other union benefits; and many newcomers to the city found that, once they secured a job, they were at the mercy of unscrupulous employers.[10] None of this fit the image of a settlers' paradise.

It was not only white settlers who subscribed to the utopian image of Los Angeles. Many African Americans, seeing L.A. as a place where segregation was at first minimal, did so too. When black leaders from other parts of the country returned home after visiting the city, they often praised the superior opportunities it offered. "One never forgets Los Angeles and Pasadena," wrote W.E.B. Du Bois in *The Crisis*, official organ of the National Association for the Advancement of Colored People (NAACP), in August 1913. "The sensuous beauty of roses and orange blossoms, the air and the sunlight and the hospitality of all of its races lingers long."[11]

These early African American visitors were followed by generations of Mexicans, Japanese, and other migrants of color who were attracted to Southern California for the same reasons as whites. Mexicans first moved north across the border to escape the turmoil of the Mexican Revolution and later to look for jobs in a modern city with a reputation for opportunity and the largest Mexican community in the West. Immigrants from China and Japan, the Philippines, and Latin America did much the same.[12] In some cases, their motives barely changed over time. In 1985, for example, a woman who had moved to L.A. from El Salvador to find peace and stability explained that there was "much danger because of the rebels and the army" in her homeland—the same reason that Mexicans had used to justify moving north in 1910.[13]

USING MYTHS TO CREATE A "USABLE PAST"

It was not unusual for promoters of an ambitious American metropolis to exaggerate its advantages over those of rival cities. For years, upstart settlements on the western frontier had proclaimed themselves great cities of the future in order to attract settlers, secure political advantages, or persuade national railroads to run their tracks through town.[14] It is also true that the warm, dry climate of Los

Angeles was good for health and that land was at first plentiful and cheap. When land values rose, as they almost invariably did, the small bungalows built by the early settlers could be traded in for bigger and better houses with yards and picket fences. Once the Pacific Electric Railway (Red Car) system had been completed, and sufficient water had been diverted from the Owens River in 1913 to irrigate the San Fernando Valley, the fertile Southern California plain afforded wonderful opportunities for suburban living.[15]

But this was only part of the story. Even during the early years of the twentieth century, much in the boosters' narrative was misleading. The downside of living in Los Angeles included political corruption, primitive working conditions, land grabs by investors intent on driving up prices to make a killing, and the spread of industrial blight to large parts of the downtown area. In addition, the city's leading employers were clearly willing to exploit workers to gain an advantage for themselves.[16] While nominally supporting "industrial freedom" (an idea that in theory gave equal rights to both employer and employee), a majority of companies opposed any form of trade unionism and brazenly recruited members of the Los Angeles Police Department (LAPD) to help them keep the unions at bay. Not until the U.S. Senate hearings held by the La Follette Committee, which investigated violations of free speech and the rights of labor in the late 1930s, was the extent of their illegal practices exposed.[17]

THE GARDEN CITY

By the early years of the twentieth century, Southern California's boosters had distilled their beliefs into three main myths in order to furnish believers with a "usable past"—a past that legitimated their view of what L.A. had been and what they hoped its future would be.[18] The first myth derived from the then-fashionable "Garden City" movement, which was espoused by Progressive reformers as well as by the business elite. The idea was to perpetuate L.A.'s image as a spacious, semi-rural metropolis where most workers owned their own homes, regular work was available, and slums were few. In 1907 Protestant cleric Dan Bartlett claimed that in Southern California the "poor live in single cottages, with dividing fences and flowers in the front yard." He acknowledged that manufacturing was growing, but he argued that it would somehow develop in "the country" and that the city's factories would be hidden behind a "wealth of climbing vines and roses."[19]

The promulgation of the Garden City image distorted reality in a number of ways. First, it neglected the efforts of *Los Angeles Times* editor General Otis and other members of the business elite to turn the city into an industrial dynamo

	Los Angeles	San Francisco
Manufacturing plants	1,325	1,796
Proprietors	1,181 (5.4%)	2,544 (6.9%)
Salaried officers	919 (4.2%)	1,653 (4.5%)
Clerks	2,448 (11.2%)	4,469 (12.1%)
Wage earners	17,327 (79.2%)	28,244 (76.5%)
Total employees	21,875	36,910

SOURCE: U.S. Bureau of the Census, *Thirteenth Census of the United States, 1910*, California Supplement (Washington, D.C.: Government Printing Office, 1913), 700–713.

that would replace San Francisco as the largest manufacturing city in the West. Although the Bay Area continued to boast more factories and workshops, by 1910 L.A.'s industrial sector had grown so fast that the proportion of the city's labor force defined as wage earners, at 79.2 percent, was higher than in San Francisco, as table 1 shows.[20] By 1920 Los Angeles had outstripped San Francisco both in number of manufacturing establishments and in the number of white-collar employees.

Los Angeles boosters also exaggerated the proportion of the city's population who owned their own homes. Although the statistical evidence shows that L.A.'s rate of homeownership ranked high among U.S. cities, it did not rank high enough to justify the extravagant claims that were made for it. Table 2, which rank-orders rates of homeownership in the country's ten fastest-growing cities between 1890 and 1920, shows that whereas Los Angeles ranked fifth in 1890, it had dropped to ninth place thirty years later.

But the most misleading impression left by promulgators of the Garden City image was the idea that most of the city's residents, including its workers, lived in salubrious surroundings with no congestion, few uninhabitable buildings, and a fully developed infrastructure. While Los Angeles certainly did not possess as many slums and immigrant tenements as New York and Chicago, its downtown area contained numerous impoverished neighborhoods where Mexicans, Chinese, and Eastern European immigrants lived cheek by jowl and where rented housing, not privately owned homes, predominated.[21] In 1910, for example, 113,673 people (36 percent of the city's population), the vast majority of them working class,

TABLE 2   Percentage of homes owned in ten cities
whose population increased more than 200 percent
between 1890 and 1920

City	Percentage of homes owned, 1890	City	Percentage of homes owned, 1920
Akron	56.2	Canton	54.0
Canton	49.2	Youngstown	47.8
Youngstown	46.9	Seattle	46.3
Oakland	40.4	Akron	44.7
Los Angeles	40.0	Portland	44.6
San Antonio	37.1	Oakland	42.0
Houston	33.2	San Antonio	37.8
Portland	30.5	Dallas	36.9
Seattle	28.7	Los Angeles	34.7
Dallas	25.5	Houston	34.2

SOURCE: U.S. Bureau of the Census, *Fourteenth Census of the United States, 1920. Mortgages on Homes: A Report on the Results of the Inquiry as to the Mortgage Debt on Homes Other than Farm Homes* (Washington, D.C.: Government Printing Office, 1923), table 20.

lived in the districts shown in map 2, an area bounded by Sunset Boulevard on the north, Temple and Figueroa streets on the west, Vernon Avenue on the south, and Indiana Street on the eastern side of the city. By this time, downtown L.A. had been zoned into several discrete districts, some of them designated for industrial development, others for residences only.

By 1910 the so-called Industrial District, in the southwestern quadrant of map 2, contained over fifty major businesses. Of the households in the district, 24 percent were headed by unskilled laborers, and only 2 percent of the district's workers held white-collar jobs. Only 17 percent of the residents owned their own homes. The Commission of Immigration and Housing in California, reporting in 1915, attributed this partly to high rates of unemployment and partly to the presence of poor white Americans as well as low-income "Japanese and blacks" in the district.[22]

The most degraded of the downtown districts was the Macy Street area, located in "De Bloody Ate" (the Eighth Ward), which included much of old Sonoratown,

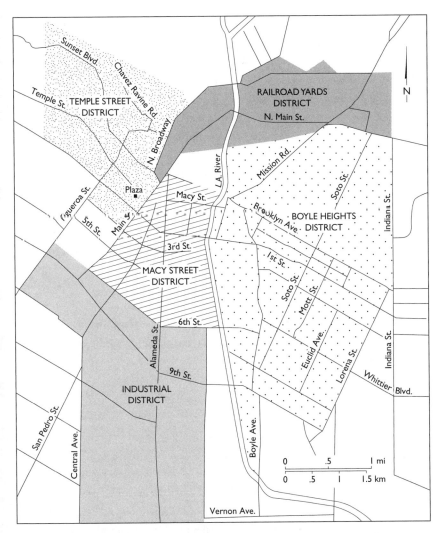

MAP 2. Downtown Los Angeles, 1910. Published in the *Los Angeles Times*, April 14, 1910.

the original Mexican area of settlement. Besides Chinatown and the decaying Plaza area, the Macy Street District contained a large slum neighborhood of some sixty-seven hundred people, who hailed from no fewer than fourteen countries. Directly contradicting the boosters' claim of "no congested districts" were the Eighth Ward's overcrowded housing courts, where dozens of poor immigrant families huddled together around refuse-strewn open spaces, sharing outside toilets and an outside water supply.[23] The 1915 commission report documented high levels of child labor, illiteracy, unemployment, and poverty in the area. Very few of the families in this district possessed any insurance or savings.[24]

Extensive unemployment in the Macy Street District, as well as in the Railroad Yards area, also contradicted the myth about the "regularity of work." More than 200 of the 688 residents in the latter neighborhood worked in nearby factories, but many of them experienced unemployment for more than three months of the year. Periodic unemployment was also endemic in the downtown garment industry, because of seasonal changes in fashion, as well as among the cannery workers and farm laborers who cultivated stretches of open land all over the Los Angeles basin. A large minority of the Mexican men in the Macy Street District were employed digging ditches or laying track for the Pacific Electric Railway.[25]

Not even the relatively attractive Temple Street District, the one district on the West Side of Los Angeles where a majority of the inhabitants were clearly middle class, lived up to the boosters' homeowning myth. Originally settled when the Temple Street cable railway opened in 1886, this neighborhood was for some years a genuine residential suburb. By 1910, however, numerous working-class German, Jewish, French, and Italian families had moved into the area. Most noteworthy, only 37 of the 294 "American" households living along Temple Street that year owned their own homes.[26]

RACIAL MIXING IN EARLY DOWNTOWN LOS ANGELES

The second myth cultivated by L.A.'s business elite was that Southern California was the "white spot of America." This phrase had several meanings, but the most popular one was that Los Angeles was a racially pure space, a city built by white Americans for white Americans. Some of the evidence already cited here shows that this assertion was misleading, but it was frequently repeated by propagandists. For example, in the 1910 edition of his popular booster tract *Land of Sunshine*, Charles Lummis reiterated his claim that "our foreign element is a few thousand Chinese and perhaps five hundred native Californians who do not speak English."[27] No one reading his account would have guessed that among the city's 319,000 residents in 1910 were 13,557 immigrants born in southern and eastern Europe as well as more than 30,000 Mexicans, Asians, and other people of color.[28]

These totals were not comparable to the hundreds of thousands of European immigrants who lived and worked in the industrial cities of the Midwest and the East, but they were significant. Nevertheless, Los Angeles civic leaders continued to promote the image of their city as a "white spot" by deliberately romanticizing—and denigrating—the role played by indigenous Mexicans, Chinese, and other subaltern groups in developing Southern California's modern infrastructure. This racially condescending image was promoted in the first "Fiesta de Los Angeles," which was held in April 1894. Invitations to Mexicans and other minority residents included a request that they dress in "native clothes." This rendered them objects of condescension instead of presenting them as they really were: urban workers with up-to-date skills who were often the victims of racial oppression.[29]

Social mixing between Anglo-Europeans and residents of color in the years before World War I was also much more extensive than contemporaries believed, throwing further doubt on the boosters' claim that L.A. was a "racially pure" white metropolis. In his *Street Meeting* (2005), Mark Wild documents numerous instances of social interactions between white families and families of color, including racial friendships between children at play and even sexual relationships between couples of different nationalities.[30] These contacts occurred most frequently around the original city Plaza. Here gossip was exchanged, friendships were made, and information was passed on about jobs and cheap places to stay, among a wide variety of people, including native-born whites, Mexican immigrants, Italian anarchists, transient farm workers, visiting tourists, and resident Chinese barrow boys.[31]

Wild also uncovered a set of interethnic social, religious, and occupational networks covering a much larger number of downtown neighborhoods than is usually supposed. The most interesting of these networks was the one established by the Church of All Nations, a Methodist congregation founded in 1918 by social reformer Reverend G. Bromley Oxnam. Though Oxnam advocated the "Americanization" of immigrants, he supported trade unions and defined education for citizenship in terms of tolerance and social justice rather than conformity to a narrow set of patriotic goals. A 1920 survey of the twenty-one-block area surrounding the Church of All Nations showed that the neighborhood was 46.5 percent "white American," 18.5 percent "Spanish/Mexican," 12.6 percent black, 7.8 percent Jewish and German, and 5.2 percent Japanese.[32]

None of this cultural mixing contradicts the fact that racial boundaries were cemented in place in much of the city by the use of housing covenants in the 1920s. Nor does it disguise the fact that many white trade unionists subscribed to the same racist ideas about L.A.'s minorities that their fellow white Angelenos held.[33] What this evidence of racial intermixing does mean, however, is that Southern California's famous "white spot" was never as "white" as its advocates claimed, and that white workers were exposed to a much wider array of intercultural contacts than has been realized.

The third myth the city's business elite promulgated in their testimony before the U.S. Commission on Industrial Relations was that most workers in Los Angeles readily accepted the open shop and were contented with their lot. Otis and his supporters provided positive evidence from their employees to support this view. But it is clear from their testimony that many of the employees had been coached beforehand in what to say. For example, Mary Horgan, a saleswoman at the A. Fusenot dry goods store, told the commission that her fellow workers were "thoroughly satisfied with the treatment they received at the hands of the owners." Her statement directly contradicted a report in the *Los Angeles Citizen* that more than a dozen saleswomen had recently struck the Fusenot store.[34]

Some of the other pro-employer testimony was genuine, and the commissioners were right to accept it at face value. But Commissioner James O'Connell (who was also president of the International Association of Machinists) invited several union leaders to testify, with enlightening results. C. F. Grow, a machinist at the Southern Pacific Railroad's repair shop, openly criticized the anti-union strategy of the Merchants and Manufacturers Association, although he did not name the organization specifically. "The prosperous condition in this city is not enjoyed by those who toil," Grow said. "We have combinations of men . . . who are very, very wealthy. They dominate all the railroad lines and everything [that] comes under their domination and power. If labor was only half so prosperous as these gentlemen, I think we would be very well satisfied."[35]

J. W. Buzzell, business agent for the Metal Trades Council, who would later become secretary of the Los Angeles Central Labor Council, was more specific. He challenged booster assertions about labor prosperity by citing state reports showing that the wages earned by metalworkers in San Francisco, Texas, and Illinois were significantly higher than those earned by metalworkers in L.A. In San Francisco, Buzzell stated, metalworkers made $5 an hour for an eight-hour day; in Texas, they made from $3.75 to $5 a day for eight hours of work. But in Los Angeles, metalworkers earned only "$2.50 a day to $4.50 a day for the same class of work." In some nonunion metal shops, Buzzell added pointedly, "they work eight hours for whatever the boss can get them to work for."[36]

Katherine Philips Edson and Frances Nacke Noel testified to the U.S. Commission on behalf of the white working women of Los Angeles. (No minority representatives were asked to give evidence.) At this early date, the number of female

Los Angeles Socialist Frances Nacke Noel and her son. Courtesy of Dr. Knox Mellon.

trade unionists in L.A. was small, no more than a few hundred garment workers, laundry employees, and waitresses. Most of the city's male unionists, caught up in the doctrine of separate spheres for men and women, were still ambivalent about organizing women, much as male unionists were all over the United States.[37]

Nevertheless, both Katherine Edson and Frances Nacke Noel were well qualified to give testimony on behalf of the city's working women. Edson, a respected leader of the statewide women's suffrage movement, had recently been appointed by Governor Hiram Johnson to the California Industrial Welfare Commission.[38] Noel, a feisty, German-born Socialist, was a protégé of Socialist Party leader Job Harriman and chairperson of the Women's Union Label League, which agitated for the sale of union-made goods.[39]

In her testimony, Edson supported Buzzell's evidence about low wages. She cited official figures showing that wages in San Francisco for most working women were significantly higher than they were in L.A. Edson also testified that in Los Angeles a higher proportion of married women went out to work than was the case in several other cities. "From our . . . experience," she added, "we do not believe that the married women are working in Los Angeles because of a so-called desire for independence, but . . . because they actually must work."[40] The reason, she said, was that the labor market in L.A. was too unstable and the level of men's pay too low for most male employees to earn a family wage.

When her turn came to give evidence, Noel also pointed to the instability of the Southern California labor market as a source of employment anxiety. She attributed the fluidity partly to the impact of the 1910 Mexican Revolution, which had drawn an increasing number of Mexican immigrants across the border to work in the city, but partly also to an oversupply of labor in Los Angeles that exerted downward pressure on wages—an oversupply created deliberately by the L.A. Chamber of Commerce, who had advertised in the East for more workers than Southern California's employers could handle.[41]

Noel also testified to the employers' growing practice of blacklisting male workers who had been on strike and also firing young female workers for joining unions. She cited the case of a group of female garment workers who, on applying to join the International Ladies Garment Workers Union (ILGWU), had promptly been dismissed by their employers. "If those girls had telephoned to the city hall to ask for the protection of their civic rights," she added, "what would our city fathers have done for them?" Nothing. And the reason that nothing would have been done to defend their union rights was that the city's favored employers had "only to press a button," as she put it, to have the girls fired. "What are we entitled to?" Noel asked the all-male panel angrily. "I ask you men to please decide that proposition from your commission work. It is a question of law and order."[42]

It is obvious from this testimony that the myth of labor contentment among much of the Los Angeles working class in the pre–World War I period was exaggerated. Despite this, the Chamber of Commerce continued to distribute misleading pamphlets all over the country about the high wages and good jobs available in Southern California. Because its reach was much greater than that of the L.A. labor press, it was able to do so without much fear of contradiction. In April 1916, the chamber declared that eastern manufacturers should open branches in Southern California because workers who migrated to Los Angeles were "pleased with what they found." They had "left behind their old labor associations" when they relocated in the "home of the open shop."[43]

FIRST MAJOR SKIRMISH:
LOS ANGELES TIMES VERSUS THE PRINTERS

In early August 1890, *Los Angeles Times* owner General Harrison Otis—a large and imposing figure with a walrus mustache—marched into the composing room of his paper on First Street and fired every member of his staff who had joined International Typographical Union Local 174. "Every man, get out of here! And get out quick!"[44] Otis's sudden burst of rage was precipitated by his employees' refusal to accept a 20 percent wage cut, which he said was necessitated by the paper's loss of advertising revenue following the collapse of a recent land boom. By dismissing his union employees, General Otis fired the first shot in a bitter campaign to transform Los Angeles from a city where trade unions were accepted to one from which they would be excluded. The resistance he met with provided further evidence that the myth of universal labor contentment was just that—a myth.

Harrison Gray Otis had not always been hostile to organized labor. In 1856, as an apprentice on the *Rock Island Courier* in Illinois, he had endorsed a union contract. Several years later, as a journeyman printer in Washington, D.C., he had become a member of the International Typographical Union. What caused Otis to change his mind? There were two basic reasons. One was his large ego and authoritarian personality, which brooked no opposition and which probably derived from his successful career as a Union officer in the Civil War, causing him to view his conflict with organized labor in military terms. Otis labeled his mansion on Wilshire Boulevard the "Bivouac" and mounted a small cannon on the roof of his automobile to dramatize his intentions.[45]

The second reason derived from Otis's passionate determination to transform Los Angeles from a rural backwater into an industrial giant that would displace San Francisco as the preeminent manufacturing city in the West. As Otis and his supporters saw it, the best way to do this was to keep labor costs low, develop a nonunion labor force, and turn the city into an exemplar of "industrial freedom." During the Gilded Age thirty years earlier, a union-free environment was a widely accepted idea. But during the Progressive period, when organized labor had greater support, it was more controversial, and Otis was somewhat exceptional among newspaper editors in pursuing it so vehemently.[46]

In theory General Otis accepted a worker's right join a union as long as the employer did not have to hire only union labor—that is, as long as the employer could avoid a closed shop (and, consequently, a stronger union). In practice, however, Otis became increasingly determined not to employ any union members at all. He was equally adamant in opposing boycotts, strikes, and any other weapons unions might use to protect the interests of their members. Strikes were "a great evil," he believed. They "disturb industry [and] beget idleness." Strikes also "harmfully affected" the loyal workingman "by throwing him out of employment, frequently against his will, annihilating his pay envelope and driving him and his family in too many cases to undeserving poverty and distress."[47]

Before he became exclusive owner of the Los Angeles Times, Otis had to move cautiously on the union front. In September 1886, for example, when Typographical Union Local 174 complained that the paper was discriminating against union members, he was forced to pay the union scale. It was only in 1890, when he had become an influential figure on the local scene, that he moved forcefully against organized labor by combining with three other newspaper editors to demand a 20 percent cut in his employees' wages. When Local 174 balked and threatened retaliatory action, his fellow editors backed down and signed a union contract. But Otis refused to do so, declaring angrily that had it not been for the "treachery" of the other newspaper editors, "we might today be complete masters of the situation."[48] Instead, he fired all of his union staff and hired a group of nonunion printers from a scab organization known as the Printers Protective Fraternity in Kansas City to run his paper.

Local 174 retaliated by striking the Times. It also obtained financial support from other printers unions and declared a consumer boycott against both the paper and the People's Store, a large downtown emporium run by D. A. Hamburger, which advertised frequently in the paper and was patronized by a working-class clientele. The boycott was effective enough to force Otis into another compromise. An 1892 agreement with Local 174 resulted in the reemployment of four union members and a promise to hire more organized printers in the future. But General Otis never implemented this promise, so the strike and the boycott were renewed, supported this time by the entire Los Angeles Central Labor Council. Angered by this response, Otis denounced the strikers as a group of "reckless and vicious radicals" who had overruled the majority of Local 174's other members.[49]

The relative effectiveness of the boycott against the Times demonstrated that, even though L.A.'s unions were still small, a spirit of community resistance to employer intransigence was available to be tapped. Otis's description of the union printers as "reckless and vicious radicals" also showed that he was now willing to employ red-baiting tactics in his disputes with labor. Incidentally, he made a poor choice in attacking the printers for their radicalism. Local 174 was composed of respectable, upwardly mobile artisans who supported the conservative wing of the

Los Angeles labor movement.[50] If Otis had intended to stigmatize the real radicals in the L.A. labor movement, he would have done better to go after the Machinists union, led by Lemanuel D. Biddle. Biddle was a skilled craftsman, an excellent speaker, and a longtime activist who ran for municipal office several times on the Socialist Party ticket.[51]

By the turn of the century, the conflict between the *Times* and Local 174 had escalated from a small, local trade dispute into a citywide struggle over the open shop, with ramifications at the state and even the national level. In October 1901, the Printing Trades Council launched a new offensive against the *Times*, and the national union sent in a new organizer, Arthur H. Hay, to try and unionize the paper. Ten thousand "I don't read the *Times*" buttons were distributed; effigies of General Otis were distributed on street corners; and the boycott of the People's Store, which was still one of the *Times*' biggest advertisers, was resumed.[52]

Equally sinister, from labor's point of view, was the entry into the dispute of the strongly anti-union Merchants and Manufacturers Association, referred to as the M&M. This organization had been founded in 1896 by a group of like-minded, conservative businessmen to boost the city's commercial and industrial enterprises. At first it steered clear of labor disputes. But not long after the M&M was founded, the *Union Labor News* criticized local firms who advertised in the conservative *Times* and followed this up with a more general attack on the anti-union views of the association. Angered by this "presumptuous critique," M&M president Niles Pease denounced labor's boycott of the *Times* as "un-American, unjust, unwarranted and illegal."[53]

Soon after this, businesses affiliated with the M&M began systematically dismissing their union employees and pressuring them to avoid all contact with labor organizers. Other businessmen started an "educational fund" to instruct employers in the evils of trade unionism. The most hostile employers hired industrial spies, enlisted the help of the LAPD to intimidate union activists, and put pressure on neutral employers to join the M&M's ranks, going so far in some cases as to persuade sympathetic banks to cut off credit to backsliders. By early in the new century, the M&M had secured the support of virtually all of L.A.'s leading shipping, lumber, oil, iron and steel, and haulage firms, as well as the citrus growers in the surrounding countryside. It was now one of the largest and most successful open shop associations in the country.[54]

Growing tensions in L.A.'s largest manufacturing firms did not mean that labor relations deteriorated all across the board. The Los Angeles labor force also included a large and growing number of white-collar workers in the sales, real estate, banking, and leisure sectors. Few of these white-collar workers wanted to be unionized. In fact, it was not until female telephone operators struck during World War I that a serious labor dispute flared up among them.[55] Employers also went out of their way to cultivate the loyalty of their white-collar employees. Their preferred method for doing this was to offer them welfare (benefit) packages containing bonuses, profit-sharing schemes, and insurance. Both Security Trust and Savings Bank of Los Angeles and Los Angeles First National Bank introduced pensions and group insurance schemes in the teens and twenties.[56] This was common practice throughout the country during this period.

Nevertheless, it was the growing number of labor stoppages in manufacturing, printing, and the garment trades that seized the headlines, especially when Otis and his allies began exercising their political muscle to elect their supporters to the Los Angeles City Council. In May 1904, for example, Otis told Henry Huntington that he would back Owen McAleer, superintendent of the Baker Iron Works, for election as L.A. mayor, "without trumpeting it in the press."[57] As it turned out, McAleer did not stand for mayor but was elected to the city council instead. Even so, Otis later expressed disappointment at his performance because, he said, McAleer had fallen under the influence of left-leaning Progressives.[58]

HENRY HUNTINGTON AND THE USES OF WELFARE CAPITALISM

The emergence of labor conflict in pre–World War I Los Angeles, and the challenge it posed to the city's image of itself, can be attributed primarily to the anti-union policies of the *Los Angeles Times* and the Merchants and Manufacturers Association. But to fully understand the dimensions of the struggle, the arrival of another major player on the scene must be considered. This was Henry E. Huntington, the nephew of Southern Pacific Railroad magnate Collis P. Huntington. Between 1901 and World War I, Henry Huntington acquired a far-flung business empire built around the Pacific Electric Railway, which turned him into an even more influential leader in the open shop campaign than General Otis.[59]

Henry Huntington was also an extensive landowner and director of numerous businesses. But his main achievement was the creation of L.A.'s interurban railroad network, which gave him a stranglehold on the city's main transportation system. His methods for developing new branch lines for his Red Cars followed a relatively simple pattern. He began by purchasing a right-of-way across an outlying area where real estate companies and settlers had already begun to move in. He then built a single hotel or lodging house at the end of the projected line to accommodate tradesmen, land agents, and construction engineers. After that, Huntington hired a mixture of laborers, soil graders, and tracklayers to build the Red Car line itself. A labor force of several hundred Mexican and Eastern European laborers would be hired and housed in labor camps, which consisted of a jumble of tents, boxcars, and shacks set up alongside the tracks. As the line moved forward, the labor camp would be dismantled and reassembled farther down the tracks.[60]

Some of these railroad labor camps, however, such as those established in Watts, Pasadena, and West Hollywood, subsequently became permanent settlements. The early establishment of these enclaves explains why some communities of color, surrounded by a sea of white suburban homes, survived even after racially restrictive housing covenants were instituted in the 1920s.[61] South Pasadena, with its African American minority, was an example. Huntington also teamed up with General Otis in several investment schemes, culminating in the giant Owens Valley water project, which opened up the San Fernando Valley to settlement. In 1902 Huntington launched the Pacific Light and Power Company, which he used to supply electricity to his Red Cars as well as to the community at large. This development, like the Owens Valley aqueduct, later became embroiled in a prolonged debate about public versus private ownership of L.A.'s municipal assets, a debate in which the unions were also involved.[62]

The first evidence of Huntington's anti-union views came with the defeat of the famous 1894 Pullman strike, which began as a boycott of Pullman railroad cars by the American Railway Union, led by future Socialist leader Eugene Debs. In Los Angeles, six ARU members were found guilty of tampering with the U.S. mails and sentenced to eighteen months in prison. The Southern Pacific refused to negotiate with the strikers. After the strike was over, Henry Huntington assured his Uncle Collis that "we have not taken an American Railway man back without his first resigning and severing his connection with the union."[63]

Huntington's anti-union views naturally appealed to General Otis, and the two men continued to correspond with each other on a wide range of topics, ranging from the profits to be earned from land investments to which Republican candidates to support for political office. A turning point in their relationship came in January 1903, when Otis and other members of the M&M joined David M. Parry's anti-union National Association of Manufacturers (NAM) and appealed to Huntington, who lived mostly in New York, for financial assistance. Huntington came up with the money, and he also donated considerable sums to the M&M and the Los Angeles branch of the virulently anti-union Citizens Alliance. Within two months of its founding in 1904, the L.A. branch of the latter organization had six thousand members, making it one of the largest affiliates in the nationwide chain of Citizens Alliances.[64]

Henry Huntington's first direct encounter with unions came in 1901 when the platform men of the Pacific Electric Railway asked for a pay raise. On this occasion he accepted a compromise settlement. But in 1902, when union organizers from San Francisco tried to organize a branch of the Amalgamated Street Railway Union in L.A., Huntington dug in his heels. He fired all of his employees who joined the fledgling union and prevented others from joining by having an LAPD officer posted on each street car, to keep union organizers from approaching them. After hiring detectives to spy on members of the Street Railway Union, Huntington rewarded his loyal employees with a 10 percent wage hike. Soon after the 1902 strike, he wrote to Otis to thank him for the *Times*' support. "I do not need to say," Huntington added, "how thoroughly my sentiments on the labor subject agree with yours."[65]

In this same letter, however, Huntington also wrote: "In time, education and good treatment will bring [U.S. workingmen] around to a right comprehension of their position."[66] This qualification suggests that, despite his display of ruthlessness in the 1902 strike, he may have been more open to cultivating good relations with his employees than some of the city's other open shop employers. In 1930 Myron Hunt, one of the architects who designed Huntington's San Marino home and library, recalled that Huntington "derived much pleasure from talks on the back platform with conductors or on the front platform with the motormen while riding into town."[67] Whatever the rationale, after the 1902 strike Pacific Electric established one of the most advanced employee welfare programs in California. Clubhouses containing libraries, restaurants, tennis courts, and even movie theaters were built at several of PE's divisional headquarters or next to its widely scattered car barns. Pacific Electric also organized an interdivisional baseball league to promote team spirit and raise company morale.[68]

Another of Huntington's employee welfare policies was the establishment of the Los Angeles Railway Recreation Association, which put on monthly dances, picnics, and "smokers" to which all of PE's employees and their spouses were invited. Like many other U.S. employers, Huntington also offered his staff a voluntary medical insurance program. In return for dues of fifty cents per month, deducted from employees' paychecks, the medical plan offered "surgical treatment, medical and surgical dressings, artificial limbs and appliances, and treatment for serious illnesses."[69] (The offer of artificial limbs was not surprising: accidents involving automobiles, pedestrians, and Huntington's Red Cars in downtown Los Angeles were quite frequent.)

However, to discourage immoral behavior, PE's medical insurance plan did not cover ailments that were considered to be anti-social in nature, such as venereal disease or injuries caused by fighting or drunkenness. Such restrictions were not, in themselves, unusual. Henry Ford's welfare benefit program in Detroit took the same approach.[70] But because of Huntington's high profile in Los Angeles, when the restrictions included in his medical benefit program became publicly known, they sparked an intense debate between workers, Progressive reformers, and employers over the purposes of social and moral reform.

"MORAL REFORM" AS A SOURCE OF CLASS TENSION

Before and after World War I, numerous evangelical Protestant ministers joined the migrant stream pouring into Los Angeles from the plains states of the Midwest. Anxious to combat social evils as well as political corruption, the ministers supported efforts by "Americanizers" and Progressive reformers to raise moral standards not only among Mexican and Eastern European immigrants but also among white working-class employees. When reformers addressed issues like slum clearance and unemployment insurance, they won the support of workers. But when they criticized saloons and other rowdy forms of public entertainment, they provoked popular anger and resentment, which added to the class tensions building in society. As the *Los Angeles Record*, a working-class paper, put it: "The saloon is the poor man's club, where he finds warmth, and light, and society, and a chance to look at the papers or play a game of cards."[71]

This negative response on the part of the *Record* did not necessarily mean that all, or even most, of L.A.'s workers opposed the regulation of drink and private clubs. What it did show, however, was their distaste for the arrogant attitude of upper-class reformers who tried to use their position at city hall to impose their values on the rest of society.

As the century came to an end, lower-class discontent continued to grow, prompted by the hostile attitude of the M&M, by Henry Huntington's refusal to provide ticket transfers from one part of his Red Car system to another (thereby increasing the cost of travel for working-class riders), and by workers' anger at the city council's decision to permit the building of noxious slaughterhouses and gasworks in the eastern parts of town.[72] At the same time, the first of many evangelical revivals swept the city, reinforcing the desire of middle-class Progressives to pursue their campaign against purveyors of vice. In 1903 the Women's Christian Temperance Union (WCTU) allied with several fundamentalist churches to propose a new city ordinance that would have abolished all the city's saloons.[73]

This time a much broader section of trade unions and workers expressed anger at the Progressives' attitude of moral superiority. The proposal to abolish saloons, the *Record* stated, was "an act of class legislation and unjust discrimination against the poor, since the rich would still be able in the restaurants and private clubs to indulge in liquor."[74] When it was put to a citywide vote, the ordinance against saloons was voted down by a large majority. In the 1902 mid-term elections, a half-hearted attempt was made by disaffected workers to unite with the city's small number of Socialists behind a United Labor Party ticket. But the unions were divided on the issue, and the ticket garnered few votes. In that year, however, fifteen new amendments to the city charter, including civil service reform and a system of direct democracy that established the initiative, referendum, and recall, were adopted by the Los Angeles electorate.[75] This marked the beginning of the high tide of Progressive reform.

At this point, the reigning city administration, led by Democratic mayor Meredith P. Snyder, had lost most of its popularity. As a result the balance of political power shifted toward the Republicans, who were divided between a conservative business element, supported by men like Huntington and Otis, and a larger group of middle-class Progressives, including various subgroups of suburbanites, skilled artisans, and white-collar workers. In the 1904 mayoral election, this moderate reform element put together a new coalition around the candidacy of Owen McAleer, the Republican councilman from the First Ward. McAleer campaigned against Huntington's efforts to secure a monopoly over the city's transportation system. He also tried to reverse the city council's decision to award the city's official printing contract to the unpopular *Los Angeles Times,* even though its bid had come in higher than that of several other papers.[76]

McAleer won the 1904 election. Soon afterward he backed a successful effort to recall Councilman J. P. Davenport, who had been instrumental in awarding the city printing contract to the *Times.* As a result of the recall, Davenport was replaced by Dr. A. D. Houghton, a liberal and a former electrician who was supported by organized labor.[77]

These political campaigns displayed the same swirl of competing interests that characterized most U.S. municipal elections at the time. Nevertheless, in the anger that working-class voters displayed over the saloon issue, over Huntington's intransigence concerning Red Car ticket transfers, and over the *Los Angeles Times* printing contract, we see signs of a distinct struggle emerging between employers and employees in which class differences played an increasingly important role.

MEXICANS SHOW THEIR METTLE:
THE "EL TRAQUE" STRIKE OF 1903

In the spring of 1903, Henry Huntington defeated a third attempt to establish a union on his Pacific Electric Railway much as he had done in previous years—by firing the strikers and refusing to meet with their representatives. Despite its brevity, this strike provides the first clear evidence of a willingness on the part of L.A.'s white trade unionists to help Mexican workers establish a union of their own. Given the ambivalent, if not outright racist, attitudes that most white workers displayed toward Mexicans during this period, the event is worth examining with some care.[78]

The story of the strike itself is quickly told. In April 1903 several hundred of PE's Mexican employees were busy laying track along Main Street in downtown L.A. They were doing the work in haste, preparing for the city's spring Fiesta and for a projected visit by President Theodore Roosevelt. On April 23 Lemanuel Biddle, who was secretary of the Central Labor Council at the time, announced the formation of a new union for the Mexican tracklayers, known as the Unión Federal Mexicanos (Mexican Federal Union), with A. N. Nieto as its executive secretary. Two days later the union claimed a membership of nine hundred tracklayers and a bank balance of nine hundred dollars, suggesting that the organization had been planned for some time. On April 25 the men asked for a wage increase. When Huntington rejected it, all the Mexican tracklayers struck, leaving about sixty Irishmen, African Americans, and a few other workers on the job. The *Los Angeles Times* immediately denounced the walkout, claiming that "radical agitators" were behind it and that they had "deluded the poor, ignorant peons employed in laying track . . . into forming a 'union'—stupid fellows, these peons, who don't know what a union is."[79]

A Pacific Electric spokesman claimed that money was not an issue in the strike and that Huntington would raise the tracklayers' wages if it were not for the presence of union agitators. Nonetheless, Huntington hired Mexican, Japanese, and African American strikebreakers from out of town to take over the tracklayers' jobs. The strikers held out for several more days. At one point they even managed to disrupt tracklaying operations and prevailed upon fifty of the strikebreakers to

Mexican tracklayers building the Pacific Electric Railway. Courtesy of Huntington Library.

lay down their tools. But Huntington responded by bringing in a large number of police from the LAPD's downtown headquarters. By April 27 full crews were again laying track, and a few days later both the strike and the Unión Federal Mexicanos collapsed. [80]

The methods employed by PE to break the 1903 tracklayers strike were by now standard practice among most of L.A.'s big employers. But the collaboration between Mexicans and white trade union leaders from the Central Labor Council (CLC) in creating the Unión Federal Mexicanos was intriguing because it was so rare. Did it occur because Socialist Lemmy Biddle happened to be secretary of the CLC at the time, or because the CLU was trying to resuscitate the white-run Amalgamated Street Railway Union and thought that organizing the Mexican tracklayers would further that goal? Or did it happen because A. N. Nieto, a talented labor organizer, happened to be in the right place at the right time?

We have no precise answers to these questions. But the *Times* was wrong to suggest that the Mexican tracklayers did not know what a union was. Granted, some of the Mexican strikebreakers that Huntington brought in from rural areas inside Mexico knew little about modern industrial life. But they were not necessarily typical of the Mexicans who stayed in the city. Most immigrant workers migrated north in stages, often in roundabout fashion. They picked up work along the way as farm laborers, metal miners, or section hands on the Santa Fe or one of the other railroads that fed into L.A.'s train depots. It is likely that during their travels they came across fellow migrants who knew about the United Mine Workers organizing campaigns in Texas, had joined a railroad workers' protest, or had met with men who worked alongside unionized metal miners in Colorado or New Mexico.[81]

Most Los Angeles employers, on the other hand, knew nothing about these traditions of cross-border solidarity. They continued to underestimate their Mexican employees, labeling them "docile and tractable" because they appeared to be willing "to work for lower wages."[82] One newspaper reporter, however, writing about the 1903 tracklayers strike, said of the Mexican workers "Their suspicions of the fairness of their employer seem easily aroused," and he noted that they were "very tenacious of their rights."[83]

By striking and joining the Unión Federal Mexicanos, the tracklayers exploded the myth of the "passivity" and "tractability" of Mexican workers. Unbeknownst to most whites, they were drawing on a tradition of resistance to oppression that went back for generations.[84] This tradition enabled the 1903 strikers to become pioneers in a century-long struggle for the rights of L.A.'s Mexicans and other immigrants of color, which has continued to this day.

COMING TO TERMS WITH REALITY

This examination of L.A.'s historical reality has exposed the set of myths, or half truths, about the city's early industrial past promulgated by the civic elite to boost the image of Los Angeles and encourage hundreds of thousands of white settlers to migrate to Southern California from the Midwest and the eastern states. The practice of exaggerating local attractions was not confined to Los Angeles; other cities did it, too. But, because of the depth and longevity of Southern California's appeal, L.A.'s utopian myths acquired a nationwide significance greater than those of any other U.S. city.

The result, until fairly recently, has been the perpetuation of a misleading narrative about Southern California's industrial history that either downplays the effects of class conflict on the city's development or ignores it altogether.[85] It would, of course, be possible to go too far in the opposite direction and claim that L.A.'s workers displayed the same level of class consciousness as their counterparts in Pittsburgh and Chicago. That too would be an exaggeration. Nevertheless, additional evidence suggests that, despite their misleading testimony to the U.S. Commission on Industrial Relations in 1914, which described harmonious labor relations, L.A.'s manufacturing elite had been aware of workers' unwillingness to accept employer domination for the preceding decade. Henry Huntington admitted as much in a letter he wrote to General Otis in December 1902: "I have been at pains to provide my men with all they could possibly need. Yet they are unwilling to settle down—something else must be done."[86]

That "something else" turned out to be Huntington's participation in building a "model factory" community outside the city limits, designed to be—or so he hoped—beyond the reach of trade union militants. In March 1903 Huntington formed a partnership with Alfred Dolge of New York to build a felt mill and factory in Alhambra, which was then in a rural area several miles outside L.A.'s city limits.[87]

Influenced in part by the Garden City movement, Huntington and Dolge hoped that by locating their new factory in the barely settled countryside, they would reduce production costs, improve productivity, and—most important—convince their employees that unions were unnecessary and that they should accept the open shop. The Alfred Dolge Manufacturing Company opened in the spring of 1904. For a time it appeared to be a commercial success. The manufacture and sale of felt slippers and piano board covers began, and three hundred workers were hired to deal with rising demand.[88] But these hopes proved to be short-lived.

Aware that the practice was unpopular with most workers, Huntington and Dolge rejected the idea of building company-owned housing for their employees. Instead, they relied on the efforts of a local Alhambra land company, in which Huntington himself had a stake, to persuade their workers to buy lots of their own and build houses on them. But the idea never took hold. By 1910 only sixty-two felt mill employees lived in Dolgeville, and only fourteen of these owned their own homes.[89]

The Dolgeville housing experiment collapsed partly because of weaknesses inherent in the Dolge Manufacturing Company itself. Equally important, however, was the unwillingness of the employees to buy property from a land company controlled by their employers. The workers preferred to continue living in cheap rental housing in downtown Los Angeles and commuting to Alhambra daily on the Red Cars. The failure of this experiment did not undermine the boosters' belief that most Los Angeles workers wanted to purchase homes of their own. What it did show, however, was that they were unwilling to commit themselves to land and housing schemes concocted by those upon whom they depended for making a living.[90]

This hostility was even more evident in the workers' response to a second, more elaborate, model industrial community, which was conceived in the aftermath of the bombing of the *Los Angeles Times* building in October 1910 and was intended, once again, to regain the loyalty of the workers after a period of industrial turmoil. This new community was the brainchild of Jared Sidney Torrance (after whom the Los Angeles suburb is named) and of shareholders from the Llewellyn Iron Works, the Union Oil and Tool Company—later Union Oil—and, once again, Henry Huntington's Pacific Electric Company.[91]

The Torrance community included a park and separate residential, civic, and industrial neighborhoods. It also contained a Red Car station for the convenience of employees, and its factories were located on the northeastern edge of the settlement, where prevailing winds blew noxious chimney smoke away from residential housing.[92] But the workers demonstrated a distinct lack of enthusiasm for buying homes in the area, even though most of them would have owned the houses themselves. By late 1914 only 170 frame and concrete houses had been purchased, out of several hundred available, and Union Oil and Tool had run short of resident employees.[93]

As in Dolgeville, a number of factors help to explain the workers' unwillingness to buy the houses, including the price of the homes and the recession of 1913–1914. But it was Frances Nacke Noel, chairperson of the local branch of the Women's Trade Union League, who identified the most important reason why so few working-class families bought houses in Torrance: they had "become wise to some of the eastern garden cities, like Pullman"—a company-owned town inside the city limits of Chicago—"and a few of those. They refused to be corralled into a territory where, when a strike breaks out, they can be surrounded by the militia or the armed guards of the companies and simply kept there."[94]

CONCLUSION

This picture of class relations in L.A.'s industrial life at the turn of the century differs markedly from the portrait the city's boosters presented in their pamphlets and in their testimony to the Commission on Industrial Relations. Contrary to their vision, pre-1914 Los Angeles was not just a privileged haven for oil speculators, real estate dealers, and white suburban retirees. As a rapidly industrializing city, it possessed a flourishing harbor, several infant movie studios, numerous metal and food-producing factories, and a large and rapidly growing construction industry that employed several thousand blue-collar workers. Inevitably, it also contained an ethnically mixed labor force and many of the same blemishes and social injustices that marred industrial cities in the East.

The workers who migrated west to take jobs in these industries, especially those who were employed in the central manufacturing district in the downtown area, were no different, in principle, from America's other industrial workers. As they developed social networks at home and at the workplace, they also developed a growing awareness of their social, cultural, and class interests and of the need to protect those interests against an increasingly aggressive business class.

The printers' struggle against the *Los Angeles Times*, the hostility of many downtown residents toward PE's control over the city's streetcar system, and the failure of "model factory" experiments to impose industrial discipline on a savvy labor force all suggested that, instead of improving, relations between L.A.'s employers and workers were growing worse. Rather than deploring this state of affairs, however, *Times* editor Harrison Gray Otis welcomed it. In October 1903 he issued a new rallying cry to the city's business leaders to reject unions altogether. Anti-picketing laws should be strengthened, strike leaders should be denied jobs, and union members should be "blacklisted and their names posted in every place of employment as dangerous men who are not to be tolerated."[95]

General Otis's appetite for industrial conflict would not go unsatisfied. In the years from 1904 to 1916, the level of class antagonism between workers and employers in the workplace, in the political arena, and in L.A.'s public life would reach greater heights than ever before.

The Open Shop Battle Intensifies, 1904–1916

THE BOMBING OF THE *LOS ANGELES TIMES* BUILDING

On the night of October 1, 1910, downtown Los Angeles was shaken by a terrifying blast. The *Los Angeles Times* building at First and Broadway had exploded. Some thought it was an earthquake. But a huge fire, fed by flammable ink, soon reduced the entire building to rubble. Giant linotype machines, heavy as railroad cars, crashed through the floor of the composing room into the basement, where they ignited the gas mains. Thousands of spectators, some in their nightclothes, stood silently, watching the disaster. By the time the smoke had cleared, twenty-one people were declared dead, including several compositors and linotype operators and two female stenographers. Dozens more were injured. The explosion occurred during the course of the most violent and extensive labor organizing campaign in the city's history to date, and it was followed by the "trial of the century," during which two leaders of the Bridge and Structural Iron Workers Union, brothers James B. McNamara and John J. McNamara, who were defended by Clarence Darrow, confessed to the bombing.[1]

The entire city—indeed, the entire country—was shocked. General Harrison Otis, owner of the *Times*, was out of town when the blast occurred. On his return, he blamed the bombing on organized labor, denouncing it in the most extreme terms. "O, you anarchistic scum! You cowardly murderers, you leeches upon honest labor, [your] hands are dripping with . . . blood."[2] The Central Labor Council,

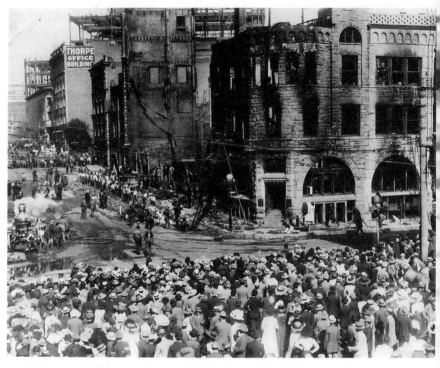

The *Los Angeles Times* building after the bombing, October 1910. Courtesy of Hearst Collection, University of Southern California, on behalf of USC Special Collections (chs-m3437).

fearing for its reputation, denied any involvement, as did the American Federation of Labor, through its president, Samuel Gompers, in Washington, D.C. After a lengthy investigation, Detective William Burns pinned the blame—correctly, it later turned out—on the two McNamara brothers, who maintained their innocence. The labor movement rallied around them, believing that they had been framed.

But on December 1, 1911, early in their trial, the McNamaras confessed to the crime. This was only four days before Los Angeles was to choose a new mayor—an election that Socialist Party candidate Job Harriman was given a good chance to win. But because he had been one of the defense lawyers at the McNamaras' trial, he lost by more than thirty thousand votes.[3]

The bombing of the *Times* building, Job Harriman's mayoral candidacy, and the strike wave that swept across the city in 1910–1911 were among the most dramatic events in Los Angeles history. How could they have happened in a city that saw itself as an oasis of calm in a turbulent world? This chapter explains how and why the social and economic tensions that had plagued the city in the preceding two decades escalated until they reached the dimensions of a class war.

STATE POWER AND THE LIMITS OF SOCIAL CONTROL

During the period of Progressive reform that preceded World War I, the first major issue to confront Los Angeles union leaders was to determine how, and to what extent, the city's public services needed to be extended and protected in order to meet the needs of its rapidly growing population. By this time, both workers and unions were keenly aware that private capitalists were eager to seize control of the city's natural resources and manipulate them to their own advantage. Labor tried, with mixed results, to prevent this from happening. That is why most workers supported public ownership and control of municipal projects like the Owens Valley water aqueduct.[4]

A majority of workers also supported the passage of new labor laws by the state legislature and new initiatives to improve the housing situation downtown. They were gratified when the mayor appointed a housing commission in 1906 to investigate slum conditions in the Macy Street District, but disappointed when the commission failed to order the removal of condemned buildings.[5] The political battle over granting streetcar franchises and the demand for a "universal transfer" that would lower costs for riders heated up again, this time with even more divisive results. Further, Henry Huntington had begun permitting freight cars to be attached to passenger trains as a cost-saving favor to his friends in the business community, even though the practice contravened state law. This led to numerous accidents on level crossings and an increase in smoke pollution.[6]

On the issue of freight cars, the unions allied with Progressive reformers in urging the city council to call the Pacific Electric Railway to account. City councilman Owen McAleer requested that the council stiffen the penalties for illegally transporting freight. But representatives of the Merchants and Manufacturers Association petitioned the council to refuse McAleer's request. This stand-off resulted in a bitter exchange of views between union representatives and employers in the Los Angeles press. The *Times,* using its customary red-baiting technique, dismissed the anti-PE agitation as "the spewings of the Socialist-Labor sons of unrest."[7] The *Los Angeles Record,* replying on behalf of the large number of working-class riders who used the Red Cars to get back and forth from work, retorted that freight transportation was "a menace to the public" and that it "served the convenience of the FEW at the expense of the MANY."[8]

As L.A.'s population grew and automobiles began to crowd the streets, the number of injuries and deaths caused by the Red Cars also rose. A study carried out by Dr. Randolph Haynes showed that PE had one of the worst safety records of any streetcar company in America. In 1904 twenty-two people were killed in streetcar accidents; in 1905 this number doubled to forty-four. In a speech in September 1905, Dr. Haynes attacked Henry Huntington for his apparent indifference to the matter: "The corporations that Mr. Huntington controls must not . . . rob us of life and inalienable rights, even though he is encouraged in this course by certain powerful newspapers, real estate men, and merchants."[9] In 1906 a city ordinance required PE to attach safety fenders to the front of its Red Cars, but it was frequently ignored.

Working-class opinion was more divided about how to improve the city's education system. The unions supported school programs that taught teenagers a sense of social responsibility. They raised no objections when the school board offered to subsidize the "Americanization programs" offered to Mexican and other foreign immigrants by the YMCA and other voluntary organizations. But they drew the line at allowing the schools to proselytize openly on behalf of capitalist values. In 1913 the school board hired a Chicago efficiency expert to teach a Mercantile Efficiency course in the city's schools. The Central Labor Council protested by urging the school board to either cancel the course or require that it include a section on the debilitating effects of factory work.[10]

Union representatives also registered their disapproval when "improving reformers" and religious leaders returned to the fight over saloon regulation and other public amusements. During this period the Progressive impulse for moral reform was at its height, and activities such as public dancing and the staging of prizefights, which were viewed by many Protestant ministers as brutal and unseemly, came under particular attack.

Early in May 1908, for example, the city council began discussing an ordinance proposed by the Sunday Rest League to limit the licensing of public dance halls. Over the next several days, representatives from the Church Federation, the Mothers Club, and the Civic Righteousness League paraded before the city council to support the proposed ordinance. Leaders from the Glass Workers Union, the Carpenters, and the German-American Liberal Alliance spoke against it. On this issue, the workers lost. In August 1908 the city council adopted the new ordinance, and Mayor Arthur Harper signed it.[11] Thenceforth police permits were required before public dances could be held; only people with written invitations could attend; no alcohol could be served; and "movies of an immoral nature" could not be shown.[12] Working-class men and women who used these facilities on their rare days off were angered by this outcome.

Working-class sports fans also lost out on the issue of prizefights, at least in public. Numerous boxing rings and other venues for staging prizefights had operated throughout L.A. for many years, especially in lower-income districts. To the consternation of conservative ministers and other upholders of moral reform, local and national fighters with names like Mince Pie Kid inspired a dedicated following, sometimes resulting in drunken street brawls following these professional matches. In July 1910 Mayor George Alexander (who by this time had replaced Harper) stepped in and persuaded the city council to pass a municipal ordinance prohibiting public prizefights and requiring that amateur fights be held in private.[13] On this occasion, however, the moral reformers did not completely prevail. The downtown Labor Temple and a number of other union halls contained entertainment facilities that were large enough to stage privately sponsored boxing matches. In January 1915, the *Citizen* boasted about a "good, clean, scientific" boxing match that had just been held in a nearby union hall.[14]

THE M&M AND THE ABUSE OF POLICE POWER

The distinction L.A. workers and their unions drew between the positive and negative uses of state power overlapped with the question of how, and to what extent, the unions should become engaged in politics. This issue became increasingly important in the early 1900s as the M&M, the Citizens Alliance, and other corporate leaders put their open shop campaign into high gear.

Not all Los Angeles employers were anti-union at the time. Family-run firms, owners of small shops, and companies where workers themselves had acquired managerial status remained neutral for the most part. Even some large companies such as Union Oil and Southern California Edison preferred a carrot-and-stick approach rather than union-bashing, in order to retain their employees' loyalty.[15] Nevertheless, by 1906 the open shop lobby had grown so strong that it was able to keep union membership in the city down to no more than about eight thousand, even though unions were growing rapidly elsewhere in the United States. Between 1904 and 1909, the city's unions lost three-quarters of the eighty-three strikes they conducted against the employers.[16]

Why did L.A.'s unions remain so weak even though the workers had strong justification for joining them? One major reason was the ability of manufacturers to import strikebreakers from outside the city and make them available through "employment bureaus," which, although nominally independent, were in reality run by the employers themselves. Companies in other U.S. cities also used this practice. But it was particularly successful in L.A. because of the proximity to the Mexican border and also because the city's employers could obtain knowledge about the state of the national labor market through the Los Angeles Chamber of Commerce, which conducted frequent booster campaigns in various parts of the country. In January 1904, for example, the *Times* urged local manufacturers to "quietly arrange with their known sources" to mobilize nonunion workers who could be "summoned at a moment's notice" from places as far away as Kansas City, Chicago, and Buffalo.[17] Local trade associations in the construction, printing, and engineering industries enhanced the effectiveness of this technique by offering financial assistance to employers who could not afford to bring in such workers themselves. According to Grace Stimson, imported strikebreakers accounted for the loss of more than a dozen strikes between 1903 and 1907 by printers, carriage and wagon makers, butcher workmen, carpenters, and longshoremen.[18]

To employ strikebreakers successfully, it was also necessary to protect them against the union pickets posted at plant gates. Employers did this by getting the LAPD to strictly enforce the city's existing picketing laws. Thus the second major reason for the success of the open shop campaign was the consolidation of the M&M's notorious alliance with the Los Angeles police force.

Before the turn of the century, the use of police to break strikes in L.A. was relatively rare. But in March 1903, Henry Huntington persuaded the LAPD to provide him with a special squad to protect the substitute workers he employed during the tracklayers' strike. When critics questioned his willingness to make officers available, Police Chief Charles Elton replied that the strikebreakers were simply exercising their right to a job and that no man should "interfere with them in the exercise of that right." The next day he revealed his pro-employer bias even more clearly when he claimed that "the large majority of the strikers would prefer being back at work."[19]

Other big employers quickly followed suit. Soon the use of city police to help break strikes became even more widespread in L.A. than it was in many other U.S. cities. In the tracklayers' strike of 1903, the LAPD managed to scare off the strikers and protect the imported scabs without using violence. But thereafter violence against labor demonstrators became increasingly common. In February 1904, for example, when fourteen members of the Culinary Workers Union, several of whom were women, struck the Spanish Grill restaurant on Olive Street downtown, a police squad attacked the female pickets and knocked several of them down. The *Record* protested indignantly that the "ladies [were] insulted" and their "eardrums . . . nearly split." But the *Times* retorted that the "union hoodlums" (union pickets) who tried to block access to the restaurant had been taught that "all who pass by have rights that must be respected."[20]

Larger and more serious strikes drew larger and more serious employer responses. In January 1906, the long-simmering struggle by the printers union to break General Otis's iron grip over the *Times*—a struggle that had now become symbolic of "open shop Los Angeles" throughout the entire country—entered a new phase when Local 174, with the support of the pressmen and machine feeders, announced a new strike and boycott against the paper. Their demands included union recognition and the eight-hour day. The International Typographical Union (ITU) provided strike benefits, and printers' locals from all over California offered financial help. In response, members of an employers' trade group, the Employing Printers Association, in over fifty cities sent money to the *Times;* L.A.'s downtown area was plastered with anti-union posters; and business leaders from the M&M got the police commission to provide "special police" to protect strikebreakers imported from the East.[21]

Organized labor was furious. In early April, Lemmy Biddle and James Roche, representing the Central Labor Council, appeared before the police commission to demand that it withdraw the "hated specials," but it refused to do so. The strikers held out as long as they could, but in October 1906 the ITU stopped sending money, other funds dried up, and the printers strike collapsed without winning the eight-hour day or recognition of the union. The boycott of the *Times* continued, but at a much reduced level. In the months that followed, the M&M raised a war chest of its own, amounting to almost one hundred thousand dollars, and virtually dared Local 174 to strike the *Times* again, which the union sensibly refused to do.[22]

Even more serious was the loss of a Teamsters strike in 1907. With five hundred members, the Teamsters local had been one of the strongest unions in the city. The Teamsters' contract with L.A.'s six major trucking companies, which was due to expire on April 30, 1907, provided for a union shop, a graduated wage scale from two dollars to three dollars a day, and overtime pay. The union asked for a fifty-cent wage increase in its new contract. Since freight rates—and the employers' profit margins—had recently gone up, the wagon drivers had good reason to believe that their demands would be met. But the M&M, backed by shipping companies from San Pedro Harbor, who employed teamsters to move imported goods, persuaded the Draymen's Association (the employers' association in the trade) not to renew its union contract, but to offer a twenty-five-cent increase if the Teamsters local gave up its contract and reverted to the open shop. The Teamsters refused and struck instead. The M&M raised a large war chest, hired deputy sheriffs to supplement those provided by the LAPD, and posted notices at freight haulage terminals in the harbor and elsewhere stating that the union was no longer recognized. Unfortunately, the L.A. Teamsters had chosen this time to withdraw from the International Brotherhood of Teamsters. Lacking external support, the union went down to a crushing defeat, losing all but fifty of its members and remaining impotent for years to come.[23]

Several other major strikes were also lost in 1907–1908. The American Federation of Labor (AFL), recognizing the gravity of the situation, sent a full time organizer out from Washington to try and repair the damage. But he could do little, in part because of the financial panic of 1907, which resulted in increased unemployment. Soon after the Teamsters' defeat, Harrison Otis triumphantly declared in the *Times* that "right-thinking employers had won the battle for 'industrial freedom' in Los Angeles."[24] Historian Grace Stimson agreed with this judgment. The loss of the Teamsters strike, she wrote, meant that "the open shop had within the space of ten days won a victory which clinched its hold over the city of Los Angeles."[25]

ARGUING ABOUT POLITICS, 1902–1906

Given these developments, the question of labor's role in politics assumed greater urgency. It seemed clear that the only effective way of combating the open shop lobby was for the unions to acquire sufficient political power to compete with it on equal terms. But how was this to be done? The attempt to unite trade unionists and radicals behind a Union Labor Party in 1902 garnered only a few hundred votes. The small group of Socialists who endorsed this effort also ran into trouble with ideological purists in the recently founded Socialist Party of America who rejected the idea of a union-based labor party—as opposed to a purely socialist one—even though Job Harriman, L.A.'s best-known Socialist, was in favor of the idea.[26]

Despite the failure of the labor party idea in 1902, most trade union leaders recognized that some form of political coalition was necessary if they were to have any chance of success. So in February 1906, despite the misgivings of the far left, a group of trade union activists and sympathizers led by Lemanuel Biddle of the Machinists and Arthur Hay of the ITU established a new political group, the Public Ownership Party (POP). The party adopted a platform that included municipal ownership of the city's gas, electric, and phone companies; direct legislation (under which voters could initiate and adopt legislation themselves); free school books; the eight-hour workday; union pay rates on public works projects; and—perhaps most important—an end to the importation of scab labor. POP's sponsors hoped that this mixture of civic and labor demands would attract left-wing Progressives as well as dissatisfied elements from the working class.[27] The party nominated Stanley Wilson, a gifted speaker and editor of the *Citizen* (the official organ of the Central Labor Council), to run for mayor.

But because of internal disagreements, POP failed to attract the ideologues on the left wing of the Socialist Party. Instead, the "impossibilists," as left-wing Socialists were sometimes called, denounced the POP as "class collaborationist" and ran a ticket of their own. The net result was that neither left-wing party even came close to winning the mayoralty. Instead, the Democratic candidate, Arthur Harper, was elected with 33 percent of the vote. None of the Public Ownership Party candidates for city council were elected either, although they did quite well in the Seventh, Eighth, and Ninth wards, where the bulk of working-class voters lived.[28] This disappointing result brought the unions no nearer to their aim of weakening the grip of the open shop.

PROGRESSIVES SHOW THEIR HAND, 1906–1908

Over the next several years, no single event turned workers' hostility toward the city's open shop employers into open revolt. Rather, a combination of several new developments finally brought matters to a head. Disillusionment with the conservative wing of the Progressive movement came first.

As a result of the 1906 municipal elections, several Progressives were elected to the Los Angeles City Council. One of their first acts was to propose that the Board of Public Works cut the wages of city employees in the name of fiscal restraint. This proposal was eventually withdrawn, but not before it drew an angry response from Fred C. Wheeler, the Central Labor Council's official spokesman, who complained bitterly that the proposed cuts threatened to deprive municipal workers of a significant proportion of their income. "What chance have the common people got when their representative lawmakers vote to rob them?"[29]

The wage reduction proposals seemed even more insensitive in light of the Panic of 1907, which had increased unemployment in several industries, most notably construction. In turn, rising unemployment increased the number of vagrants on the city streets, and the LAPD dealt harshly with them. Almost every night, police squads ranged through the L.A. riverbed, the downtown slums, and the railroad yards, arresting the homeless and the unemployed. The *Record* noted sarcastically that while being idle and wealthy was not an offense, "when allied with poverty [idleness] becomes a crime."[30]

Lower-class citizens also resented the double standard used when Henry Huntington failed to appear in court to answer charges that Pacific Electric had ignored the 1906 law requiring safety fenders on the Red Cars. According to one source, on the day Huntington was supposed to appear in court, his secretary phoned the judge to say that he was too busy to turn up. This, the *Record* observed angrily, was "class justice." At the same time, dozens of ordinary people were being arrested by the LAPD on trivial charges such as failing to hitch their horses properly when shopping downtown or picking flowers in Eastlake Park.[31]

The failure to arrest Huntington was followed by an even more disturbing incident. The police commission, worried by the recent founding of a Los Angeles branch of the Industrial Workers of the World (IWW, the Wobblies), rescinded the Socialist Party's permit to hold public meetings in the downtown Plaza. The party refused to take this lying down. At an illegal Plaza meeting, the Reverend George Woodbey, an African American Socialist, asked a nearby policeman whether he realized that, by banning meetings in the Plaza, the LAPD was violating the constitutional right of free speech. The police squad promptly arrested Woodbey and smashed up his soapbox. Undaunted, the demonstrators marched down Spring Street, calling the police "Cossacks" and singing "La Marseillaise."[32]

In addition to continuing their meetings, the Socialists took a page out of the IWW's book by insisting on lengthy jury trials for their arrestees. Especially embarrassing for the authorities was the large number of women Socialists who made use of this tactic. Aware that their presence in jail caused problems for the exclusively male LAPD, a number of arrested women refused bail and sat down on their cell floors. In September 1908 the Central Labor Council, intent on exploiting this event for publicity purposes, attacked the police commission for allowing vulnerable women to be "dragged by ruffian-looking police to the pen of criminals and exposed to foul air, fouler language, lice and rats!"[33] Faced by an overburdened court system and overcrowded jails, the city council brokered a truce with the Socialist Party. In return for restoring the permit to hold meetings in the Plaza, the Socialists agreed not to demonstrate in the white-collar districts of town.[34] But this compromise achieved little. The peremptory arrest of vagrants resumed, the importation of strikebreakers continued, and the employers' determination to destroy the trade union movement remained as transparent as ever.

The Progressive movement, both nationally and locally, in theory stood for nonpartisanship and clean government. But when representatives of the L.A. Central Labor Council turned to the Progressives for support, they found to their dismay that civic leaders who were supposed to exemplify morality in government in practice supported the police and the business elite against labor. Their anti-union stance was all the more disconcerting since on other social issues, such as protective legislation for workers and women's suffrage, the views of left-wing Progressives like Dr. Randolph Haynes were quite similar to those of moderate Socialists like Job Harriman.[35]

Trade unionists were even more shocked when several Progressive members of the Los Angeles City Council, who were thought to be pro-labor, not only refused to support the Teamsters strike of May 1907 but actively opposed it. On May 2, 1907, the *Los Angeles Express,* the Progressives' main newspaper, warned the Teamsters not to strike because it might interfere with plans for the city's annual Fiesta.[36] Even more disparaging were the paper's comments on the Teamsters strike. "We of the southland," the *Express* stated haughtily, "take a certain pride in the fact that we are not ground down under the heel of labor union tyranny as is our unfortunate sister city of the north," meaning San Francisco. "Here, *we adhere to the principle of the open shop* [my italics] and do not tolerate—and never will—that class of wild-eyed, strife-breeding, labor leaders."[37]

Not all Progressives shared these anti-union views. It is now generally accepted that the Progressive movement represented a broad range of opinions, including those of clubwomen, African American ministers, and others whose views on reform differed widely.[38] But after this attack on the Teamsters, working-class trust in the willingness and ability of the Progressives to rule the city evenhandedly rapidly diminished. Instead of trying to placate elitist reformers in the professional middle class, radical elements in the labor movement began to strengthen their relations with the Los Angeles Socialists. The result was heightened citywide tension, increased polarization of the electorate, and a hardening of class lines.

CRISIS THREATENED: SOCIALISTS, AQUEDUCT POLITICS, AND THE ELECTION OF 1909

The new political situation created by this shift in attitudes was brought to a head by an unexpected move to recall Democratic mayor Arthur Harper by referendum vote in March 1909. Democrats in the working-class Eighth and Ninth wards had often been suspected of cozying up to downtown liquor and gambling interests, and a Grand Jury investigation revealed that members of the mayor's police commission had repeatedly visited the red-light district. Mayor Harper had also improperly appointed one of his political cronies to the Board of Public Works, which was responsible for overseeing the Owens River aqueduct project.[39]

The resultant public outcry forced Harper to resign, and a special election was held to pick his successor. That election pitted Fred C. Wheeler—leader of the Carpenters Union and an avowed Socialist—against conservative Progressive George Alexander in a head-to-head contest for the mayor's seat. The elderly Alexander, who had served two terms as a county supervisor, won this election, though his margin of victory was only seventeen hundred votes. Alexander carried the West Side and most of the outlying suburbs. But Wheeler carried all five of the working-class wards downtown and on the East Side of the city.[40] Wheeler's strong showing marked the opening of a period of social tension and class conflict unprecedented in Los Angeles history.

What accounted for Fred Wheeler's political strength? First, it was clear that downtown workers and small property owners took satisfaction in expressing their feelings of pent-up anger against the LAPD and the authorities in city hall. Second, the Socialists and the unions had, for the time being, put aside their ideological differences. In 1909 the small number of Marxists and "impossibilists" in the L.A. socialist movement agreed not to run a separate candidate of their own.[41]

Third, voter support for Wheeler was bolstered by the fact that under his leadership the Central Labor Council (CLC) had broadened its appeal among Mexican and other minority workers as well as among women workers. In 1907 the CLC had established union locals among building laborers, junk dealers, and fruit and vegetable peddlers—all occupations typically dominated by people of color. Socialist unions like the International Ladies Garment Workers Union had also attempted to reach out to minority garment workers both through organizing campaigns and support for jailed Mexican liberals.[42] These outreach efforts did not mean that racial prejudice among skilled white craftsmen had altogether disappeared: white workers still complained about "Negro intruders" and the influx of *"cholo"* labor from south of the border; and in 1907, during a period of heightened anti-Asian sentiment, the *Record* (and even the *Citizen*) printed several nasty attacks on Japanese immigrants.[43] Nevertheless, these halting, early efforts at racial accommodation appeared to boost Wheeler's 1909 vote, if only slightly.

In addition, in 1908, prodded by the indefatigable Frances Nacke Noel and her

Building channels for the Owens Valley aqueduct project. From the Collection of Los Angeles Department of Water and Power.

"sisters movement" (an informal name for a group of activist women), the Central Labor Council had begun to devote increased attention to female workers. It established new union locals among laundry workers, waitresses, and telephone operators. The CLC also tried to extend its reach into the female domain of the public schools, but its efforts were stymied when the school board hastily raised teachers' salaries in order to keep the unions out.

Fourth, the most explosive question raised by Fred Wheeler during his campaign—and the one that probably won him the most additional votes—concerned the troubled state of the Owens Valley water project. Two issues drew particular attention. One was the employment status of the three thousand laborers, tunnelers, engineers, and crane operators who were extending the aqueduct channel across the long, dry, mountainous route from Mono Lake to the San Fernando Valley. Technically, the difficult working conditions faced by the aqueduct labor force were of immediate concern only to union members and their sympathizers. But because of the financial panic of 1907, several thousand nonunion tunnelers and mine diggers from the gold and silver mines of Nevada and Colorado had been brought in, making it virtually impossible for L.A.'s weak unions to exert any control over the labor practices of the Board of Public Works, which was responsible for hiring the workers.[44]

Many Los Angeles citizens also feared that, once the aqueduct was finished, land speculators and profiteers would sell L.A.'s water rights to private contractors or else divert the flow to their own landholdings in the San Fernando Valley instead of directing it to the city's main water supply.[45] In 1905, just before the aqueduct project was announced, the *Los Angeles Examiner* exposed the fact that a land syndicate had bought up 47,500 acres of San Fernando Valley land. The syndicate included some of the biggest names in L.A. public life, among them Harrison Gray Otis, Harry Chandler (Otis's son-in-law), Henry E. Huntington, E. H. Harriman, E. T. Earl, and L. C. Brand, who was president of the giant Title Insurance and Trust Company.[46] In his 1909 campaign speeches, Fred Wheeler drew applause for making this point.[47]

Other land speculators also bought dry tracts of land in the valley. Some of them sold their newly purchased lots to farmers and settlers straightaway. But others held onto their property, increasing suspicions that the aqueduct had been deliberately designed to terminate in the valley rather than in L.A. itself, so that speculators would make a killing once their lands were irrigated. To the public's anger, a subsequent inquiry showed that many of these fears were justified.[48]

CRISIS REACHED: THE TIMES BOMBING AND THE ELECTION OF 1911

Following the closely contested recall election of March 1909, December's regular mayoral election resulted in the reelection of Mayor Alexander. Hoping for a friendlier hearing from his Progressive administration, the unions opened a new front in their battle against the open shop by starting a campaign to organize more workers. The story of the struggle that unfolded, which includes the *Los Angeles Times* bombing, Job Harriman's surprising success as a Socialist Party candidate for mayor in the October 1911 primary, and the dramatic confessions of the McNamara brothers, has been told before.[49] But the significance of this two-year episode, which has usually been seen as an easy victory for the open shop movement, has been misunderstood.

According to the account by Grace Stimson, labor's organizing campaign of 1910–1911 was conceived and sustained not by the city's own unions, but by the assistance provided by the leaders of the much stronger San Francisco labor movement. The campaign was supposedly confined largely to metalworkers, and the employers were said to have defeated it relatively easily through the use of police-protected strikebreakers, court injunctions, and the financial support of the M&M. This is an oversimplification. So, too, is the argument that the McNamara broth-

Job Harriman, Socialist candidate
for mayor of Los Angeles, 1911.
Courtesy of Library of Congress,
Prints and Photographs Division,
photo no. C-B2-1238-8.

ers' confessions to the *Times* bombing guaranteed the defeat of an already weakened labor movement and helped to ensure the success of conservative politics in
Los Angeles through World War I and beyond.[50]

This traditional account demands scrutiny, beginning with the political campaign waged between Progressive mayor George Alexander and Socialist Party
candidate Job Harriman in the 1911 mayoral election. Acting as a moderate who
straddled the conservative and radical wings of the Progressive movement,
Alexander made a number of improvements in L.A.'s civic infrastructure in his
first term in office. But by the time he ran for reelection and Harriman challenged
him in the primary election of October 31, 1911, Alexander had moved to the right.
He was endorsed for reelection not only by the nonpartisan Committee of 100—
a loose coalition of middle-class professionals—but by virtually everyone who
was worried about the possibility of a Socialist victory. They included old-style
Democrats, backers of the independent mayoral candidate W. C. Mushet, right-
wing Republicans, conservative Progressives, and the entire downtown business
elite.[51]

Building on the longstanding grievances of L.A.'s workers and small business
owners who resented the power of the M&M and its allies, Harriman won the

primary election by the surprisingly large margin of 20,183 votes to 16,790 for incumbent Mayor Alexander. This result panicked the Alexander camp and gave Harriman's radical coalition good reason to believe that he would win the run-off and become the next mayor of Los Angeles.[52]

Four days before the December 5 run-off, however, James McNamara shocked the city (and the nation) by pleading guilty to bombing the *Los Angeles Times* building, while his brother John pled guilty to another bombing.[53] There is no doubt that Harriman's decision to help defend the McNamara brothers in their trial for the *Times* bombing discredited him before much of the public and contributed to his defeat in the December 5 general election, which Mayor Alexander won by a margin of 85,739 votes to 51,796 votes.[54] Harriman himself stated that anger and disgust at the McNamaras' confessions of guilt contributed to his loss. "I cannot describe how keenly I felt the blow," he stated after it was over. "I was convinced that [the confessions] would defeat us."[55]

Despite being tainted as a defense lawyer for the McNamaras, Harriman still obtained a large majority of working-class votes downtown and in the minority districts on the East Side. The persistence of this electoral loyalty suggests that the McNamara confessions did not deliver such a crushing blow to Harriman as conventional wisdom assumes. The growing power and influence of William Randolph Hearst's pro-union *Los Angeles Examiner*, which had L.A.'s second-largest circulation by 1910, also suggests the strength of the anti-Otis constituency. It explains in part how Los Angeles could simultaneously be a crucible for socialist politics and the unofficial headquarters for arch-conservative capitalism.[56] In fact, a careful examination identifies additional reasons that help to explain Job Harriman's defeat.

One factor was the red-scare tactics employed against Harriman by his opponents after the disclosure that the McNamara brothers were members of the Bridge and Structural Iron Workers Union. These tactics were hardly surprising. During the five weeks between the primary election and the run-off, the conservative coalition united behind Mayor Alexander did its best to panic the electorate, declaring that Los Angeles must be saved from the excesses of socialism. Newspaper headlines urged workers and new home buyers to "Protect Your Homes" and "Save Your Jobs."[57] General Otis, writing in the *Times*, stated that "the election of Harriman would result in an orgy of evil, in a season of stagnation for business, in the legalizing of picketings and boycotts . . . in hunger in the homes, and rioting in the highways."[58]

The use of such tactics was not, of course, unique to Los Angeles. The years between 1910 and 1914 were the high point of electoral success for the Socialist

Party of America throughout the United States, and similar attacks were made against Socialist candidates running for office in places as far apart as Milwaukee, Wisconsin, and Berkeley, California.[59] But given the atmosphere of menace generated by the *Times* bombing and the symbolic importance attached to suburban property values by Los Angeles residents, the remarkable thing was not so much that Harriman did not win the December 5 election, but that he did so well.

Female voters were also said to have contributed disproportionately to Harriman's defeat. Women secured the right to vote in California during the five-week period that fell between the 1911 primary election and the run-off, so immediately after the primary both sides in the campaign made the registration of female voters their major concern. Katherine Edson predicted that female voters were more likely to support the "safe middle ground" inhabited by Mayor Alexander and the statewide Progressive movement, which was now reaching its peak under the leadership of Governor Hiram Johnson in Sacramento, than they were to vote for the radical Harriman.[60]

On this point, it appears that Edson's prediction was justified. "Unfortunately," the *Los Angeles Citizen* reported, "the California suffragists are largely composed of society women who would rather be . . . voteless than join hands with wage workers."[61] The Socialist-labor coalition did its best to counter this argument by feverishly registering women in the working-class districts of Los Angeles. But it appears that the Harriman campaign was outmaneuvered. According to one source, when the electoral register closed on November 9, the Harriman camp had added only 28,000 women voters to the rolls, whereas the Alexander precincts had added 54,000.[62]

But the most important reason for Harriman's defeat was the opposition's tactic of establishing a fusion coalition of the Committee of 100, right-wing Progressives, and representatives of both the major parties to oppose him. The use of this fusion tactic, again, was not unique to Los Angeles. Between 1908 and 1912, Democrats and Republicans in several midwestern states combined at election time to deny victory to Socialist candidates.[63] Nevertheless, it was symptomatic of rising class tensions that the *California Social Democrat*, while regretting Harriman's defeat, actually welcomed the fusing of the Democrats, the Progressives, and the Republicans against him as a recognition of the realities of class conflict. "There was no middle ground," the paper said. "Those who stood with the Socialists stood solidly with them; those who stood with capitalism stood solidly there. The fusion was complete and it is just what the Socialists have sought all the time. It was a two-handed fight."[64]

"IT'S CLASS WAR, WITHOUT A DOUBT":
THE 1910–1911 STRIKE WAVE

Clearly, the reasons for Harriman's 1911 defeat were more complex than is usually recognized. In addition, there are several other respects in which the traditional account of the events of 1910–1911 is lacking—and in fact is misleading. For example, a careful review of the evidence suggests that, although the McNamara confessions did help to undermine Harriman's political bid for mayor, they did not weaken the strike wave that engulfed Los Angeles throughout 1910 and 1911. That strike wave, along with other signs of protest, revealed a city—and a region—that possessed a more self-aware working class, and was far more polarized along class lines, than is generally acknowledged.

The depth of this class antagonism became apparent soon after Mayor George Alexander was elected to his first full term in December 1909. At first his administration appeared to be evenhanded, balancing the appointment of numerous wealthy professionals to city commissions with the selection of Ben Robinson, a former president of Typographical Union Local 174, for a job on the fire commission. But shortly after taking office, the city council, with a majority of Progressives, passed a new licensing law that made it harder for working-class clubs downtown to secure liquor licenses than for middle-class social clubs on the city's West Side to do so. The LAPD also went unchecked when it returned to its aggressive, anti-working-class behavior. The police paddy wagons that patrolled the downtown streets, the *Record* observed bitterly in November 1910, habitually bypassed drunks in "fifty-dollar overcoats" and swept up those whose overalls and calloused hands betrayed their working-class background.[65]

The organizing drive the unions started in the spring of 1910, which continued on and off for fourteen months, precipitated the most clear-cut clash between labor and capital in Los Angeles history. Some historians attribute the start of this campaign to the June 1910 decision by San Francisco labor leaders to come to the aid of their L.A. counterparts. In reality the Los Angeles campaign began two months earlier, when Henry Huntington's Mexican tracklayers again struck for higher wages. This was followed in May 1910 by a leather workers' strike and by the brewery workers' demand for an all-union shop. The result was a major Brewery Union campaign against the city's four major brewing companies and a successful boycott against saloons that sold "unfair beer."[66]

A crisis point was reached on June 1, 1910, when fifteen hundred Los Angeles metalworkers, who were paid only $2.25 for a ten-hour day and were prevented from unionizing by their employers, downed tools in the largest strike of skilled workers that Los Angeles had yet seen. San Francisco's Metal Trades Council sent several organizers to help, but they did so only *after* the strike had already begun to show signs of success, not in preparation for it. The stoppage aimed to raise the wages of the city's metalworkers to the union scale that prevailed in the Bay Area: $3.50 for eight hours' work.[67] L.A.'s metal employers resisted and went to court to secure injunctions against the strikers. They even prevailed upon Mayor Alexander to declare that the LAPD would henceforth arrest any pickets blocking the streets.

But the L.A. strikers refused to obey the court injunctions. Instead, they continued their picketing tactics, most notably against the fiercely anti-union Llewellyn Iron Works, resulting in a growing number of violent clashes with the LAPD.[68] Frustrated by this show of resistance, Earl Rogers (attorney for the M&M) and Wheaton Gray (representing the Metal Founders Association) proposed a sweeping new anti-picketing ordinance that not only permitted scabs to cross picket lines but even prevented would-be picketers from speaking in a "loud or unusual" voice.[69] After a bitter debate, the Progressive city council adopted the ordinance on July 16, 1910, and Mayor Alexander promptly signed it. Within two weeks, the LAPD had arrested fifty-seven pickets involved in the brewery and metalworkers strikes; in less than two months, it had arrested several hundred more.[70] The *Los Angeles Times* was of course delighted by this turn of events.[71] But the thousands of metalworkers, brewery workers, railroad machinists, tailors, and other strikers in the downtown area held firm.

By the end of September 1910—a full two and a half months after the anti-picketing ordinance had been passed—the strike wave, instead of subsiding, had expanded to include a number of additional occupations, and a General Campaign Strike Committee had been established to spread the union message. Supported by trade unionists in San Francisco and elsewhere, the strike committee raised more than $330,000, a huge sum in those days. By the end of the year, the Los Angeles Central Labor Council had actually *grown* from sixty-two affiliates with 6,000 members to eighty-five unions with more than 9,500 dues-paying trade unionists, a development ignored by most traditional accounts.[72]

There is no doubt that the *Times* bombing dealt a major blow to this strike wave, particularly to the morale of the nearly two thousand metalworkers who had been trying to persuade the local foundries to recognize their unions. A number of small metal shops agreed to the eight-hour day. But later, after the McNamaras' confessions, the larger companies refused to grant union recognition, and they succeeded in forcing their employees back to work without any concessions. Many of the picketers were blacklisted, and others were driven out of town. As far as the Los Angeles metal industry was concerned, the open shop did indeed win a major triumph during these two years.[73]

However, careful examination of union sources shows that, although the L.A. metal strike collapsed at the end of 1910, by no means were all of the other strikes lost. To the contrary, the brewery workers' walkout ended in victory for the bottlers and beer drivers at the Maier and Zobelein, Mathie, and Los Angeles Brewing companies, a success that included an agreement to establish the union shop, an almost unheard-of accomplishment in Los Angeles at this time.[74] In 1912, Plumbers Local 78 also won the union shop, Local 61 of the Brotherhood of Electrical Workers secured a wage increase, and Tailors Local 81 successfully organized five new downtown garment manufacturers. In addition, the Building Trades Council (BTC) won a strike that allowed it to enforce its working card system, under which the council sometimes gave nonunion tradesmen permission to work on unionized building sites. For the first time in the city's history, the settlement that followed gave carpenters, plumbers, and other workers affiliated with the BTC the right to work with other union members only. In other words, even if the open shop continued to prevail in a majority of trades, the unions in both the brewing industry and the building trades (the city's biggest employer) were now in a stronger position than they had been before.[75]

Nor was this all. At the annual convention of the California State Federation of Labor, held in San Diego in October 1912, W. A. Engle of the Musicians Union (another trade union Socialist, and an ex-president of the L.A. Central Labor Council) reported that twenty new local unions in Los Angeles had been added to the Central Labor Council between June 1910 and December 1911 and that, despite the *Times* bombing, overall union membership in the city had risen to more than fourteen thousand. Engle added that even in the face of the enormous pressures exerted by the M&M and the anti-union press, the Los Angeles labor movement had consolidated itself into a "solid, virile working organization . . . laying a much more stable foundation for constructive work than has ever before existed in Southern California."[76] Even if we allow for a bit of hyperbole in Engle's statement, there is no reason to doubt the accuracy of his figures.

Overall, this analysis of the 1910–1911 strike wave suggests that although the bombing of the *Los Angeles Times* building and the confessions of the McNamara brothers were setbacks for the L.A. unions, these events did not destroy their determination to fight against the open shop or their ability to add a significant number of workers to their ranks. Early twentieth-century Los Angeles certainly did not witness conflicts between labor and capital on the scale of the battles in the Colorado coal mines or the textile mills of Lawrence, Massachusetts. Nevertheless, the struggles of L.A.'s workers for their union rights showed that class-conscious action—even if it was only intermittent—played a role in the city's early history that was just as important as that of cultural conflicts over temperance, religion, or race.

CRISIS AFTERMATH: GOING DOWNHILL, 1912–1916

In the subsequent years leading up to World War I, Los Angeles workers suffered setbacks. Besides the lingering effects of fusion politics, the hostility of the M&M, and the confessions of the McNamara brothers, additional explanations of this downhill slide include the changed political circumstances that resulted from the electoral success of the Progressive movement at both the local and state levels, internal conflicts within the labor movement, and the 1913–1914 economic recession.

Nationally, the high tide of Progressivism in the United States was marked by the 1912 election of President Woodrow Wilson and the passage of numerous labor reforms during his first administration, including the Clayton Act of 1914 and the creation of the Department of Labor.[77] Workers in Los Angeles also profited from new labor laws passed by Governor Hiram Johnson's Progressive administration in Sacramento. In 1911 the Sacramento legislature adopted nearly all of labor's preferred measures, including a workmen's compensation act and a law limiting the workday to eight hours for women and minors. In 1913 legislators passed improvements to the state workmen's compensation law and established the Commission of Immigration and Housing.[78]

The Progressive labor reforms adopted by the state government also shifted Governor Johnson's base of support in Los Angeles from the middle-class suburbs to the working-class neighborhoods downtown. In the 1914 election, for example, his vote totals fell in Pasadena and Long Beach but increased among workers occupying the older, less exclusive houses and apartments east of the Los Angeles River.[79] Because these legislative reforms had been secured by nonpartisan lobbying methods, their passage increased the pressure on L.A.'s trade union leaders to downplay their alliance with the Socialist Party and adopt the lobbying tactics of the AFL instead.[80]

Such were the changed political circumstances that greeted Job Harriman when he decided to make another run for the Los Angeles mayoralty in the spring of 1913. As in 1911, his platform included an eight-hour day for city workers and a publicly owned hydroelectric power system based on the Owens Valley water sup-ply.[81] However, from the start of the campaign it was clear that class lines were drawn much more loosely in the 1913 election that they had been in 1911. Some of the city's right-wing Progressives, led by Meyer Lissner, again united with the Republican old guard behind the Municipal Conference ticket, in order to ensure Harriman's defeat. The liberal Progressives, led by Dr. Randolph Haynes, endorsed a separate slate of city council candidates under the label of the People's Charter. When the primary results came out on May 6, Job Harriman had come in third and failed to qualify for the run-off. The Socialists' only significant victory was the election of Carpenters leader Fred Wheeler to the city council.[82]

A comparison with the 1911 election shows that Harriman's support was much patchier in working-class districts than it had been two years before. The unions also contributed less money to the 1913 campaign than they had in 1911.[83] Angry and frustrated by two successive failures, Job Harriman abandoned electoral poli-tics altogether. Instead, he and his followers devoted their energies to developing the Llano del Rio cooperative colony outside of town.[84]

The organizational split that now took place between the Socialist Party and the unions also proved damaging to the radical cause. In March 1914, the longstand-ing differences between the left and right wings of the party resurfaced when the Socialists refused to accept a resolution sponsored by the Central Labor Council that would have required every nominee of the party to be a member of his or her trade union. In retaliation, the Central Labor Council, deferring to the nonparti-san political policy of Samuel Gompers and the AFL (which by now had become de facto support for the Democrats), requested that its affiliates not vote for Social-ist candidates in the upcoming city elections. When longtime Socialist Party mem-ber Fred Wheeler refused to go along with these instructions, the party went one step further and called for his resignation from the city council. Wheeler refused, and in 1915 he was expelled from the party altogether.[85] This split damaged both sides in the dispute and contributed to the demise of the Socialist Party as an influ-ential player in Los Angeles politics.

Another internal conflict that helped to maintain the dominance of the open shop was the quarrel between the Central Labor Council (CLC) and the Building Trades Council. The latter (a separate body that coordinated the activities of union carpenters, plumbers, painters, and electricians) wielded an exceptional amount of power in Los Angeles because the city's construction industry was so large. In 1914 the CLC supported the passage of a $6.5 million bond issue intended to finance public ownership of the city's electricity supply. The proposal also offered the prospect of providing a great many new construction jobs for union men. Nevertheless, the BTC opposed the bond issue, accusing the council of selling out to the public power "octopus."[86]

Finally, the debilitating impact of the 1913–1914 economic recession, which affected the labor movement all over the country, appears to have hit the unions in Los Angeles particularly hard. As unemployment rates soared nationally, a disproportionately large number of jobless workers from the East moved to Southern California during the winter months to take advantage of the warm weather. In addition, employers continued their policy of advertising vacancies to job seekers all over the country during the business downturn, even though no such jobs, or very few of them, were actually available. The evidence suggests that this was done deliberately in order to maintain a labor surplus in the city. In 1914 the Central Labor Council sent out numerous appeals to trade unionists in other parts of the country, urging them to tell their members not to travel to Los Angeles, but their pleas appear to have had little effect.[87]

But the most telling blow, as far as the unions were concerned, was the way the recession drained their membership lists and undercut their attempts to resist the arbitrary firings, blacklistings, and other punitive methods the employers used to maintain the open shop. In a revealing document published in January 1914, the Central Labor Council reported that half the members of Carpenters Local 1763 were out of work. A similar percentage of Iron Workers Local 219 was unemployed. The Millmen and Cabinet Makers local reported a 45 percent unemployment rate; the Waiters and Typographical unions recorded a jobless rate of 40 percent; and so on down the list.[88]

CONCLUSION

Given these job losses, it was small wonder that between 1913 and 1915 the Los Angeles labor movement as a whole—its treasury depleted and its morale at a low ebb—was unable to prevent more than a third of its union contracts from being lost. Nor was it able to put up any meaningful resistance against the ongoing campaign of the Merchants and Manufacturers Association to keep the unions in a state of subordination. Federal control over the nation's railroads and other industries and a sympathetic hearing from the state government in Sacramento would revive labor's fortunes somewhat during World War I. But in terms of overall numbers and economic clout, the Los Angeles labor movement continued throughout the 1920s to remain a lot smaller, and a lot weaker, than its counterparts in most industrial cities in the East.

THREE

Grassroots Insurgencies and
the Impact of World War I,
1905–1924

Before World War I, the open shop empire of the Los Angeles business elite
stretched far beyond the city limits. It reached north into the citrus belt of the
San Gabriel Valley, east toward San Bernardino, and south into ranch lands on
the Mexican border.[1] In these places it was met—and frequently opposed—by
groups of peripatetic railroad workers, IWW members (Wobblies), farmhands,
and Mexican radicals who formed a small but significant minority in the deserts
and coastal plains surrounding the metropolis.

These insurgents are important to our story not only because their aims clashed
with those of the employers and the M&M. They also influenced the small but
militant group of left-wing radicals in Los Angeles itself, most notably on the San
Pedro docks.[2]

Three main groups made up this radical movement. One was the tight-knit
band of longshoremen in the harbor area who embraced the IWW's brand of militant industrial unionism and struggled openly with the shipowners for control
over the docks.[3] The second group consisted of Mexican revolutionaries known
as Magonistas, who were expelled from Mexico for plotting to overthrow the dictatorship of President Porfirio Díaz.[4] The third element was composed of itinerant anarchists, syndicalists, and insurgents[5]—many of whom were sympathetic to
the Wobblies—who ranged back and forth across the Mexican border challenging
the labor practices and "imperialist aspirations" of U.S. ranchers, mine owners,
and landholders who had bought up lucrative properties all the way from Orange

County down to the Imperial Valley. Examining these dissident groups demonstrates, as other accounts do not, the value of the Sixty-Mile Circle (shown in map 1, in this book's Introduction) in obtaining a comprehensive overview of the history of the Southern California working class.

On the surface, the three groups of insurgents had little in common: San Pedro's longshoremen were concerned with immediate workplace issues; the Magonista émigrés sought to promote revolution in far-off Mexico; and the Wobblies advocated a brand of grassroots industrial unionism that challenged the conservative policies of the American Federation of Labor (AFL). But all three were linked by a common interest in anarcho-syndicalist doctrine, grassroots militancy, and working-class internationalism. Their main haven in Los Angeles was the downtown Plaza, where Mexican immigrants, Italian anarchists, Socialists, and Wobblies gathered each weekend to listen to the speeches of fiery orators such as Ricardo Flores Magón, Bill Haywood, and Emma Goldman.[6]

WOBBLIES, MEXICAN REVOLUTIONARIES, AND CROSS-BORDER SOLIDARITY, 1905–1908

The rumblings of discontent that led to the overthrow of Mexican dictator Porfirio Díaz in November 1910 resounded on both sides of the border for some years before the actual revolution took place. Formal protests began in 1898 with a textile strike in the Mexican state of Puebla. In 1906 protest spread to Cananea (near the U.S. border close to Bisbee, Arizona), where oppressive working conditions and racist treatment of Mexican miners by Anaconda Mining and other U.S. multinational corporations led to violent upheavals.[7] Industrial cities in microcosm, these mining communities were tailor-made for the IWW's message of revolutionary industrial unionism. By 1908 the Wobblies had established dozens of locals on both sides of the border.[8]

Meanwhile, in Mexico proper, the Flores Magón brothers—Ricardo and Enrique—were among the founders of the Partido Liberal Mexicano (PLM), which held its first congress in 1901. With a program of land redistribution and social betterment, the PLM managed to survive five years in Mexico before its leaders were exiled to the United States. In July 1907 the Magón brothers moved the party's headquarters from St. Louis to downtown Los Angeles.[9] Some of the itinerant laborers who listened to revolutionary speeches in the Plaza had personally experienced the semi-feudal conditions that existed in the rural haciendas, metal mines, and textile factories of northern Mexico.

Over the next several years, the Magón brothers straddled an ideological fence. Increasingly devoted to anarchism, they made what allies they could among L.A.'s Anglo trade unionists, moderate Socialists, and left-wing intellectuals, including Job Harriman. Their middle-class supporters met weekly in Frances Nacke Noel's Highland Park home to discuss philosophical issues and pore over reports in the revolutionary newspaper *Regeneración.*[10] But most of the PLM's support came from L.A.'s three rough-and-tumble IWW locals on the docks and in the downtown area.[11] One of them was a Spanish-speaking branch, which, according to some reports, was larger than either of the other two.[12]

A common interest in "direct action" tactics and the ideas of Peter Kropotkin, Mikhail Bakunin, and other leading anarchists provided the ideological basis for this loose knit coalition between the PLM and the IWW. At the grassroots level were dozens of anonymous volunteers who traveled back and forth across the border distributing *Regeneración* and summoning support for the coming Mexican Revolution. These devotees were the real lifeblood of the Partido Liberal Mexicano.[13] By 1906, forty PLM cells were operating in Mexico, in the U.S. Southwest, and in various places in Southern California. The party planned an uprising in Mexico in June 1908. But before that could happen, LAPD detectives arrested the Magón brothers in Los Angeles, and the two were charged with treason and murder.[14]

An outcry immediately arose in the East L.A. barrio. Fearing that the Magón brothers might be kidnapped before they were brought to trial—as Bill Haywood and other IWW leaders had been several years earlier—hundreds of protesters followed the police paddy wagon taking them to jail. Labor leaders (including even President Gompers of the AFL) rallied behind the prisoners, and Job Harriman was chosen as the Magóns' main defense lawyer.[15] The *Los Angeles Times*, predictably, was infuriated by this show of public support. It called the Mexican revolutionaries who spoke at the Plaza protest meetings "greasers" and declared that the only Americans who supported Magón were "wild-eyed anarchists with smoking bombs in hand."[16]

In reply, defense lawyer Harriman portrayed Magón and his companions as innocent patriots who had been railroaded into jail on trumped-up charges. Under cross-examination, the LAPD detectives who arrested them were shown to be cops on the take; they were later tried for police misconduct.[17] The charges were dismissed.

In June 1911, however, the Magón brothers were again arrested in Los Angeles and charged with violating U.S. neutrality laws. This time there was more sub-

Ricardo and Enrique Magón in a Los Angeles jail. Courtesy of *Los Angeles Times* Photographic Archive, Department of Special Collections, Charles E. Young Research Library, UCLA (ucla_lat_1429-b770-210785).

stance to the charges, since several months earlier the two brothers, with IWW support, had sponsored an invasion of Baja California from the U.S. side of the border. The Magóns were convicted and sentenced to twenty-three months in jail.[18]

HARRY CHANDLER, THE C&M RANCH, AND THE MEXICAN REVOLUTION

Small and ineffective though it was, the Magonista incursion into Baja California in 1911 was significant for what it tells us about cross-border solidarity, anger against Anglo domination, and the development of Mexican nationalism, all of which would exert a major influence in the Los Angeles labor movement in later years.[19] The brief military incursion also threatened the investment portfolios of important members of L.A.'s capitalist elite because the insurgents threatened to confiscate ranch lands that had been purchased on both sides of the border by Harry Chandler (General Otis's son-in-law) and other L.A. land speculators.[20]

General Otis had supported the reactionary Díaz regime long before the Mexican Revolution. Commending President Díaz's program of land confiscation and enforced industrialization, no matter the cost to native Indians and the Mexican peasantry, Otis's rhetoric also revealed the transnational character of his capitalist crusade. "The triumph of the insurrectos," he wrote in the *Times*, "would be a triumph of advanced socialism. The property of foreigners and of the wealthy class of Mexicans would be confiscated. Americans would be driven out [and] while thousands of Mexicans would be relieved of peonage, they would go out of the frying pan of industrial slavery into the fires of enforced idleness, homelessness, and hunger."[21]

The possibility of a serious insurrection in Baja California also caused Otis and Harry Chandler personal anxiety when the rebels began to steal food, horses, and other supplies from the family's C&M ranch, which straddled the U.S.–Mexican border. By 1907 the Chandler syndicate owned thousands of high-yield acres irrigated by water from the Colorado River. Besides supporting large herds of cattle, the C&M ranch employed eight thousand Mexican peasants tending vegetable and cotton fields, which in one year produced $18 million worth of crops.[22] Understanding nothing about conditions on the ground, Otis was astonished when his son-in-law reported that "a majority of residents" in the Imperial Valley expressed sympathy for the Baja insurgents. Otis promptly wrote to President William Howard Taft in Washington, D.C., requesting intervention by U.S. troops to protect American interests and property. "There is an unfortunate, and, I think, amazingly disloyal and stupid sympathy existing in the Imperial Valley for the insurrecto cause," he added.[23] But President Taft was unwilling to do more than offer protection for the partly finished Imperial Canal, which was designed to bring Colorado River water to the Imperial Valley.

The L.A. land syndicate need not have worried. By May 1911, when Otis's exchanges with President Taft took place, the Magonistas' attack on Baja California was already collapsing. Despite the sympathy of the local population, the rebels could muster only a few hundred poorly armed Wobblies, anarchists, and soldiers of fortune for the military campaign. Declaring their intention to liberate the land and restore it to the Indians, the insurgents did manage to capture a few sparsely populated border towns such as Tecate and Mexicali. But later in May, when President Díaz was forced from office, a split occurred between Magón loyalists and supporters of the new president of Mexico. In June 1911, most of the remaining invaders were captured and interned at Fort Rosecrans in San Diego.[24]

If anything was needed to confirm the fear and hostility that L.A.'s business elite felt toward the Mexican Revolution and Mexicans generally, the threat posed to its land investments along the border by the insurrection in Baja California—

however brief—certainly solidified these attitudes. In addition, as William David Estrada points out, Job Harriman's defense of the Magón brothers in court and the support offered to the Mexican revolutionaries by most of L.A.'s Socialists and trade unionists "made it logical for Otis and Chandler, through their reporting in the *Times,* to draw connections between the Mexican insurrectionists and the bitter wave of labor strikes that hit Los Angeles during the same period."[25] Both the Mexican immigrants and the political radicals would become scapegoats during the anti-immigrant "brown scare" that afflicted the city in the years that followed.

THE DECLINE OF THE LEFT, AND THE "BROWN SCARE" OF 1916–1917

Chapter Two described how, in the aftermath of the *Los Angeles Times* bombing, the influence of the L.A. branch of the Socialist Party of America declined, once the reform legislation adopted by Governor Hiram Johnson's Progressive coalition in Sacramento and Woodrow Wilson's administration in Washington, D.C., made support for the far left seem less necessary than before. Between 1912 and 1916, thousands of California voters abandoned the Socialist Party. In 1916 the AFL dropped all pretense of nonpartisanship and urged all its affiliated trade union members to vote Democratic, causing a further loss of support for the Socialists.[26]

But these were not the only blows the Los Angeles left suffered in this period. Soon after the failure of the Magonistas' military incursion into Baja California, the tactical alliance between the Socialists, the IWW, the exiled Mexican revolutionaries, and the left wing of the Los Angeles trade union movement fell apart. At the national level, AFL president Gompers excommunicated the IWW from the federation, branding it as a dual-unionist organization that raided AFL craft unions for new members.[27] This made it more difficult for radical trade unionists on the L.A. Central Labor Council to assist the IWW in its efforts to recruit unskilled workers and to raise money for Wobblies who were the victims of police repression during the free speech fights. (Free speech fights were protest demonstrations by IWW members who contested municipal ordinances restricting their rights of free speech—demonstrations for which many of the protestors were jailed.)[28]

In 1912 the national leadership of the Socialist Party, seeking respectability, cut itself off from the IWW by denying membership to anyone who "opposes political action or advocates . . . methods of violence." It also dismissed IWW secretary-treasurer Bill Haywood from its executive board.[29] In Los Angeles the reaction to this new direction was mixed. The *Social Democrat* offered praise, saying that these actions would purge the party of "dangerous firebrands who believe capitalism can only be ended by violence."[30] In contrast, the Southern California correspondent of *Revolt* (a pro-IWW paper published in Oakland) wrote: "The pink tea Socialists have gone mad for respectability and driven away the only people who . . . want a real revolution."[31]

Those who wanted a "real revolution," of course, included the Magón brothers and the members of the Partido Mexicano Liberal. After the collapse of the Baja incursion, PLM leaders in Los Angeles were beset by fears that their mission had failed. Noting the internal struggles within the American Socialist camp, Ricardo Magón told his brother Enrique that "the American people, even the organized workmen of this cold-blooded country, are not susceptible to agitation."[32] He went on to criticize the Socialists for breaking with the IWW. "Look at the Socialists; they have split in a most cowardly way in their campaign for the liberty of speech."[33] In the fall of 1911, leading Socialist Job Harriman repudiated his earlier support for the PLM for two reasons. One was the PLM's recent adoption of a new revolutionary program labeled "anarcho-communism," which ran counter to Harriman's moderate socialist beliefs.[34] Harriman's other reason was his upcoming election bid for Los Angeles mayor (discussed in Chapter Two), in which he needed to present himself as a moderate in order to obtain Progressive and trade union support.[35]

Each of these developments, coupled with the rapid decline of the Socialist Party nationally, undermined the tactical alliance between the groups on the left of Los Angeles labor. They also coincided with collapsing support for the Socialists throughout California as a whole. In 1914 membership in the state party, which had been almost eight thousand in 1912, had fallen to six thousand. By 1916 it was down to twenty-five hundred, and the party's candidate for state treasurer in Los Angeles County secured fewer than a thousand votes.[36]

By this time, the Mexican Revolution had gone through several new twists and turns, some of which the Magón brothers supported, some of which they opposed. In February 1916, they were again charged in a Los Angeles federal court, this time with printing "indecent matter" in *Regeneración* and sending it through the U.S. mail.[37] Both of the brothers were found guilty and jailed. In March 1918, Ricardo Magón was charged yet again, this time under the Espionage Act of 1917, with conspiring to publish false statements that interfered with the operations of the U.S. military. He was found guilty and sentenced to twenty-one years in federal prison. Enrique Magón was deported to Mexico; Ricardo died in Fort Leavenworth prison in Kansas in 1922.[38]

In March 1916, Mexican insurgent Pancho Villa led a cross-border raid into U.S. territory in Columbus, New Mexico, in which several Americans were killed. It was this raid, coupled with the fear that Mexico would join with Germany in a wartime alliance against the United States, that triggered the "brown scare" against Mexican immigrants in the American Southwest. The backlash in Los Angeles against Mexicans suspected of supporting the raid was particularly severe. After news of the fight reached the city, Police Chief Clarence E. Snively ordered that no liquor be sold to Mexicans who showed signs of being intoxicated. "No guns can be sold to Mexicans, and all dealers who have used guns for window display have been ordered to take them from the window."[39] Chief Snively also established a special police squad to observe Mexicans on the streets and tripled the number of patrolmen in Sonoratown.[40]

In reply, the Partido Liberal Mexicano, whose offices remained open in downtown L.A., issued a circular accusing the LAPD of "a series of abuses . . . against the Mexican laborers of this city," and it urged them not to sit back and passively accept these humiliating attacks. If L.A.'s Mexican workers failed to protest their treatment, the PLM declared, they would give the city authorities reason to "continue believing that we are incapable of reclaiming our rights, to continue believing we are beasts who must be managed with clubs."[41]

Another negative consequence of this so-called brown scare was the corrupting effect it had on the Americanization movement undertaken by Progressives to help Mexicans and other immigrants secure U.S. citizenship. Initially, this movement maintained a degree of respect for foreign immigrants by accepting Jane Addams's "doctrine of immigrant gifts." But when the brown scare heated up in 1916–1917, the tone became much harsher. For example, instead of praising the positive contributions of immigrants to American society, educationalists such as Emory Bogardus at the University of Southern California focused on the dangers that poor, working-class Mexicans posed to the Protestant values of L.A.'s Anglo-Saxon middle class. Initially aimed at Mexican male employees at their workplaces, Americanization classes were now directed at the wives and daughters of these workers through the 1915 California Home Teacher Act.[42]

Whether the program was directed toward men or women, however, the message was the same. Instead of encouraging upward mobility, the program socialized Mexicans and Eastern European immigrants into accepting vocational training, low-level jobs, and obedience to employers. At the Macy Street school in downtown Los Angeles, the Americanization classes prepared Mexicans not for college but for employment in laundries, sweatshops, and factories or for household labor.[43] These educational classes had always had something of a vocational slant anyway. But the brown scare confirmed the beliefs of most of L.A.'s white residents, including many white trade unionists, that Mexicans were an inferior race whose loyalty to the United States was suspect.

SAN PEDRO LONGSHOREMEN, THE IWW, AND A FAILED ATTEMPT TO INTRODUCE INDUSTRIAL UNIONISM

Despite excommunication from the AFL, loss of Socialist support, and savage attacks by the LAPD during the free speech fights, the IWW still found a receptive audience for its message in at least one place in Southern California: among the longshoremen employed on the San Pedro docks. In fact, according to one source, it was Wobblies traveling north to Los Angeles after the 1912 free speech fight in San Diego who first convinced the San Pedro dockworkers to fight for their union rights.[44] Why did the port of San Pedro become a Wobbly recruiting ground in the years surrounding World War I?

One answer lies in San Pedro's role as an occupational community. Like logging towns on the northern California coast or coal mining towns in Appalachia, port cities like San Pedro were somewhat isolated places where two or three occupations dominated the entire economic structure. A majority of San Pedro's male residents were either sailors, longshoremen, or owners of small businesses whose livelihoods depended on the docks: rope makers, engineers, tugboat captains, flophouse owners, and bar or restaurant proprietors.[45] The result—exceptional for a suburb of Los Angeles—was a strong sense of community and workplace solidarity. Longshore work was quite often a family affair, with jobs passed down from father to son, so the sailors and longshoremen who lived in the port area provided the basis for an exceptionally strong trade union movement. As a sociologist specializing in occupational communities inelegantly puts it: "These collectively held values based on the homogeneity of life experiences enjoined mutually supportive actions which took place in a dense network of kin and neighbors on the basis of generalized reciprocity."[46]

The nature of longshore work itself also reinforced the dockworkers' sense of workplace solidarity. Until the 1960s, when mechanization transformed the industry, the loading and unloading of ships in U.S. ports was carried out either by cranes or—in the case of fruit, lumber, or packaged goods—by the use of slings, which were manhandled on and off ships by longshoremen working in gangs. The work was hard, dangerous, and demanding.[47] Given these difficulties and the employers' dependence on the individual longshoreman's skill and initiative, the dockworkers' work practices offered a perfect opportunity for the Wobblies to campaign for "workers' control at the point of production," which was one of the fundamental points in their radical philosophy. The need for a quick turnaround of the ships to satisfy business needs also made it relatively easy for longshoremen to frustrate the employers, and raise their costs, by practicing "go slows," "working to rule," or implementing some form of work sabotage.[48]

Equally significant was the hiring process in the industry, which was based on the notorious daily "shape-up." Under this system, longshoremen were required to gather at the dock gates at 6 A.M., where a number of them were selected for work and sorted into gangs at the whim of the company foreman. The system was riddled with bribes, kickbacks, and favoritism, but it also offered IWW members an opportunity to secure regular employment more easily than they could under most other circumstances. The work gangs employed on the waterfront were of two kinds: "steady" workers, who enjoyed regular employment and who were often members of the International Longshoremen's Association (ILA); and "casual" workmen, who were hired when the number of ships in port was exceptionally large. Since anyone seeking work could join "the shape," itinerant Wobblies quite often slipped past the dock gates and were chosen for casual work without their affiliation being noticed.[49]

The shape-up was universally hated by longshoremen since it led to economic insecurity, high levels of underemployment, and speed-ups on the job, in which gangs were sometimes forced to compete with one another to see who could most quickly load or unload a ship. Since whoever controlled the hiring process literally ran the docks, the shape-up system again posed the question of job control in the sharpest possible terms, and for years the main objective of the waterfront unions was to wrest that control away from the employers, or at least force them to share it with the men.[50]

The IWW was also attractive to longshoremen because of the transnational character of the maritime labor force. Many of the longshoremen who worked in San Pedro were either ex-fishermen from Dalmatia, Croatia, or Italy; ex-loggers from Oregon or Washington; or Scandinavian seamen who had sailed all over the world. This gave a transoceanic dimension to their class consciousness and enhanced the appeal of the IWW's principles of inclusiveness, direct action, and international solidarity.[51]

It seemed, under these circumstances, that IWW members who got jobs in San Pedro in the early months of 1912 might attract new recruits quite easily. "Every time a steam schooner comes in from Eureka," complained one wary shipowner, "a flood of IWW literature descends upon San Pedro."[52] But recruiting new IWW members, or even boosting the existing unions in the harbor complex, was no easy task. On July 18, 1912, some twenty-five Wobblies succeeded in halting work on the steamer *Klamath*, while others harangued longshoremen on the dockside, urging them to shut down all the ships in the harbor. They demanded an increase in wages from 35 to 40 cents an hour for regular time, 50 to 60 cents for overtime, and an hour off for meals. Some two hundred longshoremen, most of them Italians, walked off the job, but the rest of the labor force refused to support them, and the strike quickly collapsed.[53]

This lack of unity resulted partly from ethnic rivalries and partly from philosophical disagreements. Some of the Anglo longshoremen refused to follow the lead of the anarchistically inclined Italians, and the existing ILA Local 38–18 at the harbor, which was an AFL union affiliated with the L.A. Central Labor Council, opposed the IWW's revolutionary philosophy. Other longshoremen were members of the Sailors Union of the Pacific, an old-fashioned craft union controlled by the aging labor leader Andrew Furuseth in San Francisco, who disapproved of both the ILA and the IWW.[54]

As if all this were not enough, anti-union employers with close ties to the M&M controlled most of the shipping wharves in the San Pedro and Wilmington areas. Open shop lumber companies such as E.K. Wood, Banning, and Kerckhoff-Cuzner had contracts with the Southern Pacific and the Pacific Electric's railroad division to haul their lumber downtown, and they were happy to sit back and exploit the differences that existed between the small and weak maritime unions.[55] The obvious answer to these jurisdictional difficulties, as the IWW repeatedly pointed out, was to amalgamate all the separate locals in the maritime industry into a single industrial union.

But at this point neither the leaders of the ILA in Los Angeles nor the officers of the Sailors Union of the Pacific in San Francisco would consider such a step. It would not be until the 1930s, when the famed International Longshoremen's and Warehousemen's Union came into being, under the leadership of Harry Bridges, that the problem of jurisdictional conflict between California's maritime unions would be solved.[56]

WORLD WAR I, LABOR RETREAT, AND THE FEAR
OF REVOLUTION, 1917–1919

It is often assumed that the U.S. labor movement benefited from the labor shortages occasioned by World War I, from the federal government's aversion to strikes
at a time of national emergency, and from President Woodrow Wilson's assertion of federal control over major industries such as mining and railroads.[57] To
some extent this was true in Southern California, as it was elsewhere. In 1918 the
California State Federation of Labor reported a net increase of 10,000 union members in Los Angeles since its previous convention, and an additional 12,000 new
members were claimed in 1919, the year of the great postwar strike wave. But even
after taking population differences into account, this increase was far smaller than
those recorded in cities like Chicago, where the number of unionized workers went
from 114,000 to more than 350,000.[58] In Los Angeles, moreover, only rarely did
employer concessions on wages and hours lead to union recognition and permanent collective bargaining rights.

Why did Los Angeles face such disappointing results? When the National War
Labor Board (NWLB) was first established in May 1918, it generally approved
settlements that included the workers' right to organize and bargain collectively. Soon afterward, however, it qualified this positive approach by stating that
employers did not have to recognize unions unless they had done so before the war.
In Southern California, the M&M took advantage of this ruling to renew its insistence on maintaining the open shop. Since relatively few of L.A.'s large firms had
had union contracts before the United States entered the conflict in April 1917, the
city's anti-union employers were able to exploit this retreat on the NWLB's part
more easily than employers in other cities.[59]

Even when the NWLB handed down decisions favorable to the unions, Los
Angeles employers developed a habit of ignoring these dictates unless they were
backed up by legal sanctions. Given the strength of the open shop forces in the city,
the federal government, aside from registering its disapproval, could do little to
stop this practice. Additionally, in Los Angeles more than in most places, employers seized on the belief that the monopolistic practices of trade unions undermined
"industrial freedom" (the core idea behind the open shop) and expanded this logic
to argue that requests for union recognition were unpatriotic, because recognizing unions and yielding to their demands would inherently restrict needed wartime output.[60]

As a result, virtually all the major strikes undertaken by L.A. workers during and immediately after the First World War were lost. This outcome contrasted with the strike results in several other cities, a significant proportion of which were won. Take the case of the Los Angeles shipbuilding industry, which expanded dramatically during the war. In November 1917, several hundred machinists, boilermakers, and metalworkers employed by the Southern California Iron and Steel Company, which had been awarded shipbuilding contracts by the federal government, took advantage of the shortage of skilled labor to demand union recognition and a reduction in hours. The company rejected its employees' demands, and the men came out on strike. In January 1918, however, Judge Frank Finlayson issued a court injunction banning all interference with the plant's operations, stating that the strike had disrupted America's war effort. Within days the company brought in large numbers of strikebreakers, and the walkout collapsed.[61]

This negative response set the pattern for other defeats. In June 1918, metal tradesmen employed by the Los Angeles Shipbuilding and Drydock Company also walked out and demanded an upgrade in their hourly wage rates to conform with the federal government's wartime standards. But the company, which was owned by Fred Baker (who had played a key role in defeating the 1910–1911 metal trades strike), refused to negotiate. This time the NWLB agreed to hold a hearing on the matter, but it did not rule favorably on the employees' demands. Instead, it reiterated that it would not force union recognition on companies where the open shop had been in force before the war. Once more, the strikers lost.[62]

A major walkout also took place among workers employed by the Pacific Telephone and Telegraph Company, which set an interesting precedent because of the large number of women employees involved.[63] The male linemen, installers, and switchmen, who were already organized in the L.A. branch of the International Brotherhood of Electrical Workers (IBEW), at first ignored the grievances of the female telephone operators. But when a mixed labor force of twelve hundred women and five hundred men walked away from their switchboards in July 1919—during the great postwar strike wave—the IBEW gave them its support. It even approved the establishment of a new women's local. The company immediately began hiring strikebreakers from among former employees who had left their jobs to get married. Soon afterward, however, another court injunction was handed down forbidding further picketing, and the telephone strike also collapsed.[64]

The most dramatic strike in wartime Los Angeles was the two-stage walkout undertaken in 1918 and 1919 by employees of the Pacific Electric Railway. It pitted L.A.'s most determined anti-union employer, Henry E. Huntington, against fifteen hundred of his own motormen and conductors. In order to complete their runs, streetcar crews often had to work ten to eleven hours a day, and their pay was low compared to that of other skilled employees.[65] The situation was especially onerous for low-paid workers because of the high rate of wartime inflation. Huntington said that he was willing to concede a wage increase, but he remained adamant about preserving the open shop: "If the Los Angeles Railway employees strike, I would discharge every agitator, and see to it that they never have another day's work."[66]

Early in 1918, Los Angeles Division 835 of the Amalgamated Association of Electric Railway Employees petitioned the NWLB for a wage increase and the eight-hour day. The eight-hour day was granted, but Huntington refused point blank to implement it. So his streetcar crews came out on strike. Because the public was seriously inconvenienced, the U.S. naval commander at San Pedro stationed armed sailors on the Red Cars, and the local draft board threatened to force striking motormen and conductors to join the army. In addition, Judge Benjamin Bledsoe served the strikers with an injunction declaring that since the streetcar men had accepted the open shop as a condition of their employment, their demand that PE recognize their union was illegal.[67]

Faced with this injunction, the streetcar crews went back to work. But a few months later, they petitioned the NWLB a second time for union recognition. The NWLB sidestepped this request, so in August 1919 strikers shut down much of the Red Car system again. This time the battle was even fiercer. The Mexican tracklayers walked out in sympathy, the dispute spread to the steam railroads, and there was considerable violence. Strikers greased the streetcars' wheels (so they could not gain traction), trolleys were overturned, and on August 20 a riot broke out in downtown Los Angeles, when several hundred onlookers jeered at scabs who were putting their trolleys back into the car barns.[68]

Mayor Meredith Snyder, who had been elected partly with working-class votes, attempted to mediate the dispute, but the three hundred special deputies who had been hired to protect the strikebreakers managed to keep the cars running. By November 1919, the strike had been called off, streetcar service was back to normal, and the open shop lobby emerged from the conflict—as it did from virtually all of L.A.'s other wartime strikes—virtually unscathed.[69]

The First World War affected the lives of working-class Angelenos in other ways, too. Besides the draft, which conscripted several thousand young men into the army, there were housing shortages, meatless days, special programs for war relief, and endless patriotic speeches both in the community and at the workplace to encourage the purchase of Liberty Bonds. More than two hundred volunteers,

A Red Car overturned during the 1919 streetcar strike. Courtesy of the Crump family.

known as Four-Minute Men, were selected to make short patriotic speeches during the intervals between films at the city's movie houses, appealing to citizens to make sacrifices for the war effort.[70] Several of these Four-Minute Men had working-class backgrounds. Evangelical ministers and Progressive reformers also exploited the patriotic mood of the day to clamp down on vice and advance the cause of Prohibition, even though some of them had initially opposed U.S. entry into the war.[71]

But the biggest issue plaguing workers who dared to protest during World War I was the question of national loyalty and national security. In December 1917, a bomb exploded outside the governor's mansion in Sacramento, setting off a hue and cry against traitors up and down the state. The IWW was immediately suspected, and in the eyes of a majority of the public, the Wobblies came to symbolize all that was most threatening and dangerous about those who questioned America's role in the war. In his wartime speeches, Governor William D. Stephens blamed the Wobblies for a wide range of mishaps for which they could not possibly have been responsible—everything from military setbacks and bad harvests to the shortcomings of the domestic Americanization program.[72]

After the 1917 Russian Revolution and the massive strike wave that spread across the United States in 1919, the anti-radical hysteria in Los Angeles grew even more shrill. By this time General Otis was dead, but under Harry Chandler the *Los Angeles Times* continued the same conservative editorial policy. Chandler's denunciations of the IWW elevated the organization in the public mind from a minor irritant on the left wing of the labor movement to a universal symbol of the worldwide Communist conspiracy.[73] In December 1918, a month after the end of the war, superficial credence was given to the fears fanned by the *Times* when the IWW tried to organize the citrus workers employed in the San Gabriel Valley. The episode began in February 1919, when the IWW held its first rally in downtown Los Angeles in two years. The demonstrators protested the primitive conditions and extremely low wages the growers had imposed on their Mexican and Asian employees during the preceding years.[74]

About two hundred citrus workers took part in the IWW protest strike in the San Gabriel Valley and farther east in San Bernardino County. The white growers, unwilling to acknowledge substandard conditions on their ranches, blamed the strike on "outside agitators." They displayed particular hostility toward strike leaders who had leased a house near Charter Oak in the San Gabriel Valley— calling it the "Russian house" because it contained supposed revolutionaries. According to the *Los Angeles Times*, "agitators of both sexes," who "wore little or no clothing," took up residence in the house, arousing the indignation of the local populace.[75] Exaggerated or not, this vignette provides a glimpse into the overblown tales of sexual license and debased femininity that shocked bourgeois moralists contemplating the new world of the Russian Revolution.

When the IWW leaders refused to leave the "Russian house," a convoy of cars carrying hundreds of police and vigilantes descended on the building and forced the union leaders to leave, even though they had leased the house legally. This and other acts of intimidation effectively ended the citrus workers' strike without any improvement in their wages or conditions. The coercive tactics employed by the police provided a foretaste of the even more lawless behavior it would direct against the IWW later on.

The years immediately following World War I were also the period when fear of the "yellow peril" was at its height. About five thousand first- or second-generation Japanese lived in Los Angeles County, most of whom lived peaceably, producing agricultural products Southern California's residents needed. Despite this, fears among whites of some kind of "Asian takeover" were enhanced by the failure of the 1913 Alien Land Law to prevent Japanese farmers from leasing U.S. land and by the "picture bride" phenomenon, a method used by single Japanese men to bring over marriage partners from their homeland. Efforts by whites to stop the importation of picture brides resulted in considerable agitation against Japanese laborers.[76]

The African American community on L.A.'s Central Avenue was not immune from wartime tensions, either. Shocked by the race riots that broke out in East St. Louis in the summer of 1917, the black community went out of its way to show support for the U.S. war effort. Local NAACP branches sold Liberty Bonds, black women's clubs gave money to the Red Cross, and when the first batch of American draftees left the downtown railroad station, a large crowd of black citizens gathered to see them off, waving a U.S. flag that had been specially made for the occasion. But even these signs of support were not enough to dispel the doubts held by many whites about the loyalty of African Americans. Angry that qualified black women were being rejected by L.A.'s only nursing school, Joe Bass (husband of Charlotta Bass, famed editor and publisher of the African American newspaper the *California Eagle*) rejected W.E.B. Du Bois's plea that African Americans set aside the race issue until the war was over. "These people," Bass wrote, referring to white nativists and racists, "are tearing down democracy faster at home than the boys who are fighting in the trenches can build it up."[77]

All these developments, coupled with the feelings of insecurity generated by the brown scare of 1915–1917, contributed to the explosive mixture of nativism, racism, and anti-radical sentiment that prompted the California state legislature in 1919 to adopt one of the most draconian criminal syndicalist laws in the country.[78] The new state law did not simply punish acts of insurrection. It made it illegal to advocate violence or to join organizations that endorsed violence as a means of social change. In Southern California, the M&M, the Better American Federation (a right-wing patriotic organization), and the Chamber of Commerce all praised the new statute. A.S. Lavenson, director of the Better American Federation, claimed that the best thing his organization ever did was to help secure passage of the criminal syndicalism law.[79]

In the heightened atmosphere of the red scare and the perception of threats from many quarters, there was little that the unions or the liberal community could do in response. The result was another violent and climactic struggle between the longshoremen and the forces of reaction on the San Pedro docks, which ended the IWW's career, along with the post–World War I radical upsurge in Southern California, once and for all.

LONGSHOREMEN, THE KU KLUX KLAN, AND
THE WOBBLIES' LAST HURRAH, 1916–1924

Despite their failure to gain much traction on the waterfront in 1912, the remaining Wobblies in Southern California kept a weather eye open on the festering discontent of longshoremen in the following years. The rapid expansion of shipping in the build-up to the U.S. entry into World War I meant that the oversupply of labor that characterized many ports in normal times turned into a labor shortage. So in May 1916, the International Longshoremen's Association, meeting in Seattle, decided to test the waters by striking for a wage increase up and down the West Coast.[80]

In San Pedro about sixteen hundred men came out on strike, joined by the lumber handlers, millmen, and other dockside workers. A federal mediator was sent in to negotiate a raise of 5 cents an hour, pending a final settlement. While most of California's other longshoremen returned to work while awaiting a final agreement, the San Pedro men stayed out because the mediator refused to include the lumber handlers in his offer. This show of solidarity momentarily raised the workers' spirits. But as the strike intensified, the shipowners began hiring strikebreakers. At the request of the M&M, a hundred special LAPD officers were detailed to keep order on the docks, and violence grew as the strikers tried desperately to keep the scabs from taking their jobs. Strikebreakers were attacked at the Hammond Lumber Works, and fires were set on several wharves and at lumber yards.[81]

The depth of the strikers' anger against the police was shown when attempts were made to burn down the Sunshine Inn, where twenty special LAPD officers were sequestered. San Pedro's shopowners extended credit to the strikers' families, a labor dance was held to raise money, and other unions from the downtown Central Labor Council donated food. But the police, aided by strikebreakers, kept the port open. By August operations had resumed full time again, and most of the strikers had returned to work.[82]

The most important result of this 1916 West Coast dock strike was that the San Francisco longshoremen won union recognition and the closed shop, even though the San Pedro workers lost, thus demonstrating the superior strength of the Bay Area labor movement. But the problems in San Pedro, most notably shipowner control over the hated shape-up, persisted, and everyone knew that it would be only a matter of time before the struggle was renewed. Soon after the war was over, another skirmish demonstrated just how polarized the town had become. In October 1919, the San Pedro Chamber of Commerce declared its intention to restore open shop conditions throughout the entire harbor area, a decision that was endorsed by all the local shipping, lumber, and warehouse companies. Local 38–18 of the ILA responded by asking all "friends of labor" in the town to stop patronizing local businesses that supported the chamber's decision. Another brief strike followed these new declarations, but it too ended in defeat.[83]

The final showdown between the IWW, the maritime unions, and the San Pedro shipping companies was delayed until 1923. By that time, most of the Wobblies who had tried to organize Southern California's citrus workers, itinerant farm laborers, and cotton workers in the hinterland had either left the area or been arrested and convicted under the criminal syndicalism law—often on the flimsiest of evidence.[84] Despite this, in November 1922 the IWW's general executive board in Chicago, in a last desperate attempt to reassert its influence, requested all remaining Wobblies on the West Coast to rally in San Pedro to contest the open shop on the docks and also to test the constitutional limits of California's criminal syndicalism law.[85]

The IWW's one remaining advantage was that several hundred organized longshoremen from the conservative craft unions in the San Pedro shipping industry—influenced by the popularity of the One Big Union movement that spread across the country during the national strike wave of 1919—had finally recognized the need for an all-inclusive industrial union in the maritime trades. In 1919 and 1920 many of them left the ILA and the Sailors Union of the Pacific and joined the IWW's Marine Transport Workers Industrial Union (MTWIU). This union incorporated all kinds of harbor workers—longshoremen, lumber handlers, tugboat captains, oilers, cooks, and stewards—into a single organization.[86] However, in 1922 the MTWIU was still too weak to bring about a wholesale reform of the maritime unions in the port.

As more and more Wobblies arrived in San Pedro, the IWW newspaper, the *Industrial Worker*, admonished the longshoremen to be ready for a strike call, which finally came on May 1, 1923 (the historic May Day of international socialism). The strike call announced a "strike to free the class prisoners"—the Wobbly term for those who had been convicted and jailed under the criminal syndicalism act—and "to improve material conditions on the decks and on the docks."[87] Estimates of the number of longshoremen who struck in 1923 varied; a majority of the seven hundred or so who came out were probably not IWW members. Nevertheless, by May 10 more than sixty ships had been tied up, and San Pedro Harbor had been brought to a virtual standstill. To keep up the strikers' morale, the IWW leaders held rallies at Fourth and Beacon streets, including one in which the Reverend Fred Wedge, an ex-lumberjack and former pastor of the Terminal

Island Congregational Church, addressed the crowd in apocalyptic terms. Many of the two thousand persons in attendance wore red flowers in their buttonholes, and a red airplane with the word "SOLIDARITY" painted on its side flew overhead.[88]

However, the shipowners and law enforcement authorities were ready for the fight. Early in May the employers held brief negotiations with the strikers, but the talks broke down over the longshoremen's demand that the employers stop using the "fink hall" for hiring. ("Fink hall" was the popular name for the new Sea Service Employment Bureau, which had been established in 1922 to screen job applicants and which made it more difficult for IWW members to get waterfront jobs.) On May 4, 1923, the Shipowners' Association resumed its accustomed tactic of importing strikebreakers, a task made easier by the squad of 140 special police and detectives sent by LAPD chief of police Louis D. Oakes to patrol San Pedro's streets and arrest alleged troublemakers.[89]

Ten days later, the LAPD began making mass arrests. Before noon on that day, the "Wobbly Squad" raided the IWW defense office on South Broadway in downtown L.A. and picked up twenty-five persons, including staff members from the office of the IWW's chief defense lawyer. Later that day, in what the *Los Angeles Times*, with typical exaggeration, called the "greatest campaign against Reds ever made in the United States,"[90] the LAPD arrested several hundred strikers and protesters on a vacant plot of land in San Pedro known as Liberty Hill. They were taken downtown in special Red Cars, charged with violating the criminal syndicalism law, and held without bail. The next day, the celebrated muckraking novelist Upton Sinclair—who would run a spectacular campaign for governor of California in 1934—was arrested on Liberty Hill for reading aloud portions of the U.S. Constitution. So effective was the police action that by the end of the month the strike had collapsed.[91]

But not even this was enough to satisfy the open shop lobby's determination to crush dissent. In the winter of 1923–1924, the LAPD decided to run the remaining members of the IWW out of town. In this effort they were aided by a sinister new recruit to the forces of law and order, namely, the Ku Klux Klan. As noted earlier, many Italians, Mexicans, and other foreign immigrants worked alongside the European and native-born longshoremen on the waterfront, and the KKK's entry onto the scene added a depressing note of religious bigotry and nativist fervor to the anti-union campaign. The reinvigorated Klan gained quite a large following among conservative migrants from Indiana and other midwestern states who had settled in Los Angeles after World War I and who came from the areas where the Klan enjoyed its greatest postwar influence. On May 14, the day of the big police round-up, the L.A. headquarters of the KKK distributed a circular in San Pedro stating: "The watchful eyes of one thousand God-loving citizens [are] upon the law violators and foreign agitators. . . . Those who have lost God, have no country, home or family ties will do well to cease their despicable agitation."[92]

Thereafter members of the Ku Klux Klan, with or without their hoods and disguises, frequently came to San Pedro to back up police raids against radical sites. For example, in March 1924, when the LAPD conducted a raid on the IWW hall, a line of cars containing KKK members dressed in full regalia circled the block, waiting to intimidate any stray protesters whom the police did not catch. The atmosphere was made even more explosive by the presence of a Sergeant Webber, who described himself as a "fearless, patriotic, one hundred per cent American anti-red agitator."[93] Webber held several nightly meetings of his own in San Pedro that week, and a police car carried him to and from the gatherings. By January 1925, IWW influence among San Pedro's longshoremen had virtually disappeared.

CONCLUSION

The key to the crushing defeat of the 1923 San Pedro maritime strike, which posed the biggest challenge to the dominance of the open shop in Los Angeles until the rise of the CIO in the 1930s, was the overwhelming power of the forces arrayed against it. Three factors, in particular, played a critical role. One was the successful demonizing of the IWW and the longshoremen's unions, not only by the LAPD, the M&M, and other agents of the employers, but also by popular fear of disruptions to the social order stirred up by nativists, hyper patriots, and exploiters of the red scare.

The second major factor was the mass importation of strikebreakers, a familiar employer tactic that testified to the power of the Shipowners' Association and the M&M. Its impact was exacerbated by the large numbers of casual laborers looking for work on the docks. Third, there was the brutality of the LAPD and the lawlessness of the vigilantes, including the Ku Klux Klan in the latter stages, who were repeatedly allowed to beat up picketers and demonstrators, smash up the strikers' headquarters, and intimidate any outsiders who dared to show their support.[94]

As a consequence, the longshore strike went down to defeat, just as L.A.'s other post–World War I strikes had done. The net result of these losses, and of the turn to the political right that followed in the 1920s, was that the M&M and other champions of the open shop maintained their grip over the Los Angeles workforce for the next fifteen years.

FOUR · Moving to the
"Industrial Suburbs"

From Hollywood to South Gate, and from
Signal Hill to the Citrus Belt, 1919–1929

During the 1920s the population of Los Angeles grew at an alarming rate, stimulated by an oil boom, a new surge in Southern California land prices that rewarded speculators, and the rapid growth of mass production industry. Annexations increased the city's land area by approximately eighty square miles, and its population rose from 936,000 to 2.2 million. Like many who had migrated before the First World War, most of these newcomers were white Anglo-Saxon Protestants who came from the plains states of the Midwest and who brought some savings with them.[1] Among the rest, the ethnic mix differed somewhat from that of prewar days. Few African Americans moved to L.A. in the 1920s, and almost no Asians. The number of Mexican immigrants increased only modestly, as both supporters and opponents of the Mexican Revolution moved north to escape the ongoing turmoil.[2]

Throughout the decade, new arrivals streamed out of the downtown railroad depots by the thousands. Hoteliers, sales representatives, and real estate agents eagerly awaited them in the station yard, some equipped with horse-drawn buses or automobiles to whisk prospective clients off to view newly built housing tracts in places such as Glendale and Santa Monica.[3]

Growing prosperity in the 1920s also enabled many established residents to move up from their first houses and find better accommodations in the suburbs.[4] The industrial geography of the city changed, too. Older artisanal businesses such as garmentmaking, furniture manufacturing, and small metals production stayed in the downtown and East L.A. manufacturing area.[5] But this chapter leaves the

83

city center behind. It examines workers' fortunes in four widely scattered industrial suburbs that emerged in the 1920s: craft workers in Hollywood; semi-skilled autoworkers in South Gate; mixed-skill oil workers in Signal Hill; and unskilled citrus workers in the San Gabriel Valley.

HOLLYWOOD'S CRAFT WORKERS AND THEIR GRIEVANCES

At first glance, it may seem odd to describe the city of Hollywood as an industrial suburb. As the accompanying photograph demonstrates, the city remained a residential community, with open land to the east and south of it, right through the decade. Hollywood was not, of course, an industrial suburb in the sense that the factory communities in South L.A. were. Nevertheless, the advanced technology and coordinated production techniques needed to make movies were similar enough to those used in manufacturing to make movie production an industrial occupation. By World War II, with thirty thousand men and women employed in the industry, Hollywood had become the largest—as well as the most famous—employer of carpenters, electricians, painters, costumers, and other specialized craft workers in Southern California.[6]

When the market for feature films emerged after World War I, the demand for labor in Hollywood escalated dramatically. In 1921 there were over six thousand production workers. By 1928 moviemaking ranked as one of the most important industries in the city, and the number of production workers had grown to more than ten thousand. Not much is known about the background of these early film workers, except that they came from many different parts of the country. No African Americans were employed in Hollywood at this time, except for the black musicians who played in some of the studio orchestras. Reflecting the prevailing view about women's role in society, the 6 to 10 percent of studio employees who were women were limited to jobs such as seamstresses and milliners in the costuming departments, inspectors and editors in the film processing labs, or secretaries in the front office—a gender imbalance that remained in place until after World War II.[7]

Sophisticated technology and an increasingly subdivided labor force also necessitated the building of large-scale, indoor studios. Carl Laemmle, a German immigrant who began his career operating nickelodeons in downtown Chicago, was the major pioneer in this effort. In 1915 he opened his giant Universal City on a 240-acre site near Lankershim Boulevard, on the southern edge of the San Fernando

A Hollywood studio in semi-rural surroundings, 1918. Courtesy of University of Southern California Photographic Archives, on behalf of the USC Special Collections (chs-m3422).

Valley. Besides indoor and outdoor stages and enough backdrops to shoot a dozen different kinds of films, the huge site included property warehouses, carpenters' shops, stables, a zoo (for animal films), eating facilities, editing rooms, an administration building, and even a city hall. In the late 1920s Paramount and Warner Brothers followed suit. By this time, as one historian puts it, "the pre-planned regimented, 'factory-like' studio" had come to stay.[8]

The actual work of the studios largely took place indoors in an artistic setting, more white collar than blue collar. The big studios like Paramount, Warner Brothers, and MGM, all of which employed between two thousand and three thousand workers, were too far apart to be seen as a single geographical entity. Nevertheless, the workers themselves were more concentrated, as in these early days many of the studio employees lived in an area known as "Gower Gulch," not far from their workplaces.[9] Over the long run, these workers, who began joining the International Alliance of Theatrical Stage Employees (IATSE) before World War I, managed to turn the movie studios into bastions of organized labor. But their struggle for recognition proved to be extremely contentious, partly because of the hostility of the employers and partly because of internal conflicts among the employees themselves.[10]

Despite the supposed glamour of working in Hollywood, the work lives of the craftspeople were not easy. They worked long and unpredictable hours, continuing to shoot a scene until it was finished to the satisfaction of the director, and there was no extra pay for overtime or for working on weekends. The lack of disability compensation was also a source of major concern, given the dangerous working conditions employees frequently had to confront. Light operators, perched high above the set on flimsy scaffolding and working in the intense heat generated by arc lamps, sometimes fainted and fell to the floor. For stunt men, the situation was still more difficult since they were prone to serious accidents.[11]

In these early years, the studio employees' biggest grievance was the unpredictable nature of their work. The casual nature of employment in the movie industry, like that faced by the longshoremen on the San Pedro docks, resulted from the inability to predict how many workers would be needed on the set and how long it would take to shoot a particular scene. Westerns and other outdoor adventure films often required a large pool of craft workers, electricians, and costumers to be available on short notice and to travel long distances to shoot scenes far away from home. But production slumps, sudden changes in production schedules, and seasonal marketing strategies dictated that movie producers would guarantee regular employment only to a relatively small minority of their workers.[12]

Over time, the casual nature of movie employment led to an unusual division of labor between those who worked "inside" and those worked "outside" the studio gates. The minority of "insiders"—who were either favorites of the studio producers or those with special skills—worked every day and were told at the end of each shift when and where to report the following morning. But the majority of studio workers were "outsiders," who were forced to "pan the gates," that is, to wait outside the studio entrance hoping that a foreman would call them inside.[13]

Under these circumstances, it was hardly surprising that IATSE, founded in 1893 as a union for those who worked in live theater, soon acquired a following in Hollywood. In September 1916, President Samuel Gompers of the American Federation of Labor sent an organizer out to the West Coast to assist in unionizing the studio workers.[14] Local 33 of IATSE, which became the dominant union in Hollywood, with over a thousand members, followed this up with an organizing campaign of its own.[15]

Given the workers' pressing need for employment security, IATSE's basic strategy was to put pressure on the studio heads by imposing limits on the available labor supply. In addition to adopting an apprenticeship training scheme that permitted only qualified craftspeople to work in the studios, Local 33 tried to enforce what it called the "permit system." Under this plan, whenever studios needed more workers than the local union could supply, the union could issue temporary work permits to nonunion workers.[16]

When he first approached the employers with this scheme, President Charles C. Shay of IATSE Local 33 believed that the studio chiefs would readily agree because they had been accustomed to dealing with unions in New York. He was mistaken. From the beginning, the Hollywood studio heads, like L.A.'s other major employers, showed their determination to uphold the principle of the open shop. In 1917 the producers formed the Motion Picture Producers Association (MPPA) to present a united front in their dealings with the unions. Not long after that, they countered IATSE's attempt to limit their labor supply by establishing a placement bureau downtown on Hill Street, called the Mutual Alliance of Studio Employees (MASE), which supplied nonunion workers to the studios. In effect, MASE acted as a company union. When Local 33 complained about these activities to the studio bosses, it was told that the union had no right to tell the producers who to hire.[17]

Not long after this, union representative Steve Harmon reported to the national IATSE convention in New York on the problems that MASE posed to the union's organizing efforts. "Conditions here [in Hollywood] are deplorable," Harmon stated. "MASE are sending men out every day into the studios and have phoned downtown [when] they were not able to supply the demand from their own office. . . . Members of the Alliance [IATSE] have been approached by bosses on the lots to sign a long term contract with the company, but must agree to stay on the job in case of trouble and renounce their union affiliation. When they refuse, they are laid off that night."[18] The long-term contract Harmon referred to was also known as a "yellow-dog contract" (meaning: renounce your union or lose your job), which was widely used by anti-union employers as a weapon against the AFL. The National Open Shop Association also entered the fray by announcing its support for the MPPA and pledging legal and financial aid to the producers in return for a promise not to bargain with the unions.[19]

In August 1918, after the producers had rejected the union's demands, over a thousand Local 33 members walked off their jobs. A Joint Studio Strike Committee was set up, which organized a nationwide boycott of films made by the offending studios. The strike committee sent out more than fifteen thousand letters to unions all over Canada and the United States asking for support. "When the working people, who are the great majority of those who attend picture shows, refuse to view these scab-made pictures the natural result will be no sales of these unfair products."[20] Despite these efforts, the strike and boycott were lost, as were two further strikes undertaken by Local 33 against the Hollywood studios in 1919 and 1921.[21] L.A.'s open shop lobby had once more demonstrated its enormous power.

JURISDICTIONAL DISPUTES AND
THE 1926 BASIC STUDIO AGREEMENT

Employer resistance was not the only reason for these strike losses. These defeats also resulted from jurisdictional conflicts between IATSE (whose ranks included a wide range of carpenters, electricians, and other skilled trades workers) and national building trades unions such as the United Brotherhood of Carpenters and Joiners (UBCJA), which had been given the right to organize these same trades by the American Federation of Labor. For IATSE to succeed in its campaign for union recognition, it had to be able to prevent the studios from hiring enough workers to carry out their production schedules during a strike. But the Carpenters and Painters unions and the International Brotherhood of Electrical Workers (IBEW) were also determined to uphold their own organizing authority, a dilemma that resulted in prolonged and seemingly intractable jurisdictional conflicts.[22] Logic suggested that these groups of workers would have improved their bargaining position with the studios if they had all joined a single industrial union. But that possibility was not yet on the table.

So bitter did these jurisdictional disputes become that during a September 1919 strike when IATSE again demanded recognition from the studios, L.A.'s AFL-affiliated Building Trades Council and its Carpenters Union sent in scabs to replace IATSE's striking employees.[23] At the national AFL convention the following November, the AFL executive council tried to mediate the dispute. It requested that IATSE relinquish its claim over the carpenters, painters, plasterers, and other building trades workers in return for being given permission to enroll studio projectionists and set electricians. IATSE initially accepted this proposal but then failed to honor it.[24]

Exhausted by these continuous battles, IATSE and the Hollywood studio bosses decided to compromise by signing the Basic Studio Agreement of 1926, which gave the unions some measure of acceptance. Though the agreement did not grant a closed (union) shop, it did grant recognition to IATSE and the local unions of carpenters, painters, electrical workers, and musicians it had taken under its wing. The 1926 agreement, which lasted for more than twenty years, also redressed some of the workers' original grievances by providing an eight-hour day, higher wages on Sundays, and a number of rest days. However, in order to maintain union peace, the agreement also specified that negotiations between the studios and the unions should not be conducted locally, but instead by a committee of five producers and the heads of the five relevant AFL unions, who would meet in New York. Although well intentioned, the effect of this decision was to undermine local control and rank-and-file democracy in IATSE, a development that made it easier for criminals such as Willie Bioff and the Chicago mobsters to take control of the union in later years.[25]

These angry union disputes in the Hollywood studios also took place against a darkening background of political reaction and anti-radical sentiment, including the establishment of several Ku Klux Klan groups at various places in Southern California.[26] This shift to the right even affected movie content. Before World War I, the AFL and various socialist groups had sponsored a number of films that presented the labor movement in a positive light, some of which reflected real-life events. In 1911, for instance, the AFL's McNamara Legal Defense Committee commissioned a movie that portrayed John McNamara as a loyal, hard-working citizen instead of an anarchist bomb thrower. At L.A.'s 1916 Labor Day celebrations, *General Garrison Bray Who-Tis*—a satirical movie on the career of *Los Angeles Times* owner Harrison Gray Otis—was shown.[27]

But with the growing influence of the big anti-union studios and the renewed efforts of the open shop movement to stop union growth after World War I, conservative producers exploited the public fear of Bolshevism by making films depicting labor unions in a lurid and negative light. In *Dangerous Hours* (1920), the fictitious union leader Michael Reagan is portrayed as a double-crossing, cigar-chomping labor boss who incites previously contented shipyard workers to strike—likely a reference to the struggle of the IWW on the San Pedro docks (see Chapter Three). Some of these hostile depictions of union leaders may even have been inspired by real-life vendettas. For instance, the corrupt union business agent portrayed in several anti-labor films of the early 1920s bore a striking physical resemblance to the actual business agent of IATSE's Local 33, Roy Stephenson, who played an important part in union negotiations with the studio owners.[28]

BLUE-COLLAR WORKERS IN SOUTH GATE AND WATTS: "THE HOME OF THE WORKINGMAN"

During the 1920s the blue-collar workers who moved into the newly built industrial suburbs along the Alameda corridor, which ran south from Huntington Park down to Long Beach, showed little of the militancy displayed by craft workers in Hollywood. This was partly because of employer hostility to unions. But it was also because the AFL, an organization devoted to protecting the interests of skilled, white, male craftsmen, used its limited resources to consolidate its position among L.A.'s downtown tradesmen instead of recruiting semi-skilled blue-collar workers outside the existing city limits.[29]

In addition, when eastern manufacturers established their West Coast factories, they built plants in areas where even the craft unions had not yet secured a foothold. In December 1919, for example, when Goodyear Rubber built a branch factory in Vernon, its publicity magazine explained the choice in part by asserting that "free labor has always been insisted on, and attempts at strikes, whether by agitator elements within or without the city, have invariably proved failures."[30] Not until 1937, when the Congress of Industrial Organizations (CIO) established local unions in the rubber, steel, and automobile industries, did labor secure any real influence in L.A.'s southern industrial belt.[31]

In 1930 the city of South Gate had a population of 19,632, and the majority of its adult male residents held jobs in one of the sixteen steel, concrete, and paper manufacturing plants that had been established there. By that date South Gate had become the industrial hub of the Alameda corridor factory zone.[32] Its biggest employer was the huge Firestone Tire and Rubber plant, which opened in 1928 and employed 1,525 workers in fourteen shops. It manufactured tires, inner tubes, battery cases, and a range of other automotive products. The work was physically demanding and noxious—in light of the chemicals used in the distillation of rubber—but it paid well. In keeping with the welfare capitalist ethic of the time, Firestone's forty acres of grounds contained a cafeteria and an athletic field with baseball fields, bleachers, and tennis courts for the employees' use.[33]

Unlike some of the densely packed industrial cities in the Midwest, L.A.'s manufacturing suburbs did not contain only blue-collar workers. As these areas grew, commercial and white-collar jobs also became available. By 1930, for example, one-fifth of South Gate's earners held white-collar positions as professionals and managers, shopkeepers, or owners of small businesses. This may have been another reason why the union movement remained relatively weak there.

About 19 percent of South Gate's labor force, most of them women, worked as sales clerks or secretaries in the town's manufacturing plants. However, as elsewhere in the United States during the 1920s, the majority of South Gate's female residents did not work outside the home. Instead they did unpaid housework, canned fruit, looked after chickens as well as children, and did volunteer work of various kinds. By the end of the decade, the town's workforce was divided between 65 percent blue-collar workers and 35 percent white-collar employees, with the proportion of blue-collar jobs increasing as additional manufacturing plants were established.[34]

Sparsely populated Watts, on the other side of Alameda Street, which was fast becoming a critical dividing line between whites and blacks—and between relative affluence and relative poverty—acquired no manufacturing plants during this period, only a flour mill and a few canneries. As a consequence it remained a semi-rural community until the Second World War, composed of truck gardeners, railroad workers, and small farmers producing cattle, alfalfa, and fruit.[35]

Why did Watts fail to secure an industrial base of its own? First, the town had originated before World War I as a labor camp for Mexican tracklayers employed by Henry Huntington's Pacific Electric Railway. This fact gave it a somewhat shady reputation and discouraged white factory owners from establishing plants there. Second, as a result of a real estate deal in 1904, a growing number of African Americans, some of whom moved down from Central Avenue, bought lots in Watts, ensuring that it became a racially mixed community. Most white employers at that time refused to hire blacks, providing another reason why no manufacturing industries came to the area.[36]

As the twenties wore on, the white community's insistence on excluding Mexicans and blacks—and even Southern and Eastern Europeans—from their side of the Alameda corridor became even more pronounced. Huntington Park was described approvingly by one source as having a population that was "100% American of the white race." And South Gate itself was praised for having an "abundant supply of skilled and unskilled white labor . . . [and] no foreign population."[37] By this time, Alameda Street was developing a reputation as one of the most tension-laden racial barriers in Los Angeles.

RACE RELATIONS AND POLITICS IN THE WHITE INDUSTRIAL SUBURBS

Whatever their personal predilections about African Americans, local manufacturers tried to avoid incidents at work that might disrupt production and create division within the racially mixed communities of East and South L.A. This intention was confirmed by a manufacturing survey conducted in 1926 by Charles S. Johnson, an African American sociologist employed by the National Urban League. However, Johnson also found that not just employers but also white workers held racist opinions about workers of color. Among the reasons employers gave for not hiring African Americans were the objections of white employees who believed that "Negro and White Labor do not mix."[38]

The background to the increased tension lay in the deterioration of national race relations in the aftermath of World War I, including the serious race riots that occurred in Chicago and elsewhere. An added reason was that South Gate, like L.A.'s other industrial suburbs, experienced a postwar influx of poor white farmers from Oklahoma and Texas, who had come to California in search of a better life (an influx that would become a flood during the Great Depression of the 1930s). In some ways, the outlook of these southwestern newcomers was similar to that of the white Protestant migrants from the rural Midwest who had come to Los Angeles earlier.[39]

Because they were southerners, however, the former residents of Texas and Oklahoma were less willing than their midwestern counterparts to work alongside, or even live near, the African Americans who resided in Watts. As a result, they endorsed the exclusive racial covenants that had been adopted to keep South Gate's homes, and its voluntary associations, exclusively white. As one civic leader from Home Gardens (a poor neighborhood inside South Gate) put it: "Home Gardens is a town of, by, and for workingmen—and we want hundreds more of them. The only restrictions are racial—the white race only may own property here."[40] Some of these newly arrived southerners also attended the open-air meetings of the Ku Klux Klan, which occurred with increasing frequency in Maywood, Lynwood, and elsewhere up and down the Alameda corridor.[41]

As the local population grew, it was only a matter of time before the racially mixed community of Watts, just across Alameda Street (see map 3), became a target for the white residents of South Gate, especially among southerners who found the very idea of a mixed racial community offensive. Prohibition, which came into force in 1920, was poorly enforced in the southern section of Watts, where most of the African Americans lived, and hooded Klansmen made several raids on the local speakeasies there.[42] One black woman who arrived in Watts in 1923 described the atmosphere of intimidation she found, an atmosphere so highly charged that it caused some black residents to carry guns. "I came here from Natchez, Mississippi, right to Watts. We got off the traction car and began walking down Main Street. I had never seen a man in a white hood, all the time in Mississippi, but there were Ku Klux Klan men in front of the Baptist Church. . . . It made my blood curdle. It was raining and dark. I'll never forget [it]."[43]

Worse was to come. In April 1925, the *California Eagle* (L.A.'s premier African

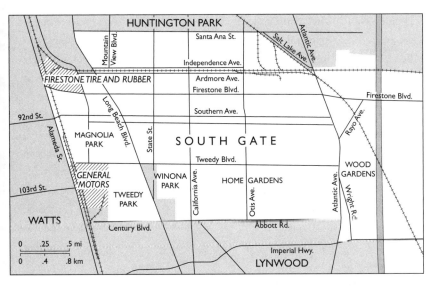

MAP 3. South Gate in the 1920s, showing the border with Watts. Courtesy of the University of Chicago Press. Becky Nicolaides, *My Blue Heaven: Life and Politics in the Working-Class Suburbs of Los Angeles, 1920–1965*, p. 314. © 2002 by The University of Chicago. Reprinted by permission of the University of Chicago Press.

American newspaper, edited by Joe and Charlotta Bass) published a letter sup-posedly written by Klan leader G. W. Price urging KKK members to frame the Reverend Knox, a respected black minister in Watts, by planting a bottle of liquor in his car. An uproar followed. Price denied writing the letter and sued the *Eagle* for libel. Although Thomas Woolwine, the Los Angeles district attorney at the time, was anti-Klan, the local courts were often guilty of prejudice. The *Eagle* eventually won its court case, but not before Charlotta Bass, working alone one night in the newspaper office, was threatened with violence by several Klansmen. Luckily she had the presence of mind to pull out an unloaded pistol from her drawer and aim it at her would-be assailants, who fled.[44]

In addition to their racial convictions and the pride they felt in their newfound economic independence, the white workers of South Gate manifested a strong sense of patriotism, including antipathy toward Communism, which was cemented in place by the red scare that followed World War I. They also shared a strong commitment to pietistic, Protestant values. In the case of migrants from Texas and Oklahoma, this was supplemented by a penchant for evangelical religion and Pentecostal religious beliefs, evidenced in the First Baptist, Bible Assembly, and

Holiness churches in Home Gardens, where many of the formerly rural southerners lived.[45] Some among them even adapted their former southern religious practices to their new urban setting by using an ecstatic, physical form of worship that gave them the same reassuring emotional sustenance they had received in Texas and Oklahoma.[46]

These racial and religious beliefs might suggest that the political views of blue-collar workers in places like South Gate were uniformly conservative. It is true that during the 1920s most voters in Southern California continued to vote Republican in congressional and presidential elections.[47] But some recently arrived migrants from the rural Southwest retained strong memories of the producer ideals that had once fueled the Populist Party in that region.[48] In 1912 the voters of Watts, many of whom still farmed the soil, gave more than 40 percent of their votes to Socialist Party candidates in the Ninth Congressional and Thirty-third Assembly districts.[49]

These same voters were also pleased when, in the presidential election of 1924, a number of Los Angeles unions endorsed Senator "Fighting Bob" La Follette on a separate third-party ticket.[50] La Follette stood for government ownership of railroads and water power—a potent issue in Los Angeles—as well as an end to the use of court injunctions in labor disputes and a guarantee of freedom for farmers and workers to organize and bargain collectively. The *California Eagle,* following the traditional loyalty of most African American voters to Republicans, endorsed Calvin Coolidge.[51] But no fewer than 41 percent of the voters in Watts, black as well as white, cast their ballots for La Follette, while 34 percent of the white working-class inhabitants of South Gate did the same.[52] It was a harbinger of Upton Sinclair's EPIC movement, which would exert a strong influence all across the Los Angeles region ten years later.

ROUSTABOUTS AND OIL WORKERS ON SIGNAL HILL

Whoosh! "Shooting oil up in the air fully 150 feet, the Shell Oil Company's well at Temple Avenue and Hill Street came in last night, just 90 days from the date of 'spudding in.' Fully two thousand persons witnessed the sight."[53] This report by the *Signal Hill Daily Telegram* on June 23, 1921, and the oil boom that followed through most of the1920s, transformed the small town from a rural, hilltop community overlooking the Pacific into a major new source of industrial wealth for Los Angeles. It also helped to transform Long Beach, just to the south, into one of America's greatest oil shipping ports.[54]

Oil well gusher and fire, Signal Hill. Courtesy of the City of
Signal Hill.

At its peak in 1928, Signal Hill boasted 828 wells producing 62,000 barrels of oil
per year. Yet it was not a typical Southern California oil town. Most of the region's
oil towns were north of Los Angeles, in the desert regions of Kern County and
the San Joaquin Valley. Demographically, however, Signal Hill—like nearby San
Pedro—became an "occupational community." According to the 1930 census,
as many as 2,214 of Signal Hill's male workers, out of a total population of about
10,000, were employed in the oil industry. An additional 870 men and 570 women
were employed as technicians, clerks, and support personnel in Long Beach, San
Pedro, Wilmington, and other nearby places.[55]

Signal Hill's prior history as a residential community meant that after oil was
discovered in 1921, real estate values skyrocketed even more rapidly than in most
other parts of Southern California. "The scramble for Signal Hill drill sites,"

wrote one local author, "became so competitive that in many cases the legs of the tall wooden derricks interlaced with each other."[56] Oil rigger Jonathan Booth told an interviewer that his father had purchased land in Signal Hill before World War I and made a killing by selling it when property values began to rise.[57] Another local resident reported that, unlike the ranchers and oil company representatives who profited from the sale of oil lands in Texas and Oklahoma, the beneficiaries of the oil boom in Signal Hill were "a cross section of the general public."[58]

The transformation of Signal Hill reflected the boom mentality of this decade, which continued to bring thousands of migrants out west from all over the country in the hope of fulfilling the Southern California dream. But even in the 1920s, the profits reaped by those who benefited from the discovery of oil did not prevent the emergence of a separate class of oil workers in Signal Hill or the division of the town into rich and poor neighborhoods.[59] Nor did it prevent the buildup of grievances held by local oil workers against the large oil companies, like Shell, that employed many of them. The big oil companies, like most other large firms in Los Angeles, insisted on the open shop. Moreover, they often treated their skilled employees like casual laborers and ignored their own safety rules. Working on an oil rig, whether one was employed as a driller, a roustabout, or in some other capacity, was dangerous, much more so than tending an overhead light in a Hollywood studio or working in a South Gate auto plant. When oil wells caught fire, as they often did, they could cause serious injury to anyone who got in the way.

In fact, in 1924 the California Bureau of Labor Statistics described oil as the second most dangerous industry in the state, after mining, with more than seventy-five deaths each year.[60] A report in the *Signal Hill Beacon* in October 1925 described the death of David Patton, age fifty-five, an oil pumper whose body was found lying on the platform of Patton and Cassidy's No 2 well. "The body, entangled in the machinery, had stopped the machine. It is supposed the dead man's body clothing caught in the cam-shaft."[61]

Most of the oil workers who lived locally, as Hollywood's studio craft workers and South Gate's factory employees did, were white, native-born Americans who had come from the Midwest or from southern oil states such as Texas or Oklahoma. Very few Mexicans were employed in the industry, and no African Americans. The most skilled workers in the industry were experienced blue-collar employees whose traditions included knowledge of underground geology, an understanding that all members of a shift depended on one another for their safety, and a masculine tradition of workplace camaraderie that included initiation rituals and private forms of language. Oil workers called each other "cocky roosters" who had to "heave up and run" to "put money in the bank." In their leisure time, Signal Hill's oil workers frequented the pool halls and boxing rings of nearby Long Beach and visited the Santa Anita race track.[62] These traditions added up to a more proletarianized form of workplace culture and a deeper sense of class-conscious solidarity than could be found either in South Gate or among the conservative building tradesmen of nearby Long Beach, a solidarity more akin to that shown by the longshoremen in San Pedro.[63]

Despite their masculine work habits, Signal Hill's male oil workers did not exclude their wives from their activities. Local 128 of the Oil Workers Union established a female auxiliary, which put on dances, raised money for oil rig accident victims, and gave its support to women's groups such as the Olinda "Get to Gether" club.[64] In an urban environment such as Signal Hill, a higher proportion of oil workers' wives were also able to secure regular employment than would have been the case in the isolated oil fields in Kern County. After marrying an oil pumper, for example, Joy Elliott worked as a clerk in a Long Beach drugstore and then kept house for a man in the oil supply business. Virginia Maxfield audited the books in her father's oil equipment firm and helped run the local women's service club.[65]

THE OIL WORKERS UNION AND THE 1921 STRIKE

The oil workers' most serious grievance stemmed from the requirement that they work a twelve-hour day and a seven-day week. It was this grievance, more than any other, that led a group of activists, meeting in Bakersfield in July 1917 and using the U.S. government's wartime need for oil as leverage, to form a union, demand a pay raise, and insist on an eight-hour shift.[66] For the next ten years, union control over Signal Hill's oil workers was divided between Long Beach Local 128 and an executive board located in Taft, seventy miles north in the San Joaquin Valley. Local 128's ablest leader was a diminutive Scot by the name of Walter J. Yarrow, a self-styled "oil geologist" and a radical whose call for government ownership of the oil industry made him a controversial figure among the rank and file.[67]

As in other industries, the anti-statist stance of the oil companies was strongly supported by the *Los Angeles Times* and the Merchants and Manufacturers Association. Nonetheless, the federal government did take control of the nation's oil fields for strategic purposes during the First World War. But this did not stop the *Times* from attacking Yarrow as a dangerous radical. In December 1917 the paper accused him of "aiding the Central Powers"—the alliance of Germany and Austria-Hungary against whom the United States fought in World War I—by threatening to strike in time of war. It alleged that the "oil agitators" had planned a strike for September, when the American Expeditionary Force was preparing to leave for Europe and when "the demand for oil [would] have become so urgent that the companies will be forced to surrender."[68]

In the short term, the wartime oil shortage enabled the oil companies to ignore their employees' demands. But the oil trust, which was later accused of war profiteering, was unpopular, and the idea of government control of the industry for the duration of the conflict had considerable public support. With oil strikes looming in Texas and elsewhere, the Wilson administration, fearful that the California oil workers would follow suit, dispatched a Mediation Commission representative to the West Coast to keep the peace. In November 1917, the mediator persuaded the Signal Hill oil companies to accept a $4 daily wage and an eight-hour shift, along with an agreement to arbitrate future employee grievances.[69] Elated by this apparent victory, oil workers began flocking to join Local 128 in Long Beach as well as the local unions in Taft and Coalinga in the San Joaquin Valley. By the end of 1919, more than four thousand had joined up. Meantime, in June 1918, the AFL issued a charter to the oil workers union (formally known as the International Association of Oil Field, Gas Well, and Refinery Workers of America), establishing its headquarters in Fort Worth, Texas.[70]

For a short time after World War I, the prospects for continuing growth in Long Beach Local 128, most of whose members came from Signal Hill, appeared bright. Structurally speaking, the oil workers union was a "natural" industrial (that is, occupationally mixed) union: the oil rig crews who joined it included not only semi-skilled oil riggers and roustabouts but also skilled machinists, blacksmiths, and engineers. Within the AFL, therefore, the union supported the postwar movement for a industrial form of unionism led by the United Mine Workers of America—an organization with which the oil workers union had much in common. It is also likely that the oil workers of Signal Hill sympathized with the radical outlook of the nearby longshoremen who took part in the San Pedro strike of 1916. Delegate Yarrow spoke passionately in favor of "new unionism" at the AFL convention in 1919, where the issue of industrial union was extensively debated.[71]

Another sign of Local 128's radicalism was its willingness to permit the wives and daughters of the oil workers to play a role in the life of the union. Soon after the war, it established a union periodical, the *California Oil Worker*, which reached a peak circulation of twelve thousand in 1922. The journal carried a women's page, which not only printed the usual notices of local dances and bake sales but also urged its female readers to study the trustification of America's oil industry and to support pro-labor candidates for political office.[72]

Once the war was over and the oil industry was returned to private hands, the open shop oil companies went back on the offensive. Their renewed hostility toward the union was made clear in August 1921, when all of the major California oil companies except Shell refused to negotiate with the union or renew the Memorandum of Agreement that had governed wages, hours, and conditions in the industry during the war. When Local 128 persisted in demanding a new agreement, several large California oil companies began discharging union members and circulated "yellow-dog" contracts among their employees that required them to give up their union membership. Even Shell refused to return to the negotiating table. Although aware of their weakened position, the eight thousand unionized oil workers in the San Joaquin Valley felt they had no choice but to strike, which they did on September 11. The result was a disastrous union defeat, followed by extensive wage cuts and a return, nearly everywhere, to the open shop.[73] In the words of an AFL representative who had been sent from Washington to aid the strikers, the union's strategy meetings were "beset with [employers'] spies" who were "bent on the destruction of the organization."[74]

Neither Local 128 in Long Beach, with its large complement of Signal Hill members, nor the other oil locals in Huntington Beach and El Segundo came out on strike during the 1921 struggle, although all three sent money and helpers to support it. As a result, after the strike was over, Local 128 was able to recruit new members from among the veterans of the struggle who had lost their jobs in Kern County and had also been forced out of their company-owned houses. Nevertheless, as reports in the *International Oil Worker* made clear, Local 128 remained in a weakened state for the rest of the 1920s. In July 1925, Secretary John C. Coulter complained bitterly that the oil companies were using detectives to infiltrate union meetings and that "intimidation [by company spies] rules upon pipe lines and in stations, upon leases, and in refineries."[75]

As a consequence, even Shell Oil, which had negotiated a limited Memorandum of Agreement with its employees after World War I, refused to recognize the union. It established "welfare committees" (a euphemism for company unions) in all of its oil camps instead.[76] In oil, as in most of Southern California's other major industries, the open shop movement clearly retained the upper hand. It was not until the coming of the CIO in 1936–1937 that the oil workers of the region began to organize again.

"FACTORIES IN THE FIELD" IN L.A.'S CITRUS BELT

The citrus industry was the last of the four major catalysts that helped to transform Los Angeles from a commercial city into an industrial powerhouse in the 1920s and 1930s. Before World War I, a number of enterprising Anglo ranchers had bought up thousands of acres of farmland in the San Gabriel and Pomona valleys and turned them into large-scale orange and lemon groves. By 1928 more than three hundred citrus ranches along the eastern edge of the L.A. basin—in valleys and suburbs as far apart as Santa Ana, Pasadena, and Santa Paula—had been planted with oranges, lemons, and grapefruit; and growers were shipping forty million boxes of fruit a year to consumers all over the United States.[77]

The ranchers who achieved this feat carried it out it with factory-like efficiency. Indeed, it was their managerial skills that provided journalist Carey McWilliams with the celebrated "factories in the field" metaphor, which he introduced to describe the techniques they used to cultivate and market their crops.[78] Having discarded the Japanese and Sikh workers they had initially employed, the growers hired hundreds of Mexican farm workers to pick and process their oranges and lemons on an assembly-line basis. McWilliams extended his factory metaphor to describe not only the harvesting of the crops but what he called the system of "theft, fraud, violence and exploitation" that the growers imposed on their seasonal employees in the 1920s and 1930s.[79]

After the defeat of the brief IWW campaign to organize the farm workers of the San Gabriel Valley in 1919 (described in Chapter Three), labor relations on the citrus farms appeared to settle down for a time. In order to maintain a good public image, the growers presented themselves as benevolent family farmers concerned with protecting the interests of their employees.[80] In reality, however, they introduced labor-intensive methods of production that were extremely demanding. In 1921 the Fruit Growers Exchange issued guidelines requiring that each individual picker must not pull oranges from a tree, but instead must cut them "across the stem right next to the button." They also admonished their employees not to allow their fruit sacks "to bump up against the ladder, box, or any hard object."[81]

The pickers lost income if any of the fruit in the boxes they turned in showed signs of damage. Payment was made on a piecework basis, the usual rate being 30 to 35 cents a box of fruit. But seasonal changes and adverse weather conditions frequently cut back on working hours, so that picking crews often averaged no more than twenty to thirty hours per week. This meant that their weekly earnings were from one-half to two-thirds lower than the wages of Anglo workers in manufacturing industry.[82]

After the fruit had been cut down from the trees by male pickers, it was piled onto flatbed trucks and hauled to the packing sheds, where it was washed, graded, and boxed by female employees before being loaded onto railroad cars and shipped east.[83] The expectation was that the entire process would be completed in a week, with an efficiency comparable to that of Henry Ford's automobile assembly lines. Lines of authority in the industry were also organized on a hierarchical basis, much as they were in urban manufacturing. Each rancher was a member of a local growers association, which controlled picking schedules, coordinated relations with the railroads and packinghouses, and supervised the marketing of fruit. At the top of the hierarchy was the California Fruit Growers Exchange, which was strongly anti-union and an active member of the Merchants and Manufacturers Association.[84]

The female employees who processed the lemons and oranges in the packing sheds were even more strictly controlled than the male crews who harvested the crops. Managers expected each female packinghouse employee, many of whom were the wives and daughters of the male fruit pickers, to fill at least fifty boxes of oranges or lemons a day. The packinghouse supervisor controlled the pace at which the fruit came down the chute onto the processing tables, and speed-ups were an ever present threat. The supervisors also kept their eyes open for "slackers," who could be punished for failing to properly insert each orange into its wrapper or for placing a piece of fruit in the box without the company's logo properly exposed.[85]

Punishment for inadequate performance was usually a reprimand. But, as in the oil industry, the growers' most powerful disciplinary tool derived from their ownership and control of the rented housing in which most of the citrus workers lived. Persistent complaints about inadequate wages by the pickers, or about a speed-up in the packing plant, could result not simply in a dismissal but in eviction from company-owned homes.[86]

Examining the living situation of first-generation immigrant citrus workers in a small Mexican barrio named Arbol Verde, on the southern edge of Claremont, provides insight into the quality of their lives and their responses to their employers. Half of this barrio consisted of company-owned houses erected by the growers to shelter their employees. These dwellings were poorly furnished, primitive accommodations under the direct control of a company foreman, with few of the amenities needed to conduct an independent life. The ranch hands who lived there, mostly single men, did little more than cook their meals, go back and forth to work, and rest until trucks took them to the fields next day.[87]

The behavior of the Mexican workers who lived with their families in the other half of the barrio was different. The houses there were not company-owned; instead, they were rented or owned by the occupants themselves. Their homes were arranged in clusters around a number of community buildings, which included a Catholic church, a cooperatively run market, and a meeting hall. This section of Arbol Verde enjoyed a vibrant community life, with saint's day celebrations, social dancing, and communal meals served outdoors. Although the children from both halves of the barrio went to the same Spanish-language school, the independent residents were much quicker to express their dissatisfaction with their low pay and poor working conditions than the men in the company-run part.[88]

It is not clear how extensively the residents of Arbol Verde participated in the numerous walkouts and protests that took place against the growers in the 1920s. What is clear, however, is that the independent residents in the barrio (which was one of about a dozen independent *colonias* in the Pomona Valley) were able to develop a separate cultural space for themselves more easily than their company-dominated neighbors were. Their autonomous way of life served as an important resource in the face of an overwhelmingly dominant and oppressive Anglo-Protestant culture.[89]

CONCLUSION

What general conclusions can be drawn from this portrait of labor relations in the emerging industrial suburbs of Los Angeles during the 1920s? First, the good news. Because of the postwar housing boom, membership in the downtown Building Trades Council rose from 8,814 to 12,328 between 1919 and 1923.[90] Local 47 of the Musicians Union was able to improve its bargaining position by controlling the supply of instrument players for the orchestras employed by the Hollywood studios, and the Typographical Union secured a forty-four-hour week for most of its members.[91] There was also the successful signing of the Basic Studio Agreement between IATSE and the Hollywood studios in 1926.

But these were about the only positive developments. In nearly every other trade, ranging from the metal shops to the electrical trades and from longshore work to the construction industry, the story was one of apathy, lost strikes, and declining union membership. The Brewery Workers Union, for example, lost more than half its members because so many Los Angeles breweries were shut down as a consequence of Prohibition. The Jewish-dominated locals of the International Ladies Garment Workers Union also lost ground after an internal conflict between the Communists and their opponents.[92] To this list of setbacks must be added the failure of the citrus workers walkout in 1919 and the disastrous defeat of the oil workers strike in Signal Hill in 1921.

The Los Angeles unions were also weakened by a bitter quarrel that broke out between the Building Trades Council and the Southern California locals of the Carpenters Union. Some of the other building trades locals on the council believed that the numerical strength of the Carpenters gave that union too much power, and in 1923 they prevailed on the AFL to rule that the Carpenters should affiliate with the county Building Trades Council rather than the one in downtown L.A. Seemingly trivial, this power play ended up with the expulsion of the Carpenters locals from the AFL, the formation of a dual (rival) Building Trades Council by the AFL, and the establishment of a new labor paper, the *Southern California Labor Press,* as a rival to the longstanding *Citizen.* The *Citizen's* existence was threatened, the labor movement as a whole was demoralized, and the Merchants and Manufacturers Association took advantage of the split to mount a ferocious new attack against the Los Angeles unions.[93]

In June 1921, the M&M opened a free employment bureau for nonunion workers at its downtown Industrial Relations Department, where the registrants were required to sign a statement saying: "I pledge myself to conform to the American Plan of Open Shop."[94] The words "American Plan" were used to give the open shop idea a patriotic flavor and to suggest that a closed, or union, shop, was somehow foreign and un-American. When the split between the two rival building trades councils occurred, the M&M launched a direct attack on the construction unions, which had been one of the Los Angeles movement's few areas of strength. In January 1924, the *Los Angeles Times* reported that the M&M had persuaded more than a thousand carpenters to abandon their union and that the M&M's employment bureau had found jobs for several large crews of nonunion plasterers, bricklayers, and cement finishers. "We have been particularly fortunate in placing some 300 superintendents, general foremen, and crew foremen on construction jobs."[95]

These attacks by anti-union forces were not, of course, confined to Los Angeles. During the 1920s the National Association of Manufacturers orchestrated an open shop drive all over the country in the name of the American Plan. It also encouraged the spread of welfare capitalism, namely, the idea that individual firms should provide their employees with insurance benefits, recreation facilities, and other services to stimulate company loyalty and counter the appeal of independent unions. In Los Angeles, this movement was pioneered by the Goodrich Rubber Company in South Gate. But the open shop drive in Los Angeles may have had an added advantage that was not available in the older industrial cities of the Midwest. This was the opportunistic mood stimulated among L.A.'s recent arrivals by the "newness" of the city, by the rise in land values, and by the possibility of making quick profits from the discovery of oil on their property.[96]

This opportunistic psychology was not immutable. Signal Hill's oil boom, for example, lasted only about a decade. But while it lasted, the psychology of abundance it fostered made it possible for the Industrial Department of the Los Angeles Chamber of Commerce in 1927 to reassure eastern manufacturers contemplating new branch plants in Los Angeles —with a considerable degree of credibility— that their new employees would have few incentives to join a trade union. Two years later, in 1929, the LACC declared that no fewer than eight out of sixteen new industrial suburbs in the Alameda corridor were free of union activity, including South Gate, Van Nuys, Torrance, Lynwood, Vernon, and Huntington Park.[97]

Most of L.A.'s established labor leaders saw through the employers' renewed emphasis on "industrial freedom" and denounced it as an "ingenious device" to trick newcomers into opposing trade unions. They were particularly incensed when the Chamber of Commerce claimed that the wages paid to workers in industrial suburbs such as South Gate were "comparatively high."[98] In fact, according to a survey published by the National Industrial Conference Board in 1930, wages in Los Angeles were 13 percent lower than in several eastern industrial cities.[99]

But in the 1920s, labor had few resources for combatting employer propaganda. There were even some members of the Central Labor Council, wrote one local journalist in 1926, who "grudgingly conceded the . . . attractions of Los Angeles to be sufficient, in the mind of a servile workingman, [to compensate] for his deprivation of the benefits of unionism."[100] It would be another ten years before labor acquired sufficient strength to mount a successful counterattack.

FIVE

· Unemployment, Upton Sinclair's
EPIC Campaign, and the Search
for a New Deal Political Coalition,
1929–1941

During the early years of the Great Depression, which started with the Wall Street crash of October 1929, the Los Angeles labor movement remained weak. It was not until the passage of the National Industrial Recovery Act in 1933 that it was able to mount a sustained–and ultimately successful—campaign against the open shop employers who had dominated the Southern California labor scene for so long. This chapter begins by describing the impact of the Depression on the Southland. But instead of turning immediately to the union upsurge, the remainder of the chapter tells the story of workers' political response to the crisis. The dynamic growth of the L.A. labor movement, including the split between the American Federation of Labor (AFL) and the Congress of Industrial Organizations (CIO), is explored in Chapters Six and Seven.

The reason for this approach is the important, and somewhat peculiar, role of Upton Sinclair's End Poverty in California (EPIC) plan in combatting the economic crisis in Southern California. EPIC itself did not last long, and its veterans eventually allied with Los Angeles Democrats and with the city's emerging CIO unions to form a New Deal coalition.[1] But L.A.'s New Deal political alliance took longer to form, and it never became quite as strong as comparable labor-Democratic coalitions did in other industrial states.

Contrary to popular impressions at the time, the Great Depression of the 1930s was just as severe in Southern California as it was in other parts of the country. It seemed at first that the mild climate, the availability of locally grown food, and the prosperity of the oil industry and the Hollywood studios might mitigate the effects of the 1929 economic crash. Indeed, in March 1930 the *Los Angeles Times* claimed that L.A. was "one of the employment 'white spots' in the entire country" and that the city was less affected than most other parts of the nation.[2] But as factories closed and the number of unemployed workers increased, even the *Times* had to admit that the situation was serious. By the middle of 1932, the nadir of the Depression, about seven hundred thousand people were out of work in California, almost half of them in Los Angeles.[3]

Homeless families established squatter camps in various parts of the city, just as they did in other parts of the United States. In 1932 sixty families built shacks and other shelters on vacant lots between Alameda and 16th streets, not far from downtown. Farther south, near Firestone Boulevard, the homeless built a community called Ragtown, where approximately seven hundred people ate, slept, and cooked over open fires. In September 1933, at the request of the landowners, a squad of sheriff's deputies evicted the squatters and burned the settlement to the ground.[4]

Equally disconcerting in a city that prided itself on the extent of working-class homeownership, rising unemployment meant that many newcomers were shut out from the cherished dream of purchasing a house and that many who already owned a home were threatened by fears of foreclosure. According to one source, home-ownership rates in the industrial suburbs fell from 89 percent of the population in 1929 to 55 percent in 1935—a huge decline.[5] Many of the lost homes were bought up by real estate speculators, who then rented them out to people looking for temporary accommodation. "With the rise in tenancy," writes Becky Nicolaides, "the very purpose of working-class suburban life began to transform—for the worse, in the eyes of many."[6]

Especially alarming for the city's building trades was the rapid decline in the demand for new housing, which resulted in major unemployment among construction workers. In August 1932 Clyde H. IsGrig, Los Angeles representative of the California State Federation of Labor, reported a 50 percent unemployment rate in the city's building trades, prompting employed union members to donate a part of their earnings to relieve the distress of their fellow carpenters. The Building Trades Council also lobbied for the speedy completion of the Hoover Dam and the

Boy being served at a soup kitchen in downtown Los Angeles, 1932. Courtesy of Library of Congress, Prints and Photographs Division, photo no. LC-USF-34-060596-D [P&P] LOT 1188.

Colorado River aqueduct—two major New Deal projects—in the hope that they would provide new jobs for Los Angeles workers.[7]

Another serious consequence of the Depression was a major contraction in city services, which prompted rising demands for relief. In 1934 the Los Angeles Council of Social Agencies reported that "the current financial depression [has] . . . made serious in-roads on the mental health of an alarming number of our applicants." The agency's medical department noted that suicide rates among the families of unemployed workers had risen and that alcoholism and divorce rates had increased.[8]

As in most cities, L.A.'s initial response to the rise in unemployment was to rely on private charity for the relief of distress. In 1931 and 1932 Goodwill Industries, the Red Cross, the Community Chest, and the Jewish Social Services Bureau were among the voluntary organizations that raised money to prevent tenants from being evicted from their homes and donated food and other services to the destitute. The Catholic Welfare Bureau, the largest private charity in Los Angeles, ministered to Mexican families on the East Side and—to the embarrassment of the city's civic elite—established soup kitchens at several locations in the center of downtown. Applicants for monetary relief who had assets of more than $250 were not eligible for assistance unless they agreed to a county lien on their property, and homeowners whose houses were worth $2,500 or more were not eligible for financial assistance at all. When benefits were granted, they were meager, amounting in most cases to no more than $10 a week.[9]

In fact, according to a comparative study of the response to the Depression in Los Angeles, San Francisco, Portland, and Seattle, L.A. took longer to invoke the power of the state to provide relief to homeowners and the unemployed than any other major metropolis on the West Coast. In 1934 the unemployment rate in Southern California stood at 16.4 percent, compared to a state average of 13.2 percent; but a report submitted to the city council revealed that L.A. "had the lowest tax rate for general services of cities over 300,000 population in the United States."[10]

Early in 1931 the city council finally bit the bullet and submitted a bond issue to the voters for $5 million to fund a work relief program, which was adopted. Predictably, however, the *Los Angeles Times* expressed skepticism about the idea of public works, remarking that Mexicans and other unemployed workers recruited to carry out city improvements were "mostly vagrants profiting from the public purse."[11] The money from this bond issue was inadequate. L.A. was finally able to provide adequate relief only when resources became available from the Federal Emergency Relief Administration in Washington and, later, from the Works Projects Administration (WPA).

TREATMENT OF WORKERS, THE UNEMPLOYED, AND MEXICANS

In the months that followed the crash of 1929, most business owners in Los Angeles supported President Herbert Hoover's belief that little could be done to alleviate the Depression and that the country simply had to wait until the business cycle recovered. But when Communists began to organize unemployment demonstrations in 1930, and when strikes began to affect local industry, what might loosely be called California's vigilante right became increasingly aggressive. It included fringe groups such as the Silver Shirts in San Diego (an echo of Hitler's Brown Shirts in Germany), a revived Ku Klux Klan in the Central Valley, and the Associated Farmers, a powerful group of right-wing growers who were affiliated with the Merchants and Manufacturers Association.[12]

The main target of the Associated Farmers in this period was the Cannery and Agricultural Workers Industrial Union (CAWIU), a Communist-led union, which in 1931–1932 led several strikes among Mexican, Filipino, and Japanese farm workers who were employed by lettuce growers in the Imperial Valley, not far from the old C&M ranch owned by General Harrison Otis and Harry Chandler. Charging criminal conspiracy, a motley crew of sheriff's deputies, hired gunmen, and vigilantes descended on rural communities such as Brawley and El Centro and made no bones about using extra-legal tactics to suppress the local farm workers, whose wages had tumbled to 14 cents an hour in the wake of collapsing farm prices.[13]

The situation in Los Angeles was not quite that dire. But given the violent traditions of the LAPD's red squad (led by Captain William Hynes) and the large influx of migrants from Oklahoma and elsewhere looking for work, it was nevertheless combustible. On October 30, 1931, Captain Hynes's men broke up a mass meeting of radicals at the Philharmonic Auditorium that had been called to demand freedom for Tom Mooney, a labor agitator jailed for allegedly throwing a bomb during the 1916 San Francisco Preparedness Day parade. Numerous demonstrators were arrested on charges of "criminal syndicalism," and several were hurt. Only when it became clear that these serious allegations would not hold up in court were the charges reduced to disturbing the peace.[14] On the night of January 3, 1932, another red squad detail dispersed a legal demonstration of unemployed workers by wading into the ranks of unarmed men and women with clubs, slingshots, and brass knuckles and beating many of them to the ground.[15]

Outrageous though the red squad's behavior was, the movement to "repatriate" Mexican residents of Los Angeles affected a much larger number of working-class families. The idea of sending Mexican workers "back to Mexico" as a means of solving the unemployment problem appealed both to city hall, which rarely had enough money for public relief, and to white trade union officials who believed that immigrants took jobs away from native-born workers. In August 1931, the state legislature in Sacramento passed a law making it illegal for any company doing business with the government to employ "aliens" on public works such as schools or highway building. The law was used illegally by private employers as well, to favor whites over job applicants of color.[16]

Even more offensive was the discriminatory treatment meted out to Mexicans when plans were drawn up to deport them from the city en masse. Because ethnic background rather than legal status was used to justify removal, the authorities frequently failed to distinguish between immigrants who were not yet citizens and Mexican Americans, whom they had no right to deport.

In January 1931, Charles P. Visel, the coordinator of unemployment relief, notified the immigrant community that suspected aliens would be sent back across the border. He followed this up by authorizing police sweeps through the Plaza area to scare Mexicans into returning voluntarily. The threat proved effective. Several thousand Mexicans had already returned to Mexico spontaneously when the Depression first hit, and the number increased markedly after the deportation notices were published.[17] At the same time, the county board of supervisors adopted a plan to send Mexicans back across the border by train, calculating that it was cheaper to get them out of town than it was to keep them on relief. The first trainload of "repatriates" left downtown Los Angeles on March 23, 1931, and was followed by several others in subsequent months. By 1935, almost a third of L.A.'s Mexican population of about one hundred thousand had left the city.[18]

The effect was quite traumatic. Fear of deportation drove many Mexicans away from the once-thriving, ethically mixed neighborhoods surrounding the Plaza into the safer but more isolated confines of the East Side barrio. Ironically, the deportation program was carried out at the same time that the new Union Station was being built and when private philanthropists were attempting to "renovate" the Plaza area by turning it into a "picturesque Mexican market place."[19] The poverty, the slums, and the life struggles of real unemployed Mexicans were swept under the rug and replaced by a sanitized—and inaccurate—portrait of romantic, "old-time" Mexico where pretty maidens danced the fandango and sombrero-clad guitar players entertained the crowd.[20]

Some sense of reality was restored to the Plaza when David Alfaro Siqueiros, the great Mexican muralist who was one of his country's fiercest social critics, was commissioned to paint a number of murals in the downtown area. Angered by what he saw going on around him, Siqueiros painted a large satirical mural on the wall of the Hammel Building, just off the Plaza, calling it *América Tropical*. The central figure, depicted in vivid colors, was an Indian peon who lay stretched out on a crucifix while an American eagle representing imperialism hovered over him. The eagle was threatened by two Mexican soldiers perched on the roof to his left.[21]

L.A.'s commercial establishment was shocked by the Siqueiros mural. Christine Sterling, the philanthropist who masterminded the restoration of the Plaza, called the mural "anti-American" and ordered a collaborator to paint over the portions of it that were visible from Olvera Street. By 1938 the entire painting had been whitewashed. As for Siqueiros himself, his six-month visa to the United States was revoked, and he was forced to leave the country.[22]

THE ROLE OF THE COMMUNISTS, 1930–1935

The most radical organization advocating solutions to the problem of unemployment during the Great Depression was the Communist Party (CP). During the 1920s the Socialists had been the larger of the two main radical parties in Los Angeles. But the social and economic reforms of Roosevelt's New Deal, coupled with the loss of Upton Sinclair (the Socialists' most prolific vote-getter in the 1920s, who withdrew from the party in 1933), undermined its remaining support.[23] In L.A. the CP was the first party to tackle unemployment head on, and it was the only one to take the special plight of racial minorities into account. Japanese American Communist leader Karl Yoneda, for example, who later helped organize California's farm workers, joined the Communist Party in part because it contained African Americans, Mexicans, and Asians in its ranks.[24]

In 1935 the Los Angeles CP, like the Communist Party nationally and the international Communist movement, adopted a Popular Front strategy. Mandated by Moscow, this strategy replaced the repudiation of Western capitalism with a policy of cooperating with the Western powers in opposing the rise of fascism in Germany, Italy, and Spain. As a result, the CP in Los Angeles became—for one of the few periods in its history—a serious player in L.A. politics, especially in the trade union councils of the newly organized CIO.[25]

Earlier, during its Soviet-mandated "revolutionary Third Period," between 1929 and 1933, the CP's trade union efforts were largely limited to organizing the dual-unionist Trade Union Unity League (TUUL), made up of relatively small unions intended to be radical alternatives to the conservative unions of the American Federation of Labor—a strategy that, according to veteran Communist Ben Dobbs, "never really took off in Los Angeles."[26] The party was also aided by the activities of several "front" organizations whose supporters were not full party members but who carried out valuable propaganda work. Thus the Southern California Scottsboro Council contributed money to the national campaign to free the "Scottsboro Boys," nine African American youths improperly jailed and tried in Alabama after allegations that they had raped two white women; the Young Communist League recruited new party members on college campuses; and the

Communist Party rally at the Los Angeles Plaza, 1934. Courtesy of Regional History Center, University of Southern California, on behalf of the USC Special Collections.

International Labor Defense recruited attorneys to defend African American victims of police brutality and immigrant workers who were in the process of being deported.[27]

But, as Mark Wild has shown, the most successful activities of the Los Angeles Communists during the early Depression years were its street demonstrations on behalf of the city's unemployed. Using the mottos "Don't Starve—Fight!" and "Work or Wages!" Communist organizers went door to door establishing block clubs to prevent tenants from being evicted in Boyle Heights, Little Tokyo, and other parts of town. Once enough members had been recruited on each block, they elected their own leaders, established unemployed councils and conducted protests in the downtown streets, at the Los Angeles welfare office, and at numerous locations where soup kitchens had been set up. Once monetary relief began flowing from state and federal coffers, the unemployed councils protested its inadequacy and demanded representation on the various bodies that distributed the aid.[28]

In April 1932, for example, representatives of L.A.'s unemployed councils urged the California State Unemployment Commission to press for a national unemployment insurance bill, complaining that the current system of state relief had "allowed thousands of workers and their families to be evicted from their homes, . . . [and has] driven many hundreds to crime and suicide."[29] In 1934, leftists seized upon the neglect of minorities by the local offices of the federally operated Civil Works Administration and proceeded to organize a short-lived Relief Workers Protection Association.[30]

Despite these efforts, the Communists failed to develop a mass following in Southern California. This was partly because the esoteric Marxist jargon the party used during its revolutionary Third Period frightened off more workers than it attracted.[31] It was partly because the party started off with a very small group of active members, consisting of a few hundred garment workers, some students and Hollywood intellectuals, and a number of Jewish tradesmen and Eastern European sympathizers from Boyle Heights.[32] And it was partly because the LAPD's red squad had no hesitation about breaking up the CP's street demonstrations wherever and whenever they appeared. The LAPD regularly beat up the marchers and took many of them into custody, making it risky for all but the most dedicated demonstrators to turn out in support.[33]

On March 6, 1930, for example, when the Los Angeles Communists led a hunger march on city hall (which was coordinated with similar hunger marches elsewhere in the country), protesting unemployment and demanding more state relief, the red squad deployed a thousand police on horseback as well as on foot, clubbed and beat many of the demonstrators, and put more than fifty of them in jail. Participant Peggy Dennis remembered envying the marchers in San Francisco on that same day: instead of attacking the crowd, the Bay Area police escorted the protest leaders to a public rostrum to present their demands to the city's mayor.[34] The greater harshness of the LAPD against these protest marches was, of course, consistent with its earlier history, and it confirms an observation William Mullins makes in his study of four western cities during the Depression. "Several marches in Los Angeles," he writes, "ended in confrontations with the Red Squad and arrests. In the other cities officials met the parades with mounting irritation but a minimum of violence."[35]

But the most important reasons for the Communist Party's limited appeal to L.A.'s working class in the early thirties were probably social and cultural rather than economic. Most white factory workers who settled in L.A.'s new industrial neighborhoods were patriotic immigrants from the rural Midwest, "plain folks"

Okies from the dust bowl states, and socially conservative Protestants from the border states to whom any talk of revolutionary action was anathema. Most historians of the Great Depression also agree that the majority of unemployed workers at first were too demoralized by their condition to consider challenging the prevailing economic system in any fundamental way. It was not until after the National Industrial Recovery Act (1933) had been adopted and President Roosevelt's other New Deal measures had begun to revive the country's belief in the future that most U.S. workers recovered their self-confidence. Contemporary researchers also found that large numbers of unemployed workers blamed themselves, not the breakdown of the capitalist system, for their plight.[36]

VOLUNTARY SELF-HELP OR STATE AID?

Radical activists in Los Angeles also found it difficult to disabuse blue-collar workers of the idea that the individual, rather than the state, should take responsibility for restoring the economy to health. The reluctance of the city authorities to provide money for unemployment relief not only resulted from the conservatism of Mayor John Porter and other municipal and county officials; it likely reflected the opinions of a majority of the local electorate as well. Even before the Great Depression hit, most blue-collar homeowners in the Alameda corridor favored low taxes and believed that the responsibility for financing welfare should be borne by local taxpayers, not provided free of charge by the state or federal government. When unemployment began to affect an industrial suburb like South Gate, for example, most residents held on to the view that urban services should be cut back to whatever the existing tax base could afford.[37] During the early years of the Depression, most of the city's AFL leaders appeared to agree with this voluntarist philosophy. In November 1930, the L.A. Central Labor Council signaled its opposition to state-mandated unemployment insurance. "The American people abhor charity," the statement read. "They must not and will not become the victims of a paternalistic policy."[38]

Given the large agricultural surpluses created by farmers in the Los Angeles basin, the initial reaction by many residents focused on how best to get these food surpluses into the hands of the unemployed without making it appear to be a form of direct relief. The answer came from an exceptionally well-developed system of local self-help cooperatives, which by 1935 had become the largest and most successful such network in the country. At their peak, these cooperatives provided some form of material assistance to more than 120,000 Southern California residents.[39]

L.A.'s self-help co-ops went through several stages of development. First came an informal network of barter associations, which exchanged surplus farm products for assistance such as barbering, shoe repairing, and auto servicing. Next came a group of so-called scrip exchanges organized by the Unemployed Cooperative Relief Association (UCRA). Under this system, unemployed workers "sold" their services in return for notes that could be redeemed at local cooperative food centers. These barter and scrip cooperatives, which dominated the movement between 1931 and 1933, established more than eighty branches all over the Los Angeles basin. Some unemployed workers provided gardening, general labor, sewing, or housecleaning services in exchange for food. Others set up small workshops that manufactured domestic articles.[40] A group of unemployed workers in Gardena operated a furniture shop; Huntington Park's jobless co-op ran two cooperative bakeries; and several individuals in Compton and South Gate rented a lean-to shed where unemployed families canned fruit and vegetables.[41]

Most of these Southern California self-help co-ops were small-scale affairs that lasted no more than a few months. The majority were located in the working-class suburbs on the south side of the city or farther west, toward the ocean. But the Unemployed Cooperative Relief Association was more substantial. Along with bodies such as the Unemployed Citizens' League, UCRA established a democratic method of self-government, with an elected council. At one point, the UCRA council included a longshoreman from San Pedro, an artist from Hollywood, and a steel mill worker from Torrance. Trade unions as such, however, had no official role.[42]

In 1932 the Communists, in an effort to expand their base, made an attempt to gain influence in the self-help cooperative movement, but they had little success. A number of private businessmen complained about the danger of left-wing producers' cooperatives undercutting their prices, which they considered incompatible with the free enterprise system. Radical leaders of cooperatives with names like Rochdale Workshop (a reference to Robert Owen's utopian cooperative movement in England) might also have been expected to treat the producers' co-ops as an embryonic alternative to the capitalist system.[43] However, the values of individualism and self-reliance held by most Southern Californians remained sufficiently strong throughout the Depression that almost no self-help co-op members made a serious move in the direction of radical politics. This was significant. A list of the party affiliations of a thousand co-op members drawn up in 1936 showed that a majority of them were Democrats and only ten or twelve were affiliated with either the Socialist Party or the Communist Party.[44]

Given the extent and persistence of the economic downturn, however, it soon became clear that the co-ops could not solve the unemployment problem by themselves. By 1932 California's city and state authorities were appropriating increasing amounts of money for direct relief; and after FDR took office in March 1933, even larger sums became available through the Federal Emergency Relief Administration, the Civilian Conservation Corps, and the WPA.[45] By the mid-1930s public works programs like the WPA, which at one time or another gave jobs to more than eighty thousand Southern California workers, undermined the cooperative movement and led to its demise.[46]

Unexpectedly, however, this was not the end of the story. Indeed, in some ways it was just the beginning. For it was just at this point that the Los Angeles public turned its attention to Upton Sinclair's panacea-like blueprint entitled End Poverty in California. What was EPIC, and why did it exert such a powerful, if temporary, influence over Southern California's politics?

UPTON SINCLAIR'S EXTRAORDINARY
1934 EPIC CAMPAIGN

Early in September 1933, the tall, bespectacled figure of Upton Sinclair—muck-raking novelist, publicist, civil libertarian, and excellent public speaker—strode into Beverly Hills City Hall and changed his voter registration from Socialist to Democrat. For nineteen years he had been a stalwart member of the California Socialist Party and had several times run for state office on its ticket. But in the presidential election of November 1932, a massive political tide had begun to move toward Franklin Roosevelt and the Democrats. Even in that Depression year, Socialist presidential candidate Norman Thomas received only nine hundred thousand votes nationwide—a drop in the bucket compared to the millions of votes that went to FDR. According to his own account, Sinclair also changed his party affiliation out of fear that if the Depression could not be cured, Hitler's fascist movement might spread from Europe to North America.[47]

Sinclair modeled his EPIC plan partly on Southern California's existing co-ops, capitalizing on their popularity to advance his candidacy when he ran for governor in 1934. A food cooperative he visited in Pomona gave him the idea for his proposed California Authority for Land, whose purpose was to establish a series of land colonies to produce food for the state's population. The metal, canning, and furniture co-ops operating in downtown Los Angeles provided the model for his California Authority for Production, which would rent or purchase idle factories in which the urban unemployed could manufacture industrial goods. The scrip used to pay for exchanging goods between L.A.'s co-ops was the inspiration for his proposed California Authority for Barter. That authority was also supposed to establish a circulating medium for the exchange of goods produced by the other two authorities. Sinclair estimated that this scheme would generate enough money not only to operate his three basic economic organizations but also to fund an old-age pension for persons over sixty-five.[48]

Despite its utopian elements, when the EPIC plan was first published in the fall of 1933 it proved to be highly popular. It is not difficult to see why. The tax breaks Sinclair proposed for property owners were attractive to L.A.'s working-class homeowners, and his plan for ending unemployment appealed to state and federal administrators, who were paying out millions of dollars in direct relief to the jobless—a task they would happily have dispensed with. In the excitement of the 1934 primary election campaign, not many people except professional economists stopped to ask how Sinclair's plan would actually work.[49]

When his campaign for the Democratic nomination started in earnest in the spring of 1934, Sinclair used what some historians have labeled America's first full-fledged media campaign to get his message across. In addition to *EPIC News*, which sold many thousands of copies, his staff established EPIC clubs in both Northern and Southern California. These clubs sponsored radio broadcasts, plays, youth clubs, speakers' bureaus, even drama groups and a rodeo. Sinclair also issued a sixty-four-page pamphlet entitled *I, Governor of California: And How I Ended Poverty: A True Story of the Future*. This pamphlet retrospectively narrated Sinclair's achievements as governor—after he had finished his term—in the manner of Edward Bellamy's utopian novel *Looking Backward* (1888). It showed how his EPIC plan had ended California's Depression and turned the state into a model for economic recovery all over the country.[50]

The utopian element in Sinclair's EPIC scheme raised the question of whether it was intended as a serious left-wing alternative to Franklin Roosevelt's New Deal or whether, as Carey McWilliams suggested, it was a propaganda vehicle designed to get Sinclair elected to office.[51] McWilliams' argument is certainly plausible. It seems difficult to believe, in retrospect, that even sympathetic members of the public could have considered it possible to create a new economic and political structure on the scale that EPIC envisaged as the result of a single election.

Nevertheless, historian James Gregory is on firmer ground when he argues that it made sense for Southern California voters to support the practical aspects of EPIC, even if they doubted that its long-range ideas were practicable. Gregory

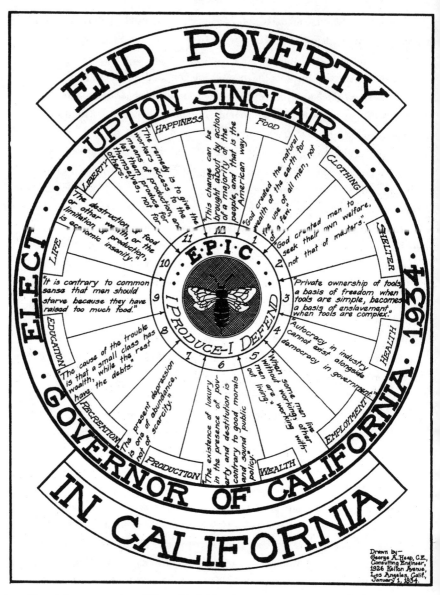

Pictorial representation of Upton Sinclair's EPIC program. Courtesy of Lilly Library, Indiana University, Bloomington, Indiana.

argues, rightly, that the large number of votes Sinclair won in the 1934 Democratic gubernatorial primary were part of a liberal tendency supported by the same constituency who had voted for Senator Robert La Follette's third-party movement in 1924 and would shortly vote for the Democratic Party and the New Deal.[52]

Voting data examined by Michael Rogin and John Shover supports Gregory's argument. Rogin and Shover found that Sinclair secured a large number of votes in working-class districts that were already responding to the union organizing campaigns spurred by pro-labor New Deal reforms. This data also challenges McWilliams's assertion that Sinclair's votes came primarily from the lower middle class. Rogin and Shover show that the more middle-class voters there were in any given precinct, the larger the Democratic drop-off was in the general election. By contrast, the larger the number of "laborers, service workers, operatives [and] craftsmen" living in a precinct, the smaller were the Democratic losses between the primary and the general election.[53]

The idea that EPIC acted as a conduit through which the working-class voters of Los Angeles were channeled into supporting the Democratic Party is also confirmed by Becky Nicolaides's study of South Gate. In the fall 1934 general election, she reports, no fewer than 61 percent of South Gate's voters cast their ballots for Sinclair, with only 27 percent going to Republican gubernatorial candidate Frank Merriam.[54] It was not surprising, either, at a time when politicians in other parts of the country were advocating far-reaching political reforms, that EPIC's far-left ideas should have proved attractive to California voters. In Minnesota, Governor Floyd Olson was urging the federal government to espouse the public ownership of several industries; and in Louisiana, Senator Huey Long was promulgating his "Share the Wealth" clubs. Dr. Francis Townsend's scheme to boost consumer spending by establishing an old-age pension system also reached a peak in popularity at this time, along with other panacea groups such as the Technocracy movement and the Utopian Society of America.[55]

What did surprise Los Angeles political observers, however, was the extent of Sinclair's victory in the Democratic primary. When the primary ballots were counted on August 29, Sinclair had received more than 436,000 votes, crushing the more moderate Democratic candidate, George Creel, a well-known New Dealer who had the personal support of President Roosevelt.[56] In Bell, for example, Sinclair defeated Creel by 1,030 votes to 158; he carried Maywood by 532 to 84; Inglewood by 3,207 to 712; and Montebello by 484 to 153.[57] These voting returns suggested that a new, class-based constituency of working-class Democratic voters was emerging in Southern California—and that it was growing rapidly. It was small wonder that Harry Chandler's conservative *Los Angeles Times*, expressing the fears of the Republican right, described Sinclair's primary victory as "a crisis for California—and for America."[58]

The Los Angeles political establishment was not going to be caught napping a second time. In the general election campaign that followed, it pursued a strategy much like the one used against Socialist Job Harriman after his surprise victory in the1911 primary election for mayor. The Republicans red-baited Sinclair mercilessly, and several moderate Democratic Party leaders, also believing that Sinclair had moved too far to the left, established a League of Loyal Democrats, which allied with acting governor Merriam's Republican Party to oppose Sinclair on the November ballot. Sinclair was also severely disappointed—indeed, made to look rather foolish—when President Roosevelt failed to endorse him after having given signs that he might do so.[59]

During the general election campaign, EPIC's relations with organized labor were also more lukewarm than might have been expected. *EPIC News* reported sympathetically on a number of strikes then occurring in Los Angeles, and it condemned the repressive behavior of the LAPD.[60] But Sinclair himself was not invited to speak to any union meetings, and few unions gave him money. For its part, the L.A. Central Labor Council thanked Sinclair for the support he gave to the city's unemployed, but it had refused to endorse him in the primary.[61]

Instead, the council followed the AFL's traditional "reward-your-friends, punish-your-enemies" political policy and endorsed a mixture of pro-labor Republican and Democratic candidates. In the general election campaign, a statewide labor committee was set up to help EPIC candidates, but the Central Labor Council held off on its endorsement and came out definitively in favor of Sinclair only one week before polling day, on October 28. It seems likely that many of the AFL's more conservative members, troubled by Sinclair's former Socialist Party activism, divided their votes between Republican candidate Merriam and mainstream Democrat Raymond Haight, who ran on a separate platform.[62] Given the massive disinformation campaign mounted against him, the remarkable thing was not that Sinclair lost the gubernatorial election in November 1934, but that he managed to secure 879,537 votes to Merriam's 1,138,620.[63]

In the Sixty-second Assembly District, which included much of Central Avenue, the young African American politician Augustus Hawkins—running as a Democrat—defeated incumbent GOP assemblyman Fred Roberts. This was the first time a Democrat had beaten a Republican elected official in L.A.'s black community—a major reversal of African American political tradition. Hawkins's victory was part of a nationwide shift in the political allegiance of African American voters from the Republican to the Democratic Party.[64]

THE LIMITS OF WHITE LIBERAL REFORM

Although Upton Sinclair and his push for reform lost in the 1934 gubernatorial election, by 1936 it had become clear that the reform programs of the New Deal were almost—if not equally—as popular in Southern California as they were elsewhere in the country. In December 1935, for example, a local leader of the Women's Trade Union League described the new pension system created by the Social Security Act (1935) as a "godsend," which would ensure that "the forgotten man is no longer a mere figure on the rolls of charity."[65] When President Roosevelt came up for reelection in November 1936, the *Los Angeles Citizen,* for the first time, urged the city's workers to turn out for the state and national Democratic ticket.[66]

At first, the 1936 election results appeared to be encouraging. Not only did FDR carry Los Angeles County by a large majority, but ten of the twelve Democratic candidates endorsed by the Central Labor Council for election to the state assembly were returned to Sacramento, some of them by large majorities. Five of these Democrats were former EPIC activists and distinctly radical in their opinions. (One, John P. Pelletier, represented the Forty-fourth Assembly District, a working-class neighborhood on the East Side; another, Jack B. Tenney, was president of the white Musicians Union.)[67] According to Michael Rogin and John Shover, the 1936 Democratic victory in Southern California showed "a trend towards a more urban-based constituency with greater labor support, greater sympathy for welfare measures, and less sensitivity to the prohibition question."[68]

Yet in some ways these victories proved to be a false dawn. It is true that two years later, in 1938, the Democratic Party in Los Angeles scored a further victory when it helped elect State Senator Culbert Olson, a Democrat and the leader of the EPIC group in the assembly, as governor.[69] But in that same year Judge Fletcher Bowron (a progressive Republican) was elected mayor of Los Angeles on a platform that nevertheless included several standard New Deal planks. In his first term, Mayor Bowron abolished the LAPD's infamous red squad, opposed a municipal anti-picketing ordinance, and saved L.A.'s city employees from retaliation by supervisors who were under investigation for corruption.[70] But the reform impulse at both the state and citywide levels soon faltered. During his first year in office, Governor Olson saw virtually his entire New Deal agenda defeated by the state legislature; and in 1942 he was defeated for reelection after only one term. Neither Olson's reform agenda at the state level nor Mayor Bowron's in Los Angeles paid much attention to issues of gender or race.[71] It is also noteworthy that some of EPIC's original activists had moved to the right by the end of the 1930s.

During the 1930s very little progress was made in Southern California on the question of civil rights, either. By the mid-1930s, racially restrictive covenants, which had begun with housing agreements in the 1920s, had been extended to apply (unofficially at least) to some of the city's schools, to most of its public swimming pools, and even to many of its parks. To white working-class families who had recently arrived in L.A. from Oklahoma and Texas, the idea of men and women of different races swimming together in revealing swimsuits was an affront to their traditional values. In 1931 Ethel Prioleau, an African American mother of two, took the city to court after being denied access to a public swimming pool and won her lawsuit. From that time on, L.A.'s public pools were officially integrated, but this did not prevent angry whites from keeping most blacks away.[72]

The same racist treatment was imposed on poor Asians and Mexicans, who had to content themselves with swimming in the Los Angeles River or in abandoned quarries such as Sleepy Lagoon, which would become famous in a World War II racial incident. Angry at being viewed as an inherently "criminal" class, some Mexicans got their revenge by taking Red Cars out to the West Side and deliberately picnicking in the front yards of wealthy white suburbanites.[73] Equally explosive was the question of public control over L.A. County's seventy-five miles of beaches, whose all-white image was seen as crucial to maintaining Southern California's reputation as the leisure mecca of the West. When rumors spread that African American entrepreneurs might buy some beach land, white politicians expressed the fear that private ownership could mean nonwhite ownership, so real estate developers stepped up their purchases of new beach land.[74] It was not until the 1960s that people of color were permitted to mix freely with whites on Southern California's warm stretches of sand.

L.A.'s overwhelmingly white bureaucracy also used more subtle methods to downplay minority demands for their fair share of leisure facilities. In the early 1930s, for example, the city's Playground and Recreation Department justified its refusal to build more than two small playgrounds in Watts, which by now was heavily African American, with the argument that its tax base was too narrow to warrant further expense. In 1937 a public swimming pool was built at 109th Street, but only after the WPA had agreed to pay most of the cost. Similarly, when it came to downtown urban renewal, the city privileged Pershing Square over the original

Mexican Plaza, especially after Pershing Square became a favorite hang-out for white-collar workers on their lunch breaks.[75]

White manipulation of the Plaza area—which, like Chinatown, was affected by the building of Union Station in 1928—went even deeper than that. In that same year, Harry Chandler, General Otis's successor as publisher of the *Los Angeles Times*, endorsed the idea advanced by Christine Sterling (the wealthy, philanthropic matron from San Francisco who had earlier protested the radical mural painted by David Siqueiros) to rescue Olvera Street from decay by "restoring" it as an "old Mexican" village with tiled sidewalks, displays of folk crafts, and strolling guitarists to entertain the tourists.[76] Just as the mistreatment of Indians by the Spaniards had earlier been swept under the rug by pageants that misrepresented mission life as benign and conflict-free, so now white fears of Depression-driven, Mexican social protest were smoothed over by transforming Olvera Street into "a beautiful little Spanish Village complete with balconies and senoritas with roses in their hair."[77] In reality, of course, no such ideal village had ever existed.

Additional evidence of both the class antagonisms and the racial conflicts that lurked beneath the surface of L.A.'s benign cultural façade could also be seen in the problems the Japanese American community encountered when it decided to stage a series of Nisei festivals in Little Tokyo, aimed at keeping second-generation Japanese Americans connected to their heritage, both culturally and economically. During the 1930s the image of the Japanese American community in Los Angeles became increasingly negative, owing to the denial of citizenship included in the 1924 Johnson Reed Act and to the diplomatic tensions that arose over Japan's invasion of China.[78] Most white employers refused to hire Japanese American workers, and many labor unions denied them membership. With no new Japanese immigrants permitted to enter the country, Little Tokyo risked the possibility of commercial decline.[79]

Faced with this dilemma, Little Tokyo's merchants staged a number of Nisei festivals to encourage second-generation Japanese to purchase Japanese goods instead of American ones. But given the hostility of the Anglo community, the festival organizers deliberately avoided displaying exhibits that might foster anti-Japanese sentiment or reveal class differences within the Japanese American community itself. Thus the 1936 festival parade featured a giant celery stalk symbolizing the skill of Japanese truck farmers in the Venice area, and wholesale merchants from the downtown Japanese produce market carried a banner boasting about their business success. But no mention was made of the poorly paid Japanese labor-

ers who loaded the produce at the downtown market, and no Japanese farm workers were invited to march in the parade.[80]

It is of course true that, with certain exceptions, the 1930s were not generally
noted for progress on civil rights at a national level. To push his New Deal agenda
through Congress, President Roosevelt needed the support of southern Democrats
too much to risk many initiatives in the area of civil rights.[81] But the racist behavior of white politicians in Los Angeles—which was, after all, a "northern" city—
was particularly noticeable.

The most obvious explanation for the failure to make any appreciable progress against institutionalized racism in Southern California during the New Deal
era lay in fears of the "yellow peril," which had long characterized L.A.'s attitude
toward the Japanese,[82] and in the deeply held racist prejudices of the white majority against Mexicans and African Americans. In his 1934 political campaign, for
example, Upton Sinclair even advised his supporters not to discuss the question
of race.[83] But after the high hopes for social reform that had been engendered by
the 1936 election, some further explanation is required for the difficulty the social
reformers experienced in creating a viable New Deal political coalition.

UNIONS, POLITICS, AND THE SEARCH FOR
A NEW DEAL COALITION

Why was the revitalization of the Southern California Democratic Party that followed Upton Sinclair's spectacular showing in the 1934 primary not quickly followed by the establishment of a New Deal alliance built around labor and the
Democrats? This, after all, was what happened in most of the industrial cities of
the Midwest and the East.

One reason was that Los Angeles had never contained the same kinds of ethnic voters who had traditionally nurtured the Democratic Party elsewhere in
the country. Historian Lizabeth Cohen has described the positive role Eastern
European immigrant voters played in creating Chicago's powerful New Deal
coalition: "Workers became drawn into an inter-ethnic Democratic machine . . .
under the leadership of Czech politician Anton Cermak that connected them
not only to a unified Democratic party on the city level but also to the national
Democratic party."[84] Los Angeles, by contrast, had far fewer Irish and Eastern
European voters with which to fashion a similar Democratic machine.

A second reason was that social and political reform in Los Angeles had traditionally been enacted by enlightened elements among the Progressives or in the

Republican Party, not through the Democrats. When L.A. historian Tom Sitton wanted to characterize the reform coalition that took office under Mayor Bowron in 1938, he called it "an odd combination of conservatives . . . , of liberals and leftists who wanted progressive change to go further, and of those who simply wanted municipal office."[85]

The persistent loyalty of reformers to the Republican Party in Southern California was also illustrated by the experience of Robert W. Kenny, a leftwing Superior Court judge who worked for the La Follette-Norris-LaGuardia Committee, a Republican policy organization that wanted to build a nationwide labor-reform alliance while maintaining its loyalty to the Progressive wing of the Republican Party. In 1936, Kenny tried to attract Culbert Olson onto this committee before he became governor, but Olson refused to join because he "could not appreciate the feelings of those of us who were ashamed to be Republicans but were still afraid to become Democrats."[86]

The effect of these shifting political loyalties on the city's trade union leaders, especially those in the conservative AFL, was to encourage individual unions to engage in pressure-group politics instead of embracing an overall commitment to the Democratic Party's program. The secretary of the Central Labor Council, J. W. Buzzell, was a particular devotee of this practice, tenaciously opposing "any ideologically oriented political activity."[87] It was quite common in this period—as it still is today—for working-class voters in cities all over the country to vote for Democratic candidates in federal elections and divide their votes between other parties at the local level.[88]

But L.A.'s working-class voters may have followed this practice even more assiduously than labor voters did in other cities. For example, it appeared in the late 1930s that a coalition of Southern California union members was actively promoting municipal ownership of the city's electric power facilities, a policy Mayor Bowron supported. In reality, however, most of labor's contribution came from a single union, the International Brotherhood of Electrical Workers (IBEW) Local 18, which represented employees in the Department of Water and Power. "Public ownership would clearly increase the local's size and power and protect its members' jobs," writes political scientist David Greenstone, but "once the battle was won, the local did not undertake any [further] significant political action."[89]

Although it was still quite small, the L.A. Communist Party, for its part, played a more influential role in local politics at this time than in earlier years. Between 1934 and 1937, the party expanded its base quite substantially among intellectuals, as well as among San Pedro longshoremen, Hollywood guild members, and

African Americans hungry for civil rights. It also commanded a significant following among unions affiliated with the Industrial Council of the CIO. By 1938 the party had grown to include approximately two thousand members.[90] Its largest units were among the "talent branches" of writers, directors, and actors operating in Hollywood under the direction of V. J. Jerome, who was known as the party's "commissar of cultural affairs."[91] Following the lead of the CIO, in 1938 the Los Angeles Communists endorsed the successful mayoral candidate, Fletcher Bowron.[92]

Probably the most important explanation for the divided loyalties of L.A.'s working-class voters in the latter part of the 1930s, however, was the limited political reach of the Los Angeles CIO. In cities such as Chicago and Detroit, it was the political clout of the CIO-affiliated unions, more than anything else, that solidified working-class support for the Democratic Party. Between 1936 and 1939, nationwide CIO unions like the United Auto Workers, the Rubber Workers, the United Electrical Workers, and the Mine, Mill, and Smelter Workers all established branches in the industrial enclaves along the Alameda corridor. So, too, did more localized unions such as the Oil Workers, which operated out of El Segundo and Long Beach, and the United Cannery, Agricultural, Packing, and Allied Workers of America (UCAPAWA), which secured a major following among farm and packinghouse workers in the citrus belt.[93]

When compared to their counterparts in other big industrial cities, however, the Los Angeles branches of these CIO unions were puny. Take the Steel Workers Organizing Committee (SWOC), for example, which later became the United Steel Workers of America. In 1937–1938, Steel Workers Local 1845 enrolled about 850 workers at the recently founded Bethlehem Steel plant in Maywood and at a few other Southern California steel mills, but the total number of steel mill employees in the region amounted to no more than 14,000.[94]

As early as 1919, by contrast, the Calumet/Gary industrial zone south of Chicago boasted five or six steel towns, each of which contained thousands of Slovakian anthracite shovelers, Croatian furnace men, Irish crane operators, and a wide range of other steel mill employees. By 1940, after the 1937 Memorial Day massacre (in which Chicago police fired on unarmed protestors, killing ten and injuring many others, during the "Little Steel" strike) and the other bloody labor struggles of 1936–1937, they added up to a total of about 114,000 militant trade unionists, virtually all of whom had been signed up by the union, and most of whom voted solidly for the Democratic Party in local, state, and federal elections.[95]

The contrast between the numerical strength of the United Auto Workers in

Los Angeles and Detroit was even more striking. After the UAW's victory in the famous General Motors sit-down strike at Flint in 1936–1937, which unionized no fewer than 80,000 assembly-line workers, the union's political influence in Detroit became so great that it was able to dominate the city's political agenda.[96] The influence exerted by the UAW in Southern California was much weaker. The General Motors factory at South Gate (which was only the second auto assembly plant established in the region) did not open until 1936, the same year as the Flint strike. In 1938 UAW Local 216 contained 1,200 members, a drop in the bucket compared to the giant UAW locals in Detroit.[97] The L.A. branches of other CIO unions such as the Rubber Workers, the United Electrical Workers, the Meat Packers, and the Amalgamated Clothing Workers were equally small.[98]

CONCLUSION

It would be wrong to argue that there was not a shift in the political loyalties of L.A.'s workers from the Republicans to the Democrats during the course of the 1930s. Such a shift did occur, and it lasted, in many instances, through the 1960s. In 1930, all of the city's twenty-two state assembly seats were held by Republicans. But after 1936, the Democrats held sixteen assembly seats, whereas the Republicans held only six.[99] But the key point in understanding the relative weakness of the labor-Democratic coalition in L.A. compared to such coalitions elsewhere is that Los Angeles had a smaller number of manufacturing workers than the large industrial cities of the East and the Midwest. Hence the Industrial Council of the Los Angeles CIO had a smaller and less disciplined body of voters at its command than did its equivalents in other industrial cities with comparable overall populations.

The political significance of this numerical imbalance becomes even clearer when we compare the limited role of the CIO-sponsored Labor's Nonpartisan League (LNPL) in Los Angeles with this organization's extensive activities in the nation's industrial heartland. Labor's Nonpartisan League was a Communist-influenced political pressure group established by the CIO in the summer of 1936 to aid in the reelection of President Franklin Roosevelt and, where possible, to bring about "a realignment of all progressives into one party."[100] Denounced by the AFL as a Communist front, the LNPL based its political campaigns on the enthusiasm of thousands of volunteers from the United Mine Workers, the Amalgamated Clothing Workers, and the CIO's other industrial unions in the Midwest and the East. In Pennsylvania, according to one authority, "the substantial majority given to the Democratic ticket . . . [was] due largely to the activities of the League."[101]

In Los Angeles, however, the Industrial Council of the CIO lacked both the money and the membership to turn the Nonpartisan League into a political force of comparable power. The LNPL's activities in Northern California, where the political side of the CIO was more developed than in the Southland, were quite extensive. In the summer of 1936, there were scattered references in the labor press to a Los Angeles branch of the LNPL being formed by Communist Party leader Don Healey. But when it came to the critical November 1936 election, the league managed to hold only three poorly attended political rallies in Southern California.[102]

Not until the massive expansion of the aircraft and shipbuilding industries during World War II did the L.A. labor movement begin to exert a degree of political clout that was comparable—although not yet as great—to the political clout exerted by its counterparts elsewhere. Even then, for reasons explored in the next chapter, the business union philosophy of the AFL remained more influential in Southern California than the broad, industrial union outlook of the CIO.

SIX · Raising Consciousness at
the Workplace

*Anglos, Mexicans, and the Founding of
the Los Angeles CIO, 1933–1938*

On June 22, 1934, J. W. Buzzell, secretary of the Los Angeles Central Labor Council, told his fellow council members that for weeks on end after the passage of Section 7a of the National Industrial Recovery Act (NIRA) in 1933, he had been pressured, day after day, "to attend meetings of groups of workers seeking to organize."[1] For the first time in American history, federal law banned company (that is, employer-created) labor unions and provided definitive support for independent union organizations. By the end of that summer, the American Federation of Labor in Los Angeles, whose ranks in 1932 had dwindled to 11,139 paid-up members, had enrolled more than 30,000 new employees among bakers, laundry drivers, cloak and dressmakers, tire and rubber workers, building trades workers, and others.[2]

Sensing his new power, Buzzell invited representatives of the Merchants and Manufacturers Association to sit down with him and discuss the new labor codes mandated by NIRA. He was curtly rebuffed. Though labor was strong enough to force employers to negotiate in a number of cities around the country, the AFL in Los Angeles was too weak to elicit a positive response. "We cannot see that the NIRA has in any way made mandatory the recognition of organized union labor," stated Edgar R. Perry, general manager of the M&M.[3] Even after President Roosevelt issued an executive order requiring employers to abide by the act, L.A.'s open shop manufacturers avoided compliance, continuing to establish company unions in numerous trades and refusing to recognize the independent labor movement.[4]

This rebuff set the stage for a decade of bitter conflict between labor and capital in Southern California—in the fields, on the docks, in the mass production industries, in the sweated trades such as garmentmaking, and in the increasingly influential aircraft and moviemaking industries. It came to a head in 1939–1940, when the revolution in labor law brought about by the New Deal and the growing power of the unions finally gave the Los Angeles labor movement enough strength to quell the power of the open shop lobby. The struggle changed Southern California from a place where unions were regarded as a threat to "industrial freedom" to one where they were accepted, albeit grudgingly, as a legitimate part of civil society.[5]

This battle between capital and labor was not only conducted at the workplace. The New Deal brought many other changes in society as well. As the groundswell of labor protest in Los Angeles grew, it became a multilayered conflict between employers and workers, between federal agencies such as the National Labor Relations Board and conservative Republican officials such as Mayor Frank L. Shaw and L.A. district attorney Buron Fitts, and between conservative craft union leaders and insurgent factory workers in South and East L.A. In 1936–1937 industrial unions such as the United Auto Workers and the Steel Workers Organizing Committee broke away from the AFL and established the Southern California branches of the Congress of Industrial Organizations (CIO).[6]

This chapter and the next focus on the resurgence of labor in Los Angeles in the 1930s and on the founding and growth of the CIO. Though the organization itself was not constituted until 1937, the influence of industrial unionism spread throughout much of the decade. Strikes and protest movements took place not only among male manufacturing workers in the Alameda corridor but also among women in industries such as garmentmaking and canning, among migrant agricultural workers in the San Gabriel Valley, and among the dockworkers of San Pedro.

DOWNTOWN GARMENT WORKERS RESPOND TO THE CALL

Most labor historians agree that the upsurge of union activity in 1933–1934 was as much a spontaneous, grassroots response to the passage of Section 7a of the NIRA as it was the result of a carefully prepared campaign.[7] The most remarkable thing about this strike wave, however, is that it was initiated not by skilled workers eager to expand their existing base but by supposedly inexperienced Mexican workers whom the AFL had hitherto largely ignored. Even more remarkable was the important part Latina workers played in the opening phases of the struggle.

Rose Pesotta of the ILGWU. Courtesy of TICOR Collection, University of Southern California, on behalf of the USC Special Collections.

Part of the explanation for their prominent role lies in the devastating effect of the Depression, in which a higher proportion of minority men than women lost their jobs. This left a significant number of Latinas and African American women, many of whom were paid less than half of what their husbands made, in desperate need of a wage increase to keep their families afloat.[8] Hence their desire for a union.

Whatever the reasons, L.A.'s most influential strike in the early days of the New Deal was the walkout of Mexican dressmakers in the downtown garment district in the fall of 1933. The dressmakers were assisted in their efforts by an energetic young organizer named Rose Pesotta, a Jewish immigrant from Eastern Europe, who had been sent out from ILGWU headquarters in New York by the union's president, David Dubinsky.[9] The International Ladies Garment Workers Union was a semi-industrial union containing Italian and Eastern European garment workers with several different levels of skill, and it was one of the few important unions in the AFL with a predominantly female membership.[10] But in Southern California it was run by a group of male union leaders, nearly all of them white and Jewish, who had moved west from New York at an earlier date and who focused on organizing the same kinds of workers who had made cloaks and suits back east. Knowing no Spanish, these union men ignored the thousands of Latinas who labored in sweatshops fabricating light dresses and summer clothes, which sold more quickly in the warm Southern California weather than the heavy East Coast garments did.[11]

When she first arrived in L.A. in September 1933, Rose Pesotta was shocked to find that the Jewish leaders of the union, many of whom were nominal Socialists, regarded the Latina dressmakers with something like contempt. "Mexican women could never be organized," said ILGWU West Coast director Louis Levy, adding that the L.A. garment manufacturers preferred to hire Mexican women rather than white, or even black, women "because they would work for a pittance and could endure any sort of treatment."[12] This condescending attitude betrayed a failure by the leadership to understand Mexican traditions of solidarity or to realize that the female sewing machine operators were just as eager to improve their wages and working conditions as the male cloakmakers were. A 1928 survey of the L.A. garment industry found that, far from being easily intimidated, most of the Mexican women and girls were "regular workers, . . . who were ready to advance."[13]

Rose Pesotta had no patience with the racist and sexist attitudes of the ILGWU's old guard. She hired Socialist Bill Busick as her assistant and implemented a consciousness-raising program among the Mexican dressmakers that stands out, even today, as a model of cultural sensitivity. Pesotta visited nearby Olvera Street to admire the Mexican-run sales booths, established after-hours socials in the garment district to which married women could bring their children, and arranged for Spanish-language broadcasts on station KELW to inform immigrant workers about the benefits of trade unionism. Pesotta was equally skillful in handling the strike for union recognition that followed in October 1933. She and her volunteer helpers established a strike headquarters at 1108 South Los Angeles Street, where the dressmakers were organized into shop groups, each of which elected its own chairperson. By the end of the first day, 3,011 strikers had registered with strike headquarters and had received a bag of groceries to help sustain their families. Most of the remaining workers in the industry honored the strikers' picket lines. Before two weeks had passed, the Garment Manufacturers Association agreed to go to arbitration and negotiate a settlement.[14]

Unfortunately for the strikers, it proved impossible to make the negotiated agreement stick. In theory, the dressmakers were to obtain union recognition, a pay hike, and wages ranging from $14 to $45 a week depending on the hours worked, in accordance with federally required labor codes for the industry. As with all the labor codes mandated by the National Recovery Administration, however, there was at first no legal machinery to enforce them. Pesotta tried to get permission from the ILGWU president to resume the strike, but Dubinsky refused. Despite this, the strike did secure some benefits. It increased the union's membership, raised the dressmakers' morale, and gave the immigrant workers valuable experience. Above all, it demonstrated that the white male leaders of the Los Angeles ILGWU had been wrong to dismiss the immigrant Mexican dressmakers as unorganizable.[15]

Rose Pesotta stressed these points in her report to President Dubinsky. She told him that the female pressers, finishers, and sewing machine operators in the L.A. garment shops were "of the same class as those in the east," and that if further efforts were made to organize them, they would become, "after the Italians, the second largest group in our national union."[16] Expressing her own frustrations with the L.A. union leaders, Pesotta added, pointedly, that most of the men who ran the Los Angeles locals of the ILGWU were "as petrified as the forests in Arizona."[17]

The 1933 dressmakers strike was not without frustrations. The Needle Workers Industrial Union, a Communist-run, dual-unionist organization, criticized the inability of the ILGWU to secure a satisfactory settlement. Pesotta herself experienced the anti-Semitism of some of the Latino strikers, and she had difficulty restraining them from rejecting the leadership of the ILGWU's white organizers and launching a separate Mexican-run union.[18] The latter point was important. At this time many of East L.A.'s Spanish-speaking immigrants were still suspicious of the white male leaders of the Central Labor Council. They were understandably more comfortable with union organizers who spoke their own language than they were with the Anglo leaders of the ILGWU.

Despite these limitations, the dressmakers strike showed clearly that the immigrant workers in L.A.'s downtown sweated trades were just as capable of pursuing their own economic interests as the white, English-speaking factory workers in the city's industrial suburbs. It also demonstrated that second-generation Mexican women in the city were beginning to respond to the same modernizing, cosmopolitan, and liberalizing influences that were affecting their male counterparts. Pesotta noted this herself when she wrote her autobiography, *Bread upon the Waters*. "Some of the women quietly admitted to me that they, too, would like to be Americans," she reported. "In Mexico women still had no freedom; a married woman could not vote or hold office without her husband's consent, and the father was still the supreme ruler over unmarried daughters until they reached the age of 29."[19]

EL MONTE'S BERRY PICKERS, LUISA MORENO, AND
THE TRANSFORMATION OF MEXICAN CONSCIOUSNESS

The growing self-confidence displayed by the ILGWU's dressmakers showed that minority women in the garment industry had moved well beyond the stereotype of the submissive immigrant. The same conclusion can be drawn regarding the Mexicans in another major strike carried out by immigrant workers in 1933: the walkout by berry pickers in El Monte, in L.A.'s eastern suburbs. Beginning in May 1933, the California agriculture industry as a whole was convulsed by a major strike wave that involved cotton workers, fruit pickers, cannery employees, and vegetable harvesters in places as far apart as San Diego and Eureka.[20] The El Monte berry pickers strike, in the San Gabriel Valley, was not the largest of these protests, but it provided an important example of militancy for immigrants and manufacturing employees who worked downtown.

The story of the El Monte strike is easily told. The fruit pickers held a mass meeting at Hicks Camp outside El Monte on June 1, 1933, at the height of the harvest season and voted to stop work unless their Japanese employers agreed to raise their wages. Their demands rejected, the Mexican pickers launched a six-week strike, which at one point swept across the entire Southern California basin to include onion and celery workers in Venice and Culver City. This fast-moving protest was typical of the spontaneity that characterized many of the organizing strikes in the turbulent years of the early 1930s. Even if Los Angeles was not a hotbed of union activity at the level of Detroit and Pittsburgh, clearly its immigrant workers were beginning to respond enthusiastically to the hope of unionization unleashed by the New Deal labor reforms. The basic issue in the El Monte strike was the wage rate to be paid for an hour's work or for picking a crate of berries. Early in the strike, the growers, fearing the loss of their crop, offered 25 cents an hour or 40 cents per crate, which was a major increase over the prevailing wage rate. Sensing victory, the strikers rejected this offer in the hope of gaining something better.[21]

Before the growers could reply, an internal dispute broke out over who should lead the strike, which ultimately compromised its outcome. The groundwork for the stoppage had been laid by the Communist-led Cannery and Agricultural Workers Industrial Union (CAWIU), most of whose leaders were Anglo. But Armando Flores, the leader of the Mexican berry pickers, was suspicious of the Communists, preferring instead to keep control in Mexican hands. In order to improve the strikers' bargaining position, Flores sought the help of the Mexican government, which responded by dispatching Ricardo Hill, the Mexican vice-consul in L.A., to assist in the struggle. Appealing to the strikers' ethnic pride, Hill denounced CAWIU as a union controlled by outsider agitators and urged the strikers to repudiate it in favor of an all-Mexican union, which would have the support of the Mexican government.[22]

Hill's appeal appeared to succeed. The Communist leaders of CAWIU tried to keep control of the strike by claiming that the "fake liberal" Hill-Flores faction was collaborating with the state authorities, a claim that turned out to have some validity.[23] In his account of the strike, Cletus Daniel suggests that the white city authorities in El Monte believed that the Mexican rank and file, being "less clever and more malleable" than their Anglo leaders, would easily be persuaded to back down once the Communists had been eliminated.[24] In this, they were mistaken. Flores and his supporters proceeded to spread the work stoppage into new areas, reconstituted their part of CAWIU into a new union known as the Confederación de Uniones de Campesinos y Obreros Mexicanos (CUCOM), and forced the growers to the bargaining table. By this time, however, several weeks had passed, and most of the El Monte berry crop had already been picked by imported scabs. Although CUCOM secured a settlement providing a standard wage of $2 a day for its members, few of the berry workers present at the time benefited from it. Most of the active unionists were fired, and the berry pickers had to wait until the following season to try and gain another contract.[25]

In spite of its mixed results, the El Monte berry strike provides another fascinating glimpse into the development of relations between employers, Anglos, and immigrant workers in Southern California agriculture. Despite evidence to the contrary, Dr. George P. Clements, agricultural manager of the L.A. Chamber of Commerce, claimed that the Mexican worker was "ignorant of values; . . . He is the most tractable individual that ever came to serve us."[26] Some white employers were forced to revise that opinion when they witnessed the role of Mexican workers in the CIO. But most of L.A.'s white employers persisted for years in the erroneous view that it was only when outside agitators seduced them that Mexicans were likely to unionize.

Though the El Monte strike once more punctured the myth of Mexican docility at the workplace, it does not justify the opposite conclusion, that all Mexican workers were seething with radical discontent. After the strike was over, the Communists, to their credit, did not simply blame "anarchists," "fake liberals," or even the "capitalist police" for their loss of control over the strike. Instead, consistent with the party doctrine concerning the need for self-criticism, they acknowledged that they had made some mistakes in their conduct of the strike.[27] Should we then conclude, as Vice-Consul Ricardo Hill appears to have done, that most of the El Monte strikers were putative Mexican nationalists?

Such a conclusion would be equally misleading. Armando Flores clearly opposed the influence of the Communists and called on the Mexican consulate for help in order to push the El Monte strike in a more nationalist direction. But later in the decade, at another farm workers strike in Riverside County in which some of the same actors were involved, Guillermo Velarde, the leader of CUCOM, argued that "a large proportion of the strikers are American citizens and [Vice-Consul] Hill and [Honorary Commissioner] Lucio have no authority . . . to negotiate for them."[28]

The operative words in Velarde's remarks were "American citizens." The strikers at El Monte, like other Mexican immigrant workers who labored in the sweated trades, were groping for a new sense of identity that was an amalgam of many elements, some drawn from their Mexican heritage and some from their U.S. experience. How should this new sense of identity be defined? To answer this question, we can look to an event that occurred later in the decade: the founding in 1939 of El Congreso del Pueblo de Habla Española (the Congress of Spanish-Speaking Peoples), the first national civil rights assembly established among Latinos in Southern California. Among those present at the founding convention of El Congreso were the cannery workers employed at Cal San (California Sanitary Canning Company) in Boyle Heights.[29] Their story throws additional light on the Mexican workers' emerging sense of identity.

As in the garment industry, an external catalyst stirred the cannery workers into action. In this case, the catalyst consisted of two feminist labor organizers— Communist leader Dorothy Healey and Guatemalan-born Luisa Moreno, who later became a vice-president of the West Coast CIO.[30] (Both of these women are commemorated in a mural located at the Southern California Library for Social Studies and Research, on Vermont Avenue in South Central Los Angeles.) On August 31, 1939, at the height of the peach-canning season, over four hundred men and women who worked at the Cal San plant in Boyle Heights left their work stations and went on strike. They wanted recognition of their union, UCAPAWA (the United Cannery, Agricultural, Packing, and Allied Workers of America); a wage hike; and the dismissal of their vindictive male supervisors. Dorothy Healey organized strategy and picket line committees, while Luisa Moreno made public speeches on the strikers' behalf. Meanwhile, CIO supporters from the white industrial suburbs in south Los Angeles joined Mexican cannery women on the picket line, and East L.A. grocers supplied them with food.[31]

The result was a remarkable demonstration of community solidarity and, since

Luisa Moreno, vice-president of UCAPAWA. Courtesy of Southern California Library for Social Studies and Research.

women constituted a majority of Cal San's employees, sisterly support. Unlike the 1933 garment workers strike, in which outsider Rose Pesotta carried most of the burden, the Mexican cannery women developed a cadre of home-grown leaders, which included Elmo Parra, Carmen Escobar, and Julia Luna Mount. In addition, rank-and-file strikers boycotted local businesses friendly to George and Joseph Shapiro, Cal San's owners, and even embarrassed the two brothers by setting up a picket line on the lawn of their home. In a preview of modern labor feminism, the women placed the dignity of Cal San's female employees at the center of their demands; for example, they asked for child care during work hours. "In [the] Cal San negotiations," Luisa Moreno recalled, "a woman remarked: 'Females includes the whole animal kingdom. We want to be referred to as WOMEN.'"[32] The result was that the strikers won most of their demands, and Local 75 of UCAPAWA became one of the most famous CIO locals in Southern California.

By adding women's rights to the list of cannery workers' demands, Moreno added a new dimension to the immigrants' task, in George Sánchez's words, of "becoming Mexican American." To put it another way, labor organizers like Rose Pesotta and Luisa Moreno helped L.A.'s minority workers of different nationalities to modify and update features of the indigenous protest traditions they had brought from their homelands into a new, "American" form of oppositional culture.[33]

Equally important was the growing political sophistication Mexican workers displayed through their association with El Congreso. In April 1939, a couple of months before the Cal San strike took place, over 130 Spanish-speaking and Anglo representatives from the I A unions as well as community organizations from elsewhere in the Southwest attended the first national convention of El Congreso in downtown Los Angeles. Built around the leadership skills of Luisa Moreno and Josefina Fierro de Bright, El Congreso put together a remarkable coalition of Mexican union organizers, civil rights activists, and social justice groups, including the Workers Alliance, the Women's International League for Peace and Freedom, and a group of left-wing Hollywood artists and writers from the Screen Actors Guild. (The latter group was included because Josefina Bright was married to scriptwriter John Bright.)[34] This new movement toward cross-cultural and cross-gender solidarity would become even stronger when it was reinforced by the industrial union philosophy of the CIO.

THE GREAT 1934 SAN PEDRO DOCK STRIKE

The next major step in the escalating struggle for trade union rights in Southern California was the longshoremen's strike, which affected ports up and down the West Coast, including the San Pedro waterfront, in the spring of 1934. The issues that sparked the strike were similar to those raised in the 1916 West Coast dock strike (described in Chapter Three): anger at the employer-controlled "fink hall" method of hiring on the docks and, in San Pedro, resentment at the longstanding domination of the waterfront by open shop shipping companies and their allies in the M&M. In addition, rank-and-file members of Local 38–92 of the International Longshoremen's Association in San Pedro (which later became Local 13 of the ILWU) had grown increasingly dissatisfied with the failure of their union leaders to resolve the conflicts between the different marine workers unions.[35]

A coastwide strike to protest the fink hall system of hiring almost broke out in March 1934, but it was delayed at the request of President Roosevelt. The employers and the dockworkers used the interval to prepare for the strike they knew was coming. A company-run union known as the Mutual Protective Association was set up to supply strikebreakers, and the Industrial Department of the M&M collected a war chest of $85,000. The shipowners also signed a secret contract with the Burns Detective Agency and Captain William "Red" Hynes of the LAPD's red squad to supply extra police and guards in the event of violence.[36]

Compared to the shipowners, the longshoremen's resources seemed puny. In the spring of 1934, the San Pedro union local had more than twelve hundred members and was supported by the West Coast district of the ILA in San Francisco. But the local had been in existence for less than a year and had very little money. Although the core membership consisted of experienced Anglo and Scandinavian maritime workers, it also included large numbers of Mexican, Croatian, and Portuguese longshoremen, who were an unknown quantity.[37] Nevertheless, as members of a tightly knit occupational community, the San Pedro dockworkers enjoyed the support of many of the town's tradesmen and shopkeepers as well as the union's own women's auxiliary. Members of the local held rallies, distributed leaflets, placed union cards in the windows of supportive bars and restaurants, and hoped for the best.[38]

When the strike began on May 9, it tied up shipping in Seattle, Portland, San Diego, and San Francisco as well as in Los Angeles. The first phase of the struggle in San Pedro, which ran from May 9 to early June, was marked by the shipowners' repeated attempts to keep the port open by importing strikebreakers. These men were barricaded behind a stockade at Berth 140, just north of the main shipping channel; the shipowners provided them with food and sleeping accommodations, and they were escorted to work by company guards and police. Unlike the situation in San Francisco, the owners did manage to keep the port of San Pedro open throughout the strike. But it was no easy task. In addition to posting official union pickets, San Pedro's union members sent out patrols to counter the activities of the strikebreakers. Occasionally, their patrols "knocked over" company guards and took small boats out into the harbor to harass the crews who were still at work unloading the ships. Quite often, there was physical violence.[39]

On the night of May 14, some three hundred strikers stormed the employers' stockade at Berth 140 and tried to expel the strikebreakers from the docks. One young striker, Richard Parker, was killed, six were wounded, and a score more were injured. Accusations were traded as to who was responsible for the death, and police detective Walter Hannefeld was eventually charged with murder. A funeral procession was held, money was collected for Parker's widow, and tension mounted on both sides. The *San Pedro News-Pilot* reported the day after Parker's funeral that its "survey of the harbor district . . . revealed a seething unrest and [a] tendency to regard the dead youth and [the] injured as martyrs."[40]

The second half of the strike witnessed a broadening and deepening of the struggle. On June 8, Secretary Buzzell of the L.A. Central Labor Council established a special support fund from the AFL's constituent unions, which raised $1,947.00. The San Pedro ILA local followed this up by holding a number of benefit shows and dances at its headquarters on Fifth and Palos Verdes streets.[41] As food supplies became scarcer, striker Alfred Langley recalled, he and his friends went over to Catalina Island to shoot wild goats for meat. "All over San Pedro, Palos Verdes—they used to pick vegetables; butchers used to give 'em meat; guys would go out in trucks and pick the stuff up."[42] The shipowners and the *Los Angeles Times* tried to tighten the screws by pressuring the county board of supervisors to stop disbursing unemployment relief to the strikers. Buzzell retaliated by urging Mayor Shaw and District Attorney Fitts to have the L.A. Grand Jury investigate the increasingly transparent links between the shipowners, Captain Hynes's red squad, and the weapons that found their way into the hands of the strikebreakers. But the Grand Jury failed to respond.[43]

As the conflict sharpened, Joe Ryan, the conservative (and corrupt) president of the ILA, who was based in New York, announced a settlement with the Waterfront Employers Association of San Francisco, which he had negotiated over the heads of the strikers. Although the terms he negotiated closely resembled the ones that were ultimately accepted, a majority of longshoremen up and down the coast voted to reject the agreement in a June 15 referendum that became a resounding rebuke to Ryan's leadership. One reason for the rejection was that the proposed settlement neglected the interests of other maritime workers who had struck in support of the longshoremen. (The mutual support built between the longshoremen and other waterfront workers reflected the growing interest in the type of industrywide union the IWW had advocated in earlier years—shorn of some of its revolutionary ideology.) However, the one exception to the decisive "no" vote on Ryan's proposed settlement was the San Pedro local, whose members voted to accept it, by a margin of 638 to 584. This signaled that the conservative leadership of the San Pedro local was out of step with the militant Pacific Coast leaders of the union in San Francisco.[44]

The dock strike finally ended on July 31, 1934, when the men went back to work after agreeing that the dispute would be referred to an arbitration board appointed by President Roosevelt. The final settlement handed down on October 12 did not give the strikers all they wanted, but it was a major setback for the Los Angeles shipowning lobby. The longshoremen had not won the strike outright, but the federal government had imposed a settlement from above that the shipowners could not afford to ignore. It included the six-hour day, a wage increase, and a reorganization of the hiring hall under the joint control of the union and the shipowners.

Ignoring employers' complaints about Communist influence and the danger unions posed to "industrial freedom," the New Deal administration in Washington for the first time forced L.A.'s open shop employers to accept a solution that weakened their authority and validated the labor movement's claims to legitimacy.[45] The government's actions reflected the growing power of the federal state as it expanded its functions during the New Deal.

The June 15, 1934, vote of the San Pedro local to accept Ryan's proposed settlement, making it the only Pacific Coast local of the ILA to do so, angered the militant minority among San Pedro's rank and file. They turned against President Walter J. Peterson and the local's other conservative leaders, whom they nicknamed the "dirty dozen," and gave their support instead to the champions of a broad-based industrial union that would include all marine workers in a single organization. These were the rank and filers, led in San Francisco by Harry Bridges, who in 1937 created the International Longshoremen's and Warehousemen's Union (ILWU), which became the most powerful CIO union on the West Coast.[46]

THE FURNITURE WORKERS AND
THE FOUNDING OF THE LOS ANGELES CIO

L.A.'s furniture workers played another important part in the movement toward industrial unionism. To a greater extent than in most other trades, the downtown furniture industry included both skilled craft workers, who were white, and semi-skilled workers, typically immigrants from the East Side barrio who worked in the less skilled segment of the industry. Their joint frustration with the divisive organizing practices of the AFL became a vital bridge that linked minority workers, both male and female, with the insurgent Anglo leaders who founded the Los Angeles CIO.

In most of L.A.'s furniture factories, skilled white migrants from the South dominated the furniture making process, Jewish cutters and seamstresses worked on the upholstery, and low-paid Mexican "helpers" were used for a variety of low-level woodworking tasks. But in typical AFL fashion, the workers were divided up between the national unions of their trades, including the Carpenters, the Painters, and the Upholsterers unions. These small, separate union locals stood little chance when they faced the united hostility of the Southern California Furniture Manufacturers Association.[47]

As the manufacturing process became more mechanized, furniture making jobs became more interchangeable, creating a second rationale for industrial unionism in the furniture industry. In the 1920s, a division of labor based on race and gender existed between the skilled white carpenters, the unskilled Mexicans employed in the woodworking section, and the male and female seamstresses who worked in the upholstery lofts. By the mid-1930s, however, it had become common for male Mexican "helpers" to be given jobs as "finishers" (skilled carpenters) in the skilled Anglo workshops, though their pay was not correspondingly increased.[48] In 1935 the Independent Furniture Workers Union (IFWU), a Communist-run local, showed the way forward when the Sterling Furniture Company cut the wages of its unskilled Mexican employees by 30 percent. The IFWU promptly brought all of the company's workforce—male and female, skilled and unskilled, Mexican and white—out on strike. Sterling's factory manager tried to divide the strikers by appealing to the racial self-interest of the white furniture makers. "What are you fellows fighting for those Mexicans and unskilled workers for?" he asked. "We're not bothering your wages."[49]

This time, however, class solidarity took precedence over race, gender, and craft divisions, suggesting strongly that the workers in the furniture industry wanted to be united under a single union banner rather than remaining divided between several different craft unions. The skilled white furniture makers stood by the Mexican woodworkers, the male upholsterers stood by their female counterparts, and, lo and behold, the wage cuts were rescinded, and the strike was won. The AFL leadership disliked the fact that the Communist-led, dual-unionist IFWU took credit for this victory. Nevertheless, the episode persuaded most of the union leaders in the industry to embrace the idea of industrial unionism. "It's time we had a completely different kind of union," stated Frank López, who was influential among the Mexican woodworkers. "We cannot go on as before."[50]

By February 1936, the movement for expansion and reform in the L.A. labor movement had gained sufficient momentum for the eastern-based Committee on Industrial Organization (the embryo CIO inside the AFL) to send a full-time organizer to the West Coast to begin an organizing campaign of its own. This was George B. Roberts of the United Rubber Workers, who also briefly represented the UAW in Los Angeles. His main task was to unionize the rubber workers at the Firestone and B. F. Goodrich tire plants in South Gate and Maywood. By August, he had succeeded in establishing Local 44 of the United Rubber Workers.[51] Roberts also met several times with Secretary Buzzell of the Central Labor Council to try and persuade him to back the industrial union organizing campaign, but to no avail.[52]

Another CIO pioneer from the East was William Seligman, a shoe workers' organizer from Boston who tried to gain the support of the L.A. Central Labor Council in his efforts to unionize the city's shoe workers, many of whom were Mexican. But he, too, failed to gain the support of the local AFL leaders, who were unwilling to create a shoe workers union in which the skilled cutters, the lasters, and the stitchers would all be included in the same industrywide organization. Seligman formed a "very poor impression" of Buzzell, whom he described as "obstinate and backward-looking." "We have the carpenters, we have the [skilled] trades," Buzzell allegedly told Seligman. "That is enough for us."[53] As a result, Seligman began organizing the shoe workers of East L.A. on his own and ultimately succeeded in creating several locals of the United Shoe Workers, which later joined the CIO.

Seligman and Roberts received support and encouragement from rank-and-file longshoremen in San Pedro, from representatives of the L.A. branch of the Steel Workers Organizing Committee (SWOC), and from the local branches of the ILGWU as well as from supporters of industrial unionism in other trades. The ILGWU played a particularly important role in the CIO's founding because, as an established industrial union that included cutters, pressers, and sewing machine operators in a single organization, it provided a living example of how industrial unionism actually worked.[54] A few weeks later, when additional representatives of other industrial unions from the Midwest, such as the UAW, came out to Los Angeles, they began to bypass the Central Labor Council altogether and organize factory workers on their own. These tactics understandably alarmed and angered Buzzell and his allies on the council, who demanded that the CIO organizers either cease their activities or divide up the workers they had enrolled among the established craft unions of the AFL or among its "federal locals."[55] (Federal locals were unions directly affiliated with the AFL, to which newly organized mass production workers were sometimes assigned until they could be distributed among existing AFL unions.)

The crisis reached a breaking point on May 14, 1937. Based on instructions it had received from President William Green of the national AFL, the L.A. Central Labor Council expelled the locals that had attached themselves to the CIO. The

Los Angeles Citizen described the scene when Buzzell read aloud the letter denying CIO locals the right of representation on the AFL's central labor body: "After
the reading of the communication from President Green, for a second or so there
was tense silence. Several delegates made efforts to secure the floor. . . . However,
President Sherman promptly ruled that the matter was not debatable and was an
order that must be obeyed, and that there was no alternative but to declare that all
locals in the Council coming under the ban be suspended, which he proceeded to
do."[56] The ban included four locals of the ILGWU, one local of the Amalgamated
Clothing Workers, and two from the United Rubber Workers. These were the
only unions at the time that were affiliated with both the AFL and the now banned
CIO.

In June 1937, the expelled CIO locals established the Los Angeles Industrial
Council and began issuing charters to separate unions of their own. By February
1938, this council claimed a citywide membership of fifty thousand. This was considerably smaller than the membership of the Los Angeles AFL.[57] Nevertheless,
the die was now cast. Competition between the two organizations precipitated
new citywide organizing campaigns by unions affiliated with both the AFL and
the CIO.

PHILOSOPHY AND TACTICS OF THE LOS ANGELES CIO

The Industrial Council of the Los Angeles CIO established its headquarters at
5851 Avalon Boulevard, in the heart of South L.A.'s factory district, where many of
its affiliated unions also had their center of operations. The social justice aspect of
unionism was more central to its philosophy than it was for the AFL, which meant
greater involvement in the broader community. The CIO's activities included
committees for political action, minority organizing, sports programs, a radio
show, and various community-based fundraising efforts. Most of them were also
directed from Avalon Boulevard.[58]

Another early feature of the CIO's work was the "dawn patrol" run by Slim
Connelly, Lew Michener, and Utility Workers union leader Jim Daugherty. These
men would drive to a nearby factory, toss union cards over the fence, repeat the
maneuver at a number of other plants, then retrace their steps and speak to the
workers who were leaving their shifts. Daugherty recalled that at first the dawn
patrol didn't care much about which union the workers joined, as long as they
signed union cards. "If we were successful in getting an organization campaign
started at a plant, then we would sit down and say, 'Well, logically, this type

of work should go to the Steelworkers,' or 'This type of work should go to the Furniture Workers,' or 'This should go to the Amalgamated Clothing Workers.' We didn't care where they went as long as they got organized."[59]

The CIO's most successful period of growth would occur later, during World War II, when a massive expansion took place in Southern California's defense plants. But by 1938 it had already begun printing a newspaper of its own, the *Industrial Unionist*, and it had begun to broaden its base of operations by taking up community issues such as civil rights, housing, and education reform.[60]

By 1941 a significant number of Mexicans and other minority workers had been elected to positions of leadership in the CIO's affiliated unions. The list included Bert Corona (Warehousemen's Local 26 of the ILWU), Luisa Moreno (UCAPAWA, and later elected to be a CIO vice-president), Tony Rios and Jaime Gonzales (SWOC), Rosendo Rivera (United Electrical Workers), and Jess Armenta (United Transport Workers).[61] For most of this period, however, the Industrial Council was dominated by white male representatives from the UAW, SWOC, the United Rubber Workers, and the Amalgamated Clothing Workers. The director of the CIO Industrial Council was a former newspaperman named Philip Connelly, who was nicknamed "Slim" (even though he weighed three hundred pounds).[62] Although two women sat on the Industrial Council, efforts to organize female workers were at first somewhat sporadic, other than work in the garment industry and an attempt to organize waitresses. But there were some successes. In April 1939, for example, two hundred members of Laundry Workers Local 357 carried out a successful strike for union recognition against the Los Angeles Wardrobe Linen and Supply Company. The strike was won with the aid of a boycott organized by the League of Women Shoppers against grocery chains such as Vons, which purchased the company's uniforms.[63]

African Americans exerted surprisingly little influence in the L.A. labor movement during the early years of the Los Angeles CIO. In the early decades of the twentieth century, many of L.A.'s black workers lived in the Central Avenue district, which was a long way from the city's major industrial plants. Also, in light of the partially southern character of the white population in factory towns such as South Gate, almost none of L.A.'s large-scale employers of blue-collar labor were willing to hire African Americans. In addition, many white AFL unions had not allowed black workers to join them. Thus, when they did join unions, African Americans tended at first to congregate in all-black unions such as their own branch of the Musicians Union or A. Philip Randolph's Brotherhood of Sleeping Car Porters.[64] Given this history, few experienced black organizers were available to assist in the multiracial efforts of the new CIO. In 1939, however, the Trade Union Committee of the National Negro Council, working with the CIO's Industrial Council, did sponsor several local community meetings in the black churches of Watts to encourage factory employment among black males.[65]

On the other hand, the CIO Industrial Council developed a fruitful relationship with El Congreso, the Congress of Spanish-Speaking Peoples, even though the number of unionized Mexican workers in Los Angeles was still quite small. The platform El Congreso adopted in 1938 described the trade union movement as "the most basic agency through which the Mexican and Spanish-speaking people became organized."[66] In response, Warehousemen's Local 26 of the ILWU, led by Bert Corona, helped establish the Committee to Aid Mexican Workers, which aimed to mobilize unions against anti-Mexican sentiment and to help Hispanic workers secure factory jobs.[67] El Congreso's activities also included a political dimension. In 1938, for example, it supported Eduardo Quevedo Sr. in his unsuccessful bid for a seat on the Los Angeles City Council—the first Mexican to run for the council in the twentieth century.[68] In such efforts, El Congreso served the same kind of function (albeit on a smaller scale) that Labor's Nonpartisan League (LNPL) did among the second-generation Polish, Slavic, and Italian factory workers it initiated into Democratic Party politics in the industrial Midwest (see Chapter Five).

Meeting in Los Angeles late in 1939, El Congreso also issued calls for affordable housing, extension of federal labor laws to include agricultural and domestic workers, rejection of the Sinarquistas (a fascist group) in Mexico, and a Spanish-language edition of the *CIO News*.[69] The reference to federal programs was important. It reflected the growing sense of entitlement to New Deal programs that was now being articulated by Mexican American workers throughout the city.[70]

The request for a Spanish-language edition of the *CIO News* also illustrates the new sense of identity that was emerging among L.A.'s Mexican workers. These immigrants still wanted to read about the labor movement in their own language, as did the Italian workers living near the Plaza who read the local Italian newspaper. But they now wanted to read about U.S. unions as well as Mexican ones and to join American-style labor organizations in order to assert—or to promote—their citizenship rights. In doing this, they rode the crest of organized labor's temporary wave of nationwide popularity. For a brief period in the 1930s, the U.S. labor movement received so much popular support that joining the CIO became an acceptable means of combining demands for high wages and better working conditions, on the one hand, with aspirations for upward mobility and acceptance as full-fledged

U.S. citizens, on the other. As historian Gary Gerstle puts it, voting Democratic and joining a union meant "authenticating a new language of 'working-class Americanism.'"[71]

In certain areas, such as issues that required a joint defense against the attacks of the open shop lobby, the AFL's Central Labor Council and the CIO's Industrial Council sometimes cooperated with each other. But in other areas they did not. As both labor federations competed for members in the late 1930s, their anger at each other over stealing recruits became more noticeable. Supporters of the CIO labeled J. W. Buzzell of the Central Labor Council "Fuzzy Wuzzy Buzzy," a man who was "not too bright" and who was supposedly in the pocket of the M&M.[72] Serious jurisdictional disputes flared up between the AFL and the CIO in the warehouse and furniture industries, in moviemaking, in the garment industry, and in numerous other occupations.[73]

Supporters of the AFL regularly accused the CIO of being dominated by the Communists. This assertion had some truth in it, although the use of the word "dominated" implied a Soviet model of trade unionism that was wide of the mark. The Communist Party in Los Angeles certainly played a major role in enrolling poorly paid workers of color into the trade union movement, especially among garment, canning, and agricultural workers. They would play an even greater role in major CIO unions such as the ILWU, the United Electrical Workers, and the UAW during and after World War II. But save among virulent anti-Communists (of whom there were plenty on the Central Labor Council), during the late 1930s the assistance of the Communist Party was welcomed more often than it was shunned.

In Los Angeles, as elsewhere, the party supplied the labor movement with some of its most effective organizers. Communists such as Slim Connelly provided important leadership on the CIO's Industrial Council. They were particularly effective in working with local community organizations and in pressing union leaders to live up to their principles on such matters as public housing, education, and interracial unionism.[74]

This is not to say, of course, that the presence of the Communists did not stir up internal controversy. Between 1935 and 1940, the California CP, like the party in other parts of the country, gave its general support to President Roosevelt's New Deal while criticizing it from the left and sometimes running its own independent candidates for political office. In the fall of 1938, for example, while the state party endorsed Democrat Culbert Olson for governor of California, Communist Anita Whitney ran for state controller. Most trade unionists in the liberal or moderate wings of the CIO, on the other hand, gave their political support to the Democrats.[75]

In the years 1936 through 1939, when the Communist Party—as part of the Popular Front against fascism—toned down its revolutionary rhetoric in favor of a united response to Hitler and Spanish dictator General Francisco Franco, most CIO members were willing to live with these divided political loyalties. But they were more skeptical about the 1937 appointment of alleged Communist Harry Bridges as West Coast director of the CIO. Most CIO members opposed the federal government's efforts to deport Bridges and send him back to his native Australia. Despite their admiration for his organizing skills, however, many considered him too controversial a figure to be West Coast director. Some union members thought his political opinions were too extreme. Others feared that Bridges's belief in rank-and file democracy and in the idea of the referendum and recall of union officers posed an indirect threat to their own jobs.[76]

Personal antipathies and jostling for power were also involved. One of the ringleaders in the anti-Bridges faction was Bill Busick of the ILGWU, Rose Pesotta's erstwhile lieutenant in the 1933 dressmakers strike. Busick was a member of the Socialist Party of America, who disliked the Communists because in earlier years they had called Socialists "social fascists." Busick personally favored the industrial union method of organizing, but in an attempt to undermine Bridges, he tried to persuade the L.A. locals of the United Auto Workers not to send delegates to the state CIO convention, which was slated for the end of August 1938. When the state convention opened on August 30, however, the only Los Angeles unions to boycott it were the ILGWU and the Rubber Workers.[77]

The internal controversy over the role of the Communists in the CIO calmed down, at least for a time, in the fall of 1938, when the Communists and their allies on the Industrial Council, who had a voting majority, agreed to place less emphasis on political issues such as the Spanish Civil War and raising money for refugees from Nazi Germany. They decided instead to devote more of their attention to workplace organizing and to local labor and community issues.[78]

CONCLUSION

The unions that broke away from the American Federation of Labor to establish the Los Angeles CIO in May 1937 did so for many of the same reasons that motivated the split in other parts of the country: discontent with the craft orientation of the AFL, dissatisfaction with the racist and sexist attitudes of its white male leaders, and a recognition of the need to organize the millions of immigrants and semi-skilled workers in mass production industry who had hitherto been neglected. If the Los Angeles labor movement was to grow, it needed to move beyond "pure and simple unionism" and become part of a dynamic social movement committed to social and political change.[79]

But in certain respects the CIO in Southern California, and in other parts of the Southwest, followed a path that differed from the pattern established in the East and the Midwest. There, the CIO's emphasis was almost exclusively urban. It focused on organizing African American workers who had migrated to large cities from the South, poor Okies who had moved into the auto industry in Detroit, and the hundreds of thousands of Polish, Hungarian, and other Eastern European immigrants who worked in the rubber factories and steel mills of Chicago and the Monongahela Valley. The CIO's rural organizing in the southern states was conducted by unions like the Southern Tenant Farmers Union, hundreds of miles away from the centers of industry.[80]

The Los Angeles CIO also devoted the latter part of the 1930s to organizing mass production workers in the auto, steel, and aviation factories of the Alameda corridor. But there were differences. Few African Americans were employed in L.A.'s industrial plants, and there was a dearth of Eastern European immigrants. In addition, the spark that set off the movement came not from factory workers in white industrial suburbs like Lynwood and South Gate, but from immigrant garment workers and from Mexican and Okie cannery workers and farmhands in the Imperial and San Joaquin valleys. It was the intertwining of agriculture and urban industry in the L.A. basin, coupled with the itinerant lifestyle of many Okie and Mexican immigrants, that made this alternative configuration possible. For example, many of the Mexicans who later worked at the Bethlehem Steel plant in Maywood began their careers as farmhands, while the wives and older children of Mexican families in the East Side barrio often "went to the fruit" in the San Gabriel and Pomona valleys to earn extra money in the summer.[81]

Thus the migratory work habits of Mexican immigrants and others became a transmission belt for the message of unionism, carrying it back and forth from the Imperial Valley to the citrus belt, and from the Cal San Canning Company in Boyle Heights to the sweatshops in the downtown garment district. It was this transmission belt that inspired the garment strike led by Rose Pesotta of the ILGWU in 1933 and the cannery workers strikes led by Luisa Moreno and Dorothy Healey. The idea for these strikes did not originate in the minds of John L Lewis and the other leaders of unionized heavy industry in the East; they came out of protest movements that were indigenous to Southern California.[82]

In their analyses of the CIO in the industrial cities of the Midwest, historians have laid great stress on the importance of second-generation Eastern European immigrants in industries such as auto and steel. Members of the first generation among these European immigrants, argues Peter Friedlander, were too tied to their homeland cultures and too scared of the boss to join a union. It was only when second-generation Poles in places like Detroit felt sufficiently self-confident that they joined unions such as the UAW.[83] No one has yet made a definitive study of the generational background of the Mexicans who participated in the strike movements in Southern California in the 1930s. It seems, likely, however, that they came as much from the first generation of immigrants as they did from the second.

Whatever their generational background, the evidence suggests that Mexican immigrants—and Mexican women, in particular—played a much bigger role in the strike waves that grew the L.A. labor movement in the 1930s than they have been given credit for. Ultimately it was the combined efforts of Anglo leaders such as Slim Connelly and Jim Daugherty, Mexicans such as Frank López and Tony Rios in furniture and steel, and feminist activists such as Luisa Moreno and Rose Pesotta in the canning and garment industries, coupled with grassroots support from the Communists and from the San Pedro longshoremen—as well as help from cultural organizations like El Congreso and the Jewish Workmen's Circle—that got the Los Angeles CIO off the ground.

SEVEN

Battle Royal

AFL versus CIO, and the Decline of
the Open Shop, 1936–1941

In some areas of basic industry in Los Angeles, the establishment of CIO unions, which were the major catalyst for union growth in the 1930s, came more easily than it did in the East or the Midwest. Once a union had won recognition as the legitimate bargaining agent in an industry's headquarters city, such as Chicago or Pittsburgh, a nationwide contract sometimes resulted, which automatically brought recognition to local unions in that industry's West Coast subsidiaries.

For example, following the dramatic sit-down strike of auto workers in 1936–1937, in Flint, Michigan, General Motors signed a historic contract with the United Auto Workers, recognizing the union at all its assembly plants throughout the country, including Local 216 of the UAW at South Gate.[1] A similar development occurred in the steel and rubber industries. In 1941 the Steel Workers Organizing Committee (SWOC) won union elections in the eastern steel plants. The collective bargaining agreement that followed included Bethlehem Steel in Maywood as well as other steel plants in L.A.'s industrial suburbs.[2]

Elsewhere in Los Angeles, however, the battle for union recognition by the local unions of both the AFL and the CIO was more bitter and more complex. It required separate, uphill conflicts with the Merchants and Manufacturers Association and its allies, who increasingly realized that they were engaged in a life-or-death struggle to maintain the supremacy of the open shop. Quite often, these struggles lasted into the Second World War and even beyond.[3] Their epicenter is reflected in the sketched map of southeast Los Angeles depicted here.

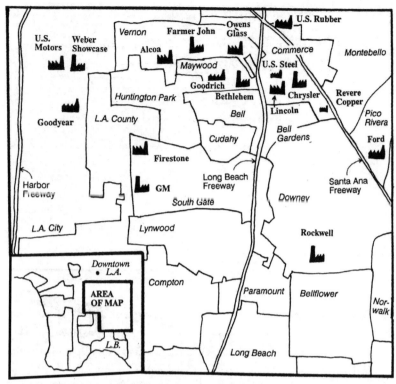

Some plants that once existed in the industrial southeast. Map drawn by SCL with the help of early CIO leader Jim Daugherty.

Core area of basic industry in southeast Los Angeles. Courtesy of Southern California Library for Social Studies and Research.

"BROTHER AGAINST BROTHER": ESCALATING RIVALRY BETWEEN THE AFL AND THE CIO, 1937–1941

As the previous chapter detailed, the roots of the CIO in Southern California were planted during the 1933–1934 labor upsurge, which included Latina dressmakers, male and female cannery workers, and Communist volunteers working among migrant farm workers on the rural peripheries of the Los Angeles basin. Because few of these workers had been organized before, their recruitment by the CIO at first caused little anxiety in the AFL's Central Labor Council. But when organizers from SWOC, the UAW, and other industrial unions began enrolling assembly-line workers from core industries in southeast L.A., J. W. Buzzell, secretary of the L.A. Central Labor Council, and other AFL traditionalists became seriously alarmed.[4]

Frantic discussions were held with AFL president William Green in Washington,

D.C., and when it became apparent that John L. Lewis, Sidney Hillman, and the other insurgent leaders of what was then known as the Committee on Industrial Organization (the precursor of the Congress of Industrial Organizations) would not back down, open conflict broke out between the two sides. AFL organizers expanded their range of recruits, while CIO sympathizers enrolled thousands of new manufacturing workers, both semi-skilled and unskilled, along the lines of industrial unionism. Meanwhile, in the National Labor Relations Board (NLRB) elections that were held to determine the workers' legal representatives, agents of the M&M and of other employer associations took advantage of the quarrel to promote company unions as "the only responsible alternative" to disorder and chaos.[5]

One of the seminal contests between the AFL and the CIO occurred in L.A.'s furniture industry. In January 1938, when the leaders of the AFL's Upholsterers Union were out of town, insurgents voted to leave the AFL union and join the CIO. Much legal wrangling followed this dubious procedure, including a violent episode in which the leaders of the AFL union barricaded themselves in the union's downtown headquarters and refused to turn it over to the insurgents. In the end, a new multiracial union, Local 576, emerged, which joined the CIO's United Furniture Workers of America (UFWA). By the start of World War II, Local 576 was the largest furniture workers union in the city.[6]

The UFWA was established in part because the AFL's white, male-dominated Carpenters Union had refused to organize the lowly furniture workers, who were mixed racially and by gender and who earned quite a lot less than the carpenters. In November 1939, when the L.A. Building Trades Council (dominated by the Carpenters) urged the furniture workers to remain loyal to the AFL, UFWA Local 576 responded by issuing a blistering attack on the "craft-minded, backward, and autocratic leaders" of the Carpenters, who had "nothing to offer but the same old, self-destructive, jurisdictional AFL messes."[7] The UFWA, by contrast, had a shop steward system of governance, which made it one of the most democratic unions in the country. Local 576 won NLRB representation elections in one after another of the city's furniture factories. The UFWA, a union circular noted proudly, was a full-fledged CIO union "with full jurisdiction over all branches of the trade—wood, juvenile, upholstered and metal furniture, mattresses, bedding and springs."[8]

The conflict between the AFL and the CIO also affected the Los Angeles clothing industry. The local unions of the Amalgamated Clothing Workers of America (ACWA), which organized garment workers who manufactured men's clothing, were among the unions that were suspended from the Central Labor Council in May 1937 (as described in Chapter Six), because they competed with the AFL's United Garment Workers.[9] The International Ladies Garment Workers Union was involved in this dispute, too. By January 1937, its leaders had learned enough from Rose Pesotta's 1933 success with the Mexican dressmakers to start a serious organizing campaign of their own among the Mexican and African American women who sewed light dresses, underwear, and blouses. Late that year, the ILGWU established Local 266, which consisted solely of cotton dress workers. But the AFL's Central Labor Council refused to seat Local 266's delegates because the ILGWU's officers, especially Bill Busick, sympathized with the aims of the CIO. In reaction to the snubbing of Local 266, all of the ILGWU's delegates withdrew from the Central Labor Council and joined the CIO, a significant move in light of the ILGWU's importance in the national labor movement.[10] (For a short time it held charters from both labor federations, making it the only major union in the United States to do so.)[11]

Because it sometimes erupted in violence, the most highly publicized interunion dispute to occur in L.A. in the late 1930s was a jurisdictional conflict between the AFL's Teamsters and the International Longshoremen's and Warehousemen's Union (ILWU), which was the CIO's flagship union on the West Coast. The clash arose because of the ILWU's celebrated "march inland" (a strategy originating in San Francisco but intended for the entire coast), in which ILWU Local 1–26 moved north out of the San Pedro Harbor area to organize warehouses throughout the entire city. These warehouses and their workers were seen as an integral part of the process of moving cargo—and thus as important elements in the event of a longshore strike. This campaign brought the ILWU into direct conflict with the AFL's powerful Teamsters, led by the aggressive Dave Beck, which also claimed the right to organize the warehouse workers. Organizers for the ILWU and the Teamsters vied with each other to enroll truck drivers and clerical employees at a wide variety of drug and paper warehouses, grain milling companies, scrap metal plants, and retail stores.[12]

In February 1937, the AFL executive board awarded the Teamsters jurisdiction over all warehouse workers except those employed on the docks. But the ILWU ignored this directive. In Los Angeles, it established its own Warehouse Local 1–26, under the leadership of Bert Corona, a prominent Mexican American union organizer. In September 1937, a dispute between members of General Warehousemen's Local 598, chartered by the Teamsters, and ILWU Local 1–26 at the Zellerbach Paper Company warehouse resulted in a street riot in which

Teamster goons beat up several of the ILWU's supporters and the LAPD was forced to intervene. This brought bad publicity to both sides. It took two representation elections scheduled by the NLRB to decide which union should represent the warehouse workers before the Teamsters won a clear victory for the AFL.[13]

The employers did not, of course, sit idly by while the AFL and the CIO increased their membership. After the passage of the National Industrial Recovery Act (NIRA) in June 1933, the M&M had issued a clarion call to employers in the Los Angeles area to maintain the open shop, protect the rights of "free and independent workingmen," and "avoid the tyranny of trade unions."[14] It had welcomed the May 1935 decision of the Supreme Court to strike down the NIRA as unconstitutional, but expressed alarm when the court upheld its successor law eighteen months later.

Eventually, however, the commitment of the New Deal administration to the cause of labor reform became so widely accepted, even in open shop Los Angeles, that the M&M was forced to begin a strategic retreat. In 1937–1938 it tried to recoup its fortunes by cooperating more closely with the Los Angeles Chamber of Commerce and sponsoring two new organizations that it hoped would stem the rising tide of trade union success. But neither had much effect. One was Southern Californians Inc., which pressured employers not to sign union contracts. The other new body was the so-called Neutral Thousands, led by Mrs. Bessie Ochs, which described itself as a voluntary association of housewives whose ostensible purpose was to protect women against fraudulent purchases, but which was in fact a propaganda organization for the open shop. It depicted unions in such a one-sided fashion on its radio show that the Federal Communications Commission ordered it off the air.[15]

The most serious—and potentially the most effective—effort to put the brakes on labor organizing in L.A. in the 1930s was the movement, led by Southern Californians Inc., to adopt a tough new anti-picketing law. Had it passed, this new law, first proposed as a municipal ordinance, would have severely limited the effectiveness of unions and strikes. After a bitter debate, the city council adopted the proposal by a vote of nine to six in December 1937, but it was vetoed by Mayor Frank L. Shaw. The city council vote showed that, whatever was happening at the workplace, anti-union sentiment was still widespread in the Los Angeles political arena.

The anti-picketing proposal reappeared in the form of Proposition 1 on a city-wide ballot in September 1938. It passed with 57 percent of the popular vote, only to be declared invalid by the L.A. County Superior Court. An alternative anti-picketing measure was then put on the California state ballot in the November 1938 election, but—with San Francisco's liberal electorate participating in the balloting—it lost by a margin of almost one million votes. By now it was clear even to some of the members of the M&M, which had dominated business life in Los Angeles for so long, that time was running out for the open shop.[16]

THE UAW FIGHTS FOR THE CIO AT CHRYSLER, 1936–1941

The second great growth spurt in labor organizing took place during the New Deal period between 1936 and America's entry into World War II. One of the most interesting examples occurred in UAW District 6, the largest and most powerful CIO regional union in Southern California, to consolidate its position at the Chrysler assembly plant in the City of Commerce.

After the UAW won an NLRB election in 1937, the Chrysler Corporation agreed to recognize UAW Local 230 as the sole collective bargaining agent for the approximately nine hundred workers in its Los Angeles plant. But this act of union recognition did not bring with it a wage increase or improved job security, which were the employees' two main objectives. What was worse, the local Chrysler management continued to operate an open shop in which other unions, including a company-sponsored one, competed for the workers' loyalty. So a new organizer was sent out from UAW headquarters in Detroit to boost the membership of Local 230 and to insist that the management live up to its commitment to recognize the local as the sole bargaining agent for the plant's employees.

As part of the new strategy, Ken Gillie, vice-president of Local 230, along with other local leaders, pressured the remaining auto assembly workers in the plant to join the union, using ostracism and sometimes physical threats to get them to do so.[17] In response, the plant manager at Chrysler secretly persuaded Paul L. Brooks, a pro-management assembly-line worker, to help set up a new company union called the Forty Hours Club to counter Local 230's organizing efforts, even though company unions had been declared illegal under federal law.[18]

The rest of the story is best told through the experiences of John Allard and other rank-and-file Chrysler workers. Allard, born in Kansas, a schoolteacher's son, had driven out to L.A. at the age of nineteen to help his aunt cultivate the large plot of land behind her house. After working briefly at an oil well, Allard took a job at a railroad siding behind the Chrysler factory, where he unloaded car bodies, axles, and other auto parts from trains that brought the parts from Detroit for assembly in Southern California.[19]

Chrysler assembly line, 1934. Courtesy of Chrysler Historical Collection, Chrysler Group LLC (CIMS 5410-11-21).

As his experience of factory life grew, Allard found his consciousness of his place in the world changing, a process resembling the one that Mexican immigrants went through when they exchanged village life in Mexico for urban occupations in L.A.'s downtown manufacturing district. At first, Allard's work on the loading dock seemed "boring and alienating" to him, but when he started attending union meetings inside the Chrysler plant, he began to identify with the pro-union faction among the workers. "I saw that I was part of something bigger," he later recalled. "Us Kansans in Bell Gardens were part of a big chain of working men which stretched all the way to Detroit, where those sit-downers were struggling for their rights."[20] Allard was later to become one of the most important leaders of UAW District 6 in the Southland.

By this time, the Chrysler management had established the Forty Hours Club as a de facto company union and had made a private arrangement with Clay Rittenhouse, a professional union buster who worked for the Neutral Thousands, to recruit dissatisfied workers into the club's ranks. The plant manager emphasized to Rittenhouse that the club's activities must be kept secret because Charles Gaebelein, Chrysler's vice-president for California, was on the board of the M&M. If Gaebelein openly promoted the Forty Hours Club, he would be breaking the law. Nevertheless, the plant manager persisted with the company union plan. He told Rittenhouse that Chrysler "did not want the union [UAW Local 230] wiped out, but merely rendered powerless," so that the NLRB could not accuse the company of being unfair to labor.[21]

Rittenhouse did convince a small number of Chrysler workers to join the Forty Hours Club. However, the plan backfired when Local 230's leaders discovered its activities, reported them to the Los Angeles office of the NLRB, and succeeded in having the company union banned. Determined not to admit defeat, Chrysler management then persuaded Paul L. Brooks, its main ally on the assembly line, to file a court injunction against the UAW for trying to force him and other workers to pay Local 230's initiation fee and dues. This time, management appeared to succeed, at least temporarily. The injunction was granted, the pro-business Los Angeles Grand Jury charged fifteen of Local 230's leaders with "extortion and conspiracy," and the union's leaders were convicted in court.[22]

The case attracted national attention because it was the first time California state law had been invoked to stop union leaders from collecting their members' dues, even though such a ban went against federal labor law. In the end, the charges against Local 230's leaders were dismissed, and the union was recognized by the NLRB as the sole legitimate bargaining agent for the Chrysler factory.[23]

However, it became clear during the course of the court trial that Brooks had not acted alone but had been persuaded to file for a court injunction by the Chrysler management. It was also obvious that L.A.'s anti-union district attorney, Buron Fitts, had played a role in the case. (Fitts was a former American Legion leader and a protégé of Los Angeles Times editor Harry Chandler, who had become the main front man for the open shop lobby in Los Angeles city government.)[24] Court papers showed that Fitts acted as a go-between for the Los Angeles Grand Jury and Chrysler management and that he gave the company confidential advice about how the Grand Jury was likely to deal with the issue.

The CIO's attorneys also argued successfully that the Neutral Thousands and Southern Californians Inc. had conspired to drive Local 230 from the plant and substitute the Forty Hours Club for the UAW, which the NLRB had previously recognized.[25]

The significance of the Chrysler episode lies not so much in what it reveals about the unscrupulous tactics open shop employers used to prevent the CIO from expanding its base among Southern California's automobile workers. These tactics were already well known. Rather, its significance lies in the fact that as a result of the growing clout of the NLRB, the M&M and L.A.'s pro-business politicians were beginning to lose out to the adherents of independent trade unionism more decisively than they had before.

AFL AND CIO BOTH CHALLENGE DOUGLAS
AIRCRAFT IN SANTA MONICA

A not dissimilar battle between organized labor and the political forces of the open shop occurred when the Los Angeles unions, aware of the large numbers of workers flooding into the rapidly growing Southern California aircraft industry, turned their attention to organizing these new recruits.[26] In this instance, however, organizers from both the CIO and the competing AFL were involved. In February 1937, Local 720 of the International Association of Machinists and Locals 683 and 188 of the Aircraft Division of the United Auto Workers began rival organizing campaigns at Lockheed in Burbank, at Northrop in Hawthorne, and at the Douglas Aircraft Company in Santa Monica.[27]

The outcome of these organizing campaigns was less clear-cut than the victory UAW Local 230 won at Chrysler. As World War II approached, the Los Angeles aircraft industry expanded much faster than the auto industry, especially after the Roosevelt administration and the governments of Great Britain and France ordered large numbers of warplanes to combat the rising power of Nazi Germany. By 1944 the number of aircraft workers had reached 160,000 in Southern California alone. As a result, the campaign for union recognition waged by both the AFL and the CIO in aircraft took much longer than it did in auto.[28]

Even though it did not secure a conclusive victory until 1944, the campaign waged by UAW Local 683 for a union contract at Douglas Aircraft in Santa Monica attracted the most public attention because it was accompanied by a sit-down strike, the first time such a militant union tactic had been employed in Southern California. Modeling themselves on the sit-down strikers in Detroit, four hundred Douglas airframe makers in Santa Monica stayed at their work stations and refused to leave the plant on February 23, 1937. Aircraft executive Donald Douglas promptly had the strikers arrested for trespassing on his property. Twenty-two of them were found guilty and fined. After prolonged wrangling between Local 683 and management, most of the strikers were reinstated. Between 1935 and 1941, several other attempts were made to organize the aircraft industry. At Vultee in Downey, for example, the UAW won a strike that secured a wage increase and union recognition.[29]

The Douglas strike was notable for several other reasons. One was the (by now familiar) political tactics the employers used to defeat it. In early February, before the sit-down strike began, the M&M established an Aircraft Committee to monitor the behavior of union activists in the local aircraft plants. Eight detectives from the Bodell Detective Agency were put on the Douglas payroll to act as labor spies. Like the executives at Chrysler, Donald Douglas established a company union at his plant in Santa Monica and maintained that it was the legitimate representative of his employees. He refused to have any dealings with either the representatives of the NLRB or the union leaders who tried to negotiate with him.[30]

On March 2, 1937, Douglas went still further and issued a statement claiming that the NLRB lacked the authority to regulate labor relations at his company because the manufacture and sale of aircraft was an "intrastate matter and beyond the jurisdiction of the Federal Congress to regulate"—even though his company had contracts with the federal government to produce planes for Roosevelt's defense program.[31] Douglas and his fellow aircraft employers also did their best to prevent the sit-down strikers from obtaining monetary relief from the L.A. County Relief Administration when they had no other source of income. In response, the UAW strike committee distributed flyers, held mass meetings in Santa Monica's public parks, and brought in speakers from SWOC, the Mine, Mill, and Smelter Workers, and the United Electrical Workers in southeast Los Angeles to champion their cause.[32]

Although the court case that followed the Douglas strike lasted for several years, the sit-down strike itself took place before the industrial union reformers in the AFL had actually broken away and formally established the CIO. Within the AFL, the conservative wing of the downtown Central Labor Council disapproved of the militant tactics of the sit-down strikers, which they considered dangerous and provocative. Nonetheless, they did not want the dispute to end in a victory for the employers. Hence, when the district attorney's office charged the sit-down strikers with felonious assault and trespassing on the Douglas plant property, J. W.

Buzzell urged District Attorney Fitts, without success, to reduce the charges to misdemeanors.[33]

But the AFL leadership was unwilling to take its support for the pro-CIO Douglas strikers too far. After a heated debate at a meeting of the Central Labor Council on March 10, it adopted a resolution stating that it would "in no wise extend aid or assistance to this, or any other outlaw strike."[34] The council wanted to use its financial resources, instead, to support AFL Machinists Lodge 720 in its own organizing campaign at Douglas Aircraft. Indeed, it is likely that the refusal of the Central Labor Council to support the Douglas sit-down strike was one of the factors that precipitated the May 1937 split between the Los Angeles AFL and the CIO Industrial Council.

The organizing campaigns conducted in the automobile, steel, and aircraft industries were by no means the only ones carried out by the Los Angeles CIO in the years between 1936 and 1941. It also made major numerical gains in meat-packing, electrical equipment manufacturing, and the rubber industry, which made tires for GM, Chrysler, and Ford. In 1937 the United Rubber Workers became the exclusive bargaining agent for the workers at the Goodyear, Goodrich, and Firestone plants in Vernon, South Gate, and Huntington Park. Competition between AFL and CIO affiliates continued in other manufacturing industries, most notably in the increasingly important aircraft industry. In addition, both sides vied for support among L.A.'s white-collar employees, with the AFL establishing two locals of the American Federation of State, County, and Municipal Employees (AFSCME) among the clerical staff in city and county offices, and the CIO orga-nizing workers in the Department of Water and Power.[35]

TRYING, AND FAILING, TO UNIONIZE OIL
WORKERS IN THE SOUTHLAND

By the time the Great Depression struck the oil fields of Southern California, the heady days of unexpected oil strikes and sudden fortunes, such as those found at Signal Hill in the 1920s, were largely over. Aside from a number of smaller wells, there were now three stable oil-producing fields in the Los Angeles basin, all located within a fifteen-mile radius of Long Beach—at Signal Hill, Huntington Beach, and Santa Fe Springs. Several modern refineries had also been built, some in the harbor area and some farther away, such as the one at El Segundo near the site of present-day LAX. New technology made working at oil rigs and refineries increasingly complex, requiring many different grades of specialist mechanics, including pipefitters, carpenters, tool dressers, welders, pumpers, and engineers.[36]

The defeat of the 1921 oil strike (described in Chapter Four), coupled with the immense power of the "Big Five" oil companies, meant that unionism remained extremely weak in the Southern California oil industry throughout the 1920s and early 1930s. Only Local 128 of the Oil Workers Union at Long Beach retained a measure of strength, and even that was minimal. The six or seven other union locals that had sprung up in Taft, Kern River, Martinez, and other oil towns in the San Joaquin Valley, fifty to one hundred miles north of Los Angeles, were even weaker. They were nominally linked to Local 128 in Long Beach as part of District 1 of the national union. But relations between California District 1 and the other districts in the Oil Workers Union, which were located many miles away in Hammond, Indiana, and in Oklahoma and Texas, were tenuous.[37]

A stark contrast also existed between the community support groups available to Local 128 in Long Beach, in the midst of a major metropolis, and the isolation of union sympathizers in Kern County, who lived in company towns vulnerable to employer pressure. A typical oil encampment in the valley, wrote Upton Sinclair in his exposé *Oil!* (1926), "was a bare wilderness of sun-baked sand and rock, with nothing but grey, dusty, desert plants."[38] The workers lived in bunkhouses owned by the oil companies and were dependent on them for many of their needs. Because the oil rigs needed constant attention, they were forced to work in twelve-hour shifts.[39] As the accompanying photograph of an oil well fire demonstrates, the work was also dangerous.

As was the case in other occupations, the election of President Roosevelt and the passage of the National Industrial Recovery Act in June 1933 brought a new surge of hope. At last the oil workers seemed to have a friend in the White House who would protect them against the anti-union policies of the oil companies. But management was also alert to the new situation and determined to quash any new organizing drives before they could get off the ground. Oil company executives from as far away as Taft negotiated with Captain Hynes of the LAPD's red squad to supply confidential agents who could infiltrate the oil workers' meetings and report on their activities.[40]

Before the end of 1933, several of these agents infiltrated union recruitment meetings called by officials of the Bakersfield Central Labor Council in Taft, Coalinga, Maricopa, and other San Joaquin Valley oil towns. In addition, oil company managers paid volunteers to "hang around the pool hall in Avenal in which union meetings are held, and sit in cars parked around the hall, to get the names

Workers examining wreckage during an oil fire. Courtesy of Doheny Memorial Library, University of Southern California, on behalf of the USC Special Collections (chs-m22503).

of the men going in."[41] Police spies also attended the business meetings of Local 128 in Long Beach, as well as recruitment meetings held at the Standard Oil refinery at El Segundo. At one El Segundo meeting in January 1934, addressed by Oil Workers Union vice-president John Coulter, it was obvious that some of the men in the audience were sympathetic but that most were unwilling to join the union because they were afraid of losing their jobs.[42]

Despite this discouraging outlook, a Petroleum Administration Board coordinated by federal official Harold Ickes held hearings on the proposed oil labor codes under the NIRA, and the Oil Workers Union submitted petitions to have their union recognized as the workers' sole bargaining agent. But as a result of poor planning by union officials, and oil company efforts to avoid coming to terms with the union, the creation of labor codes acceptable to both sides in the oil industry proved to be exceptionally difficult.[43]

The main problem was that other AFL unions had staked their claims to represent the workers on the oil rigs. The Oil Workers Union was a "natural" industrial union because of the wide range of workers it enrolled, and at the 1935 AFL convention it supported John L. Lewis and Sidney Hillman in establishing the Committee for Industrial Organization, precursor of the CIO. But several other unions, most notably the Boilermakers, the Iron Ship Builders, the Machinists, and the International Brotherhood of Electrical Workers (IBEW), also laid claim to the oil workers. They proposed a resolution at the 1935 convention urging that the Oil Workers Union charter should be withdrawn if it did not stop organizing workers within their jurisdictions. The convention shelved the matter by referring it to the AFL executive committee.[44]

When representation elections were finally held under the auspices of the NLRB, the machinists and mixed craftsmen on the Shell oil rigs chose to be represented by the Oil Workers Union—which by now had joined the CIO under the name Oil Workers International Union, or OWIU. The electrical workers chose the IBEW, and the blacksmiths and boilermakers chose (for the time being, at least) not to be represented by any union at all.[45] After the NLRB rebuked the oil companies for failing to negotiate in good faith, the newly minted OWIU did manage to increase its nationwide membership to twenty-seven thousand, including more than eight hundred members in Long Beach Local 128. It negotiated several contracts with the oil companies in Southern California, which included wage increases and the eight-hour day.[46]

However, with half a million oil workers in the United States, seven thousand of them in Los Angeles and the San Joaquin Valley, the OWIU's record in Southern California was disappointing. It was already clear from the representation elections that many of the workers on the oil rigs were divided in their union loyalties, leaving the OWIU unable to generate the same strong sense of labor solidarity possessed by the United Mine Workers, for example. This weakness was exacerbated by the geographical fragmentation of the union and by the constant harassment from company spies and vigilantes, which continued unchecked throughout the 1930s. Regional disagreements within the OWIU also made the union particularly susceptible to factionalism and to raiding by other unions from both the AFL and the CIO.[47]

Another source of internal dissension was red-baiting. After President John L. Lewis accepted known Communists as aides in his Washington office in order to build up the CIO, a favorite tactic of AFL leaders, both locally and nationally, was to attack the rival CIO as Communist-dominated, an assertion the oil companies were only too happy to endorse. At the OWIU's national convention in 1940, for example, an opposition group was elected to office on a program that promised greater democratic control of the union by the local membership. In his

Washington *Labor Newsletter*, journalist Chester Wright, who had close ties to the AFL, accused OWIU's new leaders of being Communists who had been elected to office with Standard Oil money.[48]

This rumor was almost certainly untrue. But it appears to have resulted in another round of raiding against the OWIU by other unions.[49] Altogether, it is apparent from Local 128's small size, from the entrenched hostility of the oil companies, and from the remoteness of the other oil locals in the region that the OWIU's part in developing the Los Angeles CIO was much smaller than might have been expected.

THE TEAMSTERS SAVOR A VICTORY, 1937–1939

A similar mixture of pluses and minuses attended the efforts of the AFL unions in Los Angeles as they, too, strove to increase their membership during these years. The three AFL unions that experienced the most rapid growth were the Teamsters, IATSE (International Alliance of Theatrical State Employees), and the Carpenters. The International Brotherhood of Teamsters was probably the most important of the three because of the leverage unionized truckers could exert over the movement of goods and services across the far-flung terrain of the Los Angeles basin.

Until the 1930s the Teamsters enjoyed only limited success in Southern California. But by late 1939, L.A.'s Teamsters Joint Council 42, which included short-haul drivers, long-distance operators, and deliverymen who worked for the city's dairies and bakeries, had organized more than twenty-five thousand truck drivers and had become the largest single trade union in the city.[50] How was this remarkable success achieved?

To a great extent, it resulted from the aggressive tactics employed by Dave Beck, who was the most important Teamster leader on the West Coast and who operated out of Seattle, not Los Angeles. A hard-driving business unionist who spurned the social justice aspects of trade unionism, Beck showed little interest in bottom-up methods of union organizing. Instead, he favored using top-down methods—including coercion—to pressure employers into signing union contracts. This tactic, even when it succeeded, was less likely to promote sustained, militant activity by rank-and-file workers than were direct confrontations between labor and capital. Given the power of the Teamsters, its authoritarian character may have contributed to the overall conservatism of the Los Angeles AFL.[51]

Beck prepared his 1930s organizing campaign in Southern California carefully.

First, he prevailed on the truckers in the Bay Area, with whom L.A.'s long-distance trucking companies did most of their business, to join the Teamsters. Then, in the spring of 1937, Beck's Los Angeles lieutenants called a strike at L.A.'s biggest trucking company, Pacific Freight Lines (PFL), in the hope that if the Teamsters succeeded there, other local trucking companies would fall into line.[52]

By prior agreement, Pacific Freight Lines, like L.A.'s other long-distance trucking companies, operated only over the southern portion of the state's highways. After hauling freight up to Bakersfield and Fresno, its drivers usually handed their northbound loads on to other trucking companies operating out of the Bay Area for the rest of the journey. But these Bay Area trucking companies had now been unionized. As a result, the Teamsters locals in Bakersfield and Fresno were able to persuade the northern carriers to refuse any further business with PFL until it recognized the union. The union also sent patrols out on the highways to follow PFL's trucks and pressure their crews into joining the union—often by dubious means. For good measure, if any of PFL's trucks slipped past the Teamster patrols, ILWU Local 13 in San Pedro agreed that the longshoremen would not unload their goods at the harbor, thereby squeezing PFL's business at both ends. Teamster pickets also scared nonunion drivers into joining the union by hurling bricks through their windshields as they passed by. "Bricks sailed through the windshields like rain drops through the air," one organizer recalled.[53]

Beck's tactics worked. Despite a boycott organized by the M&M against L.A.'s unionized trucking companies and the use of armed guards to protect nonunion trucks, PFL quickly lost most of its freight business to its rivals. Staring bankruptcy in the face, the company capitulated and signed a contract with the Teamsters. As Beck had predicted, most of Southern California's other trucking companies followed suit. As a result of this organizing campaign, thousands of Los Angeles truck drivers, seeking improved pay and conditions, flocked to the Teamsters in 1938–1939, thereby greatly boosting the AFL's numbers and bargaining power throughout the city as a whole.

Still more important, the strike victory delivered another major blow to the power and prestige of the open shop lobby, which permanently lost its ability to prevent unionization of one of the largest and most strategically placed elements of the Southern California labor force. "Although the M&M and other hard-core anti-union groups launched new counter-offensives . . . to 'save' other industries from domination by 'union racketeers and gangsters,'" writes Donald Garnel, "the wall of resistance to unionization in southern California had been permanently breached."[54]

IATSE AND THE CARPENTERS ALSO
EXPERIENCE SUCCESS

Similar top-down pressures enabled IATSE and the Carpenters Union, which was the largest and most powerful union in the Los Angeles Building Trades Council, to secure a union shop in most of Hollywood's major studios and the city's other construction sites during these years, even though the corrupt tactics used by IATSE in its organizing campaign were even more retrograde than those employed by the Teamsters.

In 1934 Frank Nitti, Al Capone's successor as leader of the Chicago mob, managed to get George Browne (business agent of Chicago's IATSE Local 2) and Willie Bioff (a small-time hoodlum who had earlier been convicted of pandering charges) elected as national leaders of IATSE.[55] In April 1936 these two men, meeting with Hollywood's studio bosses to renew the 1926 Basic Studio Agreement, persuaded the four largest studios to pay them $50,000 under the table in return for keeping wages down and preventing strikes. Browne and Bioff kept IATSE's members in line by a mixture of physical threats, skillful propaganda, and phony strikes, and also by placing all collective bargaining power in their own hands. In July 1936, Browne arbitrarily invoked the "emergency powers" clause of IATSE's constitution and stripped all of the studio workers' locals of their autonomy, centralizing power in his headquarters in New York—an authoritarian act by a union that was now thoroughly corrupt.[56]

In return for keeping the workers in line, the studios recognized IATSE as the sole (or almost the sole) bargaining agent for Hollywood's employees. As IATSE's membership increased to more than thirty thousand, by 1939 it too had become a vehicle for consolidating the AFL's power in the Los Angeles labor movement.[57] Morality aside, it is not difficult to see why the leaders of both IATSE and the Hollywood studios benefited from their collusion. The studios had found a way, at least for a time, of forcing their restless workers into a union controlled by men who kept the studios' costs down by preventing strikes and trading their employees' wages away in return for payoffs. For their part, George Browne and Willie Bioff received large sums of money in the form of kickbacks. They also maintained themselves in power by blacklisting studio employees who challenged their rule. As studio grip Jim Noblitt stated, people with families to support in Hollywood soon learned "whose ass to kiss" in order to keep their jobs.[58]

Some of the studio workers in Hollywood who preferred a more democratic form of trade unionism were angered by the class collaborationist tactics of

IATSE's corrupt leaders and refused to accept this new "iron law of oligarchy."[59] Between 1935 and 1939, several attempts were made by the CIO, and by Communist union organizers, to break the dictatorial grip of Browne and Bioff. In April 1937, for example, the Federated Motion Picture Crafts (FMPC), a CIO union of utility workers, painters, make-up artists, and others, struck several studios in an attempt to secure independent union recognition. But the strike was defeated when Dave Beck allied with Willie Bioff and brought in "muscle men" to beat up CIO supporters and directed Teamsters to drive supply trucks through the FMPC's picket lines at the studio gates.[60]

The willingness of the studio bosses to engage in these underhanded deals reflected the desire of L.A. employers to retain control over their economic fortunes at a time when the U.S. labor movement was growing more rapidly than ever before. The damage the corrupt practices of IATSE and the Teamsters did to the reputation of the U.S. labor movement, however, was incalculable. After World War II, nothing did more to turn the American public against unions than the corrupt and violent behavior of men like Jimmy Hoffa and unions like the Teamsters.[61]

The Carpenters' most important victory occurred in 1940. In that year, the union used both primary and secondary boycotts to starve the Griffith Construction Company, one of Southern California's largest building firms, of supplies for its building sites and forced it to recognize the union. (A secondary boycott is one in which unions boycott a company not itself involved in a labor dispute in order to pressure another firm into an agreement.) Soon afterward, industrywide negotiations produced the first master labor agreement between the Los Angeles chapter of the Association of General Contractors and all of the region's construction unions. This agreement included a union shop clause, binding arbitration, and union-controlled hiring hall arrangements for carpenters seeking work. Membership in the United Brotherhood of Carpenters and Joiners (UBCJA) in the L.A. area promptly jumped to more than twelve thousand and grew still further during the boom years of World War II. Besides adding a large contingent to the AFL's numbers, this successful agreement tore another gaping hole in the open shop defenses of the M&M.[62]

THE AFL REMAINS DOMINANT

The CIO depended primarily on grassroots enthusiasm and on the expertise of union organizers sent out from headquarters to organize factory workers.

Organizers for both the AFL and the CIO also capitalized on the enthusiasm generated by Section 7a and the legal machinery of the National Labor Relations Board. But the AFL relied more heavily than the CIO on traditional organizing methods, such as visiting with individual workers at their places of employment. The AFL also benefited from the fact that Los Angeles employers, when they were forced to deal with unions, preferred the AFL to the CIO because they believed that the moderate AFL unions were less radical and would interfere less with the operation of their businesses than the more militant CIO.[63]

Quite often, too, AFL organizers were able to persuade Los Angeles workers to choose AFL unions over those of the CIO by pointing to the influence of the Communists in the CIO and warning workers that they would be subjected to pro-Soviet political propaganda if they joined unions like the United Electrical Workers or the ILWU. John Brophy, head of the Organizing Department of the CIO, referred to this criticism in a speech he made to the Industrial Council in L.A. in August 1938. One of the problems his organizers faced in Los Angeles, Brophy said, was the "red baiting, lies and slander" that AFL organizers disseminated at union meetings, in the *Los Angeles Citizen* (the AFL's official paper), and in its radio broadcasts. "The CIO, they say, is dominated by 'reds,' 'communists,' 'dictators,' and the like. The attacks are unwarranted. These are the same groups that attack the New Deal as un-American."[64]

Despite its success in industries such as auto, steel, and rubber, the CIO never became as large as the AFL in Southern California. In this respect, its experience did not differ greatly from that of the labor movement in other cities. Between 1936 and 1937, the AFL lost about one-third of its members when the industrial unions forming the CIO were expelled from the federation. But the AFL recovered quickly from the split. Between 1937 and 1945, nearly four million workers nationwide joined unions affiliated with the AFL, whereas slightly under two million workers joined the CIO.[65]

Nevertheless, the CIO in Los Angeles remained even smaller, in relative terms, than in big industrial cities elsewhere in the country. In 1939, for example, the Los Angeles CIO Industrial Council had an affiliated membership of 39,420, compared to more than 120,000 workers in the citywide AFL. In Chicago, by contrast, the CIO alone had 278,000 card-carrying members.[66] Why was this? The most obvious reason was that the number of factory workers available to join the industrial unions of the CIO remained far lower in Los Angeles than in cities such as Chicago, Pittsburgh, and Detroit.

In addition, the decision as to whether workers would join the AFL or the CIO was not always based on a clear-cut distinction between craft and industrial union-ism. In theory, the two labor federations stood for two quite different philoso-phies of labor organizing. In reality, however, the organizing tactics employed by the two bodies were not all that dissimilar. It is true that industrial unions like the UAW often enrolled all the employees in a factory, including its white-collar work-ers, whereas the International Association of Machinists (which competed with the UAW for members in the aircraft industry) did not.[67] But the IAM also had a long history of enrolling many different kinds of machinists—including some who would otherwise have joined the CIO—ranging from railroad roundhouse machinists to engineering workers, and from small metal shop craft workers to aircraft assembly workers. Hence the proper way to view the modern IAM is as a "mixed craft union," or even as a semi-industrial union, like the modern ILGWU, not as a craft union in the classical sense.[68]

In practice, therefore, the AFL won the battle for supremacy in the Los Angeles labor movement not so much because of a conflict over trade union principles but more because of simple demographics: a higher proportion of the city's labor force worked in commercial, white-collar, and "nonfactory" occupations than in fac-tory jobs. In 1939, only 5.4 percent of Los Angeles County's total population was employed in factory production, compared to a national average of 15.4 percent.[69]

CONCLUSION: FEDERAL INTERVENTION AND THE DECLINE OF THE OPEN SHOP

As the 1930s came to an end, the M&M and its allies had lost much of their ability to enforce the open shop and prevent L.A.'s employers from negotiating contracts with organized labor. How did this liberalization of the union climate come about?

Clearly, decisions made by the federal government had begun to put limits on the power of the open shop lobby. But other factors were also involved. They included the increasing militancy of the labor movement, the growing political influence of the Democratic Party, and the arrival in Southern California of a new generation of company executives who had come to accept the legitimacy of trade unions in the East and who considered the anti-union rhetoric of the older genera-tion of L.A.'s business elite to be out of date. These modern companies included such powerhouses as RCA, Firestone Tire, Dow Chemical, and Bethlehem Steel. Additionally, the political mood of the country, including that of many Southern California small employers, had shifted toward the liberal policies of the New Deal and its legislation legitimizing trade unions.[70]

An additional blow was struck against the power of the open shop lobby in 1938–1939 by the hearings of the Senate Subcommittee on Violations of Free Speech and the Rights of Labor, better known as the La Follette Committee, which exposed the nefarious practices of the M&M, the Chamber of Commerce, and their allies in all sorts of gory detail. "Every known trick of the propagandist to create fear and hostility [was used] against those organizations which attempted to realize the fruits of the National Labor Relations Act," the committee charged. Day after day, reports appeared in the Los Angeles press about the M&M's secret deals to hire labor spies, set up illegal company unions, and fund a large network of anti-union employers in both industry and agriculture. "Important aid in this campaign," the report added, referring to the union-busting activities of the LAPD, "was given by law enforcement officers who strained every nerve and some of the commonest legal precepts to fasten the criminal tag upon union leaders."[71]

But the most crippling blow to the open shop lobby was delivered by federal legislation enacted by the Department of Labor and other federal agencies, which imposed limitations on the freedom of action of anti-union employers. Beginning with Section 7a of the NIRA in 1933 and culminating with the Fair Labor Standards Act in 1938, the New Deal administration in Washington established a new body of labor law that rendered illegal many of the practices of the open shop lobby and that was designed to protect both the safety of workers and the bargaining position of the unions. This federal legislation was then followed up by similar legislation at the state level.[72]

In addition, with the approach of World War II, many of L.A.'s open shop employers, even including some of those in the aircraft and shipbuilding industries, were persuaded to accept the principles of collective bargaining by the offer of lucrative government defense contracts, which came with labor strings attached. As James Wilburn puts it, "If the war was to remake the aircraft industry, the aircraft industry was in turn to remake the face of Los Angeles, . . . ushering in the federal government as the single most important customer and therefore the most influential regulator."[73] The influence exerted by the federal government over the hiring practices of the aircraft manufacturers in Los Angeles is a focus of the next chapter.

If there was any one year in which the open shop in Los Angeles can be said to have entered a period of terminal decline, 1937 was probably that year. No fewer than 113 organizing strikes, many of them successful, took place in the city during those twelve months, a far higher number than in any previous year. Equally significant, according to the La Follette Committee, was that the loss of the Pacific

Freight Lines strike "made the Chamber of Commerce sharply aware of the ineffectiveness of its anti-labor program."[74] The Teamsters' victory was followed by no less than three major reorganizations of the M&M as it tried to recoup its losses. The Neutral Thousands, in particular, used social events, church meetings, and other cultural activities in the Republican suburbs to try and revive the old anti-union gospel of "industrial freedom" among the white, conservative business class of Los Angeles.[75]

But none of these reorganizations did much good. To make matters worse, in 1939 not only the La Follette Committee but also the Los Angeles office of the National Labor Relations Board held several months of public hearings on the illegal activities of the M&M, the Neutral Thousands, and Southern Californians Inc. After the hearings were over, the L.A. branch of the NLRB handed down a strong public indictment of the employers' tactics and urged them, as the La Follette Committee had done, to desist from practices such as the use of labor spies, strikebreakers, company-controlled unions, and detective agencies. Its report found that these practices had for years been "part of a coordinated plan . . . of assisting all employers in Southern California in interfering with, restraining, and coercing their employees in the exercise of the rights guaranteed to such employees" under the National Labor Relations Act.[76]

The NLRB ordered each of L.A.'s open shop organizations to "cease and desist their unfair labor practices, now and in the future," to notify all of their affiliated firms of their intention to do so, and to report in writing to the board when they had taken these steps. All appeals from the NLRB's legal order were rejected. In December 1941, *Business Week* went so far as to say that even the "most enthusiastic open-shoppers in Los Angeles" were leaning toward "accepting collective bargaining as established by law."[77] By the time the U.S. entered World War II, the long reign of the open shop in Southern California was effectively over.

EIGHT

L.A. Workers in World War II

"Two Steps Forward, One Step Back"?
1941–1945

World War II brought unprecedented social, economic, and cultural changes to the way of life of most Southern Californians. But their effects on working men and women in the city began well before America entered the conflict on December 7, 1941. In the build-up to the war, the federal government awarded a substantial number of large defense contracts, particularly for ships and warplanes, to companies in Los Angeles, which brought many new migrants to the city in search of employment more than a year before Pearl Harbor. By September 1942, Los Angeles had secured 64 percent of all California's contracts for fighters and bombers as well as 28 percent of its shipbuilding awards.[1] The war plants were staggering in size, far larger than any prewar factories. At its peak, Calship on Terminal Island employed 45,000 to 55,000 riveters, mechanics, metalworkers, and engineers; and the Douglas bomber plant, located in Long Beach, took in more than 20,000.[2]

It would also be misleading to regard August 1945, when the Japanese surrendered, as an appropriate end date for the social and economic changes brought by the war. Of the 98,000 "Rosie the Riveters" employed in the Southern California aircraft industry in 1943, which was the peak year, 22,000 (or 22 percent) had already been discharged by December 1944—nine months before the end of the conflict.[3] Other effects, however, lingered well into the next decade: the debate over whether the Los Angeles City Council should authorize the building of publicly owned (as opposed to private) houses to ease the wartime housing shortage, which its opponents regarded as creeping socialism, continued until the 1950s.[4]

LABOR SHORTAGES, HOUSING, AND
THE RECOMPOSITION OF SOUTHERN
CALIFORNIA'S LABOR FORCE

By December 1941, approximately 200,000 of the 750,000 new residents who would eventually be added to L.A.'s population during World War II had already arrived. Where did these wartime migrants come from, and what did they do? Of the new arrivals, 28 percent came from cities east of the Mississippi, and 19.9 percent from the midwestern states that had supplied Los Angeles with immigrants in earlier years, such as Kansas and Iowa. Another 19.5 percent hailed from the dust bowl states of Oklahoma and Arkansas.[5]

The war created a very strong sense of common effort, feelings of patriotism, and the perception of sharing an experience larger than the individual or the group. Nevertheless, it also generated strong disagreements. Business hoped to win the war but maintain control over its own operations. Organized labor wanted to win the war but also to increase its legitimacy and its membership. African Americans and Latinos were just as patriotic as any other Americans but were additionally determined to upgrade their status, to be seen as first-class citizens. The influx of a new group of Okies, coupled with the migration of thousands of African Americans from the South, probably had the most important social effect because these population shifts contributed significantly to what became known as the "southernization" of Los Angeles and to a major increase in racial tensions.[6]

But the most startling statistics concerned the changing role of women. No fewer than 167,860 women between the ages of eighteen and sixty-four, most of whom took jobs in the aircraft, shipbuilding, and service industries, joined the Southern California labor force between 1940 and 1944. More than any other group, these women compensated for the loss of the male workers who joined the armed forces, as well as for the absence of the incarcerated Japanese Americans, who, by President Roosevelt's executive order, were rounded up and sent to internment camps in 1942, as war hysteria and anti-Japanese prejudice peaked. In fact, a census survey taken in 1944 stated that a combination of the women already living in L.A. who took jobs in the defense industries and those who came from outside constituted "the chief source of expansion in the [Los Angeles] labor supply."[7]

Map 4 shows the relative numbers and residential dispersal of a large proportion of the city's wartime employees in 1940, when the migration first began. The largest single group of wartime migrants were the 70,000 newcomers who went to Long Beach, many of whom secured jobs either in the shipbuilding industry or at

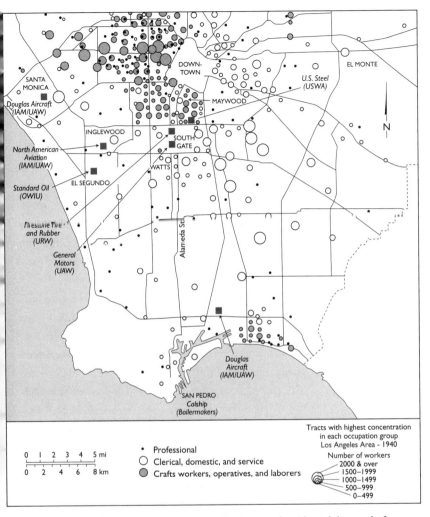

Tracts with highest concentration
in each occupation group
Los Angeles Area - 1940

Number of workers
2000 & over
1500–1999
1000–1499
500–999
0–499

• Professional
○ Clerical, domestic, and service
◉ Crafts workers, operatives, and laborers

0 1 2 3 4 5 mi
0 2 4 6 8 km

MAP 4. Major defense contractors, associated unions, and residential dispersal of employees by occupational categories, 1940. Courtesy of University of California Press. E. Shevsky and M. Williams, *The Social Areas of Los Angeles: Analysis and Typology*, p. 41. © 1949 by Regents of the University of California, renewed 1977 by E. Shevsky and M. Williams. Reprinted by permission of the University of California Press.

the Douglas bomber factory, which opened in 1941.[8] The map also lists the unions that were associated with their places of work.

In 1940 two large housing tracts, named, respectively, Westside Village and Westchester, were built near the Douglas Aircraft facility in Santa Monica and the North American Aviation plant in Inglewood.[9] In typical L.A. fashion, they did not consist of rental facilities owned by the corporations, as would have been the case in a company town, but rather were neighborhoods of private homes built for sale to incoming residents. However, only a few defense workers could afford to buy accommodations in large, new housing tracts such as these. The rest were forced to "double up" by staying with relatives or friends, by renting rooms in the city's limited stock of apartment buildings, or by moving into primitive, purpose-built accommodations near their places of work. Although shipbuilding was a cru-cial part of L.A.'s wartime economy, many of that industry's 91,000 workers (more than 5 percent of the city's population) were living in substandard accommodations next to the harbor area in Long Beach.[10]

As the demand for wartime housing grew, the city authorities began to build new apartment buildings and houses all over the city, but it took months, and sometimes years, before they became available. The Los Angeles City Housing Authority (CHA) reallocated most of its housing funds to the needs of the defense workers. But it was often hamstrung in its planning by an acrimonious debate that broke out in the city council between supporters and opponents of publicly owned housing. The liberal members of the city council, supported by New Deal Democrats, labor unions, and advocates for minority groups, favored using the federal funds that had been designated for housing to build publicly owned hous-ing projects. Their opponents, who included lobbyists for the Southern California Association of Real Estate Boards, argued that federal subsidies should be used to build additional private houses, not publicly owned housing tracts. They believed that if public housing projects were allowed to spread, the United States would "be precipitated into a socialist state."[11]

Beginning in 1941–1942, this left-right debate over publicly owned housing was complicated by the racial friction that emerged between newly arrived groups who had entered the labor force, including African Americans, Okies, and white south-erners. At first, most of the CHA's housing projects were racially integrated, as a result of federal pressure. But conservative white citizens' groups objected to hav-ing integrated housing projects located in their neighborhoods, while civil rights organizations such as the NAACP, the Urban League, and the Interracial Church Council insisted that integrated housing be preserved.

Ramona Gardens, built as an integrated wartime housing project, 1941. Courtesy of Security Pacific National Bank Collection, Los Angeles Public Library.

In January 1941, for example, the city's premier public housing project, Ramona Gardens (shown in the accompanying photograph), was opened on an integrated basis with the blessing of the Spanish-language newspaper *La Opinion*, which described the accommodations as "pleasant, healthy, and secure."[12] But soon after this, representatives of an Okie group objected to being placed in a housing project in Watts, which by then was largely African American.[13] At the same time, ILWU activist Bert Corona established a Mexican Subcommittee of the CIO Industrial Council to lobby on behalf of public housing for Mexican American war workers. At an August 1942 meeting of the City Housing Authority, Mexican families were granted permission to live in city-owned public housing provided that at least one of their children was a U.S. citizen and that someone in the family had a defense-related job.[14]

In the end, with federal backing, the CHA managed to build and operate five permanent and twenty-one temporary public housing projects for war workers, most of which were located in Watts, in the Alameda corridor, or in the San Pedro–Long Beach area. Most of these projects contained a mixture of black and white residents, together with a scattering of Latinos. "I want people to realize that public housing has come to stay," said Mrs. Virginia Lindsey in January 1944, who was the left-wing president of the residents' council at the Channel Heights public housing project. "People like having Uncle Sam as a landlord."[15] Since racial tensions persisted in both public and private housing, however, Mrs. Lindsey's opinions proved to be overly optimistic.

EMPLOYMENT, RACE, AND POPULAR CULTURE

What kind of relationships developed between L.A.'s established, white working-class residents and these new immigrant groups? Wherever they settled, the recently arrived Okies, many of whom had previously picked fruit or cotton on ranches in the San Joaquin Valley, provided a somewhat contradictory addition to the demographic mix in the defense industries. On the one hand, they were white, native-born Americans whose rural backgrounds and evangelical religion placed them in the same cultural ballpark as the former midwesterners who dominated the city's resident population. On the other hand, many of the incoming Okies were poorly educated dirt farmers, who were initially seen—unfairly—as violent, stupid, and inferior by many of the existing working-class residents. In other words, they were not quite as "white" as their supposed social superiors, and they suffered accordingly. For instance, when a new batch of Okies started working at the Calship facility on Terminal Island, one of the company's long-time employees labeled a urinal at the plant "an Okie Drinking Fountain."[16]

Many of these same Okie and Arkie migrants who were stigmatized by their better-educated, fellow white workers in the defense plants had grown up in the Southwest in a "plain folks" way of life that promoted toughness, social conservatism, and a chauvinistic form of racism that rejected any kind of contact with African Americans. During World War II, however, some of them became more sympathetic to liberal political values, particularly when such values were promoted by union organizers or broadcast over the radio by folk musician Woody Guthrie and other artists in the form of plaintive ballads about the problems and prospects of rural migrants who had recently arrived in the "big city."[17]

Mexican American workers were an equally important part of the racial jigsaw puzzle of L.A.'s wartime working class. Given the relatively strong position they had built for themselves in the CIO before the war, it seemed at first that Latino workers might not have to fight as hard as African Americans did for jobs in the defense industries. This was partly because of the perception that, as proximate Caucasians, they were more readily accepted by white employers than black applicants were. And it was partly because the federal Fair Employment Practices

Commission, which held hearings in Los Angeles in 1941 into the racist hiring practices of white factory owners, paid less attention to discrimination against Latino employees that it did to discrimination against blacks, implying that the problems faced by Latinos were less severe.[18] But these appearances were deceptive. In reality, Latino war workers suffered just as much from overcrowded housing, police harassment, and employment discrimination as other minority groups did. Like African Americans, Latinos were forced to compete in a segregated labor market where most of them were confined to unskilled, low-paying jobs.[19]

Nor was this all. In August 1942, L.A.'s Latino community was angered and humiliated when the LAPD charged twenty-three supposed Mexican gang members with the murder of José Díaz, a teenager who died after a quarrel at a swimming hole called the Sleepy Lagoon, near Slauson and Atlantic boulevards. Although no evidence of an actual homicide surfaced, the white-run press savagely attacked the defendants for their "murderous behavior," and twelve of them were later convicted in court. The U.S. District Court of Appeals eventually overturned the Sleepy Lagoon convictions for lack of evidence, and it rebuked the presiding judge for courtroom impropriety. But no other racial incident demonstrated quite as readily the ease with which the casual racism of the majority of L.A.'s white citizens could escalate into an ugly witch hunt under the pressures of war.[20]

AFRICAN AMERICANS JOIN THE ETHNIC MIX, 1942–1943

The Sleepy Lagoon case certainly highlighted the longstanding racial tensions that were widespread in Southern California, but it was the large-scale influx of African Americans that posed the greatest challenge to the white-dominated Los Angeles workforce. During World War II, the city's black population almost doubled, rising from 67,000 in 1940 to 125,000 in 1945. Hearing of high wages in the defense plants, thousands of African Americans left their homes in southern cities such as Houston, Shreveport, and New Orleans, took the train to Los Angeles, and immediately began looking for housing and jobs. This migration created a substantial black working class in Southern California for the first time. Some were able to find accommodations near the new railroad station in the neighborhood known as Little Tokyo, now largely vacated after its Japanese American residents had been removed to internment camps. But since African Americans, like Latinos, were unable to buy or rent accommodations in most other parts of the city, most of the black newcomers were forced to move in with relatives or friends in the Central Avenue neighborhood or in Watts.[21]

The arrival of so many new black workers in Los Angeles, in addition to the Okies and other job seekers, also raised the debate over public versus private housing to a new pitch. In August 1943, Mayor Fletcher Bowron called a conference to discuss the housing shortage and appointed a committee of three African American community leaders (Norman Houston, Floyd Covington of the Urban League, and Judge Edwin L. Jefferson) to consider the matter. The *California Eagle* weighed in on the side of the newcomers, arguing that "while we emphatically support the demand for increased emergency housing in the Negro districts of Los Angeles, . . . the FUNDAMENTAL housing necessity in Los Angeles is the total destruction of property restrictions [housing covenants]."[22]

This August housing conference took place in the wake of the Zoot Suit riots, which occurred in June 1943, when gangs of white, off-duty servicemen roamed through the streets of downtown Los Angeles beating up Mexican *pachucos* and African Americans who wore the specially cut, oversized garments called zoot suits. It was the city's most serious racial incident during the course of the war. Immediately after the riots, one city planner wired the City Housing Authority urging it to make available "at least 5,000 public housing units . . . for racial minorities to help relieve [a] desperate situation."[23]

In addition to housing and racist harassment, another serious problem was the failure of the city's high schools and technical institutes to provide vocational training for minority youths seeking jobs. The CIO's Anti-Discrimination Committee appeared before the Los Angeles Board of Education to complain about the lack of training classes at high schools in the East Side ghetto. But even after training facilities had been installed at Jefferson High School and elsewhere, there was no guarantee that the U.S. Employment Service (a temporary wartime agency) would recommend young Hispanic and African American trainees for jobs in the defense factories.[24]

Yet another problem resulted from the inadequate public transportation system in Los Angeles. Many of the city's biggest defense plants were located on the West Side or in the harbor area, miles away from the eastern part of the city, where most minority workers lived. In 1944, according to one estimate, more than a hundred thousand defense workers had to commute fifty miles back and forth daily to get to their jobs. For those who could afford cars (and many could not), gas rationing made things even more difficult.[25] Most defense workers relied on the Red Cars or city buses to get to work.

The problem worsened as the war progressed. Virtually all of L.A.'s prewar bus drivers and streetcar conductors were white, and after they were drafted into the military, Red Car service rapidly declined. One black defense worker from Watts complained that he had "real problems when I got a job at the Long Beach Naval Shipyard because it took the Red Car a long time to go from Watts to Long Beach and the damn thing broke down a lot."[26] Neither the Los Angeles Railway (LARY) streetcars nor the L.A. bus system would hire African American drivers to replace the white ones. In addition, Local 1277 of the Amalgamated Association of Street, Electric Railway, and Motor Coach Employees was a "whites only" union, which refused to help LARY's black workers secure promotions. It took months of pressure from other unions and an investigation by the Fair Employment Practices Commission to persuade LARY to hire African American platform conductors. Even then, the numbers hired were very small. At the end of World War II, only 113 of LARY's 2,129 drivers and platform conductors were Latino or African American.[27]

BLACK WORKERS STRUGGLE FOR DEFENSE JOBS

The biggest battle was over obtaining jobs in the defense industries themselves. In the early stages of the war, nearly all Los Angeles defense contractors refused point blank to hire African Americans until the supply of white workers had been exhausted. For example, in the spring of 1941, J.H. Kindelberger, president of North American Aviation, issued an official statement declaring, "While we are in complete sympathy with Negroes, it is against Company policy to employ them as mechanics or aircraft workers."[28] Much the same thing occurred in shipbuilding. By April 1941, only 47 African Americans had been hired by Calship on Terminal Island, out of a skilled labor force of 6,418. Many excuses were given for this dearth of minority workers: some employers claimed that no trained black workers were available to perform the skilled jobs, while other contractors asserted that no white male employees would work alongside African Americans.[29]

A spasm of hope ran through the black community when African American labor leader A. Philip Randolph announced plans for a July 1, 1941, March on Washington to protest discrimination in defense employment. Randolph's march threatened to embarrass the Roosevelt administration by pointing out the contrast between its stated war aims (opposing both the racist and the militaristic ambitions of Hitler) and its continued tolerance of racial injustice at home. By this time, many supporters of FDR's preparedness policy, as well as civil rights bodies of all kinds, were advocating the "Double V" (double victory) policy, meaning a campaign not only to defeat fascism abroad but also to advance the cause of racial justice at home.[30]

Calship shipyard on Terminal Island, where African Americans struggled to be hired. Courtesy of National Archives, photo no. NWDNS-208-YE-2B (7).

Black workers' hopes were raised again when, in order to forestall Randolph's threatened March on Washington, President Roosevelt issued his famous Executive Order 8802 prohibiting employment discrimination in defense plants. The hopes of minorities rose still higher when the president appointed the Fair Employment Practices Commission (FEPC) to enforce the order. The trouble was that although the FEPC could report examples of discrimination, at first it had no power to require the offending companies to change their hiring practices. Its efforts were not entirely without effect, however. Just before the FEPC held its first hearings in Los Angeles in October 1941, fear of negative publicity forced the Lockheed and Vega Aircraft Company to hire 54 African American workers. But this was a drop in the bucket compared to the company's overall payroll of 48,000 aircraft employees. In fact, black employment in the aircraft and shipping industries did not increase substantially until mid-1943, when the shortage of labor became so acute that employers could no longer find enough white employees, men or women, to keep the plants operating at full capacity.[31]

In the meantime, L.A.'s black community, with the help of the Anti-Discrimination Committee of the CIO, stepped up the pressure by establishing the Negro Victory Committee, under the leadership of the Reverend Clayton D. Russell, an African American minister. This committee won a small victory when it exposed the discriminatory practices of the U.S. Employment Service. In July 1942, several Los Angeles aircraft companies asked the Employment Service to provide them with female workers but insisted that they be white, in contravention of government policy. The Negro Victory Committee organized a demonstration of several hundred angry black women, who rallied outside the Employment Service office in downtown Los Angeles, proclaiming: "This is our war! . . . We cannot win it in the kitchen; we must win it on the assembly line!"[32]

The efforts of the Shipyard Workers Committee for Equal Participation (SWCEP) proved to have more far-reaching effects. SWCEP was established early in 1943 by Walter Williams, a talented African American labor organizer, who became one of the most influential voices for black equality in wartime Los Angeles. Some of the black migrants who ended up in the San Pedro area had earlier worked as longshoremen in Gulf Coast cities such as New Orleans, so they were natural candidates for jobs in the shipbuilding industry on nearby Terminal Island. A small CIO union had been established there, which was racially integrated. But it was much smaller and weaker than Lodge 92 of the AFL's large and powerful International Brotherhood of Boilermakers. Lodge 92, which was "whites only," was able to control most of the hiring and firing in the shipyards because it had negotiated a union (closed) shop agreement with the "Big-3" shipbuilding companies, including the giant California Shipbuilding Corporation (Calship), at the beginning of the war. This meant, in effect, that it could keep out any African American workers who applied for skilled jobs.[33]

For black applicants, the most galling aspect of Lodge 92's "whites only" policy was that it permitted Latino, Filipino, and Chinese shipyard workers to join as full members of the union but relegated African Americans to an auxiliary body. A-35, as it was known, denied black workers full union membership and prevented them from joining apprenticeship programs and hence from getting skilled jobs. In 1943, the several hundred African Americans employed in the shipyards worked only as janitors and unskilled laborers, at wages well below those paid to the skilled white machinists, burners, and riveters, who were full members of the union. Working with the Industrial Council of the CIO, Walter Williams and SWEPC turned the black shipyard protest into a civil rights cause célèbre. The black workers stopped paying union dues to A-35 and instead held joint rallies with other frustrated minority groups, filed complaints with the FEPC, and distributed signs reading: "JIM-CROW BELONGS IN GERMANY—NOT IN AMERICA! WE WON'T PAY DUES FOR HITLERISM!"[34]

In November 1943, the reorganized FEPC, which now had greater legal power, held new hearings in Los Angeles and ordered the Big-3 shipbuilding companies to stop discriminating against blacks. But, to the chagrin of SWCEP's members, Calship and the other companies, citing the closed shop provision in their union agreement with the Boilermakers, refused to change their hiring practices or to permit blacks to take skilled jobs. The issue then went to the courts, where it remained for more than a year.[35]

THE ANGUISH OF NOVELIST CHESTER HIMES

Conflict at the point of production was only one among many symptoms of racial unrest that afflicted L.A.'s minority communities during these years. For example, in 1941, well-known black novelist Chester Himes, who had been educated at Ohio State University, moved to Los Angeles with a letter of introduction from Langston Hughes, hoping to sell his stories to the movies. Unable to find work in the racist studio system, he was forced to labor at a low-level job in a shipyard. Angered by his experience, he later wrote the novel *Lonely Crusade* (1947), about an educated African American who was hired as a union organizer at Comstock Aircraft (an imaginary plant) specifically to recruit black workers. Published just as the House Un-American Activities Committee was beginning congressional investigations of Hollywood during the postwar red scare, *Lonely Crusade* was an anti-Marxist novel that presented Communists in the labor movement as power-hungry manipulators who were paid by the employers to spy on the workers.[36]

Himes wrote a second novel while he was still in Los Angeles, titled *If He Hollers, Let Him Go* (1945). This book was a more accurate reflection of his own experience working in the Calship shipyard two or three years earlier, including the hostile treatment of minorities that resulted from the racial conflicts stirred up by the war. During the course of a single day at Calship, Himes's protagonist, Bob Jones, who acts as his alter ego in the novel, witnesses the beating of Mexican zoot suiters, the slapping of a young Chinese girl who was mistaken for Japanese, and allegations of rape against one of L.A.'s major black entrepreneurs.[37]

If He Hollers, Let Him Go is worth analyzing in some detail because the anger expressed by its tragic anti-hero depicts better than any contemporary account the real-life dilemmas of African American workers who tried to get jobs in the defense industry. Early on in the novel, Bob Jones becomes one of the few African Americans to be promoted to the position of foreman at the shipyard. But he is soon immersed in a struggle to keep his emotional balance amid a plethora of racial, occupational, and sexual problems.[38]

Bob lives in the overcrowded black ghetto of Bronzeville (formerly Little Tokyo), as many real-life African Americans did. He commutes twenty miles each day to his job on Terminal Island, where he and his crew work on the ventilation system of a new ship. Himes's prose brilliantly evokes the atmosphere of the crowded, labyrinthine quarters of the ship's interior where Jones works. "The air was so thick with welding fumes, acid smell, body odor, and cigarette smoke even the stream [of air] from the blower couldn't get it out. I had fifteen guys in my gang, twelve men and three women. . . . Two or three guys were hand-riveting. A chipper was working on the deck above. It was stifling hot."[39] One day, during a pause in his shift, Jones comes across a white Texan woman named Madge and tries to recruit her into his crew. But she indignantly refuses, stating bluntly that she will not "work for a nigger." In response Jones calls her a "cracker bitch."[40] As punishment for this insult, he is hauled before a white supervisor, loses his foreman status, and is demoted to the position of mechanic.

Later on in the story, Jones gets trapped in a dangerous sexual triangle between Madge—the crude white woman who despises black men but finds Bob attractive—and his middle-class African American girlfriend, Alice, whom Jones's landlady describes as "the whitest colored girl you could find."[41] Alice urges Bob to leave the shipyard and get an education, but he in turn despises her as a bourgeois black woman who has sold out to "whitey" because she lives on the West Side of Los Angeles and has a white-collar job. When he takes Alice out to eat in an upscale restaurant frequented by whites, she is embarrassed to be seen with an African American who is so dark-skinned. To add insult to injury, when the white waiter brings the bill, Bob finds that he has added two lines to it: "We served you this time but we do not want your patronage in the future."[42]

If He Hollers reaches a tragic climax when Bob Jones, seeking a new job on his old ship, accidentally stumbles into a compartment where he finds Madge, asleep and alone. Madge wakes up and decides to revenge herself on Bob for his earlier insulting invitation in the most damaging way possible. She locks him into the compartment with her and screams that she is being raped—the most heinous crime a black man could have been accused of. A crowd of onlookers gathers outside the compartment, and a white navy inspector cuts through the door with a welding torch. Bob is seized, beaten unconscious by the crowd, and, after recovering in an infirmary, is brought to trial. Madge's evidence about the alleged rape is too flimsy for the judge to convict him. But the judge revokes Jones's draft exemption and sends him off to the U.S. Army, along with two Mexican shipyard workers who have also run afoul of the law.[43]

The story of Bob Jones in *If He Hollers, Let Him Go* illustrates many of the pitfalls African American migrants to Los Angeles encountered when they tried to upgrade their status during the course of the war. As historian Eileen Boris succinctly puts it in her commentary on the book: "Racialized understandings of manhood and womanhood—of the black male rapist, the pure white woman, and the uncleanly black woman [Jones's girlfriend Alice in this case] provided an arena for the wartime debate over fair employment, one connected to larger structures of power and authority."[44]

"ROSIE THE RIVETER" GOES TO WAR, 1941–1944

At first, Los Angeles defense manufacturers were loathe to hire women to work in their factories, whether the women were black, Chinese, Mexican, or white. Many expressed doubts that women could do a "man's job," while others feared that their male employees—with the experience of mass unemployment in the 1930s still fresh in their minds—would not accept women co-workers. Traditional male sex stereotyping also played a role. In January 1942, for example, Donald Douglas refused to hire women in his Santa Monica aircraft plant on the grounds that "men are more stable and efficient. Without women, no distractions are present in the canteen or the shop floor."[45]

But when the wartime draft siphoned off most male employees, and federal deadlines for the completion of defense orders loomed closer, these fears were swept aside. By mid-1943 as many as 98,000 women, the great majority of them white, had entered Southern California's aircraft factories, and another 9,749 were helping to build Liberty ships on Terminal Island. Between January 1943 and V-E Day, more than 40 percent of California's airframe employees were women, a higher proportion than in any other state.[46] Like the African American war workers who came from the South, many of these female defense workers traveled long distances to get their jobs, lured to Southern California by the prospect of high wages and by government advertising campaigns that successfully projected the

"Rosie the Riveter" at work at Vultee Aircraft in Downey, 1942. Courtesy of Library of Congress Prints and Photographs Division, photo no. LC-USE6-D-009531 [P&P].

image of "Rosie the Riveter" as a symbol of home-front patriotism.[47] Propaganda photos such as the one reproduced here, of a woman war worker at Vultee Aircraft in Downey, exalted both glamour and skill.

Contrary to popular myth, the majority of female defense workers in Southern California were not young housewives who had never worked before. Most of them were either young single women, wives whose husbands had gone to war, or married women over forty whose children were already grown. Fully two-thirds of them had worked outside the home before World War II, usually as domestics, waitresses, or in some other low-level job.[48] Connie Field's 1980 film *The Life and Times of Rosie the Riveter*, which is the best-known popular attempt to document the role of America's female war workers, is thus somewhat misleading.[49]

For example, four of the five women in the film had small children, which was not typical of the women in the defense plants. Many of the protagonists in the film have skilled jobs, when in reality most female aircraft employees worked at fairly low-level, assembly-line occupations. Virtually all the skilled craft jobs were still reserved for men.[50]

Entering the male world of the factory was a scary experience for many of these women war workers, especially those who were working outside the home for the first time. For example, when Beatrice Clifton (one of the women interviewed by Sherna Gluck for her 1987 book *Rosie the Riveter Revisited*) was shown how to use a rivet gun by an unsympathetic foreman at Lockheed, she was alarmed, "because I never worked with a man before who was not my husband."[51] Tina Hill, a black woman who worked at North American Aviation in Inglewood, found shooting hot rivets into airplane wings equally disconcerting. She stood it for two weeks, then moved on to another job.[52] In shipbuilding, where men and women were more frequently mixed together on the job because of the greater variety of tasks required, the work could be dangerous. Gladys Belcher, a deck welder who worked for Calship on Terminal Island, witnessed a male worker being crushed to death by a falling steel beam. Later she herself was injured by a heavy metal pipe and had to be hoisted off the deck of a half-completed Victory ship by crane.[53] Faced with such pressures, women workers took comfort in the sisterly relations their common experience afforded. They shared apartments, shopped together, lunched together in the plant cafeteria, and went out dancing at night in groups.

Additional difficulties arose, some of them large, others small. Some women at first balked at being required to wear slacks on the job rather than dresses. Others found carrying out repetitive tasks in a confined space over an eight- or ten-hour shift exhausting and difficult to sustain. Attractive women were subjected to constant whistling by male workers in the plants. Some of the women ignored this form of sexual harassment, while others, such as this Lockheed female employee, responded in kind: "Oh, when a fellow whistles at me," she said, "I whistle right back at him. He doesn't know what to do next."[54] Other sexual issues were more serious. Large numbers of single women and wives whose husbands were away at the front were thrown together with men in unfamiliar ways. Many defense manufacturers, along with church leaders and other conservative figures who shaped Los Angeles opinion, worried about sexual promiscuity and the increased danger of venereal disease. In May 1943, when the proportion of women at the Douglas aircraft plant in Santa Monica reached 25 percent, management locked the doors to the plant's bomb shelters to prevent sexual encounters during lunch breaks.[55]

Women's rates of absenteeism were high, given the demands of child care, the burden of housework, and the responsibility of caring for their families, a double standard that male workers rarely faced. In late 1943, several of L.A.'s biggest aircraft factories adopted a three-shift, twenty-four-hour schedule to keep up with their production deadlines, which posed a great disadvantage for women who worked the night shift but didn't have a car. Women on the day shift found it hard to do the family shopping because shops closed at 5:00 or 6:00 P.M. After pressure from some of the unions, the Los Angeles City Council requested that shopkeepers stay open later.[56] Additionally, as holders of the family purse strings, many more women than men witnessed the effects of wartime inflation firsthand as they tried to provide for their families. During World War II, the consumer price index in Los Angeles rose 31 points (100 = 1939), from 102 in 1940 to 133 in 1945. These price increases canceled out many of the benefits both men and women workers received from higher wartime wages.[57]

Despite these problems, most women workers learned their jobs quickly and took pride in their ability to perform a wide variety of tasks, which ranged from truck driving to riveting, and from lathe work to installing radar equipment on ships. Historian Sherna Gluck, who talked to more than two hundred former Southern California aircraft workers and published a dozen extended interviews, reported that many of the women "proudly proclaimed how they had held their own with men."[58] Beatrice Clifton, for example, who saw herself as "just . . . a mother of four" when she began work at Lockheed's Burbank plant, ended up as a lead person in charge of over forty assembly-line workers, more than half of whom were men. Such women gained greatly in self-confidence as a result of their own efforts and often received praise from federal authorities and from specialists in the field.[59] This was true even in the male-dominated shipyards, where the physical tasks were harder than in aircraft. "Reports from shipyards," writes historian D'Ann Campbell, "showed that women were better engineers' helpers [than men]." As one female union leader succinctly put it: "Gone is the clinging vine."[60]

The social and cultural horizons of female war workers expanded, too, especially the social horizons of single women and housewives who had come from small towns in the South and the Midwest. Each of the big Los Angeles war plants provided a variety of recreation activities, from bowling and movie shows to swimming and specialty sports. North American's recreation office even offered a dating service.[61] Other factories encouraged their single female employees to help entertain soldiers who came home on leave. The Hollywood Guild, for example, which operated one of the largest servicemen's canteens in Los Angeles, bused groups of Lockheed women workers, known as the "Blue Stars," from Burbank to their premises on Vine Street to help entertain the troops. The young women were told, "If you are young and you like to dance, you can do a good deed and while away a few lonely hours until 3 A.M."[62] Given these opportunities, it was small wonder that many young women looked back on their years of employment in World War II as the most exciting time in their lives.

RACE AND GENDER CONFLICTS AND
THE TRADE UNION RESPONSE

Despite their initial difficulties, it seems clear that white women had an easier time adjusting to their new jobs in L.A.'s aircraft factories than African American men did trying to find skilled work in the Terminal Island shipyards. Nevertheless, these two groups had many problems in common. Both were seen as temporary additions to the workforce who would leave their jobs as soon as the war was over. Another problem they both faced was the ambivalent attitude of white, male-dominated trade unions, most of which viewed the influx of women and minorities into the factories with suspicion.[63] The lengths to which Lodge 92 of the International Brotherhood of Boilermakers went to deny black men access to skilled jobs in the shipbuilding industry made its hostility toward African Americans—often disguised as fear of skill dilution—all too clear.

Part of the ambivalence, of course, came from the AFL's long history of racist and sexist treatment of minorities and women, in keeping with the culture of the times. But World War II added a new twist to the story. Before the war, most women and African Americans had been confined to traditional "female" or "colored" occupations in the lower half of a dual, or segmented, labor market (domestic or garment work in the case of women, janitorial or laboring jobs in the case of black men).[64] By 1943, however, the wartime labor shortage had become so acute that the impersonal mechanisms of the dual labor market were no longer sufficient to protect the privileges of skilled white tradesmen. Moreover, the federal government was now engaged, however half-heartedly, in an effort to integrate the shop floor. Such threats to the traditional values held by white males concerning the proper role of women and minorities in U.S. society lay behind most of the race and gender conflicts that occurred on the job.[65]

One of these conflicts involved African American men who were seeking jobs in the shipbuilding industry. As described earlier in this chapter, the Shipyard Workers Committee for Equal Participation had campaigned to force Boilermakers Lodge 92 to permit black workers to apply for skilled jobs in the Terminal Island shipyards, but these efforts stalled in November 1943, when the issue went to the courts. The first legal decision challenging this exclusion policy was made by the California Supreme Court in *James v. Marinship*, which ruled that "an arbitrarily closed union is incompatible with a closed shop."[66] The effect of this decision was to invalidate the Boilermakers' policy of confining African American shipyard workers to an auxiliary union, which had been the mechanism for keeping them out of skilled jobs.[67]

This apparent victory for interracial unionism was deceptive, however. When the legal decision was handed down in June 1945, the war in Europe was already over, victory against Japan was only months away, and both the male and female shipyard workers who had been hired earlier in the war were being rapidly laid off. By 1950 only 1,680 African American shipyard workers remained at work in the entire state of California, and most of these still labored at unskilled or semi-skilled jobs.[68] Thus, even though the "whites only" Boilermakers Union had been forced to back down, SWEPC's heroic efforts on behalf of minority employees in the shipyards ended in a pyrrhic victory because it came too late to make any real difference.

When it came to unionizing the black longshoremen of San Pedro, a more tolerant racial policy might have been expected from the CIO's left-wing ILWU, especially in light of President Harry Bridges's coastwide commitment to interracial hiring.[69] But ILWU Local 13 in San Pedro proved to be just as recalcitrant in race relations as its predecessor union had been over industrial unionism during the 1934 dock strike. When the labor shortage on the docks became acute, Local 13 found that it had to accept several thousand African American longshoremen into its ranks in order to keep ships moving and fulfill its contract with the shipowners. But Local 13's president, L. B. Thomas, made it clear that black longshoremen were temporary employees who would be required to leave the docks once the war was over. "You're only temporary workers," Thomas told Walter Williams. "This union was lily-white before you guys came down here, and after the war it is going to be lily-white again."[70]

President Thomas's racist prediction turned out to be correct. In 1945 the demand for longshoremen in the San Pedro docks declined almost as rapidly as the demand for workers in the nearby shipyards. Most of the longshoremen who had been hired during the war were discharged. Determined to maintain the lily-white status of their union, Local 13 "deregistered" the five hundred members who were lowest on the union's seniority list, which determined the order in which laid-off dockworkers were called back to work. More than half of these five hundred were African Americans. Even when laid-off black workers with some seniority came up for rehiring, however, the union gave priority to white army veterans or those who had served in the merchant marine.[71]

What accounts for this renegade behavior by one of the CIO's most progressive unions? Clearly, high-minded declarations of support for racial equality by the national leaders of the CIO—even leaders with the moral authority of Harry Bridges—were often ignored or even contradicted by the rank and file.[72] It is also true that longshore employment, like working down a coal mine, was a family-based occupation in which jobs were frequently passed down from father to son. Since the longshore industry in San Pedro had always been dominated by native-born whites, or by families from European backgrounds, tradition dictated that it should remain so. In addition, Local 13's tradition of class-conscious loyalty had been forged in the crucible of the bitterly fought 1934 West Coast dock strike, so that any new workers who sought entry into the charmed circle of the so-called '34 men were seen as outsiders. According to Bruce Nelson, this gave the '34 men who formed the core of the union not only a strong sense of class solidarity but also a *"racialized* [form of] class consciousness."[73] Whichever explanation one chooses to accept, the overall effect of Local 13's policies was to maintain racial exclusion.

The race and gender conflicts that occurred in the Southern California aircraft plants were in some ways similar to those in the shipyards, and in some ways different. For example, both white and black women workers in aircraft were treated as temporary employees just as emphatically as the black men were on the docks. Another similarity was the ambivalence shown toward the new women workers, at least initially, by the United Auto Workers and the International Association of Machinists, the two unions most responsible for organizing the aircraft factories. Of these two, the UAW, as a CIO affiliate, had a better reputation for treating women sympathetically than the AFL's IAM did. But the distinction between "women-friendly" and "non-women-friendly" trade unions did not always correspond to the distinction between the CIO and the AFL. In 1941, for example, *both* the AFL and the CIO in California had only 11 percent women members.[74]

Once they realized that the presence of women was inevitable, local unions in both the UAW and the IAM encouraged female aircraft workers to join, although very few women were elected to union office. In this respect, the aircraft locals showed greater flexibility than Boilermakers Lodge 92 had done with respect to the black male workers in the shipyards. Competition between the UAW and the IAM over which union should represent the aircraft workers remained stiff throughout the war, with each vying against the other for new members. Sometimes the rivalry was intense. Early in 1944, for example, an NLRB representation election was held at the Douglas plant in Santa Monica, which was the last of the Los Angeles airframe factories to remain unorganized. The UAW garnered 33 percent of the vote, 26 percent of the employees voted for the IAM, and 53 percent opted for no union. The anti-union *Los Angeles Times* hailed this outcome as a "victory for the American way."[75] However, in a third NLRB election, held in the fall of 1944, the IAM's giant Lodge 727, which already represented aircraft workers at Lockheed and Vega, won by a large enough majority to become the official bargaining agent in the Santa Monica plant. Interestingly, some of the credit for this victory was given to women trade union activists. In an editorial commenting on the results of the Douglas election, the *American Aeronaut* praised the role of the IAM's "unionettes."[76]

But the motives of the male union leaders in admitting women were mixed. Often, the intent was as much to protect the postwar wage levels of the male workers as it was to stand up for the principle of gender equity. For example, in February 1943, the *CIO News* reported that "the Los Angeles CIO asks equal rights for women so that there will be no repetition of the blunders of 1918 when women were used to create a fluid labor market and beat down the wages [of men]."[77] And although male leaders in both the UAW and the IAM allowed women to accumulate seniority on the job, most of them reneged on that policy when the war was over, in order to ensure that returning male GIs would get their jobs back. Overall, the idea of (male) gender solidarity outweighed the idea of cross-gender class solidarity in the minds of the men who ran the unions in the Southern California aircraft industry, just as it did in shipping and on the docks.

A good example of how racial conflicts were dealt with in the aircraft industry is provided by events that unfolded at the North American Aviation Company in Inglewood. After stubbornly refusing to accept minority workers early in the war, by 1944 North American had hired as many as 2,000 black women, a larger number than in any other Southern California airplane plant,[78] likely because the plant was located close to black neighborhoods such as Compton and Watts. At first, the racial tensions were evident. One of the union activists at North American, a young African American woman from Texas named Wanita Allen, managed to persuade the management to integrate the bathroom facilities in the plant, but it was done over the objections of the white women.[79]

The results of a survey of 225 white, African American, Latino, and Chinese women employed at North American who were interviewed between 1942 and

1944 showed that 47 percent of the white women, many of whom came from the South, at first objected to working alongside African Americans.[80] Nevertheless, because it wanted to maintain high levels of productivity, North American's management made an effort to break down the racial barriers between their white and black employees. They did so by invoking President Roosevelt's Executive Order 8802 and by appealing to the patriotism of both sides. The white employees, who were in the majority, were told that "Negro soldiers were fighting to win the war the same as white soldiers, and that therefore it was unfair to shut Negroes out of the defense jobs."[81] African American women were asked (somewhat condescendingly) to behave politely and to recognize that they were seen as intruders by the whites.

Over a two-year period between 1942 and 1944, these efforts at racial conciliation at North American slowly paid off. Fear of losing their jobs caused several white male employees who might otherwise have refused to work with Mexicans and African Americans to accept their co-workers. A black female worker was delighted and surprised when some white women made her a birthday cake. The changing views of one white female worker from Texas illustrate the process of racial accommodation: "I always thought that colored people were not clean and smelled bad," she stated when she first entered the plant. But after she had worked alongside black women for several months, she altered her opinion. "Those I have worked with are just as good as anybody to my way of thinking. There are good and bad in all races."[82]

GOVERNMENT LABOR POLICY AND THE NORTH AMERICAN AVIATION STRIKE, 1941

Concern over the presence of minorities and women in the defense plants was by no means the only problem facing Los Angeles workers during World War II. They also had to deal with issues such as organizing strategy, political action, and how best to respond to the labor policies of the federal government.[83]

Before Pearl Harbor, most trade unionists, like most other Americans, wanted the United States to stay out of the war in Europe, which had begun in September 1939. CIO leader John L. Lewis, in particular, was strongly opposed to the country aiding the western Allies. But when Nazi Germany overran western Europe and threatened Great Britain, opinion shifted in favor of U.S. involvement, and President Roosevelt made it clear that he was determined to make national defense a priority even if it meant offending some of his labor supporters in the Democratic

Party. This development had major, and somewhat unexpected, repercussions on the Los Angeles labor scene, especially at the North American Aviation plant, even though it took place several months before America's entry into the war. An important strike unfolded at North American Aviation in Inglewood in June 1941. In April of that year, UAW Local 683 had defeated Machinists Lodge 727 in an NLRB representation election at North American and had begun preparing for a strike to win its demands, which included "seventy-five and ten," meaning a starting rate of 75 cents an hour for assembly-line workers and a 10-cent raise for skilled craft workers. In response, the Roosevelt administration urged the union to refer its dispute to the government's newly created National Defense Mediation Board. FDR was particularly worried about the prospect of a strike at North American because the plant was producing badly needed fighter planes for beleaguered Britain.[84] This set the scene for a labor conflict that became a pivotal event in the development of U.S. wartime labor relations.

The most difficult issue, from labor's point of view, was how to reconcile the government's call for patriotic restraint with the militancy of the aircraft workers themselves. President Philip Murray of the CIO and the UAW's leaders in Detroit wanted the California aircraft workers' organizing campaign to succeed, but they also feared that, if the North American workers struck, Congress might retaliate by passing legislation that would prohibit strike action altogether during the approaching war crisis.[85]

On May 31, 1941, Lew Michener and Wyndham Mortimer of UAW Local 683 persuaded a mass meeting of North American employees to postpone their walkout. But when further negotiations with the Defense Mediation Board bogged down, the entire labor force at North American struck, and the aircraft assembly lines were shut down. A massive picket line of four thousand workers, bolstered by supporters from other local CIO unions, closed down the plant in the biggest demonstration of Southern California labor solidarity since the longshoremen's strike of 1934.[86]

Several members of Roosevelt's cabinet advocated sending in federal troops to break the strike straightaway, but FDR decided to let the CIO leaders try to resolve the impasse first. President Murray instructed Richard Frankenstein, who was in charge of the UAW's aircraft organizing campaign, to get the strikers to resume work, but he failed. Forced to choose between the strikers and his instructions from Murray, Frankenstein chose to support Murray. He fired Wyndham Mortimer as a UAW organizer, removed Local 683's charter, and installed new local union leaders who he believed would do the CIO leader's bidding and stop the strike.[87]

On June 7, Frankenstein followed this up with a radio speech denouncing the strike as unauthorized and publicly blaming the stoppage on the "infamous and vicious underhanded maneuvering of the Communist Party."[88] Frankenstein's radio talk caused a furor. J. W. Buzzell of the AFL's Central Labor Council, motivated partly by patriotism and partly by his desire to boost Machinists Lodge 727's prospects as a rival bargaining agent to the UAW in the North American plant, joined in the denunciations.[89] But the strikers would not budge. When Frankenstein addressed a mass meeting of strikers in a bean field next to the North American works, he was shouted down.

By this time the federal government had had enough. A presidential order was issued authorizing military force, and twenty-five hundred U.S. Army troops were dispatched to Inglewood with orders to remove the picket lines and reopen the plant for production. It was the most direct confrontation between L.A.'s workers and the federal government in Southern California since the Pullman strike of 1894. On June 9, 1941, after a struggle in which several workers were injured, the North American factory was reopened and production was resumed. During the course of the melee, some of the strikers threw tear gas shells back at the advancing soldiers, and CIO leader Philip "Slim" Connelly tried in vain to prevent U.S. Army Colonel Bradshaw from arresting the local union leaders. Mayor Bowron, who was also present, supported the use of troops to break the strike.[90]

After the plant was reopened, Frankenstein and the newly appointed leaders of Local 683 tried to rebuild support for Murray's strategy of cooperating with Roosevelt's defense policy. But Frankenstein was severely criticized by the embittered members of Local 683's rank and file, who believed that he had sold them down the river. It was several months before the furor died down and Local 683 regained its former strength.[91]

Because of both this ongoing militancy and the fear of another strike in aircraft, the decision that was eventually handed down by the National Defense Mediation Board met all of the union's demands, including the celebrated "seventy-five and ten," which brought a wage increase of 50 percent to several categories of aircraft workers. The board also instructed North American's management to recognize UAW Local 683 as the exclusive bargaining agent for the company's employees and to include a "maintenance of membership" clause and a dues check-off provision in its new union contract.[92] (The maintenance of membership clause protected the unions by requiring unionized workers who were party to a wartime contract to remain within the same union for the duration of the war, without preventing others from joining. The dues check-off mandated that union dues be automatically deducted from a worker's paycheck.) This laid the groundwork for one of the most important victories organized labor won during the war.

Six months later, America's entry into World War II temporarily put an end to the possibility of further legal walkouts, as the U.S. labor movement as a whole pledged not to strike for the duration of the conflict. However, in return for this pledge, the National War Labor Board broadened the maintenance of membership principle to include the entire labor movement. Along with the application of the "Little Steel formula" to wages in much of the rest of the economy, the maintenance of membership policy helped to stabilize U.S. labor relations as well as to increase union membership significantly throughout the country. (The "Little Steel formula" awarded wage increases to the nation's nonunion steel company employees, to bring their pay into line with wages in the industry's unionized sector.)[93] This nationwide growth was matched by a doubling in the size of the Los Angeles unions. Between 1941 and 1945, the combined membership of the AFL and the CIO in Los Angeles County rose by more than one hundred thousand, diminishing the lead the San Francisco unions had hitherto enjoyed over their Southern California counterparts and bringing the Los Angeles labor movement into line with the unions in many of the nation's other large industrial cities.[94]

This dramatic expansion of the Los Angeles unions was echoed in the large number of new collective bargaining agreements signed in Southern California during the war years. In June 1941, for example, when the Ford Motor Company conceded the union shop to the United Auto Workers at its plants throughout the country, the Ford plant in Long Beach was included in this agreement. In July 1942, the National War Labor Board ordered that maintenance of membership clauses were to be added to the contracts between the United Steelworkers (formerly SWOC) and the "Little Steel" companies, including those in Torrance and Maywood, and that the workers there would be granted a wage increase of 5 ½ cents an hour. By 1946, Local 2018 of the United Steelworkers had become the collective bargaining agent at no fewer than thirty-seven steel, foundry, and pipe-making plants all across the Southern California basin. Union contracts were also negotiated in a wide range of other industries, including meatpacking, rubber, men's clothing, and oil.[95]

These new union contracts increased the membership of the L.A. CIO Industrial Council by more than 60,000, bringing it up to 118,410 at the end of the war, despite the efforts of open shop organizations to prevent such growth.[96] Yet, as in the 1930s, it was the AFL that grew the fastest. By 1945 the L.A. Central Labor Council had an affiliated membership of 143,986, keeping its lead over the

CIO.[97] Among the AFL unions, it was once more the International Brotherhood of Teamsters, capitalizing on its strategic position in the delivery of goods, that was the most successful. In its organizing campaign of 1941–1942, the Teamsters added more than 9,000 new members by enrolling truck drivers from United Parcel Service and other delivery firms as well as the milk delivery drivers who worked at 450 Southern California dairies.[98] Never before had the Los Angeles labor movement grown so rapidly, nor has it seen such rapid growth since.

UNITY AND DIVISION IN L.A.'S WARTIME LABOR COMMUNITY

Although both the AFL and the CIO unions in Southern California strongly supported the U.S. war effort, the favorable wartime labor climate did not stop them from competing with each other for new members or from arguing over which labor organization the workers should join. The most protracted of these disputes between the two labor federations concerned the drivers and conductors who worked for the Los Angeles Railway Corporation (LARY) on the Red Cars. At first, most Red Car employees joined a company union known as the Transportation Union of California, which in June 1941 secured a union shop agreement requiring the company to fire all its other employees. Both the AFL and the CIO challenged this agreement in court, and for two years they fought a bitter jurisdictional battle over which union the Red Car workers should belong to—a dispute that ended in victory for the AFL's Amalgamated Association of Street Electric Employees.[99]

These union disagreements also included internal conflicts both within and between the AFL and the CIO. In 1942, for example, the Teamsters embarked on a campaign to strengthen their hand by ousting J. W. Buzzell from his longstanding position as secretary of the Central Labor Council. The Teamsters joined up with the Allied Printing Trades, some motion picture unions, and a number of CIO unions to create Labor's Victory Committee, whose purpose was to collaborate with the city authorities in boosting productivity, easing labor shortages, and raising money for the purchase of war bonds. However, Buzzell refused to work with the CIO's Philip Connelly, whom he labeled a Communist and with whom he continually battled over jurisdictional issues. In retaliation, the Teamsters withdrew from the Central Labor Council, complained to AFL president William Green about Buzzell's failure to cooperate, and forced Buzzell to resign his office.[100]

In electoral politics, too, the labor movement was still frequently divided. Both the Los Angeles AFL and the CIO supported the unsuccessful nationwide lobbying effort to prevent the passage of the Smith-Connally Act (1943), which limited the power of unions to call strikes. But the AFL's Central Labor Council deliberately distanced itself from the CIO's Political Action Committee, which was set up in 1944 to ensure the reelection of President Roosevelt to a fourth term.[101] While most L.A. workers continued to vote Democratic in state and federal elections, the CIO Industrial Council, adopting the Communist Party's policy of total support for the war, endorsed Republican Fletcher Bowron for mayor because he was pro-war, even though he adopted policies that were not always pro-labor. Philip Connelly became one of the mayor's advisors and was appointed to several important municipal committees. The AFL's Central Labor Council, by contrast, refused to support Mayor Bowron in his 1944 reelection campaign because he had accepted the appointment of an anti-union police commissioner.[102]

However, focusing on these internal disagreements ignores the tremendous patriotic impulse that united Los Angeles citizens of all social classes behind an Allied victory. It also neglects the efforts of Los Angeles workers in general, and its minority workers in particular, to take advantage of the spirit of unity created by World War II to play a larger role in the city's cultural life and to transcend the boundaries that had been created by racially restrictive covenants and neighborhood segregation. In this sense, the heightening of racial consciousness during the war produced both positive and negative results. On the one hand, the internment of the Japanese, the Zoot Suit riots, and the exclusionary practices of unions like the Boilermakers increased social division and racial intolerance. On the other hand, as both corporate managers and civic leaders acknowledged the contributions of minorities to the war effort, and as minorities themselves became more self-confident, the leaders of L.A.'s ethnic and racial minority communities were drawn together in efforts to secure greater recognition of their collective social and economic needs.[103]

In the spring of 1944, for example, the Los Angeles Council for Civic Unity put on a series of "National Evenings," each of which focused on the contributions to society of a single racial or ethnic group ("Negro, Mexican, Jewish, Middle European, Oakies [sic], Arkies, Americans All"). Each one offered "two hours of motion pictures, singing, dancing, and sketches designed to familiarize the audience to the cultural contributions of various sections of our national community."[104] Although the events were sponsored by middle-class leaders from each racial and ethnic group, it was hoped that by staging them in places such as Wilmington, San Pedro, Boyle Heights, and Belvedere, they would encourage working-class African Americans, Mexicans, and others to gain "a better understanding of each other."[105]

Left-wing champions of civil rights, however, wanted to go further. They hoped to capitalize on the spirit of wartime unity to put an end to all discriminatory practices against minorities, which most white middle-class Angelenos were still quite willing to accept. The main sponsors of this new, more militant civil rights program were left-wing intellectuals, El Congreso, the Communist Party, and the Anti-Discrimination Committee of the CIO. In a 1944 pamphlet entitled *Let's Continue Eight Years of CIO Progress*, the Industrial Council of the CIO published a seven-point program that included the following demands: "An End to Jim Crow, Anti-Semitism, and Restrictive Covenants," "An End to Relegating Minority Workers to 'Stoop' Jobs," "No Red Scare," and the "Unreserved Defense of CIVIL and POLITICAL RIGHTS."[106]

The organization that played the largest role in projecting this new civil rights agenda was the Civil Rights Congress (1946), a Communist-linked organization, which undertook the legal defense of numerous Latinos and African Americans who had been wrongly accused of racially motivated crimes. In the immediate postwar period, the L.A. branches of the congress exposed the violent behavior of the LAPD, picketed banks and stores that refused to hire racial minorities, and encouraged minority homeowners to challenge racially restrictive housing covenants. Its street demonstrations and its open defiance of right-wing demagogues like Gerald L.K. Smith (a Huey Long populist whose frequent speeches in Los Angeles were filled with anti-Semitism and anti-black racism) helped recruit several hundred African American members into the Southern California Communist Party.[107]

For a brief moment after the war, the Civil Rights Congress appeared to make headway. But it soon found that it was able to operate only within narrow limits, due partly to its Communist associations and partly to the fading spirit of wartime unity. For as long as the wartime alliance with the Soviet Union lasted, Communists and other left-wingers were tolerated in the labor movement and in the community at large—if they did not identify themselves too publicly. But once the Soviet-American alliance broke down and the Cold War began, this tolerance rapidly waned.[108]

In addition, the majority of L.A.'s white, socially conservative population, including many of its white workers, soon showed that they still had only a limited tolerance for racial equality. This was demonstrated by the negative response of many whites to the militant behavior of returning Latino and black GIs, who were less willing to accept their second-class status than they had been before the war. On September 13, 1946, Mayor Bowron urged the Los Angeles County Grand Jury to investigate the activities of the Civil Rights Congress, claiming that the main objective of "this Communist-inspired group" was to "stir up the local population, particularly Negroes and Jews, and cause as much distrust of established government as possible."[109] This was an ominous sign of things to come. For all the brave talk about racial progress, soon after the war was over the green shoots put forth by L.A.'s emerging civil rights movement were buried beneath an avalanche of anti-Communist propaganda.

CONCLUSION

To most returning GIs, Southern California, with its beaches, its sunshine, and its plentiful consumer goods, must have seemed an earthly paradise after what they had been through during the war. Their future seemed to be assured. But what about Southern California's wartime progress as seen by those who had stayed at home?

As far as long-term job growth was concerned, there is no doubt that the phrase "two steps forward" used in the title of this chapter is amply justified. Although some 175,000 wage earners lost their jobs in the immediate aftermath of the war, in 1946 Southern California's aircraft industry still employed four times as many workers as in 1939. In addition, World War II laid the foundations for another quantum leap in the size of the Southern California economy, which quickly absorbed the war workers who had lost their jobs. After a brief downturn, industries such as steel, garment manufacturing, petroleum refining, and—especially—aerospace grew very rapidly.[110]

The evidence concerning the postwar fortunes of the workers of color, both male and female, who entered Los Angeles defense plants during the war and were let go soon afterward is more problematic. It is clear that several leading unions, including the Boilermakers and (more inexcusably) Local 13 of the ILWU, behaved very badly toward them. The male leaders of the UAW and the IAM also showed considerable ambivalence toward the women who worked in aircraft. They welcomed the increased dues income and bargaining clout that went along with admitting women into their unions, but they also supported the widespread (though misleading) belief that the employment of women workers was only temporary.[111]

The popular idea that the vast majority of women who worked in the defense plants were eager to return home is also open to question. Most African American women who worked in the aircraft factories wanted to keep their jobs after the war. This was partly because black women were more accustomed to working outside the home than white women were, and partly because working in an aircraft factory represented a major step up in the job hierarchy. Historian Karen Anderson argues that black women "were victimized by the postwar eviction of women from jobs" more than white women were.[112] This may have been true in the short run. But the facts suggest that a modest increase in upward mobility took place among black women as a result of the war. Evidence for this is the rapid postwar decline that occurred in the numbers of African American women who worked as domestics—implying that many of them did better when they moved over to factory jobs.[113]

The evidence regarding white women is more ambiguous. Historian Alice Kessler-Harris, writing about the national scene, states: "The rate at which they chose to leave their jobs was at least double, and sometimes triple the rate at which they were discharged."[114] But this evidence does not necessarily fit with the views of women who actually worked in the Los Angeles aircraft industry. In 1944 a public opinion survey taken by the *Los Angeles Examiner* found that 62 percent of the female aircraft workers in the city wanted to keep on working after the war. On the other hand, 64 percent of them also looked forward to being at home again after the war was over.[115]

How should these contradictory results be viewed? Some feminist scholars at the time, and others in the years that followed, argued that in their hearts most women war workers wanted to maintain the financial freedom and psychological independence that working outside the home provided.[116] But to push this argument too far is to indulge in wishful thinking. Feminism as a social movement did not emerge in the United States until the late 1960s, and for years it was primarily middle class in character. A more likely explanation is that women were subjected to enormous pressures to return home immediately after the war was over, even if some of them did not want to. Among these influences were management's wish to discharge female workers in favor of returning male GIs, men's desire for women to resume their domestic duties, and intense cultural pressure in the conservative 1950s for women to resume their traditional role as wives and mothers.[117]

The evidence regarding a possible improvement in race relations as a result of social mixing during the war is also ambiguous. The activities of organizations like the Council for Civic Unity and the Civil Rights Congress were certainly useful. But these bodies were either wartime organizations as such or groups

that were founded during the war, and thus they fed off a spirit of wartime tolerance, which diminished soon after the war was over. It is true that in 1947 a South
Pasadena Japanese American couple successfully challenged a race-based real
estate covenant in court.[118] But this legal victory was counterbalanced in 1946 by
the defeat, by a large majority in a referendum vote, of a proposal put forward by
the statewide CIO Council and the NAACP to establish a California state Fair
Employment Practices Commission.[119]

In one area, however, there can be no doubt that the war resulted in two very
large steps forward and no steps back: the rapid growth in the overall size of the
Southern California trade union movement. In June 1945, the AFL and the CIO
affiliated unions in Los Angeles County had a combined membership of 382,337,
up from 170,000 in December 1939. This represented an overall union density
rate in Los Angeles of 25 percent. (Union density is the proportion of wage workers who are unionized.) While still eleven points behind the average level of union
density throughout the United States, this development was a major improvement
over prewar levels.[120] It is true, as Nelson Lichtenstein points out, that many of the
workers who joined unions during the war did so because of previously negotiated union shop agreements rather than because of new organizing campaigns.[121]

It is also true that the largest increases in minority membership in Los Angeles
unions were in "workers of color unions," which were composed of janitors, meat-
packing employees, brick and clay workers, garment and furniture workers, and
others, all of whom held low-skill, low-wage jobs.[122] Nevertheless, the strong
growth of the Southern California labor movement during the war and immediately after it, despite an employers' counterattack, showed that it was in a far
stronger position than it had been before the conflict, and that it faced the future
with confidence.

NINE

"Caught between Consumption
and the Cold War"

Rebuilding Working-Class Politics, 1945–1968

Most present-day observers, if asked to describe the impact of the Cold War in
Southern California, would probably refer to the House Un-American Activities
Committee (HUAC) hearings, which made Whittier-born Richard Nixon famous,
or to the blacklisting of the Hollywood Ten.[1] These events were important. But
however absorbing such developments were for the American public, they tell us
little about who was actually responsible for the anti-Communist crusade in California or about how it affected not just the world of high politics but also the day-
to-day world of workers and ordinary citizens.

Focusing on these events also neglects the social and economic context from
which they emerged. That context included a counterattack against the labor
movement, the retreat of New Deal liberalism, and the emergence of a new form
of cultural conservatism that was itself partially shaped by one of the greatest—if
not the greatest—consumer booms in American history.[2]

The hastily planned hearings of the California legislature's Committee on
Un-American Activities, chaired by State Senator Jack Tenney, recorded juicy
tidbits about the private lives of numerous prominent citizens. But they provided
few details about how the Cold War influenced the Democratic Party or the political left. Nor did they explain how the shift to the right intensified racial prejudice, ended the movement for public housing in Southern California, and turned
Orange County—which was already conservative in its orientation—into a bas-
tion of anti-union and anti-Communist sentiment.[3]

This chapter corrects this imbalance by examining the effect of the Cold War both on L.A.'s labor leaders and on ordinary working men and women as they struggled to maintain their civil liberties and build a new political coalition that would give them greater access to political power.

HOLLYWOOD SHOWS AMERICA HOW TO EXPLOIT THE RED SCARE, 1945–1946

The first major domestic event that sparked the emergence of red scare politics in postwar Southern California was the dramatic strike wave that swept across the nation in 1945–1946. The strikes, which affected as many as 4.6 million employees in the mass production industries, aimed to make up for four years of inflation, austerity, and wage restraint.[4] They caused less turmoil in Los Angeles than in the nation's industrial heartland, but two of them had a significant impact in the region, although for different reasons.

The first was the celebrated (or infamous) strike and lockout in the Hollywood movie industry, which began in March 1945 and lasted on and off for several years. Initially, this dramatic and violent conflict, which involved more than ten thousand studio employees, had little to do with politics, still less with any Communist plot to undermine the American free enterprise system. It arose, instead, out of a longstanding jurisdictional dispute between two umbrella organizations, the AFL's International Alliance of Theatrical Stage Employees (IATSE) and the Conference for Studio Unions (CSU), which was affiliated with the CIO. But soon after the strike began, both IATSE and the heads of Hollywood's major studios provided the public with an object lesson in employer-employee collusion and the use of red baiting to defeat a trade union opponent.[5]

The dispute that prompted the strike concerned which of two unions—IATSE or CSU—had the right to organize a specific group of carpenters and studio set decorators. Both IATSE's big Hollywood local, Local 44, and CSU's much smaller Local 1421 claimed jurisdictional oversight over both groups of workers. CSU's members struck in March 1945, when the National Labor Relations Board (NLRB) prevented the set decorators from holding a representation election and assigned them to IATSE. A no-holds-barred jurisdictional war ensued between the two unions, as both sides indulged in violence and as allegations of Communist infiltration were leveled at CSU. In the end, IATSE colluded successfully with the studio heads to defeat CSU and secured virtually complete control over the Hollywood labor movement.[6]

Although the charges of Communist influence in CSU were exaggerated, this did not mean that the union lacked support from Communists or Communist sympathizers. Several members of Hollywood's prewar anti-Nazi Popular Front groups, some of whom were members of the Communist Party, supported CSU because it upheld a more democratic, grassroots brand of trade unionism than IATSE did. John Howard Lawson, for example, who in 1947 became one of the Hollywood Ten, frequently reported for picket duty outside the studio gates when CSU struck. So too did many other, less well-known Hollywood radicals.[7]

Nevertheless, even the studio managers who were involved knew that the issue of Communist domination, invoked by the studio heads and other opponents of the strike, was a red herring whose real purpose was to destroy CSU and give IATSE full control over the Hollywood labor scene. Even an investigator for the U.S. Senate's Internal Security Subcommittee, which was considered the gold standard for veracity at the time, reported that "in no sense can it be said that the recent strike . . . was the result of a 'Communist plot.'"[8] It was a measure of the corrosive power of the Cold War that, once U.S.-Soviet relations broke down at the end of World War II and rumors began to fly about the betrayal of atomic secrets, union busters like studio mogul Jack Warner and rumormongers like Senator Jack Tenney, with his committee hearings, were able to convince the American public that the Hollywood movie industry was about to be taken over by reds.[9]

But why did IATSE collude with the studio executives to defeat its fellow trade unionists in CSU, and why did it allow itself to become caught up in the anti-Communist hysteria? The answers are not hard to find. By this time, IATSE had become a thoroughly corrupt union, accustomed to vicious jurisdictional infighting and willing to cut backroom deals with the studio heads to establish hegemonic control over all the craft workers in the industry (see Chapter Seven). It was also led by an unscrupulous official named Roy Brewer, who was familiar with the time-honored tradition of red baiting in the AFL and who would stop at nothing to get his way.[10]

Brewer had begun his career as a movie projectionist in Lincoln, Nebraska, before becoming the Hollywood point man for national IATSE president Richard Walsh, who was headquartered in New York. At first Brewer issued relatively neutral strike bulletins laying out IATSE's side of the argument in the jurisdictional dispute. But as the conflict escalated, he stigmatized CSU as a Communist-led union and argued, without any real evidence, that the strike was part of "a long-range program, instituted . . . by a certain political party for one reason: To Take Over and Control Organized Labor in the Motion Picture Industry."[11] Later in the strike, Brewer behaved in an even more outrageous manner. He persuaded the AFL's Teamsters to undermine the CIO-affiliated Conference of Studio Unions by driving their delivery trucks through the picket lines CSU had set up at the gates of the major studios.[12]

Herbert Sorrell, leader of CSU, was a well-meaning, physically combative but somewhat naive ex-boxer, who believed in democratic unionism.[13] By the beginning of October 1945, however, he realized that the strike was likely to be lost because of the combined hostility of IATSE, the studio heads, and the Teamsters who crossed the picket lines. CSU had also lost support among its allies in the talent guilds, some of whom were returning to work. Facing defeat, on October 5 Sorrell concentrated a massive picket line outside the gates of Warner Brothers in Burbank. The result was the dramatic and bloody "Battle of Warner Brothers," which shocked the nation. The violence escalated after the *Los Angeles Times* reported that a leaflet from the "North Hollywood Communist Club" had been distributed among the crowd.[14] CSU picketers tried desperately to keep scabs out by keeping the studio gates shut and battling with a churning crowd of police, Teamsters, and IATSE goons who overturned cars and turned hoses on the demonstrators. Several dozen people were hurt quite badly.[15]

The "Battle of Warner Brothers" finally forced the NLRB to rule that CSU Local 1421 was entitled to organize the set decorators. Technically, therefore, the Conference of Studio Unions won the strike. But the jurisdictional dispute over the carpenters was unresolved, and IATSE was just as determined to crush its rival union. Not long afterward, IATSE and the producers trapped Sorrell into making a false move. In September 1946, CSU labeled all movie sets constructed by IATSE's carpenters as "hot"—that is, not to be worked on by union members—only to have the producers insist that IATSE's carpenters continue to do the work. When Sorrell objected to this move, the producers locked out all CSU members and brought in scabs to replace them.

Once more violence broke out, and once more Sorrell found himself struggling to prevent scabs—this time including some of his own members—from crossing the picket lines. For example, for Jerry Kraus, a lab technician who had a wife and two children to support, the temptation to cross the picket line to get his job back proved too much; after two years without a job, Kraus could stand unemployment no longer. Knowing that he would have to join IATSE in order to go back to work, he did so, despite having to pay $700 in dues for the privilege, a fact he later recalled bitterly. "I could have fought it—a lot of people did—but I wanted back into the business, so I paid."[16]

The "Battle of Warner Brothers," October 5, 1945. Courtesy of *Los Angeles Times* Photographic Archive, Department of Special Collections, Charles E. Young Research Library, UCLA (ucla_lat_1429_b3216_37359).

The second studio strike dragged on for three years, until 1949, when CSU was finally defeated and IATSE became the sole bargaining agent for the Hollywood craft unions, a position it has maintained ever since. A major reason for CSU's defeat was that the Screen Actors Guild (SAG) allowed its members to cross the picket line and go to work. Robert Montgomery was president of SAG at the time, but as second vice-president Ronald Reagan also had a major role in the decision, and he remained convinced until the end of his life that the Communists had sponsored the strike. "More than anything else," Reagan wrote in his memoirs, "it was the Communists' attempted takeover of Hollywood . . . that, indirectly at least, set me on the road that would lead me into politics."[17]

The role of the Screen Actors Guild, Screen Writers Guild, and the other talent guilds in the history of Cold War politics is also interesting. Because of their immense popularity, the opinions of Hollywood actors, writers, and musicians have always exerted a disproportionate influence over American popular culture. During the 1930s, for example, left-wing screenwriters such as John Howard

Lawson, Abraham Polonsky, Dalton Trumbo, and Ring Lardner Jr.—all of whom were later blacklisted, some as members of the Hollywood Ten—challenged the studios' racist hiring practices, criticized movie portrayals of black characters as servants and deferential Sambos, and championed the cause of labor films such as *How Green Was My Valley* (1941).[18]

In fact, one historian describes the musicians, playwrights, novelists, and Jewish émigrés from Europe who united in Hollywood under the banner of anti-fascism as a kind of "cultural front." Their ability to popularize the social changes embodied in the New Deal was instrumental in making the 1930s one of the few decades in American history when labor unions enjoyed majority public support. The alliance between the Communists and the liberal left was temporarily reinforced when the Soviet Union became an ally during World War II. But it split apart amid great bitterness when the Cold War began and HUAC launched investigations of Hollywood and its intellectual allies.[19]

Because of its earlier reputation as a progressive studio (manifested, for example, in its hostility toward anti-Semitism and its willingness to employ Communist scriptwriters such as Lester Cole), Warner Brothers came to be seen in the postwar era as "soft on Communism," a reputation it was determined to shed. This may partly explain why, in the strike that sparked the "Battle of Warner Brothers," it was ready to collude with IATSE against the Conference of Studio Unions and why, after the strike was lost, it fired more union employees than any other studio. "Jack Warner," wrote one commentator, "was among those who retreated from liberalism . . . . After strikers picketed his studio, he claimed that he was the 'victim of a giant communist conspiracy' and vowed never to make another 'liberal' movie. From then on, he said, he would vote for Republicans."[20]

SOUTH GATE'S AUTOWORKERS DEMONSTRATE THE INFLUENCE OF CONSUMERISM, 1945–1960

The other major dispute during the strike wave of 1945–1946 was the three-month walkout at the General Motors plant in South Gate, between November 1945 and March 1946. This was part of a nationwide strike called by Walter Reuther, head of organizing at the United Auto Workers Union in Detroit, to force GM—America's largest employer—to make major concessions regarding wages, hours, and conditions of work. The strike ended successfully when GM agreed to an 18.5 percent wage increase as well as other benefits.[21] Although this was an important victory, its significance also lies in what it tells us about America's post–World War II commitment to the gospel of consumerism, its effects on L.A.'s manufacturing workers, and its role in encouraging a shift toward social conservatism.

Even before the end of the war, observers had hoped for a postwar boom that would usher in a new age of prosperity, built around the increased capacity of the U.S. economy. To a great extent their hopes were realized. Real wages rose, house sales skyrocketed, and a flood of goods ranging from cars and refrigerators to TVs and bedroom sets poured from the nation's factories, enabling unprecedented numbers of working-class families to rise into the middle class. Looking back in 1955, *Life* magazine declared that the postwar years had witnessed a revolution in consumption: instead of saving for years, "customers buy on credit and enjoy the goods while they pay for them."[22]

Not everyone in Southern California benefited equally from this consumer revolution. The rewards of the GI bill, for example, which were supposed to help all military veterans get an education, went disproportionately to white ex-servicemen who already had some resources of their own. Housing loans made by the federal Home Owners' Loan Corporation reinforced, rather than undermined, the existing system of discrimination in the sale of houses.[23] Nevertheless, the members of Local 216 of the UAW in South Gate had good reason to celebrate when the wage hike that resulted from the three-month strike of 1945–1946 boosted their purchasing power.

One South Gate autoworker noted the new emphasis on consumption when he described the following exchange between Local 216's leaders and GM plant manager H. L. Clark before the strike began: "The [union] committee stated that they were interested in the welfare of the men and also their purchasing power so as to enable them to buy the products they produced."[24] The same point was made even more explicitly in a letter Local 216 sent out soliciting donations of food and cash from local merchants in South Gate, Lynwood, Huntington Park, and Bell during the course of the strike. The letter stated that the GM strikers were "fighting the battle of the whole American people in their struggle to compel mass production employers to raise wages and *build up purchasing power* for full production, full employment, and full consumption" (italics mine).[25]

The activism displayed by the autoworkers in the GM strike was maintained in the years immediately following as CIO industrial unionism consolidated its hold in the rubber, steel, aluminum, and cement factories in South Gate and in neighboring places like Lynwood, Bell Gardens, and Huntington Park. As time passed, however, and the benefits of rising wages and stable employment were felt in the lives of working-class families, the level of commitment to union militancy—

which had never been as great in Los Angeles as it was in Detroit—began to fade. Skilled factory employees could now afford to enjoy cocktails and steak dinners at upscale restaurants, then dance to live music at the Blue Note or the Hula Inn. Some members of UAW Local 216 and Steelworkers Local 2168 bought small boats and spent the weekends out of town. Others were able to buy larger houses or even move away to more salubrious suburbs such as Long Beach.[26]

One result was a decline in attendance at union meetings and the reappearance of socially conservative habits that had not been so pronounced before. The late 1950s and the 1960s were also the years when business unionism (joining unions solely for their economic benefits) was on the rise throughout the country, even in unions like the UAW with strong traditions of social and political activism. This meant that, instead of organizing new workers, both the AFL and the CIO began to shed some of their earlier concern for social movement issues and limit themselves to enforcing their existing contracts and maintaining the economic status quo.[27] As Becky Nicolaides puts it, for many workers in L.A.'s industrial suburbs, "unions commanded loyalties inside the workplace, but not necessarily outside of it. Beyond a general inclination towards economic justice, there were few signs that the worker militancy in the factory permeated the broader community."[28]

Another sign of lessening union militancy was the decline of a public working-class culture that emphasized the values of collective solidarity over those of individual advancement. Working-class cultural activities, such as singing in labor choruses or attending study groups, had always been less prevalent in Los Angeles than they were in Chicago or New York. But after World War II they became even less frequent.[29] In the fifties, South Gate stopped celebrating Labor Day, although patriotic holidays such as Memorial Day and the Fourth of July were fervently commemorated with public parades and picnics as well as overtones of evangelical religion. For example, in a newspaper advertisement acknowledging Labor Day in September 1957, South Gate's civic leaders paid tribute to the contributions of local workers but also reminded readers that all labor should be done in the name of God. Still more revealing was the message displayed on South Gate's float in the 1947 Rose Parade in Pasadena. It depicted a blue-collar family celebrating Labor Day, not with a union demonstration but with a family picnic in the backyard of their suburban home.[30]

Among workers with a strong commitment to class solidarity, consumerism as such did not necessarily undermine support for union militancy. But among migrants to Los Angeles, who drew an explicit connection between material affluence and the culture of leisure emanating from the city, it appears to have weakened union support for social activism more rapidly than it did elsewhere. Another sign of increasing social conservatism lay in the ambivalent attitude white workers displayed toward the issue of race. Officially, South Gate's Local 216 of the UAW maintained the same commitment to civil rights it had espoused in the 1930s. By 1955 large numbers of African Americans and Mexican Americans had been hired by General Motors and Firestone Rubber, and Local 216 had won the principle of plantwide seniority, which enabled minorities to more easily transfer to better-paid jobs at GM.[31]

But this commitment to racial tolerance no longer extended much beyond the plant gates. When radical leaders from the CIO began pushing a campaign to abolish racial covenants in private housing, rank-and-file support quickly evaporated. Most white workers in the auto, steel, and rubber plants in the Alameda corridor now accepted minorities as co-workers and union members. But they were unwilling to accept them as hometown neighbors or to let them have any real influence in local politics. As the sixties began and the black citizens of Watts and Compton demanded access to South Gate's white-owned housing stock and its segregated public schools, this ambivalent attitude toward race would eventually escalate into a crisis of major proportions.[32]

THE TAFT-HARTLEY ACT, RED SCARE POLITICS, AND THE 1948 ELECTION

In November 1946 the Republicans won control of Congress for the first time since 1930, an electoral debacle that put the Democratic Party and its labor supporters on the defensive. Seizing the initiative, the nation's business leaders pushed hard for a change in federal labor laws. One result was the Taft-Hartley Act of 1947, which canceled many of the legal rights unions had acquired in the 1930s. The law expanded the list of "unfair labor practices" (practices deemed illegal) to include organizing strategies such as mass picketing, sympathy strikes, and secondary boycotts. Taft-Hartley also banned the closed shop, empowered states to adopt "right-to-work" laws permitting individual workers to opt out of contracts negotiated between unions and employers, and required union officers to file affidavits affirming that they were not members of the Communist Party or any organization supporting it.[33]

The Taft-Hartley Act placed severe limits on labor's ability to organize. Although both the AFL and the CIO continued to grow in absolute terms after they later merged in 1955, relatively speaking U.S. union membership never surpassed the 1945 peak of 35 percent of the workforce. For years, high levels of membership remained confined to the economic sectors and regions that had seen labor's strongest gains during its dramatic rise in the 1930s and 1940s.[34]

At the same time, as the Hollywood studio strike demonstrated, the Southern California labor movement—like unions elsewhere—found it impossible to avoid becoming entangled in the politics of the Cold War. Indeed, under George Meany, who became its president in 1952, the AFL became one of the foremost champions of President Harry Truman's Cold War foreign policy. The federation endorsed the 1948 Marshall Plan, an aid plan designed to prevent western Europe from falling to the Soviet Union; approved U.S. participation in NATO; and supported conservative groups who emphasized the gravity of the Communist threat at home.[35]

Somewhat more surprising, CIO leaders Philip Murray and Walter Reuther abandoned their former tolerant attitude toward the far left and followed suit. Reuther, who in 1948 was elected president of the 750,000-strong UAW, had earlier been a self-declared Socialist. But as the country moved to the right, Reuther, like many other former Socialists (who had been quarreling with the Communists ever since 1919), repudiated the influence of the extreme left in the unions and became one of the principal architects of liberal anti-Communism. This was the belief, embraced by most liberals and unionized workers in the fifties and sixties, that the Democratic Party should adopt a strong anti-Soviet stance while maintaining its commitment to full employment and the welfare state at home.[36]

The consequences of Taft-Hartley's requirement that union officials sign non-Communist affidavits caused a serious political rift in the Los Angeles labor movement, just as they did elsewhere in the country. At first it seemed that the unions might be able to finesse the affidavits issue. When Taft-Hartley was first adopted, many labor leaders refused to sign, believing that the act would soon be repealed. In addition, President Truman's early Cold War policies were not always popular with the electorate. For example, many considered his implementation of the Federal Employees Loyalty Program to be an infringement of the right to free speech, and his bellicose denunciations of the Soviet Union alarmed those who hoped that the wartime Russian-American alliance could be maintained.[37]

In fact, it seemed possible for a time that Truman's widespread unpopularity and the public's dislike of the Republican take-over of Congress might give the Southern California Communists a chance to broaden, rather than diminish, their base of support. Between 1945 and 1947, the local party secured its highest membership numbers ever, reaching just under five thousand. Among other reasons, the increase could be attributed to the warm feelings generated by U.S.-Soviet cooperation in World War II and to the strong support the party gave to minority struggles for civil rights in South Central Los Angeles. "We had a strong base in Black communities like Compton, Willowbrook, Watts, and the neighborhood I lived in, South L.A.," L.A. Communist leader Dorothy Healey later recalled. "In the late 1940s the Party led campaigns against housing discrimination and for equal employment opportunities."[38]

Two developments, however, rapidly transformed this optimistic scenario into a major crisis for L.A.'s Communists and their allies. The first was the decision of the national CIO leadership to require its affiliated union leaders to sign the Taft-Hartley non-Communist affidavits. The problem with rejecting the affidavits was that failure to sign could—and did—lead the NLRB to withdraw official recognition of a union. As a consequence, within a few months most labor leaders at both the local and national levels signed the affidavits. This retreat caused a bitter argument inside the industrial unions of the CIO and placed the (undeclared) Communist members of left-wing unions in Los Angeles in an embarrassing position.[39]

The second development began when the national leadership of the Communist Party decided to support the establishment of the Independent Progressive Party (IPP), in December 1947, and to endorse FDR's former secretary of agriculture, Henry Wallace, as a third-party candidate for the presidency. This decision ran directly counter to the political policy of organized labor as a whole, which was to reelect President Truman. Even worse, Communist support for Wallace threatened to draw enough working-class votes away from Truman to hand the election to the hated Republicans.[40]

After the 1948 election, which Truman unexpectedly won, the CIO leadership stepped up its attacks on the Communist-led unions, and in 1949 it drove eleven affiliated unions out of the CIO altogether. The list of expelled unions represented almost a fifth of the CIO's entire strength, including the United Electrical Workers, the Mine, Mill, and Smelter Workers, and the Food, Tobacco and Allied Workers.[41] The AFL had already purged its Communist-influenced unions earlier. The non-Communist unions, with the UAW's Walter Reuther in the lead, then began to raid the expelled organizations in order to increase their own membership. A virtual union civil war followed.

The consequences of this for the extreme left in the Southern California labor movement were disastrous, just as they were for Communists in other parts of the country. The first blow was the decision of CIO president Philip Murray to remove

Harry Bridges as West Coast director of the CIO. Soon after this, Philip "Slim" Connelly was fired as secretary of the Los Angeles CIO Industrial Council. Then, in May 1950, the national leaders of the CIO lifted the charter of the Communist-influenced Industrial Council and established a new body, the Greater Los Angeles Council, led by the non-Communist leader of the United Steelworkers, Albert T. Lunceford. The effect was to cut the left-wing unions in the city adrift and precipitate a long and debilitating competition between other unions for the loyalty of their members. The result, reflected L.A. Communist leader Ben Dobbs sadly, was that "these left-wing unions, in many cases, just became shells of what they had been."[42]

The experiences of two local labor leaders who were caught up in the anti-Communist purge provide greater insight into how this issue played out. One was John Allard, the Kansas-born autoworker who had helped unionize L.A. auto assembly plants in the 1930s and had risen to become president of UAW's Chrysler Local 230, in the City of Commerce. Allard was a Henry Wallace supporter and a political idealist. He opposed Truman's tough Cold War stance not because he was pro-Soviet, but because he felt that Truman had betrayed "the whole principle of what I thought the [world] war was all about."[43] Allard believed that Truman had gone back on FDR's efforts to preserve good relations with the Soviet Union in the interests of world peace.

He also believed that the political and economic aspects of labor's struggle were inseparable and that it was foolish to evict the Communists from the UAW, given that they had played such a major role in building the union in the 1930s. "Generally," Allard stated, "I found that they [the Communists] didn't have to have all the glory, but they had something to offer."[44] This moderate—and possibly naive—position contrasted sharply with the hysterical attitude expressed by *Newsweek* and most of the national press toward the Communists' role in the Independent Progressive Party. Wallace's failure to repudiate Communist support in 1948, states one historian of his 1948 campaign (probably correctly), doomed his candidacy in advance. "No repudiation, therefore domination."[45]

Equally illuminating was the part Allard played in trying to head off the decision by Walter Reuther and the other anti-Communist leaders of the CIO to conduct an all-out purge of the left. When Allard led the Southern California delegation to the November 1947 convention of the UAW in Atlantic City, his delegation sat right in front of the rostrum and voted against many of Reuther's key proposals, including the resolution requiring union officers to sign the non-Communist affidavits. Needless to say, Allard and his fellow delegates failed in their attempt.[46]

For a few months after this UAW convention—which some observers believe was the turning point in the CIO's decision to beef up its anti-Communist crusade[47]—Allard and his friends in UAW Local 230 continued to hope that the left-wing caucus in the Los Angeles labor movement could be held together. But in discussing the issue with an interviewer years later, he remembered how, not long after the convention, a group of thugs beat up several of his radical friends in the parking lot of the Chrysler plant so severely that they had to be hospitalized. Given that level of hostility, he concluded that the alliance between the Communists and the left-liberal political community, which had held together since the days of the Popular Front in the 1930s, could no longer be sustained. "Ultimately the split did come and the left was destroyed." As late as 1987, Allard continued to believe that "the trade union movement has never been quite the same since."[48]

Another victim of the anti-Communist purge was Virgil Collins, the moderate left-wing leader of UAW Local 216 in South Gate. In August 1948 Collins, then only a shop committeeman, was put on trial with some of his fellow union members for failing to sign a non-Communist affidavit. Collins refused to sign, not because he was a Communist but because he considered the affidavit a violation of his free speech rights. Technically, therefore, he was in violation of the CIO's order. But since it was publicly known that Collins was not a member of the Communist Party but was instead a champion of democratic, rank-and-file trade unionism, he personally believed that he was put on trial because Local 216's leaders wanted to get rid of him, not because of his politics. "These clowns," he recalled, "just saw a chance to get [rid of] the people they wanted to get [rid of] who had been a thorn for them . . . . They played pretty dirty, let me tell you."[49]

Leftists like Allard and Collins had played a critical role in the creation and development of the dynamic, social justice form of trade unionism practiced by the Los Angeles CIO in the 1930s and 1940s. These two men ultimately survived the red scare and went on to serve the L.A. movement for many years afterward. But dozens of others just like them, including Luisa Moreno, did not; they were expelled from the labor movement for good.[50] Only many years later, when the Southern California unions went downhill, in part through a deadening of their former militancy, did their leaders realize the true value of what they had lost.

THE COMMUNIST PURGE AND THE DEPORTATION OF "WETBACKS," 1950–1955

The red scare took an enormous toll on the political effectiveness of the Southern California Communist Party. In 1951 the four main leaders of the party were arrested and charged with violating the Smith Act (1940), which made it illegal "knowingly to advocate and teach the duty and necessity of overthrowing the Government of the United States by force and violence."[51] The leaders were targeted in order to deprive the party of its most effective members and to make it extremely difficult, if not impossible, for it to continue recruiting. The leaders were indeed found guilty and sentenced to prison, then released on bail while their appeals went all the way to the Supreme Court. Six years later, in June 1957, both the Los Angeles and the national leaders of the Communist Party had their convictions overturned when the Supreme Court threw out the government's case.[52]

Pleased though they were by this decision, when the Southern California Communist leaders were cleared, they found that in the years between their arrest and the dismissal of their case, the Los Angeles party had been devastated almost beyond the point of no return. The hostile emotions stirred up by the trials of Alger Hiss and Julius and Ethel Rosenberg, by Senator Joseph McCarthy's congressional hearings on "Communist infiltration," and by U.S. troop losses in Korea—where the Communist and non-Communist worlds collided in open conflict—had brought about a dramatic decline in the party's membership, at both the national and local levels. According to its own records, in June 1949 the party in Los Angeles had 4,332 members, 21 percent of whom were blue-collar workers. By 1956 this number had fallen to less than 1,200, a figure that was never exceeded in subsequent years.[53]

One by one, the progressive groups the Communists had worked with over the years in electoral politics, the civil rights movement, and the trade unions withdrew their support, leaving the party exposed and with no cushion of left-liberal allies. The Los Angeles branch of the NAACP, for example, which had earlier been willing to accept Communist help on minority employment and anti-lynching issues, now became explicitly anti-Communist. In 1952, it blamed the collapse of a protest against employment discrimination at the Sears store in Santa Monica on the fact that the Communists had given it public support, and it did much the same thing when the prolonged campaign to get the California legislature in Sacramento enact a state Fair Employment Practices Act showed signs of flagging.[54]

The coup de grâce to the party's fortunes was delivered by Soviet Premier Nikita Khrushchev's speech at the Twentieth Party Congress in Moscow in 1956 revealing the criminal behavior of Stalin's regime. Many of the remaining party members in Los Angeles, like party members all over the United States, quit in disgust. It was not until the first elements of the New Left appeared in the student protests and rejuvenated civil rights movement of the early 1960s that new forms of radical politics were able to take root.[55]

Another result of the right-wing offensive in the 1950s was a resurgence of nativism. Among other consequences, this revival was reflected in the decreasing ability of the L.A. branch of the Committee to Protect the Foreign-Born, an alleged Communist front organization, to carry out its stated purpose of helping to protect European Communist émigrés and Mexican immigrants from being deported.[56] Given the long history of xenophobic actions directed at Mexicans in Southern California, it was hardly surprising that bigoted white nativists used the fear of Communism to scapegoat these undocumented workers. In February 1951, for example, the *Los Angeles Daily News* published the results of an "investigation of Communist infiltration" from Mexico.[57] The article claimed that border officials had found propaganda materials from the Partido Comunista Mexicano in the possession of an unidentified *bracero* who had crossed from Mexico into the Imperial Valley—a report that stirred up memories of the long-forgotten "invasion threat" by Magonistas before World War I.[58]

There is no real evidence that the Mexican Communist Party deliberately sent propagandists into Southern California. Nevertheless, the LAPD set up road blocks, interrogated Mexican Americans on Los Angeles street corners, and entered homes to search out and arrest alleged subversives. In response the Committee to Protect the Foreign-Born (LACPFB), which relied on an informal network of family members and friendly lawyers, challenged the LAPD's cases in court. Its president, Rose Chernin, with the help of several volunteer lawyers, did manage to prevent the deportation of several targeted Mexican families.[59]

But the LACPFB had limited resources, and it was unable to protect the masses of undocumented Mexican workers against a major sweep known as "Operation Wetback," which the Immigration and Naturalization Service mounted in the summer of 1954. According to some accounts, as many as 52,374 Mexican "aliens" were arrested in Southern California and deported as a result of that sweep.[60] The LACPFB's activities were also hampered by differences of opinion within the Los Angeles labor movement over the deportation issue. Liberal or Communist-influenced unions such as Local 13 of the ILWU, the Mine, Mill, and Smelter Workers, and United Furniture Workers Local 576, which had large numbers of Mexican members, were supportive. But older and more conservative Mexican American residents of the city, especially those who were influenced by anti-Communist priests in the Catholic Church, were hostile to the work of the LACPFB. Historian Jeffrey M. Garcilazo concludes that "the mass deportation of illegals . . . reinforced the social boundary between Mexican Americans and the Mexican born."[61]

FASHIONING A LEFT-LIBERAL RESPONSE DOWNTOWN, 1947–1962

Despite protests by civil libertarians, most residents who watched the marginalization of the Communists and the deportation of Mexicans in postwar Los Angeles probably did so with a mixture of indifference and relief. Conservative organizations such as the Chamber of Commerce, the Christian right, and the American Legion were, of course, delighted. So too were right-wing nativists, most AFL members, and all rightward-leaning suburbanites who were busy building atomic bomb shelters in their backyards and firing real and imagined Communist teachers and other suspect public employees.[62]

But left liberals, Jewish activists, and politically conscious people of color downtown and on the East Side of L.A. were made increasingly uneasy by the rightward thrust of local politics. As early as 1946, a group of local civil rights leaders had watched in alarm as Proposition 11, which proposed a statewide Fair Employment Practices Commission for California, went down to a lopsided defeat. By 1950 Mayor Fletcher Bowron, who in his early years in office had been an outspoken liberal on issues ranging from police brutality to rent control, was visibly moving to the right.[63] If Bowron could no longer be trusted, and measures to protect fair employment were considered beyond the pale, who would take a stand against the increasing attacks made not only against Mexican immigrants and supposed Communists but also against New Dealers, liberal artists and educators, and cultural deviants of all kinds?[64] And where would the political supporters be found to build a new left–liberal coalition to support civil rights?

The answer, as far as East L.A. and the other working-class neighborhoods were concerned, came from a group of civil rights activists and political reformers originating in Boyle Heights, who built a new multiethnic coalition around a young Mexican American reformer named Edward Roybal. In 1949 Roybal became the first Latino to be elected to the L.A. City Council in almost one hundred years, and he later went on to become a member of Congress. During his time on the council, from 1949 to 1962, Roybal developed a citywide reputation for probity and social activism and secured the support of many white liberals as well as middle-class African American and Latino voters who had become disgusted with the excesses of the red scare and embraced the need for radical reform. Roybal's base of operation lay in the Ninth Council District, which included Boyle Heights and straddled the Los Angeles River.[65]

How and why did Edward Roybal take the lead in establishing this new civil rights coalition, and why did its center of gravity lie in East L.A.? The answers begin with the outstanding qualities of the man himself. Edward R. Roybal was a handsome, well-educated, thirty-year-old Latino who before his army service in World War II had been active in public health. He was part of a new postwar generation of Chicanos who felt comfortable with their Mexican heritage as well as with their role as professionals in U.S society and who capitalized on the militancy L.A.'s Mexican workers had shown in previous labor struggles. Roybal was also a talented politician who had been trained by the famed Chicago-based community activist Saul Alinsky. In 1947 Alinsky put an eager young organizer named Fred Ross on the payroll of his Industrial Areas Foundation and assigned him to increase the number of qualified immigrant voters in the Ninth Council District and other Los Angeles working-class neighborhoods. It was Fred Ross who was partly responsible for Roybal's political education.[66]

It was no coincidence that Alinsky chose Boyle Heights for this political experiment. Before World War II, the area had possessed the largest concentration of Eastern European Jews in Southern California, some of whom were associated with the Breed Street Shul, which was a source of recruits for the L.A. Communist Party. Boyle Heights also contained more than its fair share of Mexican, black, and Japanese community activists who were angered by the indifference and neglect shown by the Los Angeles City Council toward their largely working-class neighborhood, which was one of the oldest in the city. Most of the 184,000 residents of Boyle Heights lived in run-down rental housing or in old, dilapidated single-family houses on unlit, unpaved streets. The Ninth Council District also included part of the Central Avenue African American community, with its established tradition of civil rights activism.[67]

But the main reason Boyle Heights became the jumping-off point for a new left-liberal political coalition was that it housed the headquarters of the Community Services Organization (CSO), with the talented Fred Ross at its head. The stated purpose of the CSO was "to improve living conditions; to promote inter community harmony; to work for more adequate educational and youth welfare programs; to remedy and prevent violations of human and civil rights; and to provide a medium for 'on the spot' leadership development."[68] These goals may appear innocuous today, but in conservative postwar Los Angeles, they seemed quite radical. The CSO also gained respectability by securing support from a number of local Catholic, Protestant, and Jewish Reform congregations.[69]

Despite the group's lack of formal links with the labor movement, several of the CSO's officers had union backgrounds, and it relied heavily on organized labor for money. The CSO's president was former United Steelworkers official Tony Rios; Maria Duran, a leading figure in the ILGWU's dressmakers division, became its treasurer.[70] It also became clear from Tony Rios's involvement in a jurisdictional dispute between several unions at the Standard Coil factory in Boyle Heights that the CSO was part of a growing coalition of anti-Communist radicals who were beginning to fill the gap created by the expulsion of the Communist-led unions from the CIO.[71]

The controversy surrounding union representation at Standard Coil deserves attention because it illustrates the bitterness of the struggle for the loyalty of former members of the left-wing unions that had been expelled from the CIO. In this case, rival campaigns were run by three separate unions, competing for the support of the three thousand Chicana electrical workers employed at the factory (some of whom can be seen in the background of the photo shown opposite). The three unions were United Electrical Workers Local 1421 (UE, which was still Communist-led), the International Brotherhood of Electrical Workers (IBEW, a conservative AFL union), and the International Union of Electrical Workers (IUE, the CIO's non-Communist replacement for UE). A representation election was held at the factory in August 1952, with Catholic clergy supporting the conservative IBEW.[72]

With Tony Rios weighing in heavily on the side of the moderates, the anti-Communist IUE (not the IBEW) won the representation election in August 1952 by a small majority. The UE's defeat may well have been influenced by the fact that, a few days before the election, the House Un-American Activities Committee publicly subpoenaed three of its Los Angeles organizers (William Elconin, Henry Fiering, and Louis Torre) to appear before it. In the end, however, another representation election was held, which resulted in the victory of the anti-Communist IBEW.[73]

The CSO's main claim to fame was its pioneering role in registering Mexican American immigrants to vote in East L.A., a historic undertaking that provided a precedent for the rapid growth of L.A.'s Latino electorate thirty years later. By 1949 Fred Ross and his helpers had registered more than seventeen thousand poor Mexican Americans to vote in the Ninth District—a far larger number than ever before. The CSO also established branches in other working-class neighborhoods

Community Services Organization president Tony Rios addresses Standard Coil electrical workers in Boyle Heights, May 1952. Courtesy of Kenneth C. Burt.

such as Long Beach. It was this voter registration drive, more than anything else, that enabled Roybal, who had lost his first run for office in 1947, to get elected to the Los Angeles City Council by a large majority in the municipal elections of 1949.[74]

What we see in Roybal's successful effort to build a left-liberal coalition in the Ninth Council District—which was followed by a number of other, less well known efforts in Monterey Park and on the city's West Side—was an attempt by L.A.'s Cold War liberals to reshape the city's politics by repudiating Communism while at the same time retaining core elements of New Deal progressivism and the postwar commitment to civil rights. The red scare campaign certainly encouraged social reform organizations like the CSO and the NAACP to distance themselves from their previous associations with the Communist Party. Nevertheless, these new civil rights leaders helped to turn Southern California's fear of Communism to the advantage of the moderate left by opening up new opportunities for minorities who might otherwise have been attracted to the far left.[75] The question now became how Councilman Edward Roybal's left-liberal credentials would hold up in the larger arena of citywide politics.

COLD WAR FIREWORKS ON THE L.A. CITY COUNCIL, 1949–1959

As it turned out, Roybal's credentials held up quite well. On several important issues between 1949 and 1962, Councilman Roybal and his fellow liberals on the city council managed to defend the economic interests of L.A.'s blue-collar workers and the civil rights demands of its minority voters with principle and vigor, even though they were a minority on the council. The main issues confronting the council in these years were corruption, police brutality, rent control, public housing, and the question of whether to pass a citywide fair employment practices law. It was a measure of how deeply L.A.'s public life had been corrupted by Cold War ideology that discussion of these issues frequently came down to a verbal confrontation between Roybal and conservative Councilman Edward Davenport from the affluent Twelfth District (Westlake), who became Roybal's principal opponent in the council debates.[76]

Roybal and Davenport first crossed swords over the question of minority employment. In September 1949, only one month after he was elected, Roybal proposed a city ordinance mandating a municipal Fair Employment Practices Commission (FEPC). The *Los Angeles Times* immediately denounced the idea, employing some of the same arguments it had used to defend the open shop thirty years earlier. "Such a law," it argued, would "rob an individual of his freedom to choose his associates at work, as business partners and employees."[77] Most employers agreed with the *Times*, but the city's minority workers were angered by the failure of either the city or the state to replace the federal FEPC, which had been terminated at the end of the war, with a local commission. When four hundred people crowded into the city council chambers for a public hearing on the matter, the fears of many whites that minorities would be guaranteed jobs at the expense of the Anglo majority came out into the open, and the racist underpinnings that lay behind much of the Cold War rhetoric were revealed for all to see.

Judge Isaac Pacht, chairman of the L.A. Council on Equality and Employment, opened the debate by arguing that the only way to end employment discrimination against minorities was to adopt a municipal ordinance with legal sanctions attached. Frank P. Roberts, former president of the L.A. Chamber of Commerce, replied that the FEPC proposal would be a step toward the "stateism" of Europe.[78] Then the chairman of the meeting lost control of the proceedings, as opponents of the measure scrambled to seize the microphone. "Why do you play with these people?" shouted Earl C. Craig of the Public Affairs Forum, pointing to the Mexicans in the audience. "Kick 'em out of the . . . country. They're all treasonous." "This is a white man's country," added Alfred E. Herbert of the Christian Nationalist Party, led by Gerald L.K. Smith, "and we will keep it that way . . . . white Christians will not tolerate any n-g-r or Jew or any other minority getting preferences in jobs."[79] Councilman Davenport also spoke against the FEPC proposal, arguing that it would involve the city in major administrative costs. When order was restored and the proposal was put to a vote, it was defeated by a vote of eight to six.[80]

Roybal and the left-liberal minority on the city council next clashed with the conservative majority in the summer of 1950, when Davenport introduced a resolution requiring Communist Party members to register with the Los Angeles chief of police. On the measure's first reading, Roybal cast his single vote against its adoption, infuriating the anti-Communist majority and requiring the council to hold a public hearing. A flurry of letters on both sides of the issue reached council members before the hearing was held, including one from ILWU Local 26 urging the council "not to be carried away by the current witch-hunt hysteria and take a vigorous stand defending the rights of all people."[81]

When the public hearing on the Communist registration proposal was held on August 29, 1950, the scene was even more chaotic than the one that had taken place previously. A verbal duel ensued between Dorothy Healey (chair of the L.A. County Communist Party) and State Senator Jack Tenney (chair of the California State Committee on Un-American Activities), during which Healey called Councilman Davenport "a two-bit Fuehrer."[82] Pandemonium broke out as Davenport, showing signs of the apoplectic rage that would kill him three years later, denounced Healey and moved to have the ordinance adopted immediately. But the council majority insisted that it be properly drafted, delaying matters further. In September 1950, the registration ordinance was finally passed by a vote of thirteen to one, with Roybal casting the single negative vote. It was later declared unconstitutional by the Los Angeles Superior Court.[83]

Conservatives also accused liberals and the left of manipulating the issue of rent control to improperly extend the power of the state. During World War II, the federal government had imposed rent control throughout the United States to keep the cost of living down, and it retained its authority over the matter until the early 1950s as a way of preventing rents from going sky-high during the postwar housing shortage. After the war was over, Los Angeles landlords and real estate associations agitated repeatedly for decontrol, while, on the other side, labor unions and tenants' rights organizations sought just as fervently to preserve controls.[84]

In February 1950, Burton E. Edwards of the Los Angeles Apartment Owners Association made an impassioned public speech decrying rent control as "un-American" and an inappropriate exercise of government power. In July the city council adopted a resolution declaring (wrongly) that a housing shortage no longer existed in Los Angeles and urging the federal housing authorities to permit local decontrol to go forward. The issue then became embroiled in the courts and in a lengthy argument between local and federal government bodies, until it was finally resolved in favor of decontrol.[85]

Lying behind the issue of rent control was the even more explosive matter of public housing. The L.A. construction industry had begun building new houses again in 1945, but the influx of hundreds of thousands of additional migrants from the East, the arrival of African Americans from the South, and the return of thousands of veterans after the war meant that demand far outstripped supply. In 1949 Congress passed a new Housing Act, and the Los Angeles City Housing Authority (CHA) signed an agreement with the federal government to build ten thousand new units of public housing. Title 1 of the 1949 law also provided federal loans for slum clearance. As a result, the debate over public housing became linked to the equally contentious issue of urban renewal.[86]

During World War II, the argument over public housing and urban development had been limited to providing temporary accommodations for war workers. After 1945, however, it became part of a much larger debate over two competing visions of the city's future. One vision, supported by the labor movement and by left-liberals such as Edward Roybal, Carey McWilliams, and Judge Robert Kenny, saw public housing as a legitimate social engineering tool that would cement the New Deal order in place, based on an implicitly social democratic version of the role of the welfare state. This philosophy of "community modernism," as Don Parson calls it, envisioned Los Angeles as a diverse, socially progressive city, which would use the new public space opened up by urban renewal to accommodate minority communities and business residents in a set of mutually supportive relationships.[87]

The "corporate modernists," on the other hand, supported by the *Los Angeles Times*, the real estate lobby, and the Republican Party, rejected public housing as an un-American, socialist idea that threatened to bring about "social mixing" (in other words, racial integration) and to undermine the nation's longstanding commitment to privately built housing. They focused instead on the modernization of downtown as a great business and commercial center and on the building of secluded dormitory suburbs as havens of leisure and consumption for L.A.'s white middle class. One of the most prominent results of this modernizing vision of urban renewal was the redevelopment of Bunker Hill downtown, which caused hundreds of working-class homes (many of them belonging to poor Mexican Americans) to be razed and replaced by corporate offices, Eurocentric museums, and other public buildings.[88]

Influenced by the conservative mood in the city, most of L.A.'s corporate elite took the view that if freeway building and urban renewal meant forcing immigrants and African Americans to abandon their old downtown neighborhoods, the price was worth the cost. This privatized, pro-growth vision of L.A.'s future was the main weapon Norris Poulson used to defeat Mayor Bowron in the mayoralty election of 1953. Poulson's victory paved the way for an even more conservative era of municipal administration.[89]

Given the Cold War political climate, it was virtually inevitable that the corporate modernists would also use red scare tactics to defeat their opponents in the public housing debate. In 1950–1951 the pro–public housing group lost its majority on the city council, and the liberal minority, including Edward Roybal, came under increasing pressure to join with the majority in repudiating the city's 1949 agreement with the federal government to build ten thousand new units of public housing. In August 1952 the United Patriotic People of the USA, a right-wing propaganda group, published a pamphlet declaring that building ten thousand units of public housing "would be the *last rung* in the ladder towards complete *socialism*, one step this side of *Communism* and *Our downfall*."[90]

The public housing issue was finally resolved after a long period of wrangling between the city and the federal government. Despite a ruling by the California Supreme Court that the city's contract was binding, a majority of L.A. voters rejected the public housing commitment in a referendum.[91] After Norris Poulson was elected mayor in May 1953, he renegotiated the city's public housing contract with the U.S. government, with the result that although some housing sites on which construction had already begun were completed, more than half of the city's remaining public housing projects were abandoned.[92]

Accompanying this debate over urban renewal was a second debate, which cast a long shadow over the future of race relations in Southern California, about the treatment of the city's ethnic and racial minorities. Traditional white supremacists such as Edward Davenport believed that social conditions like poverty and criminal behavior were inherent in the immigrant populations who lived in places like Bunker Hill. Opposing this view were racial liberals, including minority leaders such as Roybal and African American journalist Charlotta Bass, who argued that ethno-racial characteristics had no bearing on urban renewal and that L.A.'s minority populations should be treated with respect.[93]

The city's Hispanic and African American workers, who stood to benefit most from public housing, were understandably angered by the city reneging on its 1949 housing agreement with the federal government. But they were angered even more by the insensitive urban renewal policies pursued by the corporate modernists. During the early 1950s, East L.A. was bisected by no less than three new freeways (the Golden State, the Santa Ana, and the San Bernadino), each of which was driven through a formerly residential ethnic neighborhood described as "blighted" by the federal Home Owners' Loan Corporation.[94]

Other minority neighborhoods suffered the same indignities. While the Division of Highways lauded the growth of the freeway system as a major step in the creation of the world's ultimate suburban city, the *Eastside Sun* lamented the loss of numerous homes, the deterioration of race relations, and the destruction of traditional, working-class ways of life. Those among the urban poor who had the money to move elsewhere did so. But the majority, who could not afford to move, remained behind, reinforcing the concentration of minority families in the downtown ghettoes and in the East L.A. barrio.[95]

But it was over the redevelopment of Chavez Ravine that the greatest conflict arose. The fight over the disposal of this hilly, eight-square-mile area just north of downtown illustrated, better than any other urban renewal project, the losing battle fought by the supporters of racial tolerance and humane development against the champions of corporate growth and racial exclusion. In 1948 most of Chavez Ravine's population of 3,764 (more than two-thirds of whom were Latino) lived in substandard wooden dwellings, many of which lacked toilets and running water but which, despite poverty, formed part of a deeply bonded, traditional neighborhood. It therefore became the perfect target for urban renewal.[96]

In December 1950, the CHA began purchasing properties in Chavez Ravine,

Evicting families from their homes in Chavez Ravine, 1959. Courtesy of *Los Angeles Times* Photographic Archive, Department of Special Collections, Charles E. Young Research Library, UCLA (ucla_mss_1429_b382_116242).

intending to replace them with the Elysian Park Heights public housing project, which was to contain more than thirty-five hundred public housing units, complete with churches, schools, a community hall, and a commercial center.[97] Although many of the residents resented being required to move, most of the immigrant families in Chavez Ravine accepted the city's promise that they would be resettled in homes superior to the ones they had left. But then came the cancelation of the public housing contract with the federal government, the CHA's sale of the land to the city, and the decision by the city that instead of using the land for residential purposes, it would be used to attract the Brooklyn Dodgers from the East to provide Los Angeles with its first major league baseball team. Influential in making this decision were *Los Angeles Times* publisher Norman Chandler and Norris Poulson, a conservative Republican who had been elected mayor, replacing the relatively liberal Fletcher Bowron in 1953.[98]

The public housing lobby, the residents of Chavez Ravine, the Community Services Organization, and numerous civil rights activists—including the left wing of the labor movement—were outraged by this betrayal of the public trust.

Using the slogan "Save Chavez Ravine for the People," they wrote letters, brought lawsuits, and demonstrated publicly against the policy change. Carol Jacques was one among several former residents of Chavez Ravine who were turned into political activists by the issue. "I was really angry," she stated. "I had lost my home, I had lost everything that I knew, everything I'd been happy with."[99] Not long after being forced to leave her home in the ravine, Carol Jacques met Cesar Chavez and began working for the United Farm Workers.[100]

The Chavez Ravine episode culminated in the summer of 1957, when a large portion of the land was sold cheaply to Walter O'Malley for a new baseball stadium, which enabled him to bring the Brooklyn Dodgers out to Los Angeles. It ended bitterly in May 1959, when television cameras showed the remaining residents being forcibly evicted from their houses, as in the photograph shown above. This defeat for the forces of racial tolerance and humane reform showed that a significant piece of the New Deal order, which Los Angeles had struggled fitfully to embrace ever since the late 1930s, had been lost.[101]

SUBURBAN POLITICS AND THE EMERGENCE OF THE NEW RIGHT

The Cold War struggles analyzed so far occurred in a relatively small geographical area bounded by Hollywood, central Los Angeles, and East L.A. But metropolitan Los Angeles was not the only area where the new conservatism flourished. A new real estate boom, accompanied by rapid growth in the aerospace, defense, and electronics industries, encouraged many business professionals to move into the dozens of new suburbs that emerged with astonishing rapidity in the San Fernando Valley and Orange County. It was conservative elements from these suburbs who became the most avid supporters of the anti-Communist crusade.[102]

By the mid-1960s, in fact, Orange County had become the launching pad for a powerful New Right political movement, which reached its apotheosis fifteen years later under Republican president Ronald Reagan.[103] Its ideology emphasized love of country, low taxes, support for traditional Protestant morality, and hostility to the growth of state power. Interest in the New Right movement was not confined to conservative Republicans, suburban housewives, or wealthy citrus growers. It was also championed by a new generation of technocratic entrepreneurs who ran the nation's burgeoning military-industrial complex, a large portion of which was centered in Southern California. Hughes Aircraft, for example, moved to Orange County in the late 1950s, creating ten thousand skilled jobs. A wide range of aerospace companies also built new facilities in the San Fernando Valley, which one observer called "the most segregated and the most conservative part of Los Angeles."[104] These developments brought new wealth and thousands of highly paid, security-conscious engineers, technicians, and scientists into the area, many of whom had a career interest in promoting America's Cold War objectives.[105]

The search for a stable and secure lifestyle in which the Cold War values of patriotism, anti-Communism, and the sanctity of the nuclear family were upheld as a model was also manifested in the cultural arena of leisure and entertainment. For example, when he opened Disneyland in Anaheim in 1955—which proved enormously popular with working-class families—Walt Disney deliberately designed it as a clean, family-oriented amusement park to distinguish it from the chaotic, tawdry, and licentious atmosphere of Coney Island in New York. Somewhat like restored Olvera Street downtown, Disneyland's Main Street, Davy Crockett, and Frontierland exhibits projected the spirit of an idealized American past, while subtly delineating racial separateness and the superiority of Anglo-Saxon civilization. To Pamela Lawton, a working-class housewife visiting from South Gate, Disneyland was "immaculate and shiny and big . . . . I just loved being out in the world like that," away from the slums and poverty of her own early life.[106]

The suburban locations of these right-wing movements, especially in Orange County and the San Fernando Valley, might lead one to suppose that the division between Democratic and Republican loyalties in Southern California corresponded to the division between the city of Los Angeles and its outer suburbs. To some extent this was true. The number of registered Democrats in Los Angeles County remained significantly higher than in the city's new dormitory suburbs.[107] Moreover, when it came to elections, suburban voters nearly always supported candidates to the right of those elected in metropolitan L.A. In the 1964 presidential election, for example, Orange County gave a plurality of votes to Barry Goldwater, whereas President Lyndon Johnson carried Los Angeles County.[108]

But a more careful look at the election results shows that the emergence of the new conservatism resulted in a political shift to the right not only in the white middle-class suburbs but also in many of the older working-class districts in the Alameda corridor. Throughout the fifties and sixties, most blue-collar workers remained loyal to the Democratic Party. But the presidential election of 1968 registered a distinct turn to the right. In that election, Richard Nixon, the Republican presidential candidate, shifted his party's rhetoric away from the evils of Communism as such, which were now taken for granted. Instead he attacked "sexual permissiveness," "welfare cheats," and the "criminal activities" of the

New Left, which he blamed on students and on the excesses of the civil rights movement.[109] In L.A.'s white industrial suburbs, the strategy worked. Hubert Humphrey, Nixon's Democratic opponent, won Los Angeles County as a whole. But the election results showed that Nixon won eight out of ten of the old industrial suburbs. In Maywood and Bell Gardens, George Wallace, the southern segregationist candidate, also won a significant number of ballots.[110]

CONCLUSION

In many ways the 1950s were highly positive years for Southern California's working men and women, especially for its white working-class families. Wages rose, unemployment remained low, and the low-tech economy—sometimes called the smokestack, or manufacturing, economy—was at its peak. Thousands of working-class families were able to purchase homes in the suburbs and enjoy the fruits of L.A.'s booming, consumer-oriented economy. As a result, many of them were able to climb up into the American middle class. This development was powerfully assisted by the growing number of women, both minority and white, who supplemented family incomes by going out to work.

Nevertheless, the evidence also shows that the Cold War had traumatic consequences for unions, for the political left, and for poor minority families caught up in the process of urban renewal. The red scare incapacitated the Communist Party and other left-wing organizations and created a crisis in the trade union movement that weakened the CIO by forcing it to expel some of its most militant and successful organizers. It also put the civil rights movement on the defensive, created serious divisions within the Democratic Party, and precipitated the birth of a new conservative movement—the seedbed for Ronald Reagan's New Right—which captured the local Republican Party and enabled it to win numerous political victories.

In addition, the corrosive political psychology of the red scare poisoned the debate over the merits of public housing and urban renewal, sacrificing the legitimate housing needs of immigrants and poor working-class families to a rhetorical (and largely irrelevant) debate about the dangers of "creeping socialism." It also led to the creation of a parochial and narrow-minded cultural climate, which rewarded conspicuous consumption, reinforced Southern California's commitment to suburban isolation, and threatened to eclipse the cosmopolitan and socially progressive policies of the New Deal.

But none of these defeats was irreversible. The Cold War did not deal a permanent setback to the cause of civil rights in Los Angeles. To the contrary, the need to defend traditional liberties gave it a new lease on life. Nor did the rise of the New Right deal a knockout blow to the liberal wing of the Democratic Party, or even to the potential for interracial politics. Not many years after Edward Roybal's Latino-white political coalition established itself in East L.A., a new and even broader interracial alliance came into being, based this time on a marriage of convenience and principle between African American voters downtown and the West Side Jewish community.[111] In 1973 this alliance elected an African American, a former police officer by the name of Tom Bradley, as mayor of Los Angeles—a development that would have seemed unthinkable at the height of the 1950s red scare.

But before that could happen, the city of Los Angeles had to cope with a traumatic event that for a time seemed to make the idea of a black-white political alliance impossible. This was the Watts uprising of August 1965. The causes and consequences of that earthshaking event are discussed in the next chapter.

The Watts riots in South Central L.A. began on the evening of Wednesday, August 11, 1965, when a white police officer on a motorcycle pulled over a young African American man named Marquette Frye for reckless driving at Avalon and 116th Street. The LAPD officer ordered Frye to get out of his car and take a sobriety test, which he failed. The officer then arrested the youth and radioed for a patrol car to take him to jail. A crowd gathered, including Frye's mother and brother, who scuffled with police. As the police car left the scene, several angry youths threw soda bottles at the retreating vehicle.[1]

Up to that point, there was nothing unusual about this event. Arrests of this kind happened daily in Watts, where police harassment was commonplace, and the onlookers usually dispersed after an arrest had been made. This time, however, the crowd did not disperse. Instead, as the evening went on, the crowd grew larger and began throwing rocks and bottles at passersby. Then someone firebombed a white-owned business, while others shot at police. Black rioters looted shops, set fire to buildings, and erected barricades in the street.[2] All hell let loose.

Arson and looting increased the following day as the number of rioters swelled to more than forty thousand. The LAPD appealed for help, and National Guard troops were rushed to the scene. By late Saturday, more than fourteen hundred armed Guardsmen patrolled the streets, hundreds of buildings had burned down, and dozens of rioters lay wounded. When the six-day uprising finally ended, 34 persons—nearly all of them African American—were dead, and 1,032 residents

Street scene during the Watts uprising, August 1965. Courtesy of *Los Angeles Times* Photographic Archive, Department of Special Collections, Charles E. Young Research Library, UCLA (ucla_mss_1429_b556_229847).

were wounded. Property damage amounted to $40 million, and over six hundred buildings were damaged or destroyed. South Central Los Angeles would never be the same again.[3]

On the surface, the Watts uprising did not appear to be prompted by competition for jobs, anger about workplace conditions, or any of the other economic grievances traditionally associated with labor protest. Instead, it seemed to be motivated primarily by racial discontent. This has led some observers to conclude that the Watts riots and the other ethno-racial protest movements of the sixties represented a turning away from the class-based movements that had played such an important role in the city's protest movements in 1910–1912 and in 1937–1941. When coupled with civil rights actions by Mexican Americans and others in East L.A., Watts seemed to represent a rejection of class-based action in favor of cultural nationalism and the politics of racial identity. During the sixties, writes political scientist Raphael Sonenshein, "the fault lines of Los Angeles politics shifted. In the process, a new and durable change in patterns of political cleavage, based on race and ideology, began to dominate city politics. New coalitions formed around these fault lines and competed for city power."[4]

In some respects, this interpretation of the city's post-Watts history makes sense. The battle to extend civil rights to neglected minorities dominated Los Angeles politics throughout the remainder of the1960s, culminating in 1973 with the election of Tom Bradley as the first African American mayor of the city.[5] The federal Immigration Reform Act of 1965, which resulted in a massive influx of poor Asian and Mexican immigrants into Southern California, turned whites into a minority in the downtown area and gave the old manufacturing district a Third World face.[6] In 1992 a new conflict broke out, between Korean shopkeepers and African American residents, which raised many of the same racial issues as the Watts uprising. Moreover, in most municipal elections during this period, cultural conflicts split the Los Angeles electorate along ethno-racial rather than income lines and pushed many white working-class voters to the right.[7] For many analysts, after 1965 the politics of race, not the politics of class, became the order of the day.

It is true that racial questions became more prominent in Los Angeles politics after 1965 than they had been in earlier years. But to treat race-based and class-based protest as an either-or proposition is to oversimplify history. Sonenshein's approach not only ignores the importance of the class conflict that spurred the revival of the L.A. labor movement in the 1990s. It also treats race and class as separate, mutually exclusive entities, when they are in fact fluid, interdependent variables that can rarely be clearly separated one from the other. Although they were expressed in racial terms, the underlying grievances of the Watts rioters were prompted as much by unemployment, bad housing, and lack of access to a decent education as they were by hatred of the white-dominated LAPD.

The same point can be made about protest movements based on gender. If the rise of feminism, which also played an important part in Los Angeles social movements of the 1960s, was partly motivated by women's lack of access to high-paying jobs, then the issue of gender discrimination at the workplace should be seen not only as a matter of gender inequality but as one of economic (that is, class) inequality as well—even if status differences between middle-class and working-class women sometimes intervened to disguise it.[8]

The salience of one or another of these three variables—class, gender, and social discontent, the basis for social protests—has certainly been greater at some points in L.A.'s history than it has at others. But their interdependence, even during the Watts uprising, can be demonstrated by referring to the 1965 report that the McCone Commission, a panel appointed in the wake of the rioting to investigate causes and recommend policy changes, submitted in 1966. The commission identified the three most important causes of the uprising as unfair housing, segregated schools, and high rates of minority unemployment. Restrictive housing covenants (a racial issue) limited both male and female minority workers to residences in the ghetto, effectively denying them access to jobs outside the old manufacturing district and confining them to the lower echelons of the working class (an economic, or class, issue). Poor schooling prevented minority girls (a gender issue) from getting the training they needed to earn a decent living. Likewise, high rates of unemployment condemned both male and female workers of color to a life of poverty at the bottom of the prevailing economic hierarchy.[9] In each of these situations, the three variables of class, race, and gender played interdependent roles.

STRUGGLING WITH MINORITY UNEMPLOYMENT

The most urgent task facing the Los Angeles city authorities in the aftermath of the Watts uprising was how to respond to the widespread property destruction and job losses. Even before the riots occurred, many middle-class white (and some middle-class black) residents of Watts had moved to the suburbs, just as other successful residents of the downtown area had done. White flight accelerated after the riots, taking with it many of Watts's better-off workers, shopkeepers, and skilled entrepreneurs. By the end of 1965, the unemployment rate in the area had risen to 10.7 percent, compared to only 4.2 percent for the city as a whole. The level of underemployment was considerably higher.[10] "The man who is still employed can hardly support his family on the low wages he receives," wrote one observer in January 1966, "and the man who is unemployed succumbs to hopelessness and despair."[11]

Fearing a new outburst of racial unrest, numerous city and state authorities, as well as local business owners and civil rights organizations such as the Urban League and the Congress for Racial Equality (CORE), rushed in with offers of help.[12] By far the best-known minority agency—as opposed to a state-sponsored body—to provide economic assistance was the Watts Labor Community Action Committee (WLCAC), which represented a wide range of local opinion and predated the uprising. Led by Ted Watkins, a Mississippi-born autoworker assigned by the United Auto Workers to be the full-time administrator of the project, the WLCAC received financial support from several blue-collar unions, including the Amalgamated Meat Cutters, the Teamsters, the longshoremen of the ILWU, the Service and Maintenance Employees (precursor of today's SEIU), and the Laundry and Dry Cleaning Workers.[13]

Labor's role in sponsoring the WLCAC and a similar organization in East L.A. provided the best evidence of trade union support for the civil rights movement during the entire decade.[14] The prime mover and shaker in the founding of WLCAC was Paul Schrade, the left-wing director of the 14,000-strong District 6 (Western Region) of the United Auto Workers. A man of broad interests and strong convictions, Schrade was also a major supporter of the United Farm Workers, a leader in the Southern California Democratic Party, and a friend of Senator Robert Kennedy.[15] So focused did Schrade become on his civil rights activities that he was sometimes accused by his fellow union officers of neglecting his duties as leader of the Los Angeles UAW.[16]

Just how many displaced African Americans actually got new jobs as a result of the relief programs set up after the Watts uprising is unclear. But several subsequent reports flatly contradicted the optimistic scenario described by the *Los Angeles Times*, which claimed that eighteen thousand new jobs had been created. In March 1967, Operation Bootstrap, a training center run by Louis Smith, the western regional director of the Congress of Racial Equality (CORE), reported that it had seventy-five people in job training and another thirty in remedial classes—a number dismissed by *Business Week* as "a drop in the bucket compared to the need."[17] The WLCAC report for 1969 was even more disturbing. It showed that the committee operated two gas stations, one grocery store, and one warehouse in the entire city, in addition to two small training workshops.[18] Although other employment centers undoubtedly existed in the area, they could hardly have created eighteen thousand new jobs in this short time.

Circumstances were not much better for poor, unskilled Latinos seeking employment in the East L.A. barrio, even though no riots had yet taken place there. In March 1966 Glenn O'Loane, a Mexican American autoworker who had worked on the same assembly line as Ted Watkins at the Ford plant in Pico Rivera, persuaded Paul Schrade to explore the possibility of opening a new community center in East L.A. Schrade put together an advisory committee and, in February 1968, the East

Ted Watkins with job applicants at the Watts Labor Community Action Committee Project Center, 1967. Courtesy of Security Pacific National Bank Collection, Los Angeles Public Library.

Los Angeles Community Union (TELACU) was established in Boyle Heights. Union support for this venture came from the Amalgamated Clothing Workers, the United Steelworkers, and other unions with Latino members in East L.A.[19]

TELACU was headed by Esteban Torres, another former autoworker who saw his task as developing a "community organization that could harness its own economic and social power."[20] This idea provided the first hint of a separatist, neo-nationalist approach to social and economic reform, which was to become a significant feature of minority protest movements in the 1960s. TELACU established a committee structure that would eventually offer housing, educational, and employment opportunities to many working-class families in the East L.A. community. But its only report dealing with employment in 1968–1969 stated that it had placed 123 male workers in "good, steady jobs."[21] This, too, was a very small number.

Of course, CORE and other civil rights organizations then active in Los Angeles did not focus their attention solely on Watts and East L.A.; they tried to boost minority employment in other areas of the city as well. Citing California's Fair Employment Practices Act (1959), civil rights activists made strenuous efforts to persuade white employers on the West Side and in the suburbs to hire Asian, Mexican American, and African American employees. Sometimes the members of CORE's employment committee acted alone, and sometimes they acted in conjunction with the United Civil Rights Committee (UCRC), an umbrella organization that included representatives from the NAACP, the International Ladies Garment Workers Union (ILGWU), the UAW, the American Jewish Congress, and several Mexican American civil rights groups.[22]

UCRC was headed by the Reverend H. Hartford Brookins—minister at the First African Methodist Episcopal Church—a politically sophisticated leader who in 1963 helped elect former police lieutenant Tom Bradley to the Los Angeles City Council.[23] Beginning in 1962, UCRC members also picketed a number of Kresge and Woolworth stores on the West Side in an attempt to persuade them to hire African American and Mexican American employees. By early 1963 CORE's L.A. membership had increased to over four hundred, and its employment committee felt confident enough to launch its own boycott campaign against retail employers who were unwilling to hire minority workers.[24]

CORE's targets included radio station KFWB, Disneyland, Norm's Restaurants, and such supermarkets as Safeway, Better Foods, Vons, and Ralphs. In conjunction with UCRC, it negotiated what it called "non discriminatory pacts" with several grocery chains and held a "shop in" at Thriftimart.[25] In its December 1963 report, CORE noted joyfully that it had increased the number of minority employees, both male and female, in the Los Angeles retail sector by "upwards of 4,000."[26] The organization's plans for 1964—announced under the slogan "Our Proposal to Make Dreams Come True"—proposed to add five thousand more minority positions to the total in the following year.[27] In 1965 the L.A. chapters of CORE joined in a statewide campaign to force the Bank of America to employ minority bank tellers and also to cease using redlining techniques when it received minority applications for home loans.[28]

Perhaps there is some relevant employment data that would demonstrate greater progress than I have described here, but I have not been able to locate it. And even if the number of minority workers who secured new or improved jobs because of civil rights pressure was twice, or even three times, the numbers presented here, it was still too small to have had a major impact on the overall employment situation. This fact is confirmed by U.S. Census data, which indicated virtually no change in the lowly status of male minority workers during the 1960s in

Los Angeles. The data showed that in 1970, as in 1960, African Americans and Mexican Americans were overwhelmingly concentrated in the bottom third of the occupational ladder.[29]

WHY SUCH A DISMAL JOBS OUTCOME?

The census figures on unemployment are somewhat crude because they deal only in broad categories. They tell us nothing, for example, about promotions *within* an employment category (moving from an unskilled job to a skilled one, for example), which for most African American and Latino workers was a more accurate measure of occupational success. In the early 1970s, however, UCLA researcher Paul Bullock published a study of employment in East L.A. and Watts that provided greater detail. Bullock found that by 1973, despite all the efforts that had been made to increase the number of jobs in these two communities, the problem of unemployment continued to grow. "The total unemployment rate[s] for all men ages 16 to 24 in our sample," he stated, "are approximately 46 per cent in Watts and 30 per cent in East Los Angeles."[30] This was more than six times the rate for whites in surrounding communities.

Why did the job prospects of low-income minorities in L.A. remain so poor (particularly among males) at a time when the rest of the U.S. economy was booming? The reasons were many. They ranged from temporary economic downturns to inadequate education, from bureaucratic neglect to family alienation, and from trade union prejudice to the growth of a "subeconomy" of drugs and petty theft that condemned increasing numbers of black and Latino youths to a life of gang violence and personal despair. Once a young man succumbed to the gang lifestyle, he was beyond the reach of the civil rights movement and sometimes even of the welfare authorities.

Bullock's research also sheds interesting light on the differences in job prospects between working-class Mexican Americans and working-class African Americans during this period. For example, in the sixties and seventies, a higher proportion of Mexican Americans than African Americans secured manufacturing jobs. By 1970 Latinos constituted almost 21 percent of L.A.'s manufacturing workers, even though they were only 14.6 percent of the city's total population. Black workers, by contrast, made up only 6.1 percent of factory employees. This disparity could be traced to both union and employer discrimination. Mexicans historically had been more readily admitted to unions such as the UAW, the Steelworkers, and the ILWU than blacks were. In addition, employers tended to prefer hiring Mexicans, particularly immigrants, because, as the civil rights movement continued to grow, African Americans had gained a reputation for greater militancy, which corporations found distasteful.[31]

As if this was not enough, getting a full-time job did not always ensure that minority workers would climb out of poverty. Studies published soon after the Watts uprising showed that many of L.A.'s minority men and women who remained poor were already working at full-time jobs. A 1967 report released by the U.S. Department of Labor revealed that the number of employed persons in South Central L.A. who failed to earn enough money to bring them above the poverty level made up 34 percent of the local labor force.[32]

But the worst fate that could befall a minority job seeker was running afoul of the law. In 1966 the new Los Angeles police chief, Tom Reddin, tried to improve relations between the LAPD and ghetto residents by establishing Community Relations Councils and by requiring police officers to wear name tags for easier identification. But these reforms made little difference. The new name tag requirement simply meant that the ACLU's police oversight office in Watts was even more flooded with complaints of physical brutality and verbal abuse than before.[33] Once a minority job seeker acquired a police record, it became virtually impossible for him or her to get a decent job. A new policy adopted by the California Fair Employment Practices Commission in 1968 was supposed to prevent employers from questioning job applicants about prior criminal activity that had not resulted in convictions. But many corporations ignored this proviso. McDonnell-Douglas, for example, continued to ask its job applicants whether they had "ever been arrested, convicted or charged . . . for any violation of any federal law, county or municipal law, regulation or ordinance."[34] Faced with this kind of hurdle, many African American and Latino job applicants with minor police records simply gave up the search.

UNIONS STRUGGLE TO MAINTAIN THEIR PRINCIPLES

The difficulties Latino and African American (and some Asian) men faced in getting even low-level industrial jobs in this period made the rewards to be gained by securing well-paid, unionized employment in an aircraft, automobile, or steel factory, or on the docks in San Pedro, all the more desirable. On paper, the AFL-CIO, the California State Federation of Labor, and the Los Angeles County Federation of Labor all supported the anti-discrimination clauses in the 1964 federal Civil Rights Act.[35] But, even in the civil rights decade of the sixties, this did not mean that all Los Angeles unions—not even all its socially conscious, former

CIO industrial unions—were equally willing to live up to their liberal principles. In fact, a nasty example of industrial union hypocrisy on the race issue occurred in 1965. The culprit was again Local 13 of the International Longshoremen's and Warehousemen's Union.

This San Pedro local had previously compromised the ILWU's reputation for being color-blind when it balked at admitting, or readmitting, minority longshoremen to its ranks after World War II ended (see Chapter Eight). In 1965 it did the same thing. Just before the Watts uprising, Local 13 had been forced to shed some of its permanent "Class A" members as a result of the Mechanization and Modernization Agreement it signed with the employers, an agreement that acknowledged the reality that new forms of mechanization were reducing the number of dockworkers required for some loading operations.[36] When a number of new dock labor jobs opened up in the summer of 1965, Local 13 asked its remaining "Class A" members, nearly all of whom were white, to "sponsor" (that is, offer vacancies to) some of the workers on its "Class B" list, many of whom were black. ("Class B" registrants worked more steadily than casual laborers, but did not receive first priority for hiring and were not yet permanent, full-fledged members of the union.) But instead of offering African American longshoremen the well-paid and highly coveted jobs, the "Class A" members offered them to the small number of white longshoremen on the "Class B" list.[37]

The civil rights community was outraged. The *California Eagle*, the city's black trade union leaders, and the NAACP all criticized Local 13 president George Kuvakas and urged ILWU national president Harry Bridges to override Kuvakas, to no avail.[38] Thirty-two aggrieved black longshoremen filed a lawsuit against Local 13, and the L.A. branch of CORE issued a blistering statement accusing the union of hypocrisy. What had happened, CORE asked, to the reputation for social justice Local 13 had acquired on Bloody Thursday in 1934, when one of its members had been shot by the LAPD? "How does Bloody Thursday stack up against the Negro that walked across Europe, fought the . . . Japanese in the South Pacific, and today has a son in Vietnam?" CORE, the statement added pointedly, "IS FIGHTING TO GUARANTEE THAT *ALL* MEN ARE TRULY EQUAL IN THE EYES OF GOD AND THE COURTS."[39]

The lawsuit was eventually settled out of court. The pressure it brought, plus Harry Bridges's successful campaign to break down racial barriers on the docks in San Francisco, Hawaii, and elsewhere, finally persuaded Local 13 to open up jobs at the San Pedro and L.A. harbors to minorities of all races. The consequence was that Local 13 was largely taken over by Mexican American longshoremen, a situation that has persisted ever since.[40] But as time passed and civil rights activists pushed the Los Angeles unions even harder to observe Title VII of the 1964 Civil Rights Act, even the UAW—which under Paul Schrade had seemed to be a paragon of virtue on civil rights—showed that it, too, had feet of clay. The problem this time concerned the employment of blue-collar women.

The United Auto Workers had been one of the first unions in the country to establish a Women's Department. During the 1960s national union leaders such as Caroline Davis and Dorothy Haener pressured both the male leaders of the UAW and the "Big Three" auto companies to hire women not just in clerical departments but on the assembly line as well.[41] In August 1969 the federal Equal Employment Opportunity Commission (EEOC) determined that Title VII overruled state laws that limited the employment of women in industrial occupations, including rules that prevented them from taking "men's" jobs unless the women were above a certain height and weight. This ruling opened the way for the full application of the 1964 Civil Rights Act to female factory employees.[42]

That same month, the leaders of Local 216 at the General Motors plant in South Gate filed a series of complaints against GM management alleging that it had violated the 1964 Act by failing to place any women on the assembly line and by refusing to let them apply for skilled jobs. By putting its women employees in a category different from that of men, GM also prevented them from exercising their seniority rights. As of December 1969, the South Gate factory had only 159 female employees, more than half of whom were in clerical positions, out of a total labor force of 3,831.[43]

The UAW's international office in Detroit followed this up, as it did in the case of complaints submitted to the EEOC by locals in other parts of the country, by filing a civil lawsuit against GM South Gate requiring it to comply with the terms of the 1964 Civil Rights Act. This lawsuit, like the one filed by minority longshoremen in San Pedro, ended in an out-of-court settlement under which GM agreed to increase the number of women in its South Gate plant, provide them with equal access to skilled assembly-line jobs, and grant them back pay to make up for their lost seniority rights.[44] The most interesting point about these reforms, however, is that they were prompted as much by complaints made by blue-collar women and minorities against the discriminatory policies of the white male leaders of Local 216 as they were by the complaints the union made against GM management. In April 1968, for example, Kathy Seal, who later became a member of Local 216's executive board, complained that the union had failed "to treat grievances filed by women and other minorities . . . in the same manner as other grievances."[45]

Not long after this, Alfred D. Rowley, an African American booth cleaner in the South Gate GM plant, alleged that Local 216 had "failed to protect the interests of women and minorities and has acquiesced in the company's discriminatory polices and practices."[46] How much of the blame for this prejudiced behavior should be attributed to General Motors and how much should be laid at the feet of the union is unclear. What is clear, however, is that despite the prominent role the UAW played in the citywide civil rights movement, when it came to sharing the shop floor with women and minority employees, the white male members of the union were by no means free of race and gender prejudice.

Despite these problems, the record of industrial unions like the UAW, the ILWU, and the Amalgamated Clothing Workers on minority rights was better than that of the old craft unions in Los Angeles. In the craft unions, the job security of the members depended—more than in the case of assembly-line workers—on their ability to maintain exclusive control over access to employment. One of the most important tools these craft unions possessed to control the labor supply was the apprenticeship system. Since, historically, most craft unions were dominated by white males, the result of their tight grip on the apprenticeship system was to prevent women and minorities from entering their trades. The most egregious offenders in this respect in L.A., as elsewhere in the country, were the building trades unions, especially the United Brotherhood of Carpenters and Joiners (UBCJA). Throughout the 1960s, the Carpenters resisted the so-called Philadelphia and "hometown" plans, which had been negotiated by the UBCJA with the federal government to persuade building trades unions to conform to the 1964 Civil Rights Act by accepting minority applicants voluntarily.[47] But these voluntary methods did not always work.

In September 1971, for example, the Office of Federal Contract Compliance asked the Building Trades Council in Los Angeles why none of its affiliated unions had submitted any plans for integrating their membership. "To date there has been no imposed plan, no bid conditions issued [for minority employment on building sites], and no minority workers have been hired as a result of this program."[48] The male leaders of the UBCJA made no reply to this request, and they expressed strong reservations about the 1973 Employment Training Act, which mandated an affirmative action program that would train women and minorities as skilled carpenters. L.A. Carpenters president William Sidell tried to duck the issue by warning "against subsidized short-term training which potentially invaded [the union's] jurisdiction and trained disadvantaged persons . . . for substandard work."[49] At the end of the 1970s, this problem remained unresolved. In 1979 the UBCJA had

21,288 members in Southern California. Latinos accounted for 5,438 of the members, and 1,991 were African Americans. Virtually all of the remaining members (more than 13,000, or 64 percent) were Anglo-American men.[50]

Why were these Los Angeles unions so unwilling to abandon their resistance to accepting women and minority employees at the workplace? Part of the reason was the longstanding racist and sexist traditions of the city's white workers, which some of the industrial unions held onto just as strongly as the craft unions did. Other, nonworkplace factors, including a backlash against the supposed excesses of the civil rights movement and the increasing pressure it put on white homeowners to abandon their support for restrictive housing covenants, no doubt played a part as well. But probably the most cogent overall explanation for the failure of minority workers to gain high-paying, skilled jobs lies not so much with the unions as it does with the way the segmented, or dual, labor market, has historically operated in the hiring practices of Southern California's employers.[51]

According to dual labor market theory, white workers in the United States have traditionally occupied the primary, or upper, half of a dual labor market, which until recent times has given them a lock on most of the skilled, well-paid jobs in the national economy. Most of the country's minority workers, on the other hand, have occupied the secondary, or lower, tier of the dual labor market, which has limited them to unskilled, low-wage employment.[52] During the 1960s state and federal regulators, making use of civil rights laws, and Los Angeles activists who exerted pressure on employers to hire more minority workers forced some modifications in this dual labor market system. But given the large scale of the problem in Southern California (and elsewhere), and the long history of racist and sexist practices that had hitherto restricted the opportunities of minorities and women, they were able to change this system to only a limited extent. For their part, the white leaders of the craft unions were loath to adopt rule changes that would undermine their monopoly over skilled jobs, such as opening up the apprenticeship system.

Taken literally, dual labor market theory suffers from several weaknesses. It fails to recognize that racial, ethnic, and gender loyalties sometimes cut across each other in contradictory ways. For example, it cannot explain why white factory workers in South Gate could agree with their employers in wanting to prevent African Americans from attending the local schools at one point, only to unite with African American workers against their employers at another.[53]

Nevertheless, if we remove the deterministic element from the theory and accord proper weight to the interactive role of class, race, and gender, the dual labor market idea does help to explain the subordinate position of minority workers in the Los Angeles labor force during this period, as well as before and after it. Empirical data published by researchers at the UCLA Institute of Industrial Relations in 1977 lend credence to this view. One researcher who examined the position of the city's African American workers reported: "Black workers continue to be disproportionately concentrated in the less desirable and marginal occupations and industries."[54] A second researcher found that "the low earnings of Chicanos are largely associated with labor market processes which allocate members of this group to low wage establishments."[55] Still a third researcher, who surveyed the job situation of Asian American workers in Little Tokyo and Chinatown, observed that "despite a high educational attainment level, Asian workers have incomes significantly lower than whites who do the same work."[56]

The determining factor in all three of these cases, the UCLA study found, was "the existence of a split or dual labor market consisting of a primary sector composed of the high status and high paying jobs," which were mostly held by whites, and a "secondary sector comprised of the low paying and low status jobs" held by Asians, Chicanos, and African Americans.[57]

SEGREGATED SCHOOLS AND THE STRUGGLE OVER FAIR HOUSING

At least two other factors limited the employment prospects of minority workers in Los Angeles, both in the 1960s and in subsequent periods. One was the inferior education provided by the city's segregated schools; the other was the use of racially motivated housing covenants to limit where minority families could live. In March 1968, a series of "blowouts" (walkouts, or student strikes) occurred in East L.A. when several hundred Mexican American students from Garfield High School and other high schools in Boyle Heights walked out of their classes and assembled in a local park to demonstrate in protest of their substandard education. Quite a lot of African American students also accompanied them.[58] What, exactly, were these minority students protesting, and why?

The root cause of the students' anger was the failure of the Los Angeles school board to implement the U.S. Supreme Court's 1954 ruling to integrate America's school "with all deliberate speed." They were also influenced by the student protests that took place in Mexico during the 1968 Olympic Games and by the "Paris spring."[59] The long delay in implementing the 1954 ruling had resulted in grossly overcrowded schools, the absence of minority teachers, inadequate textbooks, and anger that most of the teachers in the ghetto schools directed their students' aspirations toward menial occupations instead of preparing them for college. Charlotta Bass, writing in the *California Eagle,* pointed out that "more Negro children attend all-black schools in Los Angeles than attend such schools in Little Rock, [Arkansas]."[60]

This reminder of racist practices in the South had no apparent effect on the complacent attitude of the white-dominated Los Angeles Board of Education, which for years refused to accept any responsibility for the segregated state of the city's schools. In June 1962, representatives of the Los Angeles chapter of the American Civil Liberties Union prevailed upon board president Mary Tingloff to appoint a committee of inquiry. When the resulting committee report endorsed the idea of equal educational opportunity but refused to take up the issue of school desegregation, the ACLU and its allies demanded that school boundaries be revised to ensure greater racial balance, that teaching staffs be integrated, and that students from overcrowded ghetto schools be bused to white schools. The school board rejected these requests and appointed another committee to study the issue.[61]

This second rebuff disillusioned a number of minority activists and provided them with a motive for dissociating themselves from white school officials who were supposed to be enacting reforms. This pointed up a new tendency among militants to shun white liberal support and opt for autonomous action based on separatist demands. At the same time, white parents in the industrial suburbs of South L.A. expressed growing anxiety as Latinos and African Americans demanded to send their children to the exclusively white neighborhood schools in the area.[62] This intensified the conflict over unequal educational opportunities still further.

Racial tensions over school integration were particularly strong in South Gate because its all-white high school lay only a mile away from the overcrowded, all-black—and much less well equipped—Jordan High School in Watts, on the other side of the "race curtain" of Alameda Street. Several different groups were involved in opposing school integration, including a number of white migrants from the South who were out-and-out segregationists.[63] Most white working-class families in South Gate, however, claimed to base their opposition on the liberal principle of local democracy and majority rule. Ray Bradford, a South Gate accountant, told newspaper reporters that he was concerned with "the civil rights of his own children and with the rights of . . . citizens of my own community."[64] As taxpaying homeowners, South Gate's white parents, who formed a voting majority, claimed the right to control their community's schools just as they claimed the right to control the local housing stock.

In terms of employment, the obvious problem with inferior schools in minority neighborhoods was that they prevented poor children from obtaining the kind of education that would enable them to secure decent, high-paying jobs. A 1960 survey by the Los Angeles branch of the Urban League found that the overwhelming majority of low-income minority students in the city attended schools that were more than 85 percent black or brown. The reverse was true in the city's affluent white suburbs. "The result," the Urban League stated, "was that students in these schools receive an inadequate education which fits them for nothing but menial jobs."[65]

The problems of minority workers were exacerbated by the persistence of racial covenants in the sale and rental of private housing, which had already made it difficult for Latino and African American workers residing in East and South Los Angeles to travel to work in the automobile and aircraft factories during World War II. This problem grew worse as the city continued to grow in the postwar period and as new industries such as aerospace were established in the "whites only" suburbs of Orange County and the San Fernando Valley, many miles from the minority areas of town.[66]

But the inequities of racial covenants that prevented minority workers from moving into white neighborhoods went far beyond the question of traveling to work. They posed a fundamental barrier to the citizenship rights of Asians, Latinos, and African Americans, a barrier the civil rights movement was determined to tear down. The first big move came at the state level. In June 1963, after heated debate, a mixture of Democrats and liberal Republicans in Sacramento, with the support of Governor Pat Brown, succeeded in passing the Rumford Fair Housing Act. It declared "racial discrimination in housing to be against public policy and forbade owners of residential property . . . to engage in racial discrimination in its rental or sale," and it established a state commission to enforce the measure.[67] The Rumford Act was greeted as a great victory by civil rights activists, who believed that it would provide the tools to end the system of racial covenants. But it was seen as a defeat by many of the socially conservative, blue-collar, working-class families in South L.A. who feared a decline in their property values if African American families were permitted to purchase homes in the area.

No sooner had the Rumford Act been passed, in fact, than a coalition led by the California Real Estate Association came into being to oppose it. By February 1964, an umbrella organization known as the Committee for Home Protection had collected six hundred thousand signatures (far more than the number needed) to put a state constitutional amendment to nullify the Rumford Act on the November ballot. Known as Proposition 14, this measure precipitated one of the bitterest political battles in Los Angeles history, a battle in which working-class residents were heavily involved.[68]

Despite their determination to succeed in this campaign, the civil rights activists who opposed Proposition 14 did not find it as easy to build a citywide coalition as their opponents did. Although the anti–Proposition 14 campaign secured donations from the ACLU, progressive church leaders, and liberal trade unionists, the supporters of Prop 14 had access to the much deeper pockets of big business and the L.A. Chamber of Commerce as well as the resources of the real estate industry. Even some minority property owners were themselves ambivalent, or even downright hostile, toward the Rumford Act. On election day in November 1964, for example, a majority of Latinos in Los Angeles actually voted for Proposition 14, not against it.[69] This result caused resentment in the black community and provided evidence of a divergence of opinion between Mexican Americans and African Americans that was to become increasingly problematic in the years that followed.

Nevertheless, by the time the "No on 14" campaign reached its peak in the summer and fall of 1964, the opposition had succeeded in developing quite a strong coalition. Its self-confidence was boosted by the official backing of liberal trade unionists and government officials at the state and local level.[70] Equally encouraging was the circular issued by the L.A. County Federation of Labor in August 1964, urging its members not to sign petitions in favor of the proposition. Instead, all loyal trade unionists—of whatever race—were encouraged to ask their local real estate boards to stop supporting the measure. "As organizations whose very existence is predicated on the enhancement of human dignity," the circular stated, "all local unions in the county of Los Angeles have a fundamental obligation to do everything possible to prevent passage of Proposition 14."[71]

It is unclear how many individual union members acted on this suggestion. Several industrial unions, including ILWU Local 13, the United Electrical Workers, and the ILGWU contributed money and volunteers to the "No" effort. UAW Region 6, backed by Paul Schrade, lent office space to accommodate volunteers in the "No on 14" campaign.[72] Representatives of CORE and of the Student Nonviolent Coordinating Committee (SNCC) picketed the offices of realtors who opposed the Rumford Act and assisted minority families in taking possession of the houses they had bought in white neighborhoods. In May 1964, for example, CORE picketed the offices of Torrance realtor Don Wilson, a segregationist. Several CORE volunteers, who carried signs saying "DON'T LOOK, DON'T BUY!" were arrested after scuffling with the LAPD. But an angry crowd of white

Opposition to fair housing in southeast Los Angeles, 1964. Published in *California Eagle*, November 19, 1964.

residents cheered the police when officers arrested several of the volunteers. Some white working-class homeowners in the crowd shouted that the volunteers were "criminals, or even worse, Communists."[73]

As in earlier years, the socially conservative blue-collar voters in South Gate became a flashpoint in this struggle. South Gate's city council—with several working-class individuals as members—endorsed Proposition 14, and its Committee for Home Protection solidified white community support across class lines behind the "Yes" campaign by trying to turn the liberal argument against Proposition 14 on its head. "When you say 'Civil Rights today,'" one committee member declared, "it seems to be a slogan only for the Negro; how about the rest of us [that is, the white community] having some 'Civil Rights.' Why doesn't 'Civil Rights' apply to *all of us?*"[74] When Proposition 14 was put to a vote in November 1964, it came as no surprise that the white working-class residents of South Gate voted for it by a larger majority than any other South Los Angeles community.[75]

The election returns from elsewhere in the county confirmed the continuing racial prejudices of much of L.A.'s white population. In Mervyn Dymally's heavily black Fifty-third Assembly District, 80 percent of the voters opposed Prop 14, as did large numbers of Mexican Americans in the Forty-eighth District. But most of the white residents in the outlying districts of Los Angeles, whether they were Democrats or Republicans, voted for Proposition 14 by as much as 65 percent to 75 percent. The suburban districts in Orange County and the San Fernando Valley, where the New Right had its base, were also among Prop 14's most fervent supporters.[76]

Proposition 14 was subsequently struck down by the California Supreme Court by a vote of five to two, and the Rumford Act was reinstated.[77] In a literal sense, then, liberal values won the day. Nevertheless, it is clear from these election results that, on housing and education, the rightward shift of the city's white working-class voters, coupled with the financial clout of the real estate industry and vehement opposition from the white suburbs, communicated strong, ongoing opposition to the idea of racial equality. It would be many years before the demand for integrated schools, adequate minority employment, and fair housing would be fully met.

INTEGRATION VERSUS SEPARATISM: BLACK POWER, BROWN BERETS, AND THE PARADOXICAL ROLE OF THE UNITED FARM WORKERS

The high school students from East L.A. who marched in Boyle Heights to protest their inferior education in March 1968 were accompanied by a group of militant young Chicanos known as the Brown Berets, a semi-military organization modeled partly on the Black Panthers. Evoking Che Guevara and the Cuban Revolution, the Brown Berets (with branches all over the Southwest) rejected the nonviolent philosophy of Dr. Martin Luther King Jr. and his followers and fought back against the LAPD when it threatened the Mexican community. Short-lived and marginal though they both were, the Black Panthers and the Brown Berets succeeded briefly in inserting the issue of ethno-racial separatism, instead of integration, into Southern California's debate about civil rights.[78]

For example, the Brown Berets flirted with the idea of demanding that the

United States return the five southwestern states that Mexico had lost in the 1846–1848 Mexican-American War. The idea of challenging white political authority also appealed to young African Americans and Chicanos who wanted to avoid the draft and distance themselves from the U.S. "imperialist" war in Vietnam. Their anger at the disproportionate number of deaths the Mexican American community suffered in that conflict was manifested in street demonstrations, which culminated in the National Chicano Moratorium against the Vietnam War on August 29, 1970, in East Los Angeles. On that day, the crowd of thousands was violently broken up by police, resulting in many arrests and injuries as well as four deaths, including that of popular *Los Angeles Times* reporter Rubén Salazar.[79]

Curiously, African American and Latino demands for autonomous political control over their home neighborhoods were enhanced by the role of the federal Office of Economic Opportunity (OEO) in the War on Poverty, which had been introduced by President Lyndon Johnson to expand social and economic equality. In 1964 the OEO established a series of Community Action Agencies all over the United States to enable poor people's organizations to administer federal antipoverty aid for themselves instead of channeling it through the usual municipal authorities. This federal experiment in community democracy alarmed the bureaucrats at Los Angeles City Hall, as it did in other American cities. Numerous unofficial anti-poverty groups clamored for representation on the city board that distributed the funds, while Mayor Sam Yorty strove to keep control over the federal aid in his own hands.[80]

This bureaucratic tangle also strengthened the hand of radical minority leaders who had become disillusioned by the failure of the federal government to solve the problems of the inner cities, and it reinforced their demands for separatist community action. "DO NOT SOLICIT GOVERNMENT FUNDING," warned a 1967 pamphlet issued by Operation Bootstrap in Watts. "Our experience with government sponsored projects has proved them to be paternalistic, providing an approach which is the exact opposite of what is desired."[81] Other black and Chicano nationalists expressed anger and disillusionment with the meager results achieved by moderate civil rights leaders in SNCC, CORE, and the NAACP. In fact, in 1963 the Los Angeles branch of CORE went through a crisis over this issue, which resulted in a split between its main body and a dissident faction calling itself the Nonviolent Action Committee.[82] The crisis over autonomy came to a head in 1968 when the national leadership of CORE officially excluded whites from membership and became, "once and for all," a Black Power organization with "separation" as its goal.[83]

The result of this shift to the left was a growing split between moderate integrationists and militant separatists in the L.A. civil rights movement, with the moderates remaining in the majority.[84] The best-known separatist group—and the one most feared by whites because of its militaristic philosophy of self-defense—was the Southern California branch of the Black Panther Party (BPP). Despite its image as a group of violent revolutionaries, in 1968–1969 the Panthers ran several successful "survival" programs in South Central, which were designed to "uplift the black masses."[85] Their services included a health clinic, a community center, and a free breakfast program for schoolchildren, for which many poor black parents were grateful. Predictably, however, none of the white-run trade unions and very few of the mainstream civil rights organizations would have anything to do with the Black Panthers. Anathema to the police, whom it described as "pigs," the BPP had a short life in Los Angeles, punctuated by a series of savage shoot-outs with the LAPD, some of them deliberately staged by the police themselves, which crippled its effectiveness.[86]

Most of these nationalist groups were either too small, too ideological, or too fragmented to gain a serious political following. But that was not true of the cultural side of the Black Power and radical Chicano movements. Cultural symbols of resistance to white domination, ranging from new kinds of poetry, jazz, and painting to distinctive clothing and new forms of street language, became enormously popular not only among minority activists but also among a whole new generation of New Left supporters and their allies. Rejecting all forms of European culture that smacked of colonialism, thousands of L.A.'s young Chicano and African American students and ghetto dwellers embraced Aztec, African, and other Third World cultural symbols in order to raise political consciousness and boost their own separate sense of identity.[87]

It was in this context that the "third way" of Cesar Chavez and the United Farm Workers (UFW) became important. Chavez's prominence as a national figure made separatist groups on the left wing of the Chicano movement anxious to know which elements of the insurgency he would support. On the surface, there seemed little to connect the work of the urban civil rights movement with the main mission of the UFW, which was to unionize low-wage, migrant farm workers in the vineyards and vegetable ranches of the San Joaquin Valley and elsewhere, miles away from the center of action in the metropolis.[88]

In fact, however, the UFW's tactics and organizing philosophy exerted a major influence over both the civil rights and labor movements in Los Angeles. Chavez himself had been nurtured in the same school of community organizing as Fred

Ross, who had registered thousands of Mexican Americans to vote in East L.A. Large numbers of Mexican farm workers from the catchment area surrounding Los Angeles, who spent the summers working in the grape and vegetable harvests in the valleys north and south of the city, spent their winters working as laborers, gardeners, or construction workers in the metropolis. They brought with them tales of the farm workers' struggles and of Cesar Chavez's successful civil disobedience tactics (modeled on the ideas of Dr. King and Mahatma Gandhi), which helped inspire the next generation of trade union leadership.[89]

A leader first of the National Farm Workers Association and then of the United Farm Workers, AFL-CIO, Chavez developed strong ties with the Los Angeles County Federation of Labor (LACFL). Between 1961 and 1968, Max Mont, West Coast director of the Jewish Labor Committee, served as secretary of the Emergency Committee to Aid Farm Workers, which successfully lobbied for an end to the bracero program, a mechanism that had allowed employers to import temporary farm laborers from Mexico under Public Law 78. In 1965, acting as a representative of the LACFL, Mont was a key negotiator between the wine-grape growers of the Coachella Valley and striking farm workers, a battle that resulted in the first union contracts for the UFW in the Central Valley.[90] Chavez himself spoke frequently in Los Angeles, and in July 1973 he and his staff bused several hundred UFW members into downtown L.A. to picket Safeway stores where nonunion grapes were being sold.[91]

To the chagrin of organizations like the Brown Berets, Cesar Chavez never became a Chicano nationalist. Rather, he was a labor and civil rights leader for whom "La Causa" meant freeing farm workers from the economic grip of the growers through the use of strikes, boycotts, and acts of moral suasion. For public relations purposes, Chavez was willing to employ visual symbols from the *mexicano* national movement such as the Mexican flag, images of the Virgin of Guadalupe, and songs of Mexican independence. But he rejected violence as counterproductive, even though nonviolence seemed to some UFW members to be an inadequate response when they were faced with physical attacks by the police and by the competing Teamsters Union. By focusing on the needs of farm workers' families, Chavez also rejected the ideology of *machismo* practiced by young men in the urban guerilla movement, just as he shunned definitions of minority freedom that rejected collaboration with whites. To the contrary, Chavez welcomed the support of middle-class activists and white sympathizers such as Senator Robert Kennedy; such allies were critical to the success of campaigns like the UFW's grape and lettuce boycotts, which depended on winning over middle-class urban consumers.[92]

Chavez also disappointed activists on the left wing of the Chicano movement by refusing to support the political candidates of the small, independent La Raza Unida Party, which originated in Texas, in L.A.'s municipal elections. Instead, he backed the liberal wing of the California Democratic Party, led by Governor Jerry Brown (Governor Pat Brown's son). In 1975, the UFW's support for the Democrats was rewarded by the passage of the Agricultural Labor Relations Act, which allowed union representation elections and collective bargaining for California farm workers for the first time.[93] But Chavez's main significance, as far as the L.A. labor movement was concerned, lay in the influence his message exerted on a new generation of Mexican American activists who would inject life into the Southern California trade unions in the 1990s (as Chapter Twelve explores).[94]

Although she was not as famous as Cesar Chavez, UFW vice-president Dolores Huerta also played a dual role as union organizer and political activist, both in the 1960s and for many years afterward. After working for some years for Fred Ross's Community Services Organization, as Chavez himself had done, Dolores Huerta gave evidence before legislative committees in Sacramento about child labor and old age pensions and then plunged into full-time union work.[95] Proving herself a highly competent negotiator, she participated as a virtual equal with Cesar Chavez in most phases of the UFW's development. At that time, this was highly unusual. Women field hands, who had grown up in the traditional patriarchal culture of the Mexican family, were usually seen by male leaders of the union as natural subordinates. But there was very little sexual division of labor in ranch work, and a radicalization process took hold among these young Mexican women and girls as they shared the daily struggles of their fathers, uncles, and brothers against the low wages, back-breaking labor, and unsanitary working conditions imposed by the growers.[96]

This consciousness raising process was reinforced when the UFW began sending the women, along with their husbands and children, out to cities all over California and neighboring states to help organize the grape boycott against the growers. At first, the union dispatched only male members to direct the boycott efforts, but it found that morale was higher and the boycott more effective when the wives and children of the organizers went with them. While picketing local growers in the Arvin-Lamont area south of Bakersfield, for example, Conrado Rodriguez and his eldest daughter, Lupe, were arrested and jailed. His wife, Herminia, and their remaining children, together with other detainees' wives, promptly went into Bakersfield to help secure their release. The result of the

Dolores Huerta and Cesar Chavez at the UFW's 1973 constitutional convention. Courtesy of Walter P. Reuther Library, Wayne State University.

UFW's family-oriented policy of union activism was the creation of a new cadre of female leaders inside the union, who were given important responsibilities of their own. They were put in charge of running the *centros campesinos*, centers that secured housing, shelter, and food for striking farm workers up and down the state. Encouraged by Dolores Huerta and Helen Chavez (Cesar's wife), this cadre grew until it became a group of sixty or seventy self-confident trade union women with minds of their own.[97]

Historian Margaret Rose, who interviewed many of these pioneering Mexican women in the 1980s, described their painful struggle—often against deep-seated prejudice—to gain the respect of their male counterparts. Mary Carmen, for example, described her father's anger when she first asked permission to attend a union meeting. "That was men's business," he said. "He finally agreed that I could go, but not my mother. That made my mother mad. She said she was paying union dues the same as he was, and after that she went too."[98] Mary Carmen never became as famous as Dolores Huerta. But those young women from farm worker backgrounds who managed to finish high school or even go to college became role models for the next generation of Chicanas, who played an important part in reenergizing the L.A. labor movement in the 1990s.

CIVIL RIGHTS BREAKTHROUGH UNDER
MAYOR TOM BRADLEY, 1969–1980

An outsider visiting Los Angeles in 1970 could be forgiven for thinking that not a great deal had been achieved by the civil rights and labor agitations of the previous decade. The issue of segregated and unequal schools was tied up in the courts, many white realtors still refused to sell homes to people of color, and the unemployment rate in South and East Los Angeles was still unacceptably high. By the end of the seventies, however, a major breakthrough had been made. By 1980 an African American mayor was serving his second term in office, several thousand minorities had been hired into white-collar jobs in Los Angeles city government, and civil rights laws were being more fully enforced than ever before. How and why did this breakthrough occur?

Part of the answer lies in the improved racial climate. After the first shock of the Watts riots passed, and even President Johnson had begun to use the phrase "We shall overcome," moderate whites became more willing to acknowledge that an irreversible social revolution in American race relations was under way. In addition, affirmative action rules had been introduced to expand the recruitment, hiring, and retention of minority employees. In 1971 a presidential order authorized the sanctioning (punishment) of firms doing business with the federal government if they had "fewer minorities or women in a particular job classification than would reasonably be expected by their availability."[99] In 1978 the U.S. Department of Labor followed this up by adopting a verifiable standard for deciding whether minorities were being adversely affected by the employment policies practiced by private or public employers.

The adoption of these new civil rights rules did not mean, of course, that officials in every U.S. city enforced them with equal vigor. In Los Angeles, there was sometimes disagreement between the different elements in the civil rights movement about how to proceed. Some Mexican American leaders, for example, including Edward Roybal, were upset by the disproportionate amount of attention devoted to the black community in South Central because of the Watts riots. In 1972 a minority element in L.A.'s Jewish community angered both feminists and African Americans by rejecting the idea of affirmative action and suggesting that "color-blind equal opportunity was the . . . only just and fair course for liberals."[100] What tipped the balance in favor of vigorous action were three additional factors: rising political consciousness among Latino and African American voters, disillusionment with incumbent mayor Sam Yorty, and the emergence of a new interracial political alliance led by Councilman Tom Bradley and leaders of the liberal Jewish community on the city's West Side.[101]

Bradley's remarkable political ascent unfolded in two separate stages. The first stage was during the pre-Watts period, when the young ex-police lieutenant developed a following among both white and African American voters in the Tenth Council District and was elected to the L.A. City Council in 1963, the first African American to hold a council seat. During the same period, two other African Americans, Billy Mills in the Eighth District and former janitor Gilbert Lindsay in the Ninth, were also elected to the council, raising the black contingent from zero to three and turning African American voters into a major political force in Los Angeles for the first time.[102] The second stage in Bradley's rise to power took place between 1965 and 1973, when his reassuring personality and measured response to the Watts uprising enabled him to turn his interracial political alliance into an instrument of citywide victory. His long-term political base consisted of African American voters in the Ninth District, upwardly mobile black and Jewish activists in the Tenth District, and white reform-minded Democratic voters on the city's West Side. The heart of this new coalition was Bradley's own Tenth District, west of downtown, which had become home to much of L.A.'s growing black middle class.[103]

Bradley's election as mayor was also boosted by the loss of minority support for Sam Yorty, the incumbent mayor who had once been a radical but who had lost his left-wing credentials. When first elected mayor of Los Angeles in 1961, Yorty had secured quite a lot of minority and working-class votes. But he lost the respect of the African American community—and much of his white liberal Democratic base besides—when he supported Police Chief William H. Parker's tough stand on the Watts uprising.[104] When he moved to the right and became a champion of law and order, Yorty tried to build a new conservative base by exploiting the job fears of blue-collar workers in L.A.'s old industrial neighborhoods and manipulating similar racial anxieties among the affluent white voters who had moved to the San Fernando Valley to preserve their version of the Southern California dream. At first, these tactics paid off. In the general election of November 1969, Yorty secured a majority of white and Latino votes and was reelected mayor.[105]

But Yorty's shift to the right also opened up a large new political space on the left of L.A. politics, which Bradley and his new interracial alliance were able to exploit. Bradley's personal popularity was enhanced in the African American community when he, unlike Yorty, publicly criticized Chief Parker over the conduct of the LAPD in Watts. As a result, Bradley won both the primary and the general election by solid majorities, benefiting from a high black turnout, solid Jewish support, help from the unions, and an increased share of the Latino vote.[106] The *Los Angeles Citizen*—the official newspaper of the L.A. County Federation of Labor—welcomed Bradley's victory, expressing satisfaction that, for the first time, a candidate endorsed by COPE (the AFL-CIO's political arm) had been elected to the mayor's office.[107] More remarkable was that the *Los Angeles Times,* which during the 1960s had slowly retreated from the uniformly conservative positions it had maintained in its earlier history, also extended Bradley a cautious welcome.[108]

With Tom Bradley firmly ensconced in the mayor's chair—a position to which he would be reelected no fewer than four times—the civil rights movement in Southern California finally got its reward. His administration quickly set about using federally mandated affirmative action rules to provide employment for minority men and women in city government. Of the 140 city commissioners appointed during Bradley's first term, 21 were black, 13 were Latino, 10 were Asian American, and 45 were women. These changes made influential bodies such as the Police Commission, the Public Works Commission, and the Human Rights Commission much more receptive to the needs and requirements of the inhabitants of minority, working-class neighborhoods.[109]

CONCLUSION

In many respects, the early years of Mayor Bradley's administration represented a vindication—or perhaps even an apotheosis—in the long struggle for social and economic equality that organizations such as CORE and the NAACP had fought in Los Angeles and other cities for more than twenty years, one that progressive elements in the labor movement also supported. By enforcing affirmative action rules and other civil rights laws, the Bradley administration opened up new avenues of upward mobility for minority individuals and businesses and brought a growing number of African American, Asian, and Latino civil servants into the upper echelons of city government for the first time. By 1980 more than 40 percent of all black working women and nearly 20 percent of black working men nationwide were employed in social welfare, teaching, or public health service jobs.[110] In Los Angeles, the proportions were about the same.

L.A.'s newly minted African American and Latino officials also made use of their patronage powers to increase the number of minority employees—especially women—in the city's welfare offices, which resulted in a sea change in the attitude of government agencies toward the minority and working-class families who used their services. Many of these public service jobs provided decent wages and benefits, so public service unions such as the American Federation of County, State, and Municipal Employees (AFCSME), the Service Employees International Union (SEIU), and the American Federation of Teachers began to recruit minorities on a significant scale, laying the foundations for the powerful position the public service unions assumed in Los Angeles politics in the 1990s and beyond.[111]

But it is important to add that these benefits were not distributed evenly across the city's entire minority population. The main beneficiaries of Bradley's affirmative action programs were public employees, small entrepreneurs, and women of color who became teachers, secretaries, and salaried members of the urban middle class. They were not the uneducated, the unskilled, or the inner-city poor, even though those populations constituted a majority of the city's underprivileged African American and Latino working men and women. During his first term, Bradley prided himself on providing money to train a new cadre of unskilled black workers in South Central L.A.[112] But he did very little to advance school desegregation or alleviate the plight of those who remained in Watts or East L.A. as a consequence of white flight. The net result was a growing split between better-off, upwardly mobile minority residents who moved to the suburbs and the majority of poor families who remained behind. This laid the foundation for the creation of the large pool of underemployed (or unemployed) working-class families still present in the city today.[113]

Equally unfortunate, as his administration progressed, Bradley moved away from his base of support among minorities and the lower middle class and began to collaborate with the downtown business elite in redeveloping the central city. These urban renewal projects, like the earlier debacle in Chavez Ravine, could have been carried out more sensitively if the city authorities had set aside sufficient money for low-income housing and established a viable plan for relocating the minority families who were displaced by new construction projects.[114] But instead, like Mayor Poulson in the 1950s, the Bradley administration permitted large-scale property developers to raze old working-class neighborhoods in areas such as Little Tokyo and the Temple-Beaudry district and to replace them with expensive high-rise office and apartment buildings without an adequate supply of low-income houses to replace the destroyed residences. "Amid such an acute crisis of affordable housing," writes Mike Davis, with only slight exaggeration, "the labor-market fragmentation of the L.A. working class between privileged and oppressed strata is [being] redoubled by . . . mass homelessness and mass landlordism."[115]

The Bradley administration's loss of reforming zeal had serious political consequences. As crime rates and gang violence in the inner city grew, and as the redevelopment of both downtown and the West Side ran into opposition from the preservationist middle class, Bradley's original black and Jewish coalition—including its labor union component—began to fall apart. In the late 1960s, urban renewal had been a shared value for both African Americans and white liberals. But by the 1980s, redevelopment was a major cause of friction between the two groups. The building trades unions, whose members secured many new jobs as a result of the schemes, favored downtown redevelopment. So, too, did the Teamsters and the ILWU, whose members profited from processing lumber imports at the Los Angeles harbor. The ILGWU and the Hotel and Restaurant Workers, on the other hand, whose members lived and worked in the downtown area and whose homes were threatened by redevelopment, were opposed.[116] At the same time, African American voters became less important to up-and-coming Jewish politicians such as Zev Yaroslavsky on the West Side of town, who began constructing a new political base with other white suburban homeowners around the issues of improved education, improved leisure facilities, and "slow growth." By the mid-1980s many of the black and Jewish groups in the original Bradley coalition had gone their separate ways.[117]

By this time, however, the reform goals of the civil rights movement had been pushed into the background by the onset of a nationwide social and economic crisis, which gave the Los Angeles working class a whole new set of problems to deal with.[118] The causes and consequences of this far-reaching new development are considered in the next chapter.

ELEVEN

Globalization, Labor's Decline, and the Coming of a Service and High-Tech Economy, 1970–1994

"If we read our stars aright, the seventies ought to see, not the dawning of the Age of Aquarius, but a new age for workingmen," prophesied two labor intellectuals at the beginning of the new decade. "If history moves on its present course, the worker and his union will again have a place in the sun."[1] For a time, as the country struggled to move beyond its preoccupation with Vietnam and the racial turmoil of the sixties, that prediction seemed to be justified. The record of U.S. labor protest in 1970 alone was remarkable. The early seventies witnessed 2.4 million American workers out on strike, more than at any time since 1946–1947.[2]

By the end of the seventies, however—and still more so by the end of the eighties—hopes for labor's continued advance had been shattered by a social and economic crisis of unprecedented proportions. The recessions of the mid-1970s and 1980s, and the renewed economic downturn in 1991–1992, were not just ordinary dips in the business cycle. They involved nothing less than the loss of U.S. hegemony as the world's leading producer of manufactured goods. The export of manufacturing jobs to Japan, South Korea, and elsewhere and the circulation of cheap labor around the Pacific Rim—including California—had a devastating effect on blue-collar workers and posed a serious threat to their hopes of retaining their middle-class lifestyle.[3]

Of course, these changes also affected manufacturing workers in the "rust belt" of the Midwest, sometimes with results even more serious than those in California. Nevertheless, three specific developments had particularly severe consequences in

Los Angeles. First, the 1965 federal legislation that reformed the Immigration and Nationality Act released a flood of low-wage Mexican, Asian, and Central American immigrants—perhaps as many as half a million—into the Southern California labor market. Some of these new immigrants were Asian professionals who secured good jobs in white-collar occupations or the developing high-tech industry. But the majority were poor Mexican and Central American immigrants who took minimum-wage jobs in the rapidly growing service sector of the L.A. economy. The result was a major restructuring of the labor market, in which women and workers of color for the first time became a majority of the Los Angeles labor force, even as thousands of white manufacturing workers found their jobs disappearing.[4]

The closing down of smokestack industry made possible the second major development, namely, the movement of capital from Southern California's declining auto and steel factories into the hundreds of small electronics and other high-tech plants that sprang up in the San Fernando Valley and in Orange and Ventura counties.[5] The electronics industry in Los Angeles, coupled with the rapid proliferation of new service jobs, drew thousands of poor Latinas and Asian immigrant women into low-wage employment for the first time and forced many formerly unionized blue-collar workers, now desperate for employment, into low-paying service jobs on the bottom rungs of the economic ladder.[6]

The third major development was political rather than economic. It was the final collapse of the Democratic Party's New Deal coalition and the election of Republican Ronald Reagan to the presidency in 1980. Reagan's election was a triumph for conservatism all over the country, but it had a particularly powerful impact in Southern California because the New Right already had a strong base in Orange County and the San Fernando Valley. Temporarily at least, it drove many of the blue-collar workers in L.A.'s declining manufacturing industries into supporting the nativist backlash that erupted against the influx of undocumented Mexicans and other immigrants, once more undermining the efforts of civil rights activists to promote racial unity among the Los Angeles working class. It was small wonder—in light of all this—that Jim Estrada, spokesperson for Centro de Acción Social Autónomo (a Mexican American political group) stated in May 1992 that "everything is topsy turvy."[7]

PLANT SHUTDOWNS IN AUTO AND STEEL

Anxiety about the future of factory employment first surfaced in the industrial suburbs of South L.A. in the mid-1970s, when car imports from Japan and South

Korea deluged the U.S. market and the Big Three automobile companies decided to cut their costs by moving production back to their factories in the Midwest and closing their West Coast facilities. In the early 1980s, Goodrich Rubber and a number of other rubber and glass factories located on the Alameda corridor decided to follow suit.[8]

Foreign imports and the export of jobs also led to losses in the steel industry. When Bethlehem Steel closed its plant in Maywood in 1982 and U.S. Steel shut down in the City of Commerce, a few former employees managed to find jobs by transferring to the giant Kaiser Steel plant in Fontana, which was the last fully integrated steel-producing facility in the region. But that lifeline was lost when the Kaiser plant itself shut down a year later, with the loss of as many as fifty-three hundred jobs.[9] So traumatized were Bethlehem's steelworkers by being laid off that they wrote a play called *Lady Beth* about the impact of the closing. The play's title, a longstanding nickname for the factory, suggests that the workers saw the plant as a maternal figure who had nurtured its male employees for a generation and had now withdrawn her favors. *Lady Beth* was performed on Capitol Hill during federal hearings on plant closures, and it toured several rust belt cities in the Midwest to considerable acclaim.[10]

For a time the autoworkers in South Gate appeared to be more sanguine about their future. When rumors circulated that the General Motors plant in South Gate might close, President Sal Astorga of United Auto Workers Local 216 reminded his members that their assembly line had shut down several times since World War II, only to start up again when demand for cars picked up. "Don't worry," Astorga told a crowd outside the plant gates after the graveyard shift closed in 1979, "it'll open up again when sales improve."[11] But Astorga was wrong. Local 216's members were shaken in January 1980, when Ford announced the permanent closing of its Pico Rivera plant, and they were devastated later that year when GM put the South Gate plant itself on its "endangered" list. The union immediately increased its support for the Los Angeles Coalition Against Plant Closings (LACAPS), which had been established to protect the workers' jobs. It issued leaflets, held demonstrations, and met with local politicians to plead for their support. Besides passing resolutions, however, little practical aid was forthcoming from the municipal authorities.[12]

In June 1982, UAW Local 216 and United Steelworkers Local 1845 sent delegations to Sacramento to lobby for a bill introduced by Assemblywoman Maxine Waters to require advance notice of future plant closings. It was a measure of how far the political pendulum had swung to the right that, when the measure came up for a vote, the Democratic majority in the state assembly allowed the bill to fail. The excuse given to the unions was that, with the gubernatorial election coming up in the fall and with President Reagan so popular, "we don't want the Democrats to appear to be anti-business." [13]

Later that same year, when the GM plant in South Gate shut down for good, many of its workers displayed a response similar to that of Sal Astorga in 1979: they refused to believe that it would never reopen. Some of them were so confident about this that they declined to sell their houses in South Gate even after they transferred to new jobs at the GM plant in Van Nuys, twenty miles to the north. "I can handle this lousy job because in a year or so I'm going back to South Gate," averred one former employee. [14] Only when GM finally sold the property in 1986 did the autoworkers' dream of going back to work there finally die.

Altogether, eight major plants employing more than twelve thousand blue-collar workers closed down in South L.A. between 1975 and 1986, devastating their local communities. [15]

With GM South Gate gone, Van Nuys was the only auto assembly plant left in Southern California, and it became a symbol of a vanishing era of broad-based prosperity. "Working at GM gave me a chance to own a home," stated one worker. The wages he brought home were "enough to support my family, enough to send my kids to the state university, enough to allow me to be a good father and husband." [16] Because of its symbolic value as well as because of the jobs involved, UAW Local 645 and its supporters were determined not to let the Van Nuys plant go down without a fight.

At first it appeared as though the union might win the day. The "Keep GM Van Nuys Open" campaign put together a coalition of two hundred local organizations, including African American Baptist churches, sympathetic Catholic priests, union leaders, and representatives of the Mexican American Political Association. It also produced an award-winning video, *Tiger by the Tail*, to publicize its cause. Partly as a consequence, the management at GM restored the second shift and agreed to direct talks with the union. [17] In November 1982, in fact, it seemed as though the struggle to keep Van Nuys open would succeed.

But then things began to go wrong. The two main leaders of the campaign, Eric Mann and Local 645 president Pete Beltran, succeeded for a time in persuading the membership that because they had helped to create the wealth of the community from which GM profited, they should also have some say in determining the plant's future. But Mann and Beltran, who represented the left wing in the union, appeared to go too far when they suggested that the plant was not "private property" at all, but "a joint venture between capital, labor, and [the] minority communities."[18] They also alarmed the moderates in the union when they proposed a boycott of GM products by local consumers if GM refused to keep the plant open. Both of these proposals were seen as too provocative in the conservative political atmosphere of the time. In the next union election, a majority of Local 645's members withdrew their support for Beltran and Mann and voted for a different set of union leaders.[19]

This split within Local 645 of course delighted General Motors' top-level management, who exploited it to the fullest. GM president James McDonald expressed indignation at the idea of a boycott and in December 1982 informed the union that if it did not accept the Japanese-inspired "team concept" of production, it would almost certainly be shut down. This "team concept," which divided the assembly-line workers into separate competitive groups, was anathema to most UAW members because it encouraged workers to compete against each other to achieve the highest level of productivity. But the members of Local 645 became so fearful of losing their jobs that they voted to adopt it. To make matters worse, the district office of the UAW, backed by the international administration in Detroit, also urged compliance. Under protest, Local 645's members did change over to the "team" method of production, only to have GM close the Van Nuys plant anyway, five years later. This outcome was typical of the defeats that labor sustained nationally during this period, as concessionary bargaining spread throughout the labor movement and the crisis in basic industry continued to grow.[20]

"NO WAY YOU CAN FEEL LIKE A MAN"

Losing one's income was not the only consequence of the plant shutdowns. For men (and some women) who had worked for many years in the same factory, job loss had profound psychological consequences as well. This became painfully clear in the case of the skilled machinists, drafters, engineers, and mechanics who lost their jobs when McDonnell Douglas and the giant naval shipyard in Long Beach were forced to discharge thousands of employees after the military cutbacks that followed the end of the Cold War.[21]

In September 1994 the federal government gave the Long Beach Naval Shipyard, whose fortunes had always been dependent on the country's defense needs, two years to finish all of its existing ship repair contracts before closing down. Soon afterward, over half of the shipyard's labor force of sixteen thousand skilled employees were laid off, with the rest to follow later.[22] It was clear from the loving care the shipyard workers devoted to repairing their last ship, and from the way many of them hung on to their tools even after the job was completed, that they, like the displaced autoworkers, were loathe to acknowledge that they had actually lost their jobs. Weeks after the discharge date for the first batch of laid-off employees, writes Susan Faludi, "Ben Francisco, a boilermaker turned Excess Labor Supervisor, showed me a thick list of men and the tools they still had in their possession—drills, grinders, chisels, clamps, sanders, torches, and gauges . . . . They just want to hold on to their tools till the last day, like a security blanket."[23]

Thanks to civil rights laws, by 1990 the labor force at the shipyard was more than 60 percent black, Latino, and Asian. For these men of color, working in the shipyard had become a means of acquiring fundamental attributes of American manhood that white employees might have taken for granted but that workers of color had often been denied: pride in learning and practicing a skilled craft; pride in working alongside co-workers of other races as equals; pride, in a word, in becoming full-fledged American citizens. For these men, losing their jobs was particularly tragic because it meant returning to a world in which their competence as adult men could be questioned, their self-respect and their self-confidence shaken. Of course, the white pipefitters, boilermakers, and other skilled tradesmen in the naval shipyard were equally concerned about losing their jobs, but for some of them, especially the old-timers, there were different reasons. Some of these men had been working in the shipyard since President Franklin Roosevelt had first called for sacrifice in World War II. They had repaired ships for the navy during the Korean and Vietnam wars, and they saw themselves as part of a "heroic generation" that had helped to bring victory to their country but had now been cast aside. When Luis Rodriguez, president of the Boilermakers Union local, heard that the yard would close down, he cried. "Everyone was crying. We felt we had been stabbed in the back by our own government, by the country we served."[24]

Few of the workers in the McDonnell Douglas plant in Long Beach had been employed there as long as the men in the shipyard. But as first one group, then another, of the aircraft company's electricians, riveters, and engineers were let go—until twenty-seven thousand, or a third of the labor forces had departed—the problem arose of discharged workers hanging around the plant gates in the forlorn hope that they would be rehired. "We have men here," the plant's placement director, Shirley Judd, told a reporter, "who have not told their families. They get dressed and come in every day [hoping to be rehired]."[25] But the McDonnell Douglas workers were more explicit than the naval shipyard workers about the personal problems they faced. Some talked to their placement counselors about lost paychecks, lost cars, and the houses they had been forced to sell. One of them expressed frustration, as naval shipyard personnel had, that the federal government had awarded warplane contracts to McDonnell Douglas for thirty years to defeat the Soviets and then sold the workers down the river. "Back in the fifties," he said angrily, "a man was able to be a man—and the government supported that."[26]

But the touchiest topic was the impact of job loss on their relationships with their wives and families. Some of the discharged workers avoided telling their wives for weeks, or even months, after they had been told to leave. In some cases, their fears turned out to be fully justified. When aerospace worker Don Motta finally told his wife he had lost his job, she locked him out of the house and began dating another man from the plant who was still employed. Asked for his reaction to this disaster, Motta replied that he had once been proud of his wife, of his home, and of his daughter attending college. But now? "I'll be very frank with you. I feel I've been castrated."[27]

McDonnell Douglas had more women on its payroll than the naval shipyard did, about 15 percent of the total workforce. Most of these women were part of the clerical staff, but some were employed on the factory floor. Those laid-off men who had to watch their wives or girlfriends remain at work felt the most shame. Judd reported that some of the men who fell into this category could become quite misogynistic. "All of a sudden," complained James Lawrence, whose marriage had ended in divorce, "my wife became—I don't want to say the breadwinner, but the focal point of our earning a living. She was serving both roles. And all of a sudden, I'm trying to justify what my purpose is—and couldn't."[28]

However, it should not be assumed that all, or even most, of McDonnell Douglas's male employees disapproved of their wives going out to work. By the mid-eighties, 50 percent of U.S. women with children under the age of six held paid jobs, and public opinion polls showed that most male workers, whether married or not, welcomed the presence of women in the labor force.[29] In fact, the 1992 L.A. County Aerospace Task Force report described the "typical defense worker" as "married to a spouse who also works."[30] Nevertheless, federal officials reported a spike in the number of sexual harassment and discrimination complaints that were received from the McDonnell Douglas plant—more than 330 in five years.[31] A coincidental survey of trade union opinion by researchers in 1993 did not report any particular increase in male resistance to women's employment. However, the survey did state that women frequently needed to use the threat of filing a complaint before the federal Equal Employment Opportunity Commission (EEOC) before unions would open up new categories of skilled work to women applicants.[32]

One effect of the recession: downsizing America's manhood. Courtesy of Jim West Photo.

IMPACT OF THE CRISIS ON MINORITY WORKERS

Plant closings and the disappearance of high-wage jobs were not the only reasons working-class standards of living either stagnated or fell during the last decades of the twentieth century. Deregulation of industry and the dismantling of New Deal social welfare policies put added downward pressure on wages and led many firms to reduce their workforce. During his first term in office, President Reagan cut housing subsidies for low-income families and reversed the government's policy of raising the minimum wage to keep pace with inflation, which was running at an all-time high in the late seventies and early eighties. The latter move reduced the value of the minimum wage by as much as 25 percent—no small matter for an immigrant family living at or below the poverty line.[33]

But in Los Angeles it is likely that structural changes, which reduced the number of high-end blue-collar slots and replaced them with thousands of low-wage service jobs, played a more important role. A few of the factory workers displaced by plant closings were able to retire to the suburbs or maintain their wage levels by moving laterally into new positions as machinists, electricians, or craft workers in expanding occupations like the Hollywood movie industry. But many others were forced to take manual jobs at less than half of what they had formerly been paid. When he was laid off from McDonnell Douglas in Long Beach, for example, Owen Benson reluctantly took a job at $4.75 an hour on the graveyard shift at nearby Pride Plastics, a factory that made plastic video cases. "I feel bad that there's not anything for us," he told author Susan Faludi, "that there isn't any clear place for us to go."[34]

In some cases this was literally true. Very little new public housing was built in Los Angeles after the controversies of the post–World War II period, and all over town the existing stock of older rental property was being depleted by the newly fashionable trend of converting apartments into condominiums, which few working-class families could afford. An L.A. County report published in 1980 stated that, due to inflation, rents had increased more than 150 percent in the previous eight years, while wages had risen only 14 percent.[35] The result, wrote one observer, was that thousands of immigrant families with children were forced to live in "a dense, continuous ring of slum housing around downtown, with filaments and tentacles reaching out to Hollywood and the eastern San Fernando Valley in the north, the San Gabriel Valley as far as La Puente in the east, and Lynwood in the south."[36]

Unlike Detroit or Youngstown, the old industrial suburbs of Los Angeles were not simply abandoned. Almost as fast as giant eastern corporations shut down their

Southern California branches, business interests and speculators from downtown L.A. and elsewhere rushed in to take advantage of the cheap leases and tax incentives that the affected cities offered in a desperate attempt to recoup municipal income and stem the population slide.[37] But very few of the new employers who moved into the depleted areas offered the kind of high-wage jobs that enabled an individual worker to earn a family wage. Most of the new businesses that migrated to southeast L.A. in the 1980s were retail outlets, furniture makers, storage companies, and food processing firms, which demanded long hours and paid minimum wage. Thus the old Firestone Rubber plant in South Gate was converted into a nonunion furniture factory, and the buildings that formerly housed Bethlehem Steel on Slauson Avenue were rented out to a hot-dog distributor, a Chinese food products company, and a maker of rattan patio furniture. U.S. Steel was turned into a warehouse complex, and the famous "Assyrian" wall of Uniroyal Tire became the façade for a designer outlet chain. None of the employees in these new businesses were paid more than $7 or $8 an hour.[38]

Evidence of the reduced earning power of the reconstituted Los Angeles working class also showed up in the statistical record. Between 1969 and 1990, the percentage of L.A. workers earning less than $15,000 a year more than doubled, rising from 7 percent to 19 percent, while the proportion of workers who earned between $30,000 and $44,999 a year fell from 38 percent to 26 percent.[39] Popular images of the poor in the seventies and eighties often focused on welfare-dependent single mothers with several children, whose "irresponsible behavior" was blamed for the decline of the nuclear family by conservative sociologists and politicians. But this stereotype oversimplified a complex reality. Men constituted 43 percent of the poor in Los Angeles County, not women, and although female-headed households were more likely to be poor than other households, they accounted for a small proportion of all working-class families. Also, contrary to popular belief, most L.A. families in poverty did not depend on government assistance to survive. According to the Current Population Survey for 1984, only a minority of the adult poor in the city collected any form of public assistance from such programs as Aid to Families with Dependent Children, General Assistance, or Medi-Cal.[40]

Occupational differences in income between different racial and ethnic groups in the working class also appeared in the Southern California data. There were a few encouraging trends. Owing to the growth of the black middle class, the long-standing earnings gap between African American and white workers showed signs of narrowing: in 1989, African American men in L.A. earned 69 percent of the median earnings of white males, an improvement over previous years. Black women, who had made significant inroads into such fields as government employment, did well too, as did Asian male workers. Large numbers of white women also reached the higher echelons of the white-collar labor force—a factor that boosted middle-class family income among whites.[41]

For recent immigrants from Mexico and Central America, however, the income trend was in the opposite direction. By 1989 their average wage had fallen so far that Mexican men and women earned 46 percent and 50 percent, respectively, of the earnings of whites. Some of this widening gap resulted from the massive influx of undocumented immigrants, who typically earned 6 percent less than U.S. citizens and whose presence dragged down the average wage of all Mexicans in statistical reports. But some of the advances that had been made by immigrant workers in the preceding period also appear to have been reversed. By 1980 recently arrived Mexican men earned as much as 50 percent less in real wages than the Latino men who had immigrated twenty years before, creating concerns among economists and sociologists that large numbers of newer immigrants would remain stuck at the bottom of the income hierarchy in a new "underclass."[42]

This new ethnic division of labor also had a spatial dimension. Recent Asian arrivals, especially Koreans, now lived side by side with middle-class Latinos in Hollywood and in a dozen other neighborhoods west of downtown. Upwardly mobile U.S.-born Chicanos with some education mingled together with affluent Chinese in Monterey Park and in new tract housing in the suburbs of the San Gabriel Valley. But the cultural heart of the Mexican community still remained in East L.A. and Boyle Heights, and poor Latino families now inhabited not only the central city area but also large parts of the extended metropolis. They dominated most of the neighborhoods from El Monte in the east to Pico Union in the west, and from Echo Park north of downtown all the way down to San Pedro and Long Beach.[43] Map 5, which superimposes neighborhoods with a poverty rate of 25 percent or more over areas of the city with a majority Latino population, based on 1990 U.S. Census data, demonstrates the trend.

Not all of these Latinos came from the same cultural background or lived in the same areas. Central Americans from Guatemala and El Salvador, for example, tended to congregate in the MacArthur Park and Pico Union areas, whereas undocumented immigrants from Mexico settled wherever they looked inconspicuous and could get a job. Nor did they all work in the same occupations. Mexican men were overrepresented in the construction industry, while Salvadoran women tended to work as domestics in private houses.[44] The vast majority of these new workers were nonunion.

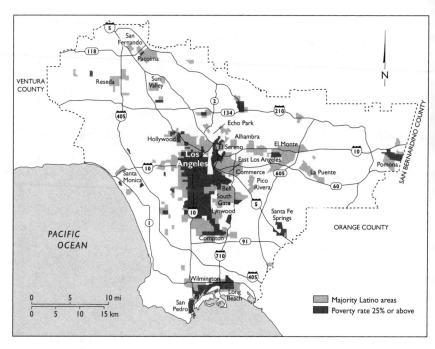

MAP 5. Los Angeles neighborhoods with a poverty rate of 25 percent or greater, superimposed over residential areas with a majority Latino population, 1990. Mike Davis, *Magical Urbanism: Latinos Reinvent the US City,* p. 57. Reprinted by permission of Verso Books.

GLOBALIZATION AND THE RISE OF THE HIGH-TECH SWEATSHOP

The "Latinization" of central Los Angeles, and the concentration of most of the newly arrived undocumented immigrants in poorly paid service and manufacturing jobs, was the major social development of the seventies and eighties. But what about the workers in the other half of the megalopolis, which now stretched not only into Orange County but also into Ventura, Riverside, and other counties? It was in these new suburban neighborhoods—or, more properly termed, satellite cities—that many of the new high-tech plants were located.[45]

By the end of the 1970s, the high-tech industry in Southern California had been divided up into three main branches: aerospace and missile parts, medical devices, and consumer electronics. The first two of these branches were relatively small, employing a high proportion of Asian and white technicians in modern glass-and-steel structures under relatively good conditions. The third branch, consumer electronics, by contrast, which assembled huge quantities of printed circuit boards, semiconductor microchips, and television parts, employed a much larger number of workers, but under much less attractive conditions. In 1989 there were 262 such plants scattered all over Orange, Riverside, Ventura, and San Bernardino counties, employing approximately 180,000 workers.[46]

Despite this rapid growth, in 1993 one specialist noted that "the electronics assembly industry is a typical example of an unstable, low skill sector . . . it constitutes an element of the lower stratum of sweatshops and secondary labor-market activity within the high technology complex of Southern California."[47] How did a supposedly "clean" industry that prided itself on producing shiny, innovative gadgets for a brave new world find itself categorized as part of the "lower stratum of sweatshops"?

The answer lies partly in the structure of the industry and partly in the working conditions on the job. Electronics assembly was a highly competitive business, with each company vying with others for orders and operating against strict deadlines. Most of the electronics assembly plants had no more than forty to forty-five employees; but some were fly-by-night enterprises with as few as ten workers operating out of a loft or garage. A great deal of subcontracting also took place, especially by small firms that lacked the specialist equipment to complete all stages of an assignment.[48] The pressure of intense competitiveness led small employers to neglect minimum-wage laws, speed up work to beat the competition, and ignore relevant health and safety standards. For example, the use of chemicals such as trichloroethane (TCA), a solvent used to remove grease from printed circuit boards, became a serious issue, both for the workers who inhaled it on the job and for the surrounding communities when it polluted their water supplies. But few small employers believed that they had the resources, even if they had the incentive, to deal with the problem.[49]

Despite its up-to-date pretensions, in fact the structure and practices of the electronics industry in Southern California strongly resembled the organizing practices of the much older garment industry, both in Los Angeles and elsewhere. So, too, did the composition of its basic labor force, which consisted largely of young Asian and Latino women.[50] But structural factors were not the only source of exploitation in electronics. L.A.'s assembly plants also had to compete in a global market that included plants in Mexico's border states. Indirectly at least, the California plants also had to compete with electronics factories in China, Thailand, and the Philippines, where wage levels, working conditions, and environmental regulations were inferior to those in the United States, creating added pressure for L.A.'s assembly facilities to keep their costs as low as possible.[51]

Among the most famous—or infamous—manifestations of this global, free-trading system of which the L.A. electronics industry formed a part, were the notorious *maquiladoras* (low-wage assembly plants) established in Mexico, just across the U.S. border in places such as Tijuana (across the border from San Diego) and Cuidad Juárez (across from El Paso, Texas). In the 1990s approximately 1,080 *maquilas*—one-quarter of all the electronics plants in Mexico—and more than 215,000 workers were "strategically located" in four Baja California cities near the border: Tijuana, Tecate, Mexicali, and Ensenada.[52]

In Tijuana, for example, U.S. and Japanese multinational corporations who owned the maquiladoras provided most of the investment capital and equipment for building the electronics plants but nothing for housing, sewage plants, or other basic infrastructure. They considered these expenditures to be Mexico's responsibility, but the Mexican authorities did not do much about it either. The result was that hundreds of poorly maintained electronics shops coexisted alongside garment factories, Coca-Cola bottling plants, and other manufacturing establishments in a degraded environment without proper housing, paved streets, or sanitation. Some of the young women who worked there—many of whom came from the rural Mexican hinterland—earned so little that they could make ends meet only by engaging in part-time prostitution in nearby San Diego. In 2001 the *New York Times* reported that assembly workers in Tijuana "earn such miserable wages and American companies pay such minimal taxes that its schools are a shambles, its hospitals crumbling, its trash collection slapdash and its sewer lines collapsed."[53]

Labor laws often went ignored and unenforced in the maquiladoras. This affected everything from health and safety and the right to unionize to the issue of women's rights. When Mexican electronics companies were criticized for paying their female employees less than men, for example, their spokesmen used the same hoary excuse for exploiting the women that American employers used in the years before World War I: "Maquiladora management holds . . . that women do not support families; they are secondary earners whose income is optional. Thus it is 'all right' to offer them dead-end jobs, because they have limited financial responsibilities and no career aspirations."[54]

In reality, of course, this was untrue. Just as Chicanas in Los Angeles service industries were often the only earners in their extended families, so too many of the young Mexican women in the electronics plants in northern Mexico had aspirations of their own, and they often traveled back and forth across the border to fulfill them. A good example of a cross-border worker with a desire for independence was Mexican-born Fermina Calero. As a girl, she attended school in her home state of Jalisco and then worked for three years in an electronics factory in Tijuana to help support her family. In 1982, however, the devaluation of the peso brought inflation to Mexico and lowered the value of her wage. So she crossed the U.S. border illegally and got a new job at Nova Tech, a small company producing personal computers near San Diego.[55]

At Nova Tech, the twenty-four-year-old Fermina earned $5 an hour, a far better wage than she had earned in Mexico, but she dared not go back to visit her family for fear of being arrested at the border as an undocumented worker. Her plant was raided twice by *la migra* (the Immigration and Naturalization Service), but Fermina avoided arrest by hiding in a closet. "I came to this country to work hard," she remembered, "and I am still determined to succeed." Fermina had not married or started a family of her own because of her fear of deportation. But several years later she became a supervisor at Nova Tech, continued to send money back to support her parents in Mexico, and expressed pride at what she had been able to achieve.[56]

As in the borderland maquiladoras, the labor force in the L.A. electronics industry was divided between a managerial cadre of white and Asian managers, a group of well-paid male technicians and quality-control personnel, and a much larger shop floor workforce of young, unskilled immigrant women whose median wage was $6 an hour. One study of the industry cited a sample of female workers of whom 54 percent came from Mexico, 23 percent from the United States, 9 percent from either Guatemala or El Salvador, and the rest from China or Southeast Asia.[57]

The electronics industry throughout California was notoriously anti-union. The owners and managers of electronics companies were dead set against trade unions, and virtually none of the attempts to organize electronics workers into unions in the 1970s and 1980s succeeded, in part because of the uncompromising hostility the pioneers of the industry showed toward organized labor from the very beginning. In 1963, for example, Robert Noyce, a cofounder of Intel Corporation, declared that "remaining non-union is essential for the survival of most of our companies."[58]

The same anti-union bias was displayed thirty years later at the San Jose hearings of the Dunlop Commission on the Future of Labor-Management Relations. There, Doug Henton, of Joint Venture, tried to argue that labor-management relations in the industry were so good that "unions as they have existed in the past are no longer relevant."[59] Henton's opinions were fiercely contested by the union officials at the convention. One of them was Romie Mahan, a shop floor leader who had himself been fired after he established a United Electrical Workers Electronics Organizing Committee at the National Semiconductor Corporation a few years before.[60]

A second reason for union weakness was the fragmented state of unions in the electronics industry after the United Electrical Workers was expelled from the CIO during the Cold War because of its Communist connections. As a result, the organizing abilities of the electrical workers' unions were hamstrung just at the time when the new high-tech industry was most vulnerable. Other unions, such the Glaziers and the Machinists, sometimes attempted to enroll electronics workers, but they never devoted sufficient resources to the campaigns. These early organizing efforts also took place at a time when most unions shunned the idea of enrolling immigrant women.[61] In addition, some of the immigrant women themselves displayed contradictory attitudes toward unions. Female assembly workers who came from Mexico or the Philippines, countries with a tradition of union militancy, were willing to join up. But those who came to the United States from rural Mexico or from patriarchal Southeast Asian countries such as Thailand saw themselves as temporary workers whose main role was to help their husbands get established in the United States. Still others, including those who had fled from South Vietnam in the late 1970s, tended to equate unions with Communism.[62]

Another reason unionization proved to be so difficult in electronics resulted from the same problem that dogged the garment trade. This was the reality that large segments of the electronics industry, like garment, were controlled by multinational corporations who, if their U.S. employees threatened union action, had the ability to transfer their production to a Third World country where costs were lower. In the Los Angeles garment industry, this practice first took the form of outsourcing, under which U.S. manufacturers were permitted to design and cut garments in California and then send them out to low-wage countries for completion. By 1984, 32 percent of all garments sold on the Southern California market had been completed in Mexico. Similar outsourcing practices were used in the electronics trade.[63]

BUSINESS RETURNS TO THE OFFENSIVE, 1972–1985

In order to cope with increased foreign competition during the transition to a postindustrial economy, U.S. firms were forced to improve their efficiency, experiment with new products, and cut their labor costs at the expense of their employees. But they also had an ideological motive for renewing their anti-labor stance.

The return to popularity of the idea of a free, unregulated market and the presence in the White House of a conservative, pro-business president permitted the national Chamber of Commerce and other anti-union organizations greater freedom of action. Soon after President Reagan took office in January 1981, a variety of business organizations—many of them employing professional union busters—launched a direct attack on the AFL-CIO.[64]

The employers' basic strategy was to shut down their uncompetitive plants, demand "give backs" from organized labor, and support the Republican Party and its pro-business agenda. In 1972 a new consultative body known as the Business Round Table, led by corporate giants such as AT&T, General Electric, and U.S. Steel, had been established to push for these ends. In addition to recommending anti-union strategies to its members, the Business Round Table established a Political Action Committee, which lobbied Congress to cut taxes, deregulate business, and frustrate the AFL-CIO's political agenda.[65]

The anti-union philosophy of the Business Round Table fit well with the emerging free-market philosophy of the New Right. But it also proved surprisingly popular among moderates in the Democratic Party, which in the late seventies still controlled the presidency and both houses of Congress. The Democratic Party's growing conservatism stemmed partly from the declining popularity of the welfare state and partly from the growing appeal of less government and lower taxes. Hostility toward raising taxes was particularly strong in California, where in 1978 the voters approved Proposition 13, which placed severe limits on future increases in property taxes. Over the long run, the tax revolt had an increasingly negative effect on the provision of public services and on liberal reform projects such as providing funding for the integration of L.A.'s public schools.[66]

The ease with which many Democrats accepted the growing influence of the business community also reflected major changes in the party's demographic base. By the late 1970s the original basis of the New Deal coalition—which had united liberal reformers, organized labor, and the "Solid South"—had completely broken down. Most southern whites now voted Republican, not Democratic; and many frustrated northern workers either stopped going to the polls or actively voted Republican, as "Reagan Democrats." To make up for these losses, the Democratic Party devoted more attention to the needs of women, minorities, and the rapidly growing number of L.A.'s suburban voters. These changes led to the rise of a new kind of Democratic politician—such as Zev Yaroslavsky, on L.A.'s West Side—who had no tradition of loyalty to the labor movement and who catered, instead, to the consumer interests of the suburban middle class.[67]

Translated into the idiom of Southern California politics, these moves to the right naturally appealed to the leaders of L.A.'s business community, who included several hold-over figures from Reagan's "kitchen cabinet" during his days as California governor as well as the CEOs of the city's major banks, oil conglomerates, and real estate companies. In the late 1970s *Southern California Business* (the organ of the L.A. Chamber of Commerce) repeatedly attacked the Democratic administrations in both Sacramento and Washington and eagerly awaited the coming of the Reagan administration. The journal also opposed union-sponsored legislation in Sacramento such as a proposed law to prevent firms from requiring their employees to work overtime. It also waxed indignant about AFL-CIO sponsored bills in Congress like the one that proposed to change the certification procedures used by the National Labor Relations Board in union elections, changes that would have made it easier for labor to secure recognition.[68]

The reason the AFL-CIO sponsored the NLRB reform legislation, *Southern California Business* believed, was because it was finding it harder and harder to win union elections.[69] The business journal was right on this point. Union organizers in Southern California, like union organizers elsewhere, were winning far fewer union elections than in the past. This was not necessarily because worker sentiment had turned against unions; rather, it could usually be traced to the increasingly brazen (and frequently illegal) tactics employers used to prevent workers from transforming a positive card vote into the formal recognition of a union. There were echoes here of the old open shop movement of the pre–World War II period.

Employers' tactics included denial of job seniority rights, threats of demotion or dismissal, and anti-union pep talks to captive worker audiences during lunch hours or after work. In L.A., as in other cities, these tactics led to frustration for union organizers, a loss of faith in the legal procedures governing union elections, and a determination in some cases to bypass them altogether. They also led to a rise in minor acts of sabotage on the shop floor as workers found outlets for expressing their dissatisfaction.[70]

In the late 1970s the main consequence of this shift to the right was the political defeat of most of the AFL-CIO's national political agenda, even while President Jimmy Carter was still in office. Labor's bitterest moment came after the defeat of the NLRB reform bill that had angered the L.A. Chamber of Commerce. This reform bill was not particularly radical. It merely called for expedited union elections, sanctions against employers who discharged union activists, and the denial of business agreements to federal contractors who violated labor law. The bill passed the House of Representatives easily in the fall of 1977, but in the summer of 1978 it lost by a narrow margin in the Senate, following a filibuster, after representatives of the Business Round Table conducted an effective lobbying campaign against it.[71]

Shortly after this defeat, Douglas Fraser, president of the UAW, angrily resigned from an organization called the Labor-Management Group, which been set up in 1976 by AFL-CIO president Lane Kirkland and a number of business leaders to discuss matters of common concern. In his letter of resignation, Fraser argued (correctly) that the corporations had given up on the compact of "mutual understanding" that had been negotiated between labor and capital after World War II and had deliberately set out "to wage a one-sided class war . . . against working people, the unemployed, the poor, the minorities, . . . and even many in the middle class of our society . . . . I would rather sit with the rural poor, and . . . working people seeking a better life than with those whose goal is profit and whose hearts are cold," Fraser declared.[72]

These were rousing words. With them Fraser seemed to throw in his lot with militant rank and filers all over the country, including Los Angeles, who were urging the AFL-CIO to stand firm against the corporations and to revitalize the labor movement by broadening its base, reinforcing union democracy, and adopting a more progressive social agenda. In January 1979 the UAW helped establish the Progressive Alliance, a national organization of thirty unions and groups of women, minorities, and environmentalists, which looked for a time as though it might offer an alternative to the stand-pat policies of the established labor leadership. There was even talk of a new labor party to challenge the hegemony of the Republicans and Democrats.[73]

But the Progressive Alliance ran aground on two problems: how to organize a separate, left-wing party without forfeiting labor's position within the Democratic Party; and how to reform the AFL-CIO itself without weakening it still further. When the 1980 presidential election came around, most labor reformers ended up voting for the incumbent Democratic president, Jimmy Carter. But they were unable to avert a nationwide defeat for the Democrats, the victory of Ronald Reagan, and—within months—the firing of 11,300 federal air traffic controllers and the destruction of the Professional Air Traffic Controllers Association (PATCO). Soon after this came a major increase in the number of corporate attacks on the labor movement, forcing the AFL-CIO leadership into a cascading series of concessions over wages, benefits, and working conditions in industries all over the country. The pace of union decline accelerated, especially in the private sector, until by 1990 AFL-CIO membership had fallen from twenty-eight million to less than fifteen million.[74] In the 1990s and 2000s, it would fall even further.

How were these developments received in Southern California? Were any efforts made, as they were elsewhere in the country, to stave off the attacks of big business by reforming and strengthening the labor movement from within?

LIMITED SUCCESS OF UNION REFORM EFFORTS

Declining membership, coupled with a loss of militancy, had begun to weaken the Los Angeles labor movement well before the economic crisis of the mid-1970s. Union density in Southern California had fallen from its peak of 37 percent of all eligible workers in 1955 (the time when the AFL and CIO merged) to 28 percent in 1970—although the absolute numbers of union members had risen slightly as the city's economy expanded.[75] In addition to the cultural factors discussed earlier, the loss of militancy stemmed from the complacency built up during the years of prosperity following World War II, the failure of the AFL-CIO to organize new members, and the growing dominance of a narrow-minded form of business unionism. In 1972 AFL-CIO president George Meany went so far as to disparage the need for new organizing drives altogether: "I used to worry about the size of the membership. But quite a few years ago, I just stopped worrying about it, because . . . it's the organized voice that counts."[76]

During the prosperous 1950s and 1960s, many blue-collar families had left their old factory neighborhoods on the Alameda corridor and moved to more comfortable suburbs. Living farther out, fewer and fewer attended local union meetings, which left the running of the locals to small groups of union stalwarts and an increasingly middle-aged labor bureaucracy.[77] In this more polarized atmosphere, opposition movements emerged that challenged the complacency of the labor leadership and criticized its failure to address questions like union democracy and workplace control.

Local union discontent first surfaced publicly in Los Angeles in November 1972 at the end of a national strike conducted by the UAW against General Motors. Before accepting a final agreement, the Detroit leadership promised to review workplace grievances submitted by the local unions, many of which involved speed-ups and insufficient relief time on the assembly line. However, because so many local grievances were submitted, time ran out at the strike settlement conference before they could all be dealt with. Sal Astorga of Local 216 in South Gate, who was a member of the national negotiating committee, expressed the cynicism many local union leaders felt about the decline of rank-and-file control, even in a liberal union like the UAW: "We just sat around . . . [for the benefit of] the news media," Astorga said. "The real meetings took place some place else . . . . The International Exec. is like a caucus within a caucus. They're a union within a union, an elite group. They're just like a corporation."[78]

Soon after this, grassroots caucuses appeared in a number of other Los Angeles unions, organized around reinforcing democratic unionism and returning to a more militant stance. Sometimes the aims of these local reform movements, which were often led by young leftists or workers of color, were relatively straightforward. For example, the stated purpose of the Los Angeles branch of Teamsters for a Democratic Union (TDU) was to oust corrupt leaders and restore internal democracy to Teamsters Local 692 at Long Beach Harbor, whose members delivered freight from the docks to their inland destinations. In 1975 Sharon Cotrell, the first woman to get a job loading and unloading trucks at the Sea-Land Terminal in Long Beach, and Bilal Chaka, a Black Power leader with experience in the L.A. civil rights movement, exposed the fact that Local 692's leaders had taken kickbacks from the Port Authority and had used violence to protect their own favored set of union drivers. "I am committed," said Chaka, "to fight against goon tactics . . . and for making elected officers responsive to the membership who pay their salaries."[79] In January 1976, Cotrell and Chaka lost their bid to become trustees of Local 692. But in December of that year, TDU elected one of their own, Monty Ogburn, as president of the local, to try to bring democratic governance back into the union. How successful he was is unclear.[80]

In the steel industry, seniority and safety issues were the most common sources of local discontent. As more and more workers were laid off along the Alameda corridor, the management at Bethlehem Steel frequently required its remaining employees either to work alone or to transfer to other jobs in the mill for which they had not been trained. Both of these changes posed increased safety hazards, which were ignored for years. In 1975, however, a new, racially mixed set of officers, led by African American Bill Bratton, was elected to lead Local 1845, and they proved to be more responsive to the membership than their predecessors.[81] This was exactly the kind of union revival that militants in the United Steelworkers, under the leadership of Ed Sadlowski, were aiming at all across the country.[82] When Bratton took office, he succeeded in getting a plantwide promotion system instituted that removed barriers faced by workers of color who attempted to transfer from low-level departments to better-paying and more highly skilled jobs. He also persuaded Bethlehem's management to take the issue of safety more seriously.[83]

But despite a serious commitment to institutional change, few of these reform efforts had much effect either in Los Angeles or at the national level, at least in the short run. Many of the plants in industries such as auto and steel, whose unions the reformers tried to change, simply closed down, cutting the ground from under their feet. In addition, several of the unions they sought to reform were simultaneously under attack by the employers, resulting in accusations of disloyalty against would-be reformers who criticized the leadership. For example, after the passage of the Motor Carrier Act of 1980, which deregulated the trucking industry (a prime example of President Reagan's deregulation policy), Teamsters Local 692 in Long Beach was weakened by an influx of owner-operated, nonunion truckers. This external attack made life more difficult for TDU reformers like Sharon Cotrell, who nevertheless remained committed to her role as a "troublemaker."[84]

Over the long run, these reformers did help to create a new cadre of union progressives, who worked to restore a measure of local democracy and grassroots militancy in the unions, both in Los Angeles and at the national level. But they were able to do so only after realizing that their goals depended on the unions allying themselves more deeply than before with community organizations such as the women's, civil rights, and immigrant rights movements. It was not until the 1990s that the need for this new vision was fully grasped.

LOS ANGELES UNIONS IN FULL RETREAT

In the meantime, Southern California unions, like unions in other regions, endured another decade of headlong retreat. In Los Angeles, the consequences were particularly severe for unions in heavily government-regulated industries: the trend toward deregulation loosened old structures and sometimes shifted the entire playing field, undercutting the traditional leverage of union power. The deregulating effect of the 1980 Motor Carrier Act, for example, enabled small firms that contracted out jobs to independent, nonunion carriers to capture a rapidly growing segment of the short-haul trade in places like Long Beach, weakening the power of the Teamsters union.[85]

At the same time, many of the large unionized trucking firms elsewhere in Southern California began a practice known as "double-breasting." This policy permitted commercial shippers to keep some of their business in the hands of unionized truck drivers, but to delegate a growing proportion of it to independent nonunion truckers who bought their own rigs. To many truck drivers, the idea of becoming independent owner-operators was highly attractive, especially since it freed them from the threats of violence that were sometimes used by Teamsters officials to keep their members in line. "You had people coming into the industry who saw this as an opportunity," stated one observer. "They thought, 'Hey, I'll be my own boss!'"[86] In practice, however, competing for business without the protection of a union contract led to a major decline in wages, driving (that is, working) hours, and conditions. Between 1965 and 1985, the membership of the Teamsters in Southern California fell from 68,900 to 56,600, and union density in the local trucking industry declined from 91 percent to 46 percent.[87]

Labor's bargaining power declined in the construction industry, too, when union membership among carpenters in Los Angeles fell from nearly 100 percent in 1955 to less than 40 percent in 1985. "Double breasting" became popular in this industry also, with the added twist that many of the nonunion carpenters and drywallers who entered the trade were undocumented immigrants from Mexico and Central America who were eager to set themselves up in their own businesses. Starting a small, family-owned construction business, which could be done out of the back of a truck, was relatively cheap and easy. But, by underbidding unionized contractors and paying low wages to the immigrant crews they picked up off the streets, these *"coyotes,"* as they were called, undermined—and, in some cases, virtually destroyed—several L.A. locals of the Carpenters Union.[88]

If anything, the situation was even worse in the Los Angeles garment industry, where membership in the International Ladies Garment Workers Union fell from 7,000 in 1962 to 3,700 in 1979, even as the city's clothing industry continued to grow.[89] Because its rank and file was now overwhelmingly Latino, the ILGWU became one of the first unions in Los Angeles to begin the painful, but necessary, process of replacing its white, male (and largely Jewish) officers with Mexican Americans, who understood barrio culture and spoke to the union members in their own tongue. In 1974, for example, Juan Ortega, Cesar Reyes, and Christina Vasquez were all added to the ILGWU's payroll, a move that presaged the immigrant-based union revival of the 1990s. But despite this increased cultural sensitivity, membership in the L.A. branches of the union continued to decline.[90]

With unions on the defensive, employers also took advantage of the episodic recessions during this period to replace unionized, native-born workers with cheap immigrant labor. In the 1970s, for example, Service Employees International Union (SEIU) Local 399, the longtime union stronghold of L.A.'s downtown janitors, included five thousand white and African American members, some of whom earned as much as $12 an hour. The 1980s saw an office building boom downtown and on the West Side, which should have enabled Local 399 to grow still larger.

Instead, by 1985 the union's membership had fallen to a mere eighteen hundred, and most of the city's white and African American janitors had left the trade. Black workers resented the loss of these high-wage jobs as well as the Latinization of many of their home neighborhoods in South L.A. Developments such as these created new tensions between the Latino and African American communities, which union leaders in the 1990s would sometimes find it difficult to resolve.[91]

The flouting of union rules regarding hours, wages, and the enforcement of health regulations also had serious consequences for the immigrants who were brought in to replace union labor. One male janitor described its impact on his new fellow employees this way: "He [or she] works the midnight shift seven nights a week, stripping, waxing, and buffing the floors. Strong chemicals make his nose bleed, burn his fingers and eat the soles of his cheap sneakers. . . . They told of wrapping steel wool pads around their sneakers when stripping floors, to keep them from slipping on the slick chemicals. They told of weeks they went unpaid, of arbitrary schedule changes."[92]

One of the few L.A. unions to escape the employers' onslaught in this period— or at least to come out of it no worse off than when it went in—was Local 13 of the ILWU in San Pedro. This was not because of employer altruism. It was because the ILWU, unlike other industrial unions, did not abandon control over the work process to the shipowners of the Pacific Maritime Association (PMA). Instead, the dockworkers made use of their bargaining clout to come to terms with automated production *before* containerization and new methods of loading and unloading ships ate up too many of the industry's old hand-based jobs. Since the 1950s the PMA had been pressuring Local 13 to end the restrictive work practices the union had put in place to protect the safety of its members. These practices included limiting the size of sling loads, repackaging off-shipped goods at the wharfside, and the famous—or notorious—"four-on-four-off" gang system, under which only four members of a work gang of eight unloaded a ship while the other four rested, later trading places, with all being paid full wages. Under the terms of the 1960 Mechanization and Modernization Agreement, negotiated by the national union for dockworkers up and down the entire West Coast, the ILWU agreed to accept the introduction of labor-saving machinery in return for guaranteed employment, increased benefits, and improved pensions for retirees.[93]

At first, old-time radicals in Local 13 resisted the M&M Agreement, as they were suspicious of any concessions to the employers and unwilling to abandon any of the privileges that had made them "Lords of the Docks" in the 1930s and 1940s. "If we go into a full mechanization program," stated one Local 13 member, "[we lose] 40 percent of the work of the port."[94] Over the long run, however, the new arrangement worked well. The agreement cut back the labor force on the docks significantly, and it took some years before the older generation of longshoremen in San Pedro were reconciled to it. But once they accepted it, they enjoyed higher wages and greater job security than any other group of workers in Southern California.[95]

By the end of the 1980s, however, most Los Angeles unions, like organized labor throughout the United States, were in free fall. This collapse did not occur, as many believed at the time, because America had entered a world in which manufacturing was no longer important. Old-fashioned smokestack industries like auto and steel were indeed under threat, but much of what passed for high-tech production was, in effect, manufacturing on a reduced scale and under a different guise.[96] In addition, as Ruth Milkman points out, the biggest drop in L.A.'s union membership occurred not in industries that were vulnerable to the export of jobs but in occupations such as trucking, construction, and building services. All of these were "nontradable, place-bound" occupations.[97] As Michael Goldfield puts it, the main reason for union decline was "neither de-industrialization nor job relocation offshore, but a broader shift in the power balance between labor and capital."[98]

CULTURAL BACKLASH AND THE RETURN OF NATIVISM, 1986–1994

What could be done to stop the union decline? One answer was to strengthen public employee unions such as the American Federation of State, County, and Municipal Employees (AFSCME) and the teachers unions, which were not vulnerable to the export of jobs. A second strategy was to reach out to the huge number of recently arrived, low-wage immigrants from Asia, Central America, and Mexico, who now constituted more than a quarter of the Los Angeles labor force. In the long run, both of these approaches were used. The strategy of appealing to public employees paid off after changes in the law in the 1970s made it possible to organize teachers, health care workers, and city employees on a large scale.[99] But before either of these strategies could reap major rewards, another episode of nativism and immigrant bashing had to be dealt with. Even in the ILGWU, the idea of organizing undocumented garment workers at first had met with considerable resistance.[100] It would take another cultural leap of major proportions before the long tradition of racism and sexism that afflicted L.A.'s white workers had diminished sufficiently to make organizing immigrant workers of color a top priority.

Most white union leaders in the 1970s and 1980s still believed that undocumented immigrants were difficult, if not impossible, to organize, either because the immigrants feared arrest by the Immigration and Naturalization Service (INS) or because, as temporary residents, they had no compunction about breaking strikes and working for longer hours and lower pay than U.S. citizens.[101] In some industries such as grape growing and vegetable farming, the use of undocumented immigrants to break strikes was indeed a problem, which was the main reason Cesar Chavez and the United Farm Workers—for a time at least—were so hostile to them.[102]

Anti-immigrant sentiment was also based on the widespread belief that undocumented workers took jobs away from the native-born. This belief, too, contained a measure of truth, but it oversimplified a complex problem. Under certain circumstances—for example, when L.A.'s cleaning companies undermined SEIU Local 399 by replacing white and African American janitors with low-wage Mexican workers—the immigrants did indeed take jobs away from native-born employees. However, the practice of "niche employment," under which specific immigrant groups specialized in, or even dominated, certain occupations—such as Filipinas in the case of nursing—meant that competition for jobs between native-born workers and the foreign-born was less widespread than it appeared to be. The rising level of education required for upper-level high-tech jobs also rendered many native-born or second-generation workers, especially white-collar workers, immune to competition from uneducated newcomers.[103] Nevertheless, during the 1980s complaints about jobs being taken by undocumented immigrants appeared with increasing frequency in political speeches, in official reports, and in the labor press.[104] In July 1979, for example, the L.A. Human Relations Commission published a report citing the lost earning power of white unemployed mechanics including Jake Anderson, whose experience was typical of many others: "I used to sell parts to body shops, and I knew Americans who were making $20 an hour repairing dented fenders. Now, ninety percent of South Central body-shop jobs are held by recent immigrants making $7 or $8 an hour."[105]

For as long as L.A.'s economy continued to grow, the threat to social harmony posed by the rising anti-immigrant sentiment could be more or less contained. After economic restructuring began to have serious effects in the 1980s, however, the nativist movement became harder to ignore. "You can absorb immigrants without displacing natives in an economy that's growing," states Michael Fix of the Urban Institute in Washington, D.C. "In a stagnant economy, it's a lot more difficult."[106] As a result, most leaders of the L.A. County Federation of Labor supported legislative measures designed to limit the influx of undocumented immigrants from abroad.

Perhaps the most significant measure was the Immigration Reform and Control Act (IRCA), passed by Congress in November 1986, which was intended to reduce the flow of immigrants across the Mexican border by imposing fines on employers who hired undocumented workers and providing amnesty for those immigrants who could prove they had lived in the United States continuously since 1982.[107] Despite its good intentions, IRCA was largely a failure. To avoid breaking the law, many employers shifted to subcontractors for their labor supply. In return for absorbing the legal risk, these subcontractors kept a share of the migrants' earnings, exerting further downward pressure on wages. In addition, about 40 percent of the approximately two million illegal immigrants who qualified for citizenship under the new law settled in the five-county Los Angeles area, releasing a new stream of legally eligible employees onto the labor market.[108] This increased competition for jobs among low-wage workers made life even more difficult for labor organizers who were trying to rebuild their unions. In October 1988, for example, Jesse Martinez, who was financial secretary of Carpenters Local 309 in the San Gabriel Valley, expressed anger over the entry of unqualified laborers into the construction industry: "They say you're never going to do this [organize a union] as long as the Mexicans keep coming in."[109]

In 1991–1992 came the videotaped beating of African American motorist Rodney King by white police officers, and the acquittal of those officers a year later, after the trial venue had been moved from multiracial Los Angeles to white-dominated Simi Valley. This verdict outraged African Americans as well as liberals throughout L.A., and for a time it threatened to throw the city back into the same racial cauldron that had precipitated the Watts uprising of 1965.[110] In fact, the verdict sparked several days of rioting, which ended with more than fifty people dead, thousands arrested and injured, stores and homes burned and looted; the damage and loss of life were even greater than in 1965. But it was symptomatic of the loss of social idealism on the part of the unions that, aside from general expressions of regret, the L.A. County Federation of Labor played almost no part in the effort to rebuild the damaged neighborhoods. Paul Schrade, the left-wing director of UAW District 6, by now had retired; and no new funds were offered by the unions, as they had been in 1965 when the UAW went to the aid of the Watts Labor Community Action Committee.[111] In the aftermath of the riots, racial tensions and polarization in the city remained heightened for some time.

Despite this recent history of racial strife, conservative politicians decided in 1994 to exploit the immigration issue for political purposes, and it was then that the new nativist movement really came into its own. Disappointment with President Carter and anger at economic dislocation had already caused significant numbers of white working-class men to abandon the Democratic Party and vote for the Republicans in the presidential election of 1980. In 1984, the election had had little to do with immigration as such. But although Walter Mondale carried Los Angeles County as a whole, President Reagan once again carried twelve out of the fourteen working-class districts in South L.A.[112] By 1990 the glory days of the "Reagan Democrats" had passed, at least on economic policy. But the cultural effects of the Reagan revolution meant that many white—and some Mexican American—working-class families continued to support a socially conservative agenda, whether it was offered by local Democrats or local Republicans. Hence, in the summer of 1994, when California's Republican governor, Pete Wilson, attempted to revive his lagging reelection campaign by endorsing Proposition 187—the anti-immigrant measure drafted by former INS officials Alan Nelson and Harold Ezell—he tapped a huge reservoir of white voter discontent.[113]

The idea behind Proposition 187 was simple: to stem the flow of undocumented immigrants and save the state billions of dollars. This was a worthy goal in times of economic distress. But even before the political campaign began, it was obvious that most, if not all, of Prop 187's provisions were either unconstitutional, counterproductive, or inhumane. Preventing undocumented children from attending school would have turned thousands of them, unfairly, into scapegoats because their parents had entered the country illegally; denying proper health care to undocumented families would have posed a serious threat to the health of the general population and diverted critical care to emergency rooms, increasing costs.[114]

But nativist movements are rarely based on rational analysis, and none of these objections prevented Governor Wilson from adding the anti-immigrant "Save Our State" label to his campaign.[115] His supporters on the far right, who included Harold Ezell, former GOP Republican candidate Patrick Buchanan, and numerous other racially motivated politicians, used even more hysterical language. Barbara Coe, who had helped draft Proposition 187, showed how far nativist supporters of the measure were willing to go when she defended the schools-exclusion proposal with these words: "You're not dealing with a lot of shiny-faced, little kiddies. . . . You're dealing with Third World cultures who come in, they shoot, they beat, they stab and they spread their drugs around in our school system."[116] Despite the obvious falsity of these statements, when the statewide election took place on November 9, Proposition 187 was adopted by a vote of 59 percent to 41 per-

Garment workers demonstrate against Proposition 187. Courtesy of UNITE.

cent. Soon afterward, nearly all of the provisions of Proposition 187 were declared unconstitutional by the courts.[117] No attempt was made to press for another legislative measure along the same lines, even though support for many of the sentiments that had inspired Proposition 187 remained high throughout the 1990s.

Did the response of Los Angeles unions to Proposition 187 show a significant rise in nativist sentiment? The answer to this question is not as easy to obtain as one might suppose. The main unions supporting "Taxpayers Against 187," an umbrella organization opposing the proposition, were progressive organizations such as AFSCME, SEIU Local 660, the ILGWU, and the United Food and Commercial Workers. By this time, all four of these unions had begun to organize undocumented workers.[118]

Somewhat surprisingly, the majority white Carpenters Union, which had suffered major losses of membership as a result of the activities of undocumented construction workers, also joined in the opposition to Proposition 187. It did so, according to Tim Cremins of the Building Trades Council, because the proposition did nothing to stem the tide of undocumented immigrants who were crossing the border, and also because the Carpenters believed that the frustrations of native-born workers "shouldn't be taken out on innocent people and children."[119] Members of some other unions, such as nurses and schoolteachers, appeared to vote against Proposition 187 because their jobs would have been made much more difficult if the restrictions on public services for immigrants had been implemented.[120]

Sixty percent of Southern California's white residents voted for Proposition 187—not an overwhelming majority—including, predictably, most of the residents who lived in Orange County and the San Fernando Valley. Among both African American and Asian voters, 53 percent supported it. L.A.'s Latino citizens, however, voted against it by a majority of 72 percent to 23 percent, and the voters in virtually all of the working-class assembly districts in the central and southern portions of the city opposed it.[121] This result suggests that the extent of the cultural backlash displayed against undocumented immigrants in the mid-term elections of 1994 may have been exaggerated.

CONCLUSION

Ironically, it was the very intensity of the attacks on undocumented immigrants and the anger these attacks aroused in L.A.'s immigrant community that helped to pave the way for the recovery of the city's labor movement in the 1990s. Only 8 percent of eligible Latino voters in Los Angeles cast their ballots in the November 1994 election. But during that fall campaign, thousands of Latino high school students walked out of class to support the protests against Proposition 187, in places as far apart as Huntington Park, Pacoima, and the San Fernando Valley, reminding some observers of the militant social protests of the sixties. And on October 24, 1994, the largest rally of Mexican immigrants Los Angeles had yet seen, with over seventy thousand attendees, paraded through downtown. Union members, church groups, youth organizations, civil rights activists, and multigenerational Latino families marched and sang together, waving Mexican and American flags and denouncing Proposition 187 and the nativist policies of Governor Wilson and the Republicans.[122]

By this time, the immigration issue had assumed an important role in national politics. The GOP's mid-term election victory of 1994 pushed the Republican Party still further to the right. Robert Dole, the party's standard bearer in the presidential election of 1996, believed that anti-immigrant television and radio advertisements would reap the same political rewards for him that Governor Wilson's support for Proposition 187 had done in 1994. But Dole misjudged the California electorate. On election day in 1996, most of L.A.'s Latinos, African Americans, and white liberal voters returned to the Democratic fold.[123]

The anger that had been stirred up among Latinos and their liberal supporters by Proposition 187 and by the anti-immigrant rhetoric voiced at the national level marked a turning point in Latino attitudes toward politics both in California and elsewhere. This was most evident in the sudden and dramatic increase in the number of immigrants who applied for U.S. citizenship and in the growing size of the Latino vote in Southern California in subsequent elections. According to one source, both of these figures doubled in just two years between the elections of 1994 and 1996.[124]

Latino representation on L.A.'s elected bodies had already begun to grow even before the debate over Proposition 187 took place. When Richard Alatorre was elected to the city council in 1992, he represented the avant-garde of a whole new generation of Mexican American political activists, not just in the downtown areas of Los Angeles but in many formerly lily-white areas in Orange County and the San Fernando and San Gabriel valleys, where Latinos were now a significant presence. Mexican American politicians also replaced white incumbents on the city councils of many of the old blue-collar suburbs on the southeast side—including Bell, Huntington Park, and South Gate.[125] But it was the furor generated by Proposition 187 that was the decisive event. "Gov. Wilson will one day go down as the father of Latino politics in California," prophesied Gregory Rodriguez of Pepperdine University.[126]

Increasing the political clout of L.A.'s Latino voters did not, by itself, guarantee the revival of the Southern California labor movement. The unions needed to change their organizing tactics and enroll a much larger number of immigrant workers before that could happen. The next chapter examines the revival of the Los Angeles labor movement in the years between 1990 and 2008. It also explores the reasons for the limited extent of that revival and the new problems that arose as organized labor, both nationally and locally, struggled to maintain its relevance in a largely hostile world.

L.A.'s Labor-Latino Alliance Takes
Center Stage, 1990–2010

On March 14, 2006, the *Los Angeles Times* described the recovery of Southern California unions from the years of stagnation and decline they suffered in the 1970s and 1980s—a recovery resulting largely from an unprecedented effort to organize immigrant workers. As evidence, the *Times* pointed to the recent and successful Justice for Janitors campaign, to the rapid growth of public employee unions, and to the May 2005 election of former union organizer Antonio Villaraigosa as the first Latino mayor of Los Angeles in more than a hundred years. The newspaper reminded its readers that until the 1930s, Southern California workers had been in the grip of the country's most virulent open shop movement, led by the paper's own former editor General Harrison Otis.[1]

"Today, however," the *Times* continued, "the city's historic, Republican, anti-labor politics have given way to the opposite." With an energized labor force and a powerful immigrant rights movement, Los Angeles had become "a model for labor organizing in the United States."[2] Scarcely two years after this editorial was printed, however, a new book entitled *Unions in Crisis* voiced skepticism about organized labor's apparent recovery, both in Los Angeles and elsewhere. Pointing to ongoing employer hostility and a serious nationwide split between the AFL-CIO and a new labor federation called Change to Win, the author predicted that unless organized labor in the United States changed course, its decline "[would] continue unabated."[3]

How could the *Times* celebrate the advance of organized labor in Los Angeles and note that it had caught up with unions elsewhere in the country, while only a short time later a leading labor expert predicted its decline? Was the labor upsurge of the 1990s in L.A. an anomaly? Did it, perhaps, represent a temporary recovery in a period of ongoing union decline? Or did it signal a major revival of the labor movement as a whole? Today, the last of these three alternatives seems increasingly unlikely. Nevertheless, this chapter tries to explain why the labor movement in Southern California began to grow again in the years between 1990 and 2005 and why, soon after that, the recovery appeared to stall.

IMMIGRANTS AND UNION SUCCESSES, 1989–2005

The union revival in Southern California is sometimes said to date from the series of marches and demonstrations held by immigrant office cleaners who were striking for a union contract in the summer of 1990. Better known as the Justice for Janitors campaign, this organizing drive by the Service Employees International Union culminated in a much-publicized march in Century City on June 15, 1990, at which protestors were clubbed and arrested by Los Angeles police. The beatings sparked considerable sympathy for the workers and prompted Mayor Tom Bradley to call for an official inquiry, which put much of the blame on the police. This publicity and growing public support for the strikers helped persuade International Service Systems (ISS), the Danish-owned company that supplied janitors for many of the hotels and office buildings in Century City, to sign a contract with SEIU Local 399, which granted union recognition and raised the wages of its employees.[4]

The Century City victory was not the first time the unions had deployed direct action techniques to organize low-income service workers. That effort had begun several years earlier in Detroit and Pittsburgh, when SEIU—America's second largest union—centralized its leadership, committed additional funds to organizing, and trained a new cadre of organizers who reached out to workers of color in their own neighborhoods for support. The union's new approach also included acts of civil disobedience, research into the strengths and weaknesses of targeted employers, and a plan to circumvent the cumbersome rules used by the National Labor Relations Board for processing union elections.[5]

Not long after the 1990 confrontation at Century City, L.A.'s union upsurge picked up added momentum when twelve hundred undocumented immigrant workers at the American Racing Equipment Company, a manufacturer of bicycle wheel rims based in Compton, staged a successful five-day walkout to protest

Police beat protesting janitors at a Century City march during the Janitors for Justice campaign, June 14, 1990. Courtesy of UCLA Labor Center.

job cuts and low pay. In December 1990, these workers joined the International Association of Machinists and six months later secured their first union contract.[6]

Then, in the summer of 1992, four thousand Mexican drywall workers, most of whom were in the country illegally, left their jobs at construction sites throughout Southern California to protest low wages and poor working conditions. After a five-month work stoppage, which included mass picketing at job sites, hundreds of arrests, and class action lawsuits against employers for violations of federal law on overtime pay, the Carpenters Union was called in to help negotiate a settlement. The result was an agreement with more than thirty major building contractors to recognize the Carpenters Union; the strikers became union members, won medical benefits, and almost tripled their wages.[7]

Drawing on the same huge pool of undocumented immigrants, Local 11 of the Hotel Employees and Restaurant Employees (HERE, which organized porters, housekeepers, dishwashers, and food servers in the city's hotels), UNITE (created by the merger of the International Ladies Garment Workers Union and the Amalgamated Clothing and Textile Workers Union), and several other predominantly Latino unions adopted many of the same organizing techniques SEIU was employing. Using Spanish-language volunteers, union organizers carried their message into the workers' communities in East L.A. and secured moral support from sympathetic clergy in the Los Angeles Catholic diocese, headed by Archbishop Roger Mahony. Following in the footsteps of the old ILGWU, union officials encouraged the organization of female employees, championed social justice issues such as health clinics and improved welfare benefits, and encouraged undocumented workers to become citizens and vote in local elections.[8]

In 1992, HERE Local 11 conducted a ten-month boycott against the Koreana Hotel in downtown Los Angeles that mixed union organizing with support for political action. It persuaded Asian visitors not to use the hotel for meetings, and it even conducted a sit-in at the Korean consulate. Soon afterward, the Koreana Hotel signed a contract with the union.[9] HERE's Local 814 in Santa Monica used similar direct action tactics when it staged sit-ins and conducted acts of civil disobedience outside local hotels. On one occasion Local 814 brought seven or eight neatly dressed chambermaids out onto the sidewalk and introduced them to the crowd. The maids hastily made up a number of mock beds right there in the street, to demonstrate the work pressure they were under.[10] Local 814 also challenged Santa Monica's anti-union Hotel Employers Council by distributing a controversial video showing how low-wage jobs undermined service in the city's hotels and urged hotel owners to raise wages for the benefit of the community as a whole.[11]

By the turn of the century, these innovative tactics, coupled with more traditional forms of union pressure, had won a series of new contracts and increased the membership of SEIU Janitors Local 399 by several thousand members. HERE Local 11's membership also grew, although by a smaller amount.[12] Overall, a 2008 review of the Los Angeles labor scene estimated that the new burst of union activity had put a halt to the seemingly relentless decline of the AFL-CIO in Southern California. "Both in the state as a whole and in the L.A. metropolitan area," the report stated, "the rate of unionization has ... edged significantly upward in the past few years. The 2008 unionization rate [that is, the union density rate] is 17.0 percent in the L.A. metropolitan area, up from 15.9 percent in 2007. ... Los Angeles currently has an estimated 1,227,600 union members, or nearly half of the 2,633,600 union members in the state of California. California in turn accounts for about 16 percent of all the nation's union members, more than any other state."[13]

CORE REASONS FOR THE UNION UPSURGE

The main reason for the emergence of the "new unionism" in Southern California, which also influenced the Bay Area, was the rising economic and political consciousness of immigrant workers from Mexico, Central America, and (to some extent) Southeast Asia who had settled in California in the preceding decades. This awakening represented the culmination of a historical process that stretched back over several generations. In Los Angeles, it began with the Mexican track-layers' militancy in the 1903 "El Traque" strike against Pacific Electric Railway, reemerged in the famous ILGWU strike of Mexican dressmakers in 1933, and reaped its first political reward with the election of Mexican American civil rights activist Edward Roybal to the Los Angeles City Council in 1949.[14] Along the way, Latino immigrants discarded the home-country loyalties typical of many first-generation settlers, digested the process of "becoming Mexican American" described by George Sánchez in his book on the subject, and reached a new plateau of self-confidence in the civil rights movement of the 1960s.[15]

Sociologist Ruth Milkman adds three further reasons for the union upsurge. The first is the "shared experience of stigmatization"—the common sense of alienation from U.S. society that many undocumented workers feel, especially when they are confronted with hostility from American citizens. Second, Milkman cites the "stronger social networks" that exist among immigrant workers, compared to the networks of L.A.'s white workers. (An example might be the "home team" soccer clubs organized by Salvadoran immigrants living in downtown L.A.) The third factor is what Milkman calls the "immigrant political experience," which includes both the growing size of the Latino vote in Los Angeles elections and the arrival in Southern California of a group of radical activists from Central America who either had helped to organize unions in their native countries or had been victims of right-wing military dictatorships in El Salvador and elsewhere.[16]

All three of these reasons make good sense, and they can be developed even more fully. For example, the shared experience of stigmatization among recent immigrants would also include the anxiety and fear generated by the passage of the Immigration Reform and Control Act (IRCA) in 1986, which increased the danger of deportation. To combat this threat, several Los Angeles unions established the California Immigrant Workers Association (CIWA), which provided legal help to immigrant workers whose citizenship status was in doubt.[17]

Several additional factors help to account for the 1990s union upsurge in Southern California. One especially important influence was the organizing legacy left by Cesar Chavez and the United Farm Workers (UFW). The power of this legacy stemmed in part from the high personal esteem in which Cesar Chavez was held by the city's Mexican American population. Among immigrant workers, however, his influence was more concrete. Many of the tactics adopted by L.A.'s service unions in the 1990s were shaped—either directly or indirectly—

by the organizing traditions of the UFW. The boycott, for example, which Cesar Chavez made famous during the UFW grape boycott in the 1970s, became a standard organizing tool used by HERE to put pressure on nonunion hotels. So, too, did workers' use of civil disobedience and street theater as ways of educating the public and drawing attention to their grievances.[18]

Equally important were the alliances immigrant workers developed with both Protestant and Catholic clergy, including such influential public figures as Archbishop Mahony. Most of the clergy-labor alliances forged in Los Angeles during the 1990s were based directly on the example of the California Migrant Ministry (later renamed the National Farm Worker Ministry), which supported the organizing demands of farm workers in rural California in the 1960 and 1970s. These alliances became a source of volunteers and built community outreach.[19]

The realization by undocumented immigrants that it was not illegal for them to join unions was also significant. In terms of the law, the right of undocumented workers to join unions was established in California in 1988 by the U.S. Court of Appeals in *Patel v. Quality Inn South*, which found that their right to organize was protected by federal labor law.[20] That legal opinion, however, was somewhat esoteric, and it did not readily filter down to the rank and file.

More important was the evidence gathered by Héctor Delgado for his 1993 book, *New Immigrants, Old Unions*. Delgado documented a successful organizing campaign carried out in the 1980s by the ILGWU to unionize the Camagua Mattress Company, a waterbed company in East L.A. Virtually all of Camagua's employees were undocumented, but Delgado's interviews showed that very few of them were deterred from joining the union by fear of deportation. One worker stated that "the chances of being surveyed or raided is very, very small." Another, speaking of possibly being arrested, said that he had a "better chance of being hit by a car—and he didn't worry about [that], either."[21]

Delgado concluded that undocumented workers' fear of *la migra* did not make them any more difficult to organize than native-born employees or immigrant workers who already had citizenship papers. Fear of being deported may have prevented some undocumented immigrants from joining unions until after the U.S. Court of Appeals found in their favor. But as more and more of them joined up in the early 1990s without suffering any penalty, their fear of arrest continued to decline.[22]

Finally, there were the creative efforts of lobbying organizations such as the Los Angeles Alliance for a New Economy (LAANE), led by economic justice advocate Madeline Janis. Among other things, LAANE helped build public support for HERE Local 11's hotel organizing campaign, and it persuaded the city council to adopt a living wage ordinance sponsored by Councilwoman Jackie Goldberg. This ordinance, which was passed over the veto of Mayor Richard Riordan in 1997, required private contractors receiving $25,000 or more in city funds to pay their employees a minimum wage of $7.25 an hour with health coverage, or $8.50 without health benefits. The measure also included job retention provisions for city workers who provided cleaning and food services at LAX and other public venues.[23]

In addition to boosting the standard of living and providing stable employment for several thousand (frequently exploited) low-wage immigrants from Mexico, Central America, and the Philippines, the living wage ordinance also gave a tremendous shot in the arm to the organizing efforts of service workers unions throughout the city.[24]

THE GROWING POWER OF L.A.'S PUBLIC EMPLOYEE UNIONS

In its March 2006 comments on the recovery of unionism in Southern California, the *Los Angeles Times* also referred to the growing size and influence of the region's public employee unions. A survey published in December 2003 showed that the three largest unions in the Los Angeles County Federation of Labor were SEIU 434B (with seventy-four thousand homecare and nursing home workers), SEIU 399 (with forty-five thousand health care and other employees), and the United Teachers of Los Angeles (with thirty thousand teachers from the American Federation of Teachers and the National Education Association).[25] This survey confirmed the large, and growing, gap between the relative success of trade unionism in the public sector and the ongoing weakness of unions in private industry. An earlier survey, taken in 1981, showed that as many as 56.4 percent of L.A.'s public employees had become union members, compared to only 9.4 percent of workers in the private sector.[26]

Why was it so much easier to organize unions in the public rather than the private sector? Certainly the issue of accountability is key. The services provided by state and city workers, which are indispensable to the public welfare, are run by government officials who are directly responsible to the electorate. Any breakdown in health services resulting from, say, a county hospital workers strike, would expose local politicians to the wrath of the voters in ways that private business executives do not face.[27]

In addition, unlike private employers who aim to keep labor costs down to maximize profit, elected officials have no inherent reason to be anti-union. This does not mean, of course, that all publicly elected officials are pro-union, any more than the general public is. In 1978, for example, a large majority of L.A. voters adopted a proposition authorizing the L.A. County Board of Supervisors to contract out government services to private companies when the supervisors deemed it "more economical" to do so.[28] Nevertheless, once a legal framework was established permitting city, county, and state employees to engage in collective bargaining (a framework that had largely been put in place by the end of the 1970s), public employee unions grew much more rapidly than unions in the private sector. In Los Angeles, the three largest of these unions, representing teachers and health care workers, played a particularly important role in the revival of the Southern California labor movement.

The rapid growth of public sector unions did not necessarily mean that their organizers faced less of a struggle with state and municipal governments than private sector organizers encountered in their dealings with business executives. Among teachers, for example, disputes over professionalism, community control, and affirmative action frequently led to conflict with the authorities. In 1978 the passage of statewide Proposition 13, limiting property taxes, began an era of conflict over school funding between the unions and county and state governments, a conflict that has grown increasingly serious over the years. Nevertheless, by the end of the 1990s, the United Teachers of Los Angeles had become one of the most powerful unions in the Los Angeles County Federation of Labor (LACFL).[29]

Until the early 1990s, when the janitors and other groups split off to form their own union, SEIU Local 399, with its headquarters in downtown Los Angeles, was a multi-occupational organization that included clerical and office workers, leisure industry employees, social workers, and librarians in its ranks. Its core membership, though, consisted of hospital workers "in every medical vocation,"[30] on whose behalf it negotiated contracts covering wages, health insurance, pensions, and other benefits with over forty hospitals in the five-county Southern California region, ranging from Kaiser Permanente to the City of Hope Medical Centers. As the largest service employees union in the region, Local 399 battled with a wide range of government agencies as it became the largest trade union in the area.[31]

But labor's most stunning victory among public sector workers came in 1999, when seventy-four thousand homecare workers in Los Angeles County voted to join SEIU Local 434B.[32] On the face of it, these homecare workers, most of whom were poor African American, Latino, and Filipino women, were privately

You know what? If you work as a live-in domestic worker, you have legal rights regarding the hours you work and the salary you receive.

REMEMBER:
- At the end of each day write down the date, the time you started to work and the time you finished.
- Each time you get paid, write down how much they paid you and how much they owe you.
- Make copies of all checks that your employer gives you.
- Make copies of any accounting that you and your employer have done regarding your hours and salary.

The information above is necessary to:
- 1. Calculate the exact amount of your claim.
  2. To use as evidence in court.

- The more information you have, the greater chance of getting your money.

Novela (cartoon pamphlet, English-language version) distributed by the Domestic Workers' Association to inform members of their rights. Courtesy of CHIRLA.

employed domestic workers who assisted elderly or disabled persons in their homes. How could they qualify as public employees? The answer lies in some shrewd political maneuvering carried out by SEIU Local 434B and its political allies, which took more than ten years to complete. In 1991, Local 434B had managed to persuade the state legislature in Sacramento to define California's counties as employers of record for homecare workers. In addition, the union prevailed upon the L.A. County Board of Supervisors to be recognized as their bargaining agent.[33]

Most individual domestic workers, however, including the maids and live-in housekeepers who worked in white suburban homes, continued to be employed in the private rather than the public sector of the economy. In answer to this, SEIU established the Domestic Workers' Association, which hired several organizers to distribute *novelas*—cartoon pamphlets, typically in Spanish—along with notices of union meetings and social events, in public parks, where nannies and other domestic workers congregated, to inform them of their rights. The association also handed out advisory materials on the east-west city buses that carried thousands of maids, housekeepers, cleaners, and nurses from East L.A. to their jobs in Beverly Hills and West Los Angeles. In 1994 the association held a series of training seminars for domestic workers, meeting in local Catholic churches, which taught the participants how to file a claim for back pay and how to redefine their status so that they could qualify as a public employee. When the meetings ended, each member of the class went through a graduation ceremony and was given a certificate of personal accomplishment.[34] Here, in embryo, was another element in the growing cadre of undocumented women who were proud of their achievements and taught others how to live a life of dignity and self-respect in their adopted country.

"IT'S TIME TO LEAVE MACHISMO BEHIND!" THE ROLE OF LATINA LEADERS IN THE UNION UPSURGE

As Southern California unions began to strengthen in the 1990s, the emergence of Latina leadership, especially in the service sector, was critical. By 1980 Latinas constituted more than 40 percent of the janitorial workforce in Southern California, and an even higher proportion of the housekeepers, maids, and dishwashers who worked in the hotel and restaurant trades.[35] The support of these women workers was essential to the success of the organizing campaigns launched by SEIU, HERE, and other service unions.

By the late eighties, several women of Mexican descent were already serving as role models for female leadership in the labor movement, including Maria Elena Durazo, head of HERE Local 11; Dolores Huerta, the veteran leader of the UFW; and Christina Vasquez and other leaders who had come up through the ranks of the ILGWU. A significant minority of the women who helped lead the Justice for Janitors campaign had come from Central America, where they had battled with employers even under the duress of politically repressive regimes. Out of a sample of forty-two female union members studied by Cynthia Cranford, 9 percent hailed from Guatemala and as many as 23 percent came from El Salvador.[36]

The unions' commitment to leadership training programs also helped to develop a cadro of a new female organizers. The program that exerted the most influence in Los Angeles was the one offered by SEIU, which was so successful that by the year 2000, Latinas had been appointed, or elected, to almost half of the leadership positions in Local 1877.[37] How was this advance achieved?

The first task in training women for leadership positions was to persuade them of the value of becoming involved. This was not always obvious to women workers who came from rural backgrounds or were influenced by the patriarchal values of the traditional Latino family. Several of the women interviewed by Cynthia Cranford reported that their interest in unionism had first been piqued not by the desire for gender equality, but by the idea that it would alleviate the feelings of isolation new immigrants often experience in an alien society. Delia, a janitor, activist, and mother of four children, described the appeal of working for SEIU this way: "I say the union takes you out of the closet because it's like being locked up. . . . And in our countries, politics is almost always left to the men. Few women participate. So you ignore these things; politics doesn't interest you. To organize? Forget it! But here, suddenly, I have done a million things."[38]

The next task was to persuade the husbands and children of Latina workers that it was desirable for women to take a leading role. Many family members were likely won over when they saw how effective women could be in emphasizing issues that protected the interests of the family. For example, male activists sometimes saw health care as a "woman's issue" that did not receive top priority. But women leaders were more likely to insist on including demands for health care and other family benefits in union negotiations. Through their advocacy, it became clear to the employers that health care was one of the immigrant labor movement's key family demands.[39]

The fight for a living wage fell into a similar category. A single worker earning minimum wage could not support a spouse, let alone several children. For those with access to grandparents or other members of an extended family, two combined incomes might make it possible for a couple to get by. But for those women who were divorced, had lost their partners, or had no extended family, a living wage (that is, a wage capable of sustaining the head of household and two children) was indispensable. This fact, in itself, provided an incentive for women to get involved in their union locals.[40]

Most union men readily agreed with the programmatic goals of these changes. But they often resisted the threat to their prerogatives when their wives and daughters began to assert their right to participate in union meetings—or to run for union office. Lupita, a Salvadoran émigré, reported that when she asked her husband to clean the house so that she could go to a union meeting, he refused, saying that if he did so he would be regarded by his workmates as a *mandilón*, a slave to his wife.[41]

But because SEIU's Justice for Janitors training program had already developed a culture of women's participation before it came to Southern California, male resistance to the advancement of women appears to have broken down more quickly in Los Angeles than in some other cities. As Cranford researched gender relations in Janitors Local 1877, she found that by the end of the century most of its male members had come to accept women as equals in the union. In 1998, Sylvia, an immigrant Latina who had been elected to not just one but several union committees (and was therefore in a good position to judge) summarized the new situation this way: "Those of us on the committees now, we are working together well. And the men give the women the opportunity, as we women give the men. I think that we are winning this. In the committees, we are very much on the same level."[42]

MIGUEL CONTRERAS AND THE RISE OF THE LABOR-LATINO POLITICAL ALLIANCE, 1996–2005

As a result of the nativist campaign that had been waged against them by bigoted white politicians during the preceding years, Latino voters expressed increased interest in political action and in electing their fellow Latinos to political office in the 1990s. Their interest in politics also reflected the need to influence the content of federal, state, and municipal laws concerning Workers' Compensation, Social Security, and unemployment insurance, which affected the workers that union leaders were trying to organize.[43]

Like unions throughout the country, the Committee on Political Education (COPE) of the L.A. County Federation of Labor had continued to maintain a political alliance with the local Democratic Party. Besides influencing the city council, this arrangement had succeeded over the years in electing several progressive city mayors, including Fletcher Bowron (1938–1953) and Tom Bradley (1973–1993). But with the passage of time, this political alliance had become a routine, bureaucratic exercise that lacked community involvement and depended heavily on televised appearances by political candidates at election time. As one critic put it: "Labor in Los Angeles . . . paid a price for its close relationship with the . . . Bradley administration, as it became accustomed to operating largely without a field mobilization capacity."[44]

In mid-1995, however, the LACFL's executive secretary-treasurer, Jim Wood, unexpectedly died. The need to elect his successor gave the immigrant-based unions their first chance at top-level power, and they ran Miguel Contreras as their candidate. Wood's predecessor as secretary-treasurer, Bill Robertson, opposed the move, saying that Contreras was "not qualified."[45] But despite the racial overtones of the campaign, Contreras won the May 1996 election, bringing a Latino to power as head of the LACFL for the first time, a highly significant development.[46]

Forty-one-year-old Miguel Contreras, who had acquired his leadership skills under the direction of Dolores Huerta and in HERE Local 11, proved to be the ideal leader to fashion a new, broadly based labor-Latino political coalition. He had been appointed political director of the LACFL in 1994, and when he became secretary-treasurer, his focus on politics continued. In particular, he placed increased emphasis on the need for Latino immigrants to become citizens and go to the polls.[47] Many of L.A.'s Latino voters favored the Democrats because of labor's traditional support for the party and because of their anger with the Republican campaign of immigrant-bashing, which continued at both the state and federal levels.[48]

In the mid-1990s, however, the proportion of eligible Latinos who voted in elections—about 10 to 15 percent—was still quite small. Contreras and his staff decided to raise that number in whatever way they could. They resurrected the door-to-door voter registration drives that had proven effective twenty years earlier, established workshops to help immigrants apply for citizenship, and made a special effort to attract first-time and "intermittent voters," a group that included many Mexican Americans. By 2000, the LACFL was able to field several hundred full-time precinct walkers at election time, concentrating them in specific wards in East L.A. Most of these precinct workers were "paid loss timers," who were compensated for their time away from work with money provided from a special union fund.[49] By 2005, the citywide Latino vote in city council elections had risen from under 10,000 ten years earlier to 27,500.

Miguel Contreras, executive secretary-treasurer of the Los Angeles County Federation of Labor, with Assemblyman-elect Gilbert Cedillo, 1997. Courtesy of Slobodan Dimitrov Photography.

The LACFL's political staff also raised political consciousness by getting each Latino family to treat voting as a collective, social duty. Door-to-door volunteers urged voters to sign forms stating that they were "Por la amnistía, por derechos, mi familia vota 100 por ciento [For amnesty, for rights, my family is voting 100 percent]." As one volunteer put it: "We tried to make everything a family act to magnify the work and make it resonate."[50] This campaign was also linked to the unions' attempts to enhance the role of women in the movement.

In addition, the Contreras regime did its best to increase the number of committed union leaders who were elected to political office, even when it meant opposing more traditional Latino candidates. For example, in a 1997 special election held in East L.A., the LACFL backed the general manager of SEIU Local 660, Gilbert Cedillo, for a state assembly seat against the "establishment" Latina candidate, Vickie Castro. Cedillo won handsomely, partly because he had helped to avert bankruptcy for the nearby County General Hospital, which many Boyle Heights families relied on for their health care needs.[51]

Gilbert Cedillo's come-from-behind victory shocked L.A.'s political establishment and served notice that Contreras and his supporters had put together a formidable political machine. In 2000 Contreras, Maria Elena Durazo, and

SEIU vice-president Eliseo Medina established the Organization of Los Angeles Workers to coordinate future political campaigns. "Supporting a candidate is no longer about bringing them to our banquet so that they can take a grip-and-grin photograph for our newspaper," Contreras told an interviewer. "It is about what you, the candidate, are going to do to level the playing field of organizing for the workers."[52] It would no longer be enough for political candidates to simply vote for specific bills in Sacramento or support pro-labor measures on the L.A. City Council. Now they would be expected to attend union demonstrations and even participate in acts of civil disobedience. As Contreras explained, "We expect them to be on the line. In the [2000] janitors' strike we had six or seven of them—city council members, state legislators—being arrested with us to show the plight of the janitors."[53]

Building an effective labor-Latino political alliance also required negotiating the thorny terrain of black-brown relations. Until 1990, the African American community in Los Angeles had effectively had two city council seats at its disposal, and its influence in the city employee unions and other organizations meant that it was still a major player in the LACFL. But the ongoing demographic shift toward a Latino majority in the city, and the anger that had been generated by the transfer of traditionally African American jobs to nonunion Latino immigrants, caused deep tensions over housing, jobs, and politics to surface in neighborhoods, in schools, and between gang members in the streets. In the 2001 mayoral election, for example, most African American voters supported James K. Hahn (who won the election), son of legendary county supervisor Kenneth Hahn, not the LACFL's preferred candidate, former union activist Antonio Villaraigosa. This racial division threatened to undermine the progress of the labor-Latino alliance.[54]

The Contreras administration recognized this danger. Although it never succeeded in dispelling black voters' fears entirely, in 2003 it helped to allay them by uniting behind the successful city council candidacy of African American union leader Martin Ludlow—former political director of the LACFL—in the mixed black and Latino Tenth Council District. Ludlow had established good credentials with the Latino community by working for SEIU and by acting as political director of Villaraigosa's 2001 mayoral campaign. The following year, Latino politicians helped to elect another African American, Karen Bass, to the state assembly, even though a recent reapportionment had transformed her constituency in the Forty-seventh Assembly District from majority black to a slim majority of white voters.[55]

The labor-Latino political alliance also extended its influence beyond Los Angeles by helping to elect a growing number of union leaders to county offices and to the state legislature in Sacramento, thereby shifting the entire center of political gravity of California to the left. In 1998 it played a major role in electing former assembly speaker Cruz Bustamante as lieutenant governor, and in the same year it deployed hundreds of staffers in cities up and down the state to help defeat an anti-union proposal, Proposition 226. If this proposition had passed, it would have prevented unions from spending money on political campaigns without securing the written permission of each member, every year.[56] Proposition 226 had been put on the ballot by conservatives hostile to organized labor, a fact that testified to their fears about labor's growing political clout.

In May 2005, the labor-Latino political alliance achieved its greatest success to date when Antonio Villaraigosa was elected to the mayor's office by a vote of 58 percent to 41 percent, a larger margin than the one secured by Tom Bradley in 1973. Villaraigosa, running against incumbent mayor James K. Hahn, swept all of the old downtown working-class neighborhoods and also expanded his victory farther west to win majorities in all but two of the city's fifteen council districts. The new mayor won 84 percent of the Latino vote and 60 percent of the union vote, and he increased his share of the black vote from 20 percent in the 2001 race to 58 percent.[57]

INTERNAL UNION CONFLICTS POSE A THREAT

Villaraigosa's election to the mayoralty was a major achievement. It was the main reason why the *Los Angeles Times* used the words "labor town" when it considered the results of the election in May 2005.[58] But there are good reasons for believing that this election may have been the high point of the Los Angeles labor movement's post-1990 upsurge. Soon afterward, a series of internal labor disputes, coupled with growing societal pressures, threatened to bring further union progress to a halt.

To make matters worse, the severe economic recession that began in 2008 unleashed a determined effort by corporations and anti-union conservatives to cut wages, lay off large numbers of workers, and undermine the collective bargaining rights of public employees. This campaign once more put the already weakened U.S. labor movement—including the Los Angeles County Federation of Labor—on the defensive.

The internal conflicts that erupted in the labor movement, both nationally and in Southern California, in the years following 2005 were both ideological and structural.

One key to the organizational success of the "new unionism" of the 1990s was the internal reforms initiated by SEIU and a number of other service and public employee unions. Besides spending more money on organizing and retraining staff members to emphasize the recruitment of new members instead of simply servicing existing contracts, the reforms included the consolidation of a large number of small union locals into much larger ones in order to bargain successfully with America's giant national corporations. "We call for . . . a massive refocusing of unions on growth," declared SEIU's aggressive and far-sighted union president, Andy Stern. He urged the national leaders of the AFL-CIO to reorganize their patchwork of small craft unions—and some industrial unions—into larger units, "so that workers who have strength can share it with others who do the same jobs."[59]

Given the rapid consolidation of ownership in California's hospital, supermarket, and hotel industries, SEIU's rationale for combining its smaller locals into large state or regionwide bargaining units made a great deal of sense. The trouble was that this amalgamation policy was largely imposed from above by the union's headquarters in Washington, D.C., instead of being negotiated at the level of the rank and file.

Consolidating SEIU's numerous small affiliates into giant, single-purpose locals with fifty thousand or more members also meant breaking up many existing multi-occupational locals and dismissing some locally elected officials. These changes may have made collective bargaining sense. But they offended many progressive union members and clashed with rank-and-file demands for local autonomy and union democracy. In January 2006, for example, SEIU's Washington leaders combined the fifty-five thousand members of Local 399 in Los Angeles County with six other California locals to create the largest health care union in the state. The merger was voted up in 2007, creating United Healthcare Workers West, which, with one hundred fifty thousand members, became the largest health care local in the nation.[60]

Despite its increased bargaining clout, United Healthcare Workers West was unpopular from the beginning. It was seen by many, if not most, of its affiliated members as bureaucratic, unwieldy, and uncaring. Rank-and-file members of the union, in both Los Angeles and San Francisco, argued that it would "threaten their democratic rights, diminish the quality of local representation, and make it difficult to hold leadership accountable."[61] In L.A., rank-and-file health care workers were also upset when SEIU official Annelle Grajeda was appointed, not elected, to run the giant local, and fifty longtime staffers were dismissed. In addition, United Healthcare Workers West was governed from Oakland, not Los Angeles. The idea was to free up staff members from representation duties so that they could concentrate on organizing new members. But Catherine Lefkowitz, a registered nurse at Kaiser Sunset, was only one of many critics who complained that the local's officers had lost touch with their members and ignored the needs of the rank and file. Since the merger, they complained, Annelle Grajeda had gone "from being our employee to our boss, and she reports only to [SEIU president] Andy Stern, not the members."[62]

Another controversial element in SEIU's reform philosophy was its abandonment of the AFL-CIO's traditional policy of adversarial unionism, which acknowledged inherent class differences of interest between workers and employers, in favor of what Stern called "value-added unionism." By this he meant that, in the current anti-union climate, unions would be more likely to succeed in winning improved pay and conditions if they proposed contracts that would also bring economic advantages to the employers, such as improvements in productivity or agreements not to challenge the workplace prerogatives of management. In the last fifteen years, SEIU has secured numerous contracts in its various divisions throughout the United States that reflect this philosophy. But in California, as elsewhere, these contracts have provoked opposition among rank-and-file union members who consider them too generous to the employers.[63]

For example, in 2006 Los Angeles health care workers expressed widespread indignation when SEIU negotiated an agreement with the California Nursing Home Association that outlawed strikes, permitted owners to choose which nursing homes could be unionized, and agreed not to damage the profitability of the homes. In exchange for wage and benefit improvements, the agreement even suggested that normally pro-union Democrats in the state legislature in Sacramento should vote against a bill that would have allowed patients to sue their nursing homes for inadequate care. Stern saw this agreement as an example of approaching the employers in a spirit of cooperation.[64] His opponents saw it as a sell-out or an example of class collaboration. Rose Ann Demoro, executive director of the California Nurses Association, expressed the anger of the rank and file at a press conference: "You can't be on the side of the public and on the side of the corporation at the same time."[65]

In May 2006, when Stern's critics in United Healthcare Workers West refused to back down over the amalgamation issue and the question of "value-added unionism," he placed the local under trusteeship, meaning that it lost the right to govern itself and instead was run from the national SEIU headquarters in Washington. Within days, a large minority of its members left and established the rival National Union of Healthcare Workers, led by Stern's former ally Sal Rosselli, with whom SEIU's international leadership battled over the loyalty of California's health care workers for several years.[66]

STRUCTURAL SPLIT BETWEEN THE AFL-CIO AND CHANGE TO WIN

These ideological quarrels inside California's unions were compounded by the structural split that took place between the leaders of traditional unionism inside the AFL-CIO and insurgents in SEIU and their allies in reform-oriented unions such as the International Brotherhood of Teamsters, the United Food and Commercial Workers, the Carpenters, the Laborers International Union, and UNITE-HERE.

During the 1990s and early 2000s, reformers in the national labor movement, led by Andy Stern and a number of other college-educated labor leaders such as John Wilhelm of HERE, lamented the parlous state of the AFL-CIO, whose numbers had fallen from 35 percent of the U.S. labor force in 1955 to 14 percent. They urged AFL-CIO president John Sweeney to recognize that unless sweeping reforms were undertaken, the federation would lose all of its remaining bargaining power. The reforms they advocated derived from the same set of ideas SEIU had adopted within its own nationwide jurisdiction. They included the need to compel small national unions with overlapping jurisdictions to consolidate into a much smaller number of occupationally distinct union blocs with greater bargaining power; to commit approximately $50 million to new organizing campaigns to slow down or halt the AFL-CIO's numerical decline; and to reassess labor's support for the Democratic Party. (The last of these suggestions was later abandoned.)[67]

These proposals were vigorously debated at the November 2005 AFL-CIO convention in Chicago. President Sweeney and several other members of the executive board expressed support for the reforms in principle but argued that they went too far, too fast. "Any attempt to dictate the merger of unions," stated one delegate, "would from the start be doomed to fail."[68] Other delegates pointed out that the AFL-CIO had come into being as a federation of independent trade unions and that attempts at coercion would undermine the sovereignty of many valuable—if small—craft unions. Still others argued that the AFL-CIO could not afford to devote such a large proportion of its income to new organizing campaigns without compromising its other activities.[69]

Acting on a threat that had been made public by several dissenting leaders before the 2005 convention took place, SEIU and three others among the above-named unions, joined later by several other organizations, seceded from the AFL-CIO after the convention was over and established Change to Win (CTW) as a rival trade union federation.[70]

Predictably, this split brought consternation to the national labor movement and inflicted considerable damage both in Southern California and around the country. In theory, the split placed all seven of CTW's affiliated national unions outside the bounds of the official labor movement, which prevented them from participating in the national councils of the AFL-CIO. It also divided the national labor movement at a moment of critical weakness, opened up unions in both federations to employer manipulation, and exposed them to the danger that unions in one of the rival federations would try to raid members from unions in the other.

In Los Angeles, where secessionist locals joining Change to Win made up about 40 percent of total union membership, Miguel Contreras tried to prevent conflict from developing between the two groups by negotiating an understanding with local CTW leaders before the split actually occurred. But his efforts were vetoed by Sweeney.[71] To the relief of many observers, however, most of the L.A. local unions in Change to Win continued to collaborate with the AFL-CIO–affiliated Los Angeles County Federation of Labor on many issues. The two federations also worked together on electoral politics, and both sides spent large sums of money helping to elect President Barack Obama in the fall of 2008.[72]

Nevertheless, the division into two separate federations raised numerous organizational problems, including duplication of effort. The split also threatened to complicate organized labor's relations both with employers and with the city, state, and federal governments. The results in the following years were numerous inter-union and intraunion conflicts, the diversion of valuable time and resources from new organizing campaigns, and the threat of employers playing one set of unions off against the other.[73]

In Los Angeles, perhaps the most serious intraunion conflict was the one that erupted in 2009 between the two halves of the merged union UNITE-HERE. UNITE was made up of garment workers locals that had formerly belonged to the Amalgamated Clothing Workers and the ILGWU, whereas HERE consisted of hotel and restaurant employees. Although UNITE-HERE reaffiliated with the AFL-CIO as a single union during the course of that year, the two sides of the union quarreled over organizing tactics and the expenditure of funds, and increasingly serious differences persisted.[74]

For grassroots activists in Southern California, this quarrel, along with the internal battles of SEIU, was an especially bitter blow. The successes of HERE Local 11 in the hotel industry, the victories won by Justice for Janitors, and the role of former ILGWU members in developing the core ideas of social justice unionism had given them some of their proudest moments. But here were the leaders of all three unions, who had united behind the 1990s upsurge, engaged in internecine conflict. "For people who believe in the American labor movement," wrote one observer, "and who've seen the positive changes that these unions have made in the lives of their members, watching this battle unfold is like watching two good friends caught up in a vicious divorce."[75]

CONCLUSION: AN UNCERTAIN FUTURE

These interunion conflicts are not the only problems Los Angeles workers have faced in recent years. They have had to cope with lost jobs, declining family income, the threat of layoffs by L.A. city government, increasing attacks on public employee unions, and a wide variety of burdens imposed by the severe economic crisis.

Some progress, to be sure, has been made. As a result of determined efforts by UNITE-HERE and other unions, Las Vegas now has the largest concentration of unionized hotel and restaurant employees in the country.[76] In 2006 SEIU succeeded in organizing four thousand African American security guards into Security Officers United in Los Angeles (SOULA). In the last couple of years, a number of informal support groups have also been established among new groups of immigrant workers, such as the Los Angeles Taxi Workers Alliance, the Los Angeles Car Wash Campaign, and the Pilipino Workers Center.[77] In Hollywood, the Writers Guild of America recently secured one of the best contracts it had obtained in years. Against that, though, one must set the growing number of films that have been made in nonunion settings outside the United States.[78]

Perhaps most encouraging, the conflict between the AFL-CIO and Change to Win has faded into the background. Although no formal reconciliation has occurred, Andy Stern has resigned as head of SEIU and has been replaced by Mary Kay Henry, who has tried to negotiate an end to the conflict between United Healthcare Workers West and the National Union of Healthcare Workers.[79]

The labor-Latino political alliance has also retained most of its clout at the ballot box, although as L.A.'s budget woes mount, Mayor Antonio Villaraigosa has come into increasing conflict with municipal unions representing such groups as firefighters and engineers. To the chagrin of the United Teachers of Los Angeles, Villaraigosa also took the side of education critics who favor using standardized school test results as a criterion for the promotion and dismissal of teachers.[80]

Other serious problems remain. For example, despite some desultory efforts, the vast majority of high-tech workers in the electronics industry remain unorganized, even though most of its female employees have the same ethno-racial background as the Latino and Asian service workers employed downtown, who readily joined up with SEIU.[81] Still more disturbing is that the new culture of organizing promulgated by SEIU and its allies has not yet spread from the service unions to more established unions such as the International Association of Machinists, the Operating Engineers, or those in the building trades. Most of these older unions operate in the private sector of the Los Angeles economy, which has sustained major union losses in recent years. Some of them are demoralized. But unless these older unions, which still account for about a third of the membership of the L.A. County Federation of Labor, devote more money to enrolling new members, the numerical gains won by the immigrant-based service unions could be undercut. Gains made on the roundabouts can very easily be lost on the swings.

The most serious example of this imbalance between public and private sector organizing is that no attempt has yet been made to compensate for the 1996 defeat of the Los Angeles Manufacturing Action Project (LAMAP). This was one of the few efforts the LACFL has so far made to organize the huge pool of blue-collar workers now employed in the old industrial zone along the Alameda corridor. The employees there are no longer well-paid white union members working in auto and steel. Rather, they are low-wage Latinos employed in tortilla plants, warehouses, food packaging sheds, and other light manufacturing outlets. In 1996 Peter Olney and other labor organizers established an interunion organizing committee composed of leaders drawn from the UAW, the Machinists, the Teamsters, and other industrial unions on the model of the old CIO.[82] The idea was to attempt to reunionize this traditional union area. But LAMAP collapsed when several of the contributing unions disagreed over jurisdiction issues, quarreling about which unions the newly recruited workers should join. Ominously, this refusal to compromise jurisdictional sovereignty in support of a common goal reflected the same parochialism and insularity that had earlier plagued the U.S. labor movement.[83]

As if these internal problems were not enough, in the last few years the nation's public employee unions—the one area where labor is still strong—have also been attacked from the outside. The loss of tax revenues resulting from the current recession has led to a public backlash and to demands that union members pay a higher proportion of the costs associated with their pensions and other benefits. In Wisconsin these demands have even led to the cancelation of public employee collective bargaining rights, and similar measures are being proposed in other states.[84]

In Los Angeles, at the time of this writing, the situation has not yet become that dire. But the struggle to prevent lay-offs among teachers and other city employees has diverted attention from organizing new union members, created growing tensions between the LACLF and Mayor Villaraigosa (who has lost his reputation as a pro-labor mayor), and further stalled the hoped-for recovery of the L.A. labor movement.

It is of course possible that these internal conflicts will soon be resolved and that the L.A. movement will continue to grow and even provide an example for the rest of the country to follow. But it is increasingly difficult to remain optimistic. Luckily, prediction is not part of the historian's task. But evaluation of the past is. The final section of this book returns to some of the generalizations made in the Introduction about the peculiar structural, ethno-racial, and cultural attributes of Los Angeles and examines how valid they remain in light of the historical narrative that has intervened.

Conclusion

Comparative Reflections

This volume has described both the strengths and the weaknesses of the Los Angeles labor movement over the years. Though its strengths were many, it is indisputable that for much of its history unions in Southern California were relatively weak in comparison to those in America's other great industrial cities. To what extent did this relative weakness result from obstacles faced by the entire U.S. labor movement, and to what extent did it result from features that were special to Los Angeles?

This concluding section argues that both sources of weakness were involved, though to varying degrees. Although more research needs to be done before any definite conclusions can be drawn about the supposed "exceptionalism" at work in Los Angeles,[1] this section examines both the "internal" and "external" reasons for the historic weakness of L.A. labor and illustrates them by referring to three other cities where the labor movement has always been stronger: San Francisco, Chicago, and Detroit.

.   .   .

The open shop lobby was undoubtedly a significant force in inhibiting the rise of unions in Southern California. The first two chapters of this book showed that while, in theory, General Harrison Otis and the Merchants and Manufacturers Association claimed they allowed their workers to choose whether or not to join a union, in practice they did no such thing, frequently firing union supporters and organizers at will. They used the open shop to prevent unions from gaining a major foothold in the city, with considerable success.

The open shop movement was not, of course, confined to Los Angeles. But in most of the United States, it was powerful only from about 1903, when the National Association of Manufacturers (NAM) took up the cause, to the mid-1920s.[2] In Los Angeles, by contrast, the open shop lobby kept unions at bay from the 1890s until the mid-1930s—a period of forty years. Not until the New Deal came along and a decisive shift occurred in Southern California, from small-scale production for local markets to large-scale industrial production for a national market, were the open shop policies of the M&M overcome.

In addition to General Otis's personal commitment, the open shop movement in Los Angeles drew its particular force from three sources. One was the bombing of the *Los Angeles Times* building in 1910, which reinforced the image of trade unionists as violent anarchists who had no respect for the law. The second was the long-standing subservience of the L.A. Police Department to the business elite. Judicial corruption was common in U.S. political life during the Gilded Age. But the circumstances in which the LAPD was founded may help to explain its repressive and violent behavior. It was established in 1877, a time when Los Angeles, unlike eastern cities, was a "wide open" frontier town, still subject to raids from Mexican "banditos" and other marauders.[3] These origins helped consolidate the LAPD's militaristic form of organization and its greater willingness to follow repressive policies, in comparison to the police in many other cities.

The third source, which is less frequently mentioned, was the complicity of the Los Angeles court system with the open shop movement and business interests. Such complicity was much less marked in San Francisco, where the unions were much more powerful. Throughout the period when the Union Labor Party was in power in that city (1902–1911), and for some time afterward, the San Francisco police force remained relatively neutral during strikes. It arrested strikers when they were disorderly or violent, but it did not escort strikebreakers across picket lines and into struck premises, and it denied gun permits to company guards. In L.A., however, the courts regularly granted employer requests for regular or special police protection. Equally important, in San Francisco business owners frequently applied to the courts for injunctions to prevent their employees from striking, whereas in Los Angeles employers made surprisingly little use of court injunctions. This was not because the Southern California courts were unwilling to grant them, but because the unions in that region were so weak that employers did not need court orders to get their way.[4]

Despite these differences, it would be misleading to suggest that the influence of the open shop lobby was confined to Los Angeles alone. In the mid-1920s the open shop movement was almost as powerful in a number of other areas as it was in Southern California. For example, New York State had more than fifty open shop associations, Massachusetts had eighteen, and Illinois forty-six.[5] In 1928 the Open Shop Committee of the NAM reported that as many as 81 percent of U.S. manufacturing workers were employed by open shop establishments.[6]

A sub-theme of state complicity in the employers' anti-union policies was the extensive use of red scare tactics to subdue the unions. This has led some to argue that anti-Communism played a more powerful role in the politics and culture of Southern California than it did elsewhere.[7] Red-baiting began with the fulminations of General Otis in the *Los Angeles Times*, picked up steam with the "brown scare" of 1916–1917 that accompanied the turmoil of the Mexican Revolution, and then escalated still further in 1919 and in the 1950s. The brown scare started the L.A. tradition of associating radical politics with racial minorities—especially Mexicans and African Americans—which has lasted to this day.[8]

Another special feature of anti-Communism in Southern California was the fear that L.A.'s most famous industry—moviemaking—would be taken over by Communists. Red-baiting was used against the radical supporters of the Screen Actors Guild and other Hollywood trade unionists as early as the 1930s, which is usually regarded as a liberal decade.[9] From the 1920s on, anti-Communism acquired the trappings of a civil religion not only in affluent Orange County and the San Fernando Valley but also in many of the city's white working-class neighborhoods. In a 1938 speech to the South Gate Kiwanis Club, for example, the club's president was already warning that Communism was a "serious peril to government" because it fomented "agitation among Negroes."[10] This speech, delivered fifteen years before the emergence of McCarthyism on the national scene, neatly elided racism with anti-Communism. This combination appealed to those in the Kiwanis Club audience who still cherished L.A. as America's "white spot," to be protected from all outside influences—including Communist-influenced African Americans.

Nevertheless, it cannot plausibly be suggested that using red scare tactics against organized labor was special to Southern California. Fear of conspiracy and hostility to foreign ideologies such as Marxism have been endemic in U.S. history ever since the American Revolution.[11] One has only to cite the hysteria that enveloped Chicago after the Haymarket riot of 1886 or the accusations of complicity in the Russian Revolution that were hurled by U.S. Steel against the Slavic immigrants who joined the great steel strike of 1919 to reject the idea that red-baiting was more extensively employed in Southern California than elsewhere.[12]

. . .

A better case can be made for four other factors as special—but not unique—explanations for the early weakness of the Los Angeles labor movement: the late arrival of smokestack industry, the fragmented character of the metropolis, the ethno-racial peculiarities of its labor force, and the ubiquity of its suburban values.

By 1930, 28 percent of L.A.'s workers were employed in manufacturing—the largest concentration found in any occupational classification in the city.[13] However, this transformation occurred almost three generations later than the industrialization of Chicago and Detroit. In 1920, when the industrial labor force in Los Angeles numbered only 106,000, Detroit already had a total of 286,000 blue-collar workers, with 83,000 of them employed in fourteen automobile plants, eleven metal rolling firms, eight chemical companies, and two other manufacturing firms.[14] Chicago's industrial development began even earlier: in 1873 it already had sixteen companies employing more than 275 workers each. By 1924 Chicago's eight largest firms employed no fewer than 370,000 workers, 94,000 of whom were unionized.[15] The Southern California trade union movement at that time counted only 13,000 workers in its ranks.[16] Thus, during the crucial formative years of the American labor movement, L.A.'s industrial proletariat (if one could call it that) was far smaller, and less militant, than its counterparts in the industrial cities to the east.

Because of L.A.'s early preoccupation with real estate, commerce, and home building rather than manufacturing, it has nearly always had a higher proportion of real estate, leisure, and clerical employees than blue-collar workers in its labor force. In 1970 white-collar employees, the vast majority of whom were nonunion, outnumbered blue-collar workers by a ratio of eight to six.[17] The fact that Los Angeles was still a sleepy cow town with a tiny manufacturing sector at the time of the Haymarket riot (1886) and the Pullman strike (1894) in Chicago not only guaranteed that the CIO—which was the real driver of union militancy in the 1930s—would be much smaller in Southern California than in the great cities of the industrial Midwest. It also meant that, until the recent immigrant-based union movement, L.A.'s manufacturing workers lacked a strong tradition of working-class sacrifice and solidarity to draw upon for inspiration and support.

As Eric Hobsbawm puts it: "Shared traditions of success or failure, such as occurred in [British] miners' strikes in the nineteenth and early twentieth centuries, are essential to the development of class consciousness that is more than skin-deep."[18] For many years after the Haymarket affair, when a group of anarchists were wrongly condemned to death for throwing a bomb at the Chicago police during a labor rally, hundreds of labor activists made annual visits to Waldheim Cemetery, where the Haymarket martyrs are buried.[19] In fact, so powerful a symbol of class injustice did Haymarket become that it resonated beyond America's shores. In an article published several years later, José Martí, the Cuban poet and revolutionist, wrote: "An enormous event took place in Chicago, but even more enormous was its inspiration to revolutionaries throughout the world."[20] What did L.A.'s white workers have to look back on as a source of inspiration for the future? A small plaque erected in San Pedro to Dick Parker, the young longshoreman shot during the 1934 strike. It is almost never visited.

Numerous writers, most notably Robert Fogelson, have commented on the fragmented character of Los Angeles as a postmodern metropolis.[21] But few have seen it as a source of labor weakness. Since World War II, several other "sunbelt" cities, such as San Jose, Phoenix, and Houston, have emerged with some of the same ecological characteristics as Los Angeles.[22] But during the formative years of the labor movement, between 1890 and 1938, L.A.'s urban sprawl—in which manufacturing zones leapfrogged over residential suburbs, cutting workers off from each other—was rare.

The fragmented metropolis argument has two elements, one cultural, the other geographic. Fogelson captures the cultural aspect when he describes the sense of isolation that recent arrivals—including many working-class migrants—often felt when they settled in one of L.A.'s spread-out suburbs. "Why, I don't even know the name of my next-door neighbor," one interviewee stated.[23] Citing the exceptional frequency with which Angelenos sold their homes to move to more desirable neighborhoods, Fogelson argues that "residential mobility" stunted the development of "voluntary associations and neighborhood ties," an observation that clearly also applied to trade unions.[24]

Since Fogelson published his book in 1967, the fragmentation argument has been subjected to criticism. Greg Hise, for example, has shown that many of the factory workers who lived in L.A.'s industrial suburbs in the 1920s and 1930s resided not in isolated housing developments but in purpose-built housing tracts located near their places of employment.[25] Becky Nicolaides has also demonstrated that new arrivals in places like South Gate helped each other construct their own self-built homes, thereby creating a viable sense of community.[26]

Nevertheless, both the geographic and cultural sides of the fragmented metropolis argument retain much of their explanatory power. In cultural terms, Ruth Milkman points out that Latino immigrants in the Los Angeles barrio live in more compact neighborhoods and are frequently more committed to community action than Anglo-American workers. "Among the native-born population," Milkman writes, "neighbors and co-workers rarely know one another well; transience, fragmentation, and instability are the norm. . . . In sharp contrast, vibrant ethnic social networks and tight-knit communities are thriving among the state's vast population of working-class Mexican and Central American immigrants."[27]

In addition, certain features of Los Angeles industrial geography are, if not unique, highly exceptional. As Fred Viehe has shown, the scattered nature of the oil fields in Southern California, which stretched all the way from Beverly Hills up to Kern County, Isolated the rouotabouts, machinists, and laborers who tended the oil rigs, making them difficult to organize.[28] The higher rate of automobile ownership among workers in Los Angeles compared to other cities and the large amount of territory covered by the Pacific Electric Railway (Red Car) system also loosened the urban fabric and extended the distance between home and work. In 1903 Henry E. Huntington, owner of the Pacific Electric system, boasted that his company, which was one of the city's largest employers, would never be unionized owing to the scattered nature of its workforce, which was divided up between car barns and depots all across the L.A. basin.[29]

Becky Nicolaides, despite acknowledging the mutual assistance that residents of the industrial suburbs offered each other, also points out that South Gate—the location of GM's biggest assembly plant—was not a physically compact community. In 1960, U.S. Census Bureau data showed that the vast majority of South Gate residents commuted to work by automobile or Red Car; nearly one-third of its residents worked in downtown Los Angeles. Unlike the hundreds—or even thousands—of workers who walked the half-mile or so from their homes to the steel mills in South Chicago or Homestead, Pennsylvania, only 5 percent of South Gate residents walked to work. "This diversity of work experience," Nicolaides concludes, "meant that no unified work-based culture dominated in South Gate. Instead, work—and unions—represented one realm among several that competed for the attention . . . of residents."[30]

The best evidence of how L.A.'s fragmented geography limited the growth of class solidarity is found by comparing the 1934 longshore strike in San Pedro with the same strike in more densely populated (and more liberal) San Francisco. This coastwide stoppage was one in which dockworkers in both places had the same goal—to end employer control over the "shape-up" hiring process. Complicating the dispute were conflicts over the need to create a single maritime union.[31]

During the 1934 strike, San Pedro's Local 13 was the only local of the coastwide longshoremen's union to vote to accept an interim settlement deemed inadequate by Harry Bridges and the radical leaders of the maritime unions in San Francisco and other West Coast cities, testimony that the leaders of the San Pedro local were more conservative than their Bay Area counterparts. More important, however, were the contrasting responses to the bloody confrontations that took place in both cities between strikers and the police, which resulted in workers being killed. Although these attacks generated outrage and support for the strikers in both locations, the response in San Pedro was focused in the local dockside community, whereas in San Francisco the dockworkers joined with other Bay Area workers in a citywide general strike.[32]

There were many reasons why San Pedro's longshoremen failed to follow San Francisco's example and declare a general strike in Los Angeles, including interunion conflict, hostility toward Communist influence in the dispute, and the refusal of the Central Labor Council to sanction such a walkout.[33] But it was not inconsequential that Long Beach/San Pedro Harbor was fifteen miles from downtown and that the strikers had little contact with the council's leaders. Although San Pedro itself was an occupational community whose residents were loyal to the strikers, it was surrounded by sparsely settled residential suburbs whose citizens most emphatically were not. At the height of the strike, when Local 13 was desperately battling against the police and company thugs, union militants in San Pedro complained that the downtown labor leadership "did not back us up because they had no real idea of what was going on."[34]

In San Francisco, by contrast, the waterfront zone was an organic part of the densely populated South of Market area, where not only the entire maritime labor force but many of the city's other workers—skilled German craftsmen, tough Irish teamsters, Swedish sailors, Filipino hotel workers, and common laborers of many nationalities—all lived and worked together in the same neighborhood. As one historian puts it, because they saw (or overheard) the maritime workers being beaten up by the police, "most of the city's work force joined in the three-day General Strike."[35] Here, surely, is convincing proof of the relevance of the fragmented metropolis argument in explaining the overall weakness of Los Angeles labor in its early years.

A third special factor influencing labor organization in Los Angeles has been the ethno-racial character of the city's labor force. In the 1920s and 1930s, large numbers of rural midwesterners, along with migrants from Oklahoma and the Southwest, moved north to cities like Chicago and Detroit, just as they traveled west to L.A.[36] But there were at least two major differences between the labor force in these two midwestern cities and the workers in Southern California. One was that L.A. lacked a large cadre of poor African American workers, a group who played a vital role in the development of a mass labor movement in Chicago and Detroit.[37]

Most early black migrants to Los Angeles came from the urban South, not its rural hinterland. They were better educated than the former sharecroppers who moved to Chicago and Detroit, and quite a few of them were middle class. In 1910, a striking 36 percent of L.A.'s black families were homeowners—one of the highest percentages of African American homeownership in the nation. Like some of the white migrants from the rural Midwest, many African Americans saw moving to Los Angeles, where segregation at first was limited, as an act of self-redemption from the poverty and stigma of second-class citizenship.[38]

The advantages they enjoyed can easily be exaggerated. One has only to recall the racial housing covenants that trapped African American residents in the Central Avenue area after World War I, or the discrimination Chester Himes encountered when he tried to get a factory job during World War II, to realize that many of the supposed advantages African Americans gained by moving to Los Angeles were illusory rather than real. Nevertheless, historian Douglas Flamming makes an important point when he writes: "Black Angelenos experienced no 'proletarianization'—no shift from farmwork to factory labor—such as that experienced by many blacks who followed the Great Migration north."[39]

These differences contributed to the emergence of a mass (or a radical) labor movement in Detroit—and to the lack of such a development in Los Angeles. In the 1960s, both cities experienced widespread rioting in African American neighborhoods, Watts in 1965, Detroit in 1967. The causes of both riots were similar: anger in the black community over police violence, bad housing, unemployment, and white privilege.[40] But the African American population in Detroit was far larger, far more individuals were from poverty-stricken backgrounds on the lower rung of the class ladder, and far more workers were likely to have been employed in the automobile industry than in South L.A. The implications of these differences for labor emerged in 1968, when four thousand black workers at the Dodge Main plant in Detroit established the Dodge Revolutionary Union Movement (DRUM) to protest the UAW's inattention to race. In 1969 DRUM united with dissidents from other Detroit auto plants to create the League of Revolutionary Black Workers, which was committed to "waging a relentless struggle against racism, capitalism, and imperialism."[41] No such radical black caucus, as a left wing of labor, emerged from the General Motors plant in South Gate, or from any of L.A.'s other manufacturing plants.

Another contrast could be seen in the behavior of white workers in L.A. and Detroit who fled their damaged neighborhoods after the riots to live in the suburbs. The white workers who left Watts for places like Long Beach generally did well, and in some cases experienced upward mobility: in a sample of thirty-four white residents who left Watts for the suburbs in the late sixties, seventeen became owners of small businesses, garage owners, or well-paid machinists in L.A.'s burgeoning aircraft industry. The majority of white workers who left downtown Detroit, on the other hand, continued to work in the auto plants. "You can't think of getting out of the shop," said one. "You've got family responsibilities, and they come first."[42] Unlike many of their L.A. counterparts, these Detroit workers remained firmly attached to the working class.

Another distinguishing feature of blue-collar workers in L.A. was the relative absence of the thousands of Irish, German, and Eastern European immigrants who flocked to the factories in cities like Pittsburgh, Detroit, and Chicago between 1880 and 1924 and who provided the building blocks for both the AFL and the CIO.[43] This difference in part reflected the distance between Los Angeles and the East Coast ports where European immigrants landed, but it was also a result of the much smaller size of L.A.'s manufacturing base. Only the longshoremen who arrived to labor on the San Pedro docks and the Jewish employees who moved west to work in the garment industry appeared to fill the same roles on the West Coast that they had in the East.[44] It was Dutch-English immigrants like Samuel Gompers and Germans like Adolph Strasser of the Cigarmakers who built the AFL in the 1880s and 1890s. Similarly it was Irish leaders like Mike Quill, Jewish refugees like Rose Pesotta, and Yorkshire-born miners like John Brophy who built up the CIO.[45] All of these individuals, at some point in their lives, had firsthand experience of a European class system that was far more rigid, and far more unjust, than the class system in America.

In the 1930s and 1940s, almost none of L.A.'s labor leaders came from a similarly class-conscious European background. Most of them were native-born Americans or migrants from small towns in the Midwest. There is, of course, a strong tradition of indigenous American unionism, manifested in the Knights of Labor and other nineteenth-century labor organizations, which had its followers in Los Angeles, just as it did elsewhere.[46] But without the aid of African Americans and European immigrants, the AFL-CIO would never have built the level of mass support that it secured at its height in the mid-twentieth century.

It is true that the Latinos who led the 1990s trade union upsurge in Los Angeles in the 1990s, whose radical heritage derived from the Mexican Revolution and

Central American political struggles, have frequently acted as a "substitute proletariat" in place of the absent Europeans.[47] They have acted as a catalyst for union militancy since the time of the tracklayers strike in 1903, and in recent years they have come to dominate a significant portion of the city's labor movement.[48] But in the formative years of the L.A. labor movement, Latino workers were few in number, and they were shunned by the white leadership. By the time they became influential in the life of Southern California unions, the halcyon days of the AFL-CIO were long since over.

A final, idiosyncratic feature of L.A.'s civic culture was the peculiar mixture of possessive individualism, moral evangelism, and fixation on suburban privacy that characterized much of the city's settler class. None of those attributes was unique to Los Angeles. But all of them, in one way or another, were antithetical to the collectivist ideas underlying the philosophy of trade unionism. Especially during the period of white domination and Southern racial influence, between 1890 and 1936—which was also the gestation period of the modern labor movement—these values appear to have permeated the entire community, including many of its workers, more completely than they did in most of America's other great industrial cities.

. . .

Is it too late for America's first- and second-generation Latino workers, together with their Asian, African American, and white allies, to drag the U.S. labor movement back from the brink? Today they are forced to operate in a political climate that is far more hostile to organized labor than the one workers faced in the 1930s. Over the last fifteen years, L.A.'s newly energized service workers have certainly given it a try. Or has history, perhaps, passed the trade union movement by? For the sake of America's working families, I certainly hope not. We must wait and see.

NOTES

INTRODUCTION

1. *Los Angeles Times,* August 17, 2011, A14.

2. See, for example, Mark Wild, *Street Meeting: Multiethnic Neighborhoods in Early Twentieth-Century Los Angeles* (Berkeley: University of California Press, 2005); William David Estrada, *The Los Angeles Plaza: Sacred and Contested Space* (Austin: University of Texas Press, 2008); Raphael J. Sonenshein, *Politics in Black and White: Race and Power in Los Angeles* (Princeton, N.J.: Princeton University Press, 1993); and Nora Hamilton and Norma Stoltz Chinchilla, *Seeking Community in a Global City: Guatemalans and Salvadorans in Los Angeles* (Philadelphia: Temple University Press, 2001).

3. For a book that describes the current negative attitudes toward unions, see Lawrence Richards, *Union-Free America: Workers and Antiunion Culture* (Urbana: University of Illinois Press, 2008).

4. Ruth Milkman, *L.A. Story: Immigrant Workers and the Future of the U.S. Labor Movement* (New York: Russell Sage Foundation, 2006). See also Ruth Milkman, Joshua Bloom, and Victor Narro, eds., *Working for Justice: The L.A. Model of Organizing and Advocacy* (Ithaca, N.Y.: ILR/Cornell University Press, 2010).

5. See Susan Garea and Sasha Alexandra Stern, "From Legal Advocacy to Organizing: Progressive Lawyering and the Los Angeles Car Wash Campaign," in Milkman, Bloom, and Narro, *Working for Justice,* 125–140.

6. See, for example, the account in Sonenshein, *Politics in Black and White,* passim.

7. Readers looking for additional historical detail on workers, industries, and

occupations should consult works such as Grace Heilman Stimson, *Rise of the Labor Movement in Los Angeles* (Berkeley: University of California Press, 1955); and Louis B. Perry and Richard S. Perry, *A History of the Los Angeles Labor Movement, 1911–1941* (Berkeley: University of California Press, 1963). Detailed studies of the more recent period include Milkman, *L.A. Story;* Milkman, Bloom, and Narro, *Working for Justice;* and Robert Gottlieb, Mark Vallianatos, Regina M. Freer, and Peter Dreier, *The Next Los Angeles: The Struggle for a Livable City* (Berkeley: University of California Press, 2005).

8. For an analysis of the impact of global restructuring and the role of Pacific Rim migration on L.A.'s garment manufacturing and other exportable industries, see Marta Lopéz-Garza and David R. Diaz, eds., *Asian and Latino Immigrants in a Restructuring Economy: The Metamorphosis of Southern California* (Stanford, Calif.: Stanford University Press, 2001).

9. These "Rosie the Riveter" women of the aircraft industry constituted the largest number of female factory workers employed in one industry up to that time. The best book about them is Sherna Berger Gluck, *Rosie the Riveter Revisited: Women, the War, and Social Change* (New York: New American Library, 1987).

10. On the topic of electronics workers employed by the maquiladoras on the Mexican border, see Emilio Pradilla Cobos, "The Limits of the Mexican Maquiladora Industry," *Review of Radical Political Economics* 25, no. 4 (1993): 91–105.

11. For the early development of the Hollywood film industry, see Mae D. Huettig, *Economic Control of the Motion Picture Industry: A Study in Industrial Organization* (Philadelphia: University of Pennsylvania Press, 1944).

12. On the economic growth of Orange County, see Rob Kling, Spencer Olin, and Mark Poster, eds., *Postsuburban California: The Transformation of Orange County since World War II* (Berkeley: University of California Press, 1991).

13. For a study of the development of the electronics industry in the Los Angeles suburbs, see Allen J. Scott, *Technopolis: High-Technology Industry and Regional Development in Southern California* (Berkeley: University of California Press, 1993).

14. See, especially, the preface in Kevin Starr, *Coast of Dreams: California on the Edge, 1990–2003* (New York: Vintage Books, 2006), x-xii.

15. Mike Davis, *City of Quartz: Excavating the Future in Los Angeles* (New York: Vintage Books, 1992); and Mike Davis, *Ecology of Fear: Los Angeles and the Imagination of Disaster* (London: Picador, 1999). See also Peter Schrag, *Paradise Lost: California's Experience, America's Future* (Berkeley: University of California Press, 1998); and Jeremiah B. C. Axelrod, *Inventing Autopia: Dreams and Visions of the Modern Metropolis in Jazz Age Los Angeles* (Berkeley: University of California Press, 2009).

16. For the "L.A. school" of urban historians, see Allen J. Scott and Edward J. Soja, eds., *The City: Los Angeles and Urban Theory at the End of the Twentieth Century* (Berkeley: University of California Press, 1996). For discussions of "Los Angeles

exceptionalism" by Carey McWilliams and others, see McWilliams, *California: The Great Exception* (Berkeley: University of California Press, 1999); Michael Kazin, "The Great Exception Revisited: Organized Labor and Politics in San Francisco and Los Angeles," *Pacific Historical Review* 55, no. 3 (August 1986): 371–402; and Robert A. Schneider et al., "Historicizing the City of Angels," symposium in *American Historical Review* 105, no. 5 (December 2000): 1668–1691.

CHAPTER ONE

1. A convenient summary of the findings of the Commission on Industrial Relations can be found in Graham Adams, *Age of Industrial Violence, 1910–1915: The Activities and Findings of the United States Commission on Industrial Relations* (New York: Columbia University Press, 1966).

2. William Alexander McClung, *Landscapes of Desire: Anglo Mythologies of Los Angeles* (Berkeley: University of California Press, 2000), chap. 1.

3. Ibid., 21–22. See also Peter Schrag, *Paradise Lost: California's Experience, America's Future* (Berkeley: University of California Press, 1998), chap. 1; and David Fine, *Imagining Los Angeles: A City in Fiction* (Albuquerque: University of New Mexico Press, 2000), passim.

4. The literature on Los Angeles boosterism is voluminous. A sampling includes Edna Monch Parker, "The Southern Pacific and Settlement in Southern California," *Pacific Historical Review* 6, no. 2 (June 1937): 103–199; Gloria Ricci Lothrop, "The Boom of the Eighties Revisited," *Southern California Quarterly* 75, nos. 3–4 (Fall/Winter 1993): 263–278; Glenn Dumke, "The Boom of the 1880s in Southern California," *Southern California Quarterly* 76, no. 1 (Spring 1994): 99–114; Tom Zimmerman, "Paradise Promoted: Boosterism and the Los Angeles Chamber of Commerce," *California History* 64, no. 1 (Winter 1985): 22–33; and William Deverell and Douglas Flamming, "Race, Rhetoric, and Regional Identity: Boosting Los Angeles, 1880–1930," in *Power and Place in the North American West*, ed. Richard White and John M. Finley (Seattle: University of Washington Press, 1999), 117–153.

5. Quoted in *Final Report and Testimony Submitted to the U.S. Commission on Industrial Relations*, 61st Cong., 1st sess. (Washington, D.C.: Government Printing Office, 1916), 5222.

6. Having taken advantage of the reduced, one-way "homeseeker" fares offered by Southern Pacific or other transcontinental railroad companies, migrants to Los Angeles were targeted by low-cost housing and finance companies such as the Los Angeles Investment Company or the Brady Janss Investment Company, who urged the migrants either to buy a home directly from them or to invest their savings with these companies until a down payment could be accumulated. Between the late 1890s and the depression of 1913–1914, hundreds of these companies were established in L.A., nourished by lenient state banking and finance laws. See Glenn S. Dumke, *The*

Boom of the Eighties in Southern California (San Marino, Calif.: Huntington Library, 1944); James M. Guinn, *A History of California and an Extended History of Los Angeles and Environs* (Los Angeles: Historic Record, 1915), vol. 2; *American Globe Investment Magazine* (Los Angeles) 8, no. 6 (April 1911); and Janss Investment Company, *A Short History of Los Angeles* (Los Angeles: Janss Investment Company, 1926).

7. *Final Report and Testimony*, U.S. Commission on Industrial Relations, 5228.

8. Ibid., 5244.

9. Ibid., 5501, 5706, 5860.

10. Ibid., 5227, 5245–5248, 5706, 5862–5863, 5868. For additional material on the numerical weakness of L.A.'s early unions and the failure of strikes, see California Bureau of Labor Statistics, *Twelfth Biennial Report, 1905–1906* (Sacramento: State Printing Office, 1907), 184–211. On relative wages, see U.S. Department of Commerce, *Earnings of Factory Workers, 1890–1927* (Washington, D.C.: Government Printing Office, 1929), 149–150 (table 68), 392 (table D).

11. Quoted in Deverell and Flamming, "Race, Rhetoric, and Regional Identity," 126.

12. On the appeal of L.A. to migrants of color, see Douglas Flamming, *Bound for Freedom: Black Los Angeles in Jim Crow America* (Berkeley: University of California Press, 2005), chap. 1; Peter La Chapelle, *Proud to Be an Okie: Cultural Politics, Country Music, and Migration to Southern California* (Berkeley: University of California Press, 2007), chap. 2; George Sánchez, *Becoming Mexican American: Ethnicity, Culture, and Identity in Chicano Los Angeles, 1900–1945* (New York: Oxford University Press, 1993), chap. 2.

13. Quoted in Leo Chavez, *Shadowed Lives: Undocumented Immigrants in American Society* (Fort Worth: Harcourt Brace Jovanovich, 1992), 36.

14. Reviewing the claims of more than twenty small cities vying to become the state capital of Kansas, a reporter for the *Kansas City Star* noted in 1857: "On paper, *all* these towns were magnificent. Their superbly lithographed maps adorned the walls of every place of resort. The stranger studying one of these fancied the New Babylon surpassed only by its namesake of old" (quoted in Daniel J. Boorstin, *The Americans: The National Experience* [New York: Vintage Books, 1965], 162). See also Charles N. Glaab, "Visions of Metropolis: William Gilpin and Theories of City Growth in the American West," *Wisconsin Magazine of History* 45 (1961): 21–35.

15. Robert M. Fogelson, *The Fragmented Metropolis: Los Angeles, 1850–1930* (Berkeley: University of California Press, 1993), chaps. 6, 11–12; Schrag, *Paradise Lost*, pt. 2; Martin Schiesl and Mark M. Dodge, eds., *City of Promise: Race and Historical Change in Los Angeles* (Claremont, Calif.: Regina Books, 2006).

16. Robert Gottlieb and Irene Wolt, *Thinking Big: The Story of the Los Angeles Times, Its Publishers, and Their Influence on Southern California* (New York: Putnam, 1977), chaps. 7–8.

17. William B. Friedricks, "Capital and Labor in Los Angeles: Henry E. Hun-

tington vs. Organized Labor, 1900–1920," *Pacific Historical Review* 59, no. 3 (August 1990): 375–395; Richard Connelly Miller, "Otis and His *Times:* The Career of Harrison Gray Otis of Los Angeles" (PhD diss., University of California, Los Angeles, 1961), passim. For an exposé of the illegal acts of the Merchants and Manufacturers Association, see U.S. Senate, "Employers Associations and Collective Bargaining in California," *Report of the Committee on Education and Labor, Subcommittee Investigating Violations of Free Speech and the Rights of Labor,* 78th Cong., 2nd sess. (Washington, D.C.: Government Printing Office, 1944), passim.

18. On the idea of a "usable past," meaning the legitimization of a favorable but sometimes fictional historical narrative, see Eric Hobsbawm and Terence Ranger, eds., *The Invention of Tradition* (Cambridge: Cambridge University Press, 1992).

19. Quoted in Greg Hise, "Industry and Imaginative Geographies," in *Metropolis in the Making: Los Angeles in the 1920s,* ed. Tom Sitton and William Deverell (Berkeley: University of California Press, 2001), 13.

20. Robert Alan Phelps, "Dangerous Class on the Plains of Id: Ideology and Home Ownership in Southern California, 1890–1920" (PhD diss., University of California, Riverside, 1996), 49. Carey McWilliams, among others, described the process by which Otis and his supporters undercut San Francisco's industrial supremacy. Their "only chance to establish Los Angeles as an industrial center," he wrote, "was to undercut the high wage structure of San Francisco, long a strongly unionized town." This was accomplished by attracting two streams of immigrants from the rural Midwest: "tourists to provide the capital and revenue," and "homeseekers to provide a pool of cheap labor." See Carey McWilliams, *Southern California: An Island on the Land* (Salt Lake City: Peregrine Smith Books, 1973), 274–276. See also Frank L. Beach, "The Transformation of California: The Effects of the Westward Movement on California's Growth and Development" (PhD diss., University of California, Berkeley, 1963), passim.

21. *First Annual Report of the Commission of Immigration and Housing in California,* pt. 4: *Housing* (Sacramento: State Printing Office, 1915), 228–229.

22. Ibid., 241.

23. Ibid., 250–251. This 1915 commission report also contained a detailed account of degraded housing conditions, poor sanitation, employment patterns, and inadequate schooling in the Macy Street District; for further details, see ibid., 228–255. Additional evidence of poor housing and poor health among Mexicans in East L.A. can be found in Sánchez, *Becoming Mexican American,* 78–83.

24. *First Annual Report of the Commission of Immigration and Housing,* 243.

25. Phelps, "Dangerous Class," 124–130.

26. Ibid., 132–133.

27. Quoted in Marco R. Newmark, "La Fiesta de Los Angeles of 1894," *Historical Society of Southern California Quarterly* 29 (March 1947): 103.

28. Fogelson, *Fragmented Metropolis*, 76–77.

29. William Deverell, *Whitewashed Adobe: The Rise of Los Angeles and the Remaking of Its Mexican Past* (Berkeley: University of California Press, 2004), chap. 2. See also Norman M. Klein, *The History of Forgetting: Los Angeles and the Erasure of Memory* (New York: Verso, 2008), chap. 1.

30. Mark Wild, *Street Meeting: Multiethnic Neighborhoods in Early Twentieth-Century Los Angeles* (Berkeley: University of California Press, 2005), passim.

31. William David Estrada, *The Los Angeles Plaza: Sacred and Contested Space* (Austin: University of Texas Press, 2008), chap. 4.

32. Wild, *Street Meeting*, 26.

33. For a compelling account of the racialization of California's minorities, see Tomas Almaguer, *Racial Fault Lines: The Historical Origins of White Supremacy in California* (Berkeley: University of California Press, 1994).

34. *Final Report and Testimony, U.S. Commission on Industrial Relations*, 5896. Also see the account in the *Los Angeles Citizen*, April 14, 1914, 4.

35. Quoted in *Final Report and Testimony, U.S. Commission on Industrial Relations*, 5565.

36. Quoted in ibid., 5586.

37. For a discussion of male attitudes toward women working outside the home, women's wages, and equal pay for equal work during this period, see Alice Kessler-Harris, *In Pursuit of Equity: Women, Men, and the Quest for Economic Citizenship in 20th-Century America* (New York: Oxford University Press, 2001), passim.

38. Judith Raftery, "Los Angeles Club Women and Progressive Reform," in *California Progressivism Revisited*, ed. William Deverell and Tom Sitton (Berkeley: University of California Press, 1994), 158–164.

39. Sherry Katz, "Frances Nacke Noel and 'Sister Movements': Socialism, Feminism, and Trade Unionism in Los Angeles, 1909–1916," *California History* 67, no. 3 (September 1988): 181–208.

40. *Final Report and Testimony, U.S. Commission on Industrial Relations*, 5720.

41. Ibid.

42. Quoted in ibid., 5722.

43. Quoted in Zimmerman, "Paradise Promoted," 29.

44. Quoted in Gottlieb and Wolt, *Thinking Big*, 32.

45. Grace Heilman Stimson, *Rise of the Labor Movement in Los Angeles* (Berkeley: University of California Press, 1955), 38. For other accounts of General Otis's life and times, see Gottlieb and Wolt, *Thinking Big*, chaps. 1–6; Errol Wayne Stevens, *Radical L.A.: From Coxey's Army to the Watts Riots, 1894–1965* (Norman: University of Oklahoma Press, 2009), 36–39; and Miller, "Otis and His *Times*," passim.

46. For an analysis of how the attitudes of business and government toward trade union rights evolved in the late nineteenth and early twentieth centuries, see Bruno

Ramirez, *When Workers Fight: The Politics of Industrial Relations in the Progressive Era, 1898–1916* (Westport, Conn.: Greenwood Press, 1978).

47. Quoted in Gottlieb and Wolt, *Thinking Big*, 44.

48. Quoted in ibid., 36.

49. Ibid. See also "Mr. Otis and the *Los Angeles Times*," pamphlet published by the International Typographical Union in 1915, 5–6, file 25, box 209, *Los Angeles Times Company Records*, Huntington Library, San Marino, Calif.

50. Grace Stimson notes that when Local 174 was first established in 1874, it held a "typographical ball," which "attracted prominent citizens who made it a fashionable event in the social season." This language reflects the relatively high social status of skilled typesetters in the mid-Victorian age. See Stimson, *Rise of the Labor Movement*, 33.

51. Jeffrey D. Stansbury, "Organized Workers and the Making of Los Angeles, 1890–1915" (PhD diss., University of California, Los Angeles, 2008), 214–221.

52. Stimson, *Rise of the Labor Movement*, 250–252; Gottlieb and Wolt, *Thinking Big*, 42–43.

53. Quoted in Stimson, *Rise of the Labor Movement*, 73.

54. Ibid.

55. Louis B. Perry and Richard S. Perry, *A History of the Los Angeles Labor Movement, 1911–1941* (Berkeley: University of California Press, 1963), 140–144.

56. Ibid., 140.

57. Harrison Otis to Henry E. Huntington, May 2, 1904, box 125, Henry E. Huntington Collection, Huntington Library, San Marino, Calif. See also Gottlieb and Wolt, *Thinking Big*, 66–70.

58. Otis to Huntington, April 5, 1905, box 125, Huntington Collection. For the influence of the Progressives on Los Angeles city politics, see Tom Sitton, *John Randolph Haynes: California Progressive* (Stanford, Calif.: Stanford University Press, 1992).

59. William B. Friedricks, *Henry Huntington and the Creation of Southern California* (Columbus: Ohio State University Press, 1992), chaps. 2–4.

60. Ibid., 328. See also William B. Friedricks, "Henry E. Huntington and Real Estate Development in Southern California, 1898–1917," *Southern California Quarterly* 71, nos. 2–3 (Summer/Fall 1989): 327–340.

61. Patricia Ray Adler, "Watts: From Suburb to Black Ghetto" (PhD diss., University of Southern California, 1977), 68–69; Becky M. Nicolaides, "'Where the Working Man Is Welcomed': Working-Class Suburbs in Los Angeles, 1900–1940," *Pacific Historical Review* 68, no. 4 (November 1999): 543–545.

62. Friedricks, *Henry Huntington*, 328.

63. Quoted in Friedricks, "Capital and Labor in Los Angeles," 378. See also William N. Ray, "Crusade or Civil War? The Pullman Strike in California," *California History* 58, no. 1 (Spring 1979): 20–37.

64. Friedricks, "Capital and Labor in Los Angeles," 380–382.

65. Otis to Huntington, January 8, 1903, box 165, Huntington Collection.

66. Ibid.

67. Quoted in Spencer Crump, *Ride the Big Red Cars: How Trolleys Helped Build Southern California* (Glendale, Calif.: Anglo-American Books, 1983), 63.

68. Friedricks, "Capital and Labor in Los Angeles," 382. On company welfare programs generally, see Stuart D. Brandes, *American Welfare Capitalism, 1880–1940* (Chicago: University of Chicago Press, 1976); and Gerald Zahavi, "Negotiated Loyalty: Welfare Capitalism and the Shoemakers of Endicott Johnson, 1920–1940," *Journal of American History* 71, no. 3 (Fall 1977): 602–620.

69. Quoted in Friedricks, "Capital and Labor in Los Angeles," 384.

70. For Henry Ford's discriminatory welfare benefit system, see Stephen Meyer, *The Five Dollar Day: Labor Management and Social Control in the Ford Motor Company, 1908–1921* (Albany, N.Y.: SUNY Press, 1981).

71. Quoted in Daniel Jon Johnson, "A Serpent in the Garden: Institutions, Ideology, and Class in Los Angeles Politics, 1901–1911" (PhD diss., University of California, Los Angeles, 1996), 88.

72. Ibid., 84–90.

73. See the following essays in Deverell and Sitton, *California Progressivism Revisited:* Sherry Katz, "Socialist Women and Progressive Reform," 117–143; Judith Raftery, "Los Angeles Club Women and Progressive Reform," 144–174; and Mary Odem, "City Mothers and Delinquent Daughters: Female Juvenile Justice Reform in Early Twentieth Century Los Angeles," 175–202.

74. Quoted in Johnson, "A Serpent in the Garden," 86.

75. Stimson, *Rise of the Labor Movement,* 184–186.

76. Stevens, *Radical L.A.,* 46–50; Stimson, *Rise of the Labor Movement,* 226–232.

77. Johnson, "A Serpent in the Garden," 163–184.

78. For a history of the strike, see Charles Wollenberg, "Working on 'El Traque': The Pacific Electric Strike of 1903," *Pacific Historical Review* 42, no. 3 (August 1973): 365.

79. Quoted in ibid., 365.

80. Ibid., 364–365.

81. Sánchez, *Becoming Mexican American,* chap. 1. On Mexican coal miners who joined the United Mine Workers of America, see Roberto R. Calderon, *Mexican Coal Mining Labor in Texas and Coahuila, 1880–1930* (College Station: Texas A&M University Press, 2000), passim. For information on Mexican metal miners and the Western Federation of Miners, see Carlos E. Cortes, *The Mexican Experience in Arizona* (New York: Arno Press, 1976), passim; and Manuel P. Servin and Robert L. Spude, "Historical Conditions of Early Mexican Labor in the United States: Arizona—A Neglected Story," *Journal of Mexican American History* 5 (1975): 44–56. For a description of the

circular migratory patterns of Mexican migrants, see Benny J. Andres, "Invisible Borders: Repatriation and Colonization of Mexican Migrant Workers along the California Borderlands during the 1930s," *California History* 88, no. 4 (2011): 5–21.

82. Quoted in Sánchez, *Becoming Mexican American*, 190.

83. Quoted in Victor S. Clark, "Mexican Labor in the United States," *Bulletin of the Bureau of Labor* 17, no. 77 (July 1908): 496.

84. Included in this tradition of resistance were so-called *mutualistas*, which were partly insurance societies and partly organizations for developing community solidarity. See Emilio Zamora, "Labor Formation, Community, and Politics: The Mexican Working Class in Texas, 1900–1945," in *Border Crossings: Mexican and Mexican-American Workers*, ed. John Mason Hart (Wilmington, Del: Scholarly Resources, 1998), 154–157.

85. In the first volume of his multivolume work on California, Kevin Starr mentions the Merchants and Manufacturers Association and the *Times* bombing of 1910, but he says almost nothing about unions or the life and labor of L.A.'s workers. See Starr, *Americans and the California Dream, 1850–1915* (New York: Oxford University Press, 1986), passim.

86. Huntington to Otis, December 3, 1902, box 9, Huntington Collection.

87. See Margaret Crawford, *Building the Workingman's Paradise: The Design of American Company Towns* (New York: Verso, 1995), 89–90.

88. Phelps, "Dangerous Class," 176–184.

89. Ibid., 194–204.

90. Ibid., 196–197.

91. For a study of the Union Oil Company's origins in Southern California, see Frank Taylor and Earl M. Welty, *Black Bonanza: How an Oil Hunt Grew into the Union Oil Company of California* (New York: Whittlesey House, 1980).

92. Crawford, *Building the Workingman's Paradise*, 90–91. See also Walter Willard, "Moving the Factory Back to the Land," *Sunset*, no. 30 (March 1913): 300–301; and Dana Bartlett, "An Industrial Garden City: Torrance," *American City*, no. 10 (October 1913): 308–314.

93. Robert Phelps, "The Search for a Modern Industrial City: Urban Planning, the Open Shop, and the Founding of Torrance, California," *Pacific Historical Review* 64, no. 4 (November 1998): 511–529.

94. Quoted in ibid., 530.

95. Quoted in Gottlieb and Wolt, *Thinking Big*, 50.

CHAPTER TWO

1. Howard Blum, *American Lightning: Terror, Mystery, Movie-Making, and the Crime of the Century* (New York: Crown, 2008), chap. 7.

2. *Los Angeles Times*, October 14, 1910, 2. For more on the *Times* bombing, see Robert Gottlieb and Irene Wolt, *Thinking Big: The Story of the* Los Angeles Times,

Its Publishers, and Their Influence on Southern California (New York: Putnam, 1977), chap. 5; and Sidney Fine, *"Without Blare of Trumpets": Walter Drew, the National Erectors' Association, and the Open Shop Movement, 1903–1957* (Ann Arbor: University of Michigan Press, 1995), chaps. 3–4.

3. For a discussion of the rise of the Socialist Party in Los Angeles, see Errol Wayne Stevens, *Radical L.A.: From Coxey's Army to the Watts Riots, 1894–1965* (Norman: University of Oklahoma Press, 2009), chap. 3; and Paul Greenstein, Nigey Lennon, and Lionel Rolfe, *Bread and Hyacinths: The Rise and Fall of Utopian Los Angeles* (Los Angeles: California Classic Books, 1992), 62–69.

4. For an introduction to the tensions that arose over the Owens Valley aqueduct project **and** the sale of land in the San Fernando Valley, see Catherine Mulholland, *William Mulholland and the Rise of Los Angeles* (Berkeley: University of California Press, 2000), chaps. 9–20.

5. Daniel Jon Johnson, "A Serpent in the Garden: Institutions, Ideology, and Class in Los Angeles Politics, 1901–1911" (PhD diss., University of California, Los Angeles, 1996), chap. 5.

6. Ibid., 244–255.

7. Quoted in Gottlieb and Wolt, *Thinking Big*, 86.

8. Quoted in Johnson, "A Serpent in the Garden," 245.

9. Quoted in ibid., 244.

10. Ibid.

11. Los Angeles City Council Minutes, vol. 76, June 15 and 22, 1908; July 6, 1908; August 3, 1908; archived at Los Angeles City Hall.

12. Ibid.

13. Los Angeles City Council Minutes, vol. 81, July 5, 12, and 19, 1910; August 23, 1910.

14. *Los Angeles Citizen,* January 18, 1915, 3.

15. Clark Davis, *Company Men: White-Collar Life and Corporate Cultures in Los Angeles, 1892–1941* (Baltimore: Johns Hopkins University Press, 2000), 127–128.

16. For further background on L.A. unions and strikes, see Grace Heilman Stimson, *Rise of the Labor Movement in Los Angeles* (Berkeley: University of California Press, 1955), chap. 18; Greenstein, Lennon, and Rolfe, *Bread and Hyacinths,* 32–42.

17. *Los Angeles Times,* January 4, 1904, 8.

18. Stimson, *Rise of the Labor Movement,* 114–115.

19. Quoted in *Los Angeles Record,* February 18, 1904, 3. See also Charles Wollenberg, "Working on 'El Traque': The Pacific Electric Strike of 1903," *Pacific Historical Review* 42, no. 3 (August 1973): 365.

20. Quoted in Thomas R. Clark, "The Limits of Liberty: Courts, Police, and Labor Unrest in California, 1890–1926" (PhD diss., University of California, Los Angeles, 1994), 415.

21. Stimson, *Rise of the Labor Movement*, 121.

22. Ibid., 298–299; *Report of the Proceedings of the Twenty-sixth Annual Convention of the American Federation of Labor*, Indianapolis, Indiana, 1907, 99–100, 321–322.

23. Stimson, *Rise of the Labor Movement*, 310–312; Clark, "The Limits of Liberty," 417–419.

24. Quoted in Stimson, *Rise of the Labor Movement*, 312.

25. Ibid.

26. Stevens, *Radical L.A.*, 46–48; Greenstein, Lennon, and Rolfe, *Bread and Hyacinths*, 37–38.

27. Stimson, *Rise of the Labor Movement*, 306–308.

28. Johnson, "A Serpent in the Garden," 308–309.

29. Quoted in ibid., 342.

30. Quoted in ibid., 374–375.

31. Ibid.

32. Mark Wild, *Street Meeting: Multiethnic Neighborhoods in Early Twentieth-Century Los Angeles* (Berkeley: University of California Press, 2005), 157.

33. Quoted in Johnson, "A Serpent in the Garden," 361.

34. Wild, *Street Meeting*, 157.

35. Tom Sitton, "John Randolph Haynes and the Left Wing of California Progressivism," in *California Progressivism Revisited*, ed. William Deverell and Tom Sitton (Berkeley: University of California Press, 1994), 17.

36. Johnson, "A Serpent in the Garden," 338.

37. *Los Angeles Express*, May 2, 1907, 4.

38. For an up-to-date treatment of the varieties of Progressivism in Los Angeles and California generally, see the essays in Deverell and Sitton, *California Progressivism Revisited*.

39. Stevens, *Radical L.A.*, 59–60.

40. Ibid.

41. David Montgomery, *Workers' Control in America: Studies in the History of Work, Technology, and Labor Struggles* (Cambridge: Cambridge University Press, 1979), 72.

42. John Laslett and Mary Tyler, *The ILGWU in Los Angeles, 1907–1988* (Inglewood, Calif.: Ten Star Press, 1989), 14; Luis Leobardo Arroyo, *Mexican Workers and American Unions: The Los Angeles AFL, 1890–1933* (Berkeley: Chicano Studies Library Publications, 1981), 13–19.

43. Johnson, "A Serpent in the Garden," 377.

44. Mulholland, *William Mulholland*, 162–167. See also William L. Kahrl, *Water and Power: The Conflict over Los Angeles' Water Supply in the Owens Valley* (Berkeley: University of California Press, 1977), passim.

45. Gottlieb and Wolt, *Thinking Big*, 131–143; Stevens, *Radical L.A.*, 60–62.

46. In May 1907, to quiet fears about his role, Mayor Harper asked General Otis

to repudiate rumors that were circulating about the syndicate's intentions. Otis replied that he had sold his share in January 1905 and thus was no longer part of the syndicate. In August 1906, however, a rival newspaper discredited this assertion. See Gottlieb and Wolt, *Thinking Big*, 136–137.

47. Mulholland, *William Mulholland*, chap. 18.

48. For a discussion of the culpability of the speculators who tried to siphon off aqueduct water to irrigate their land in the San Fernando Valley, see ibid.

49. Standard accounts of these events are contained in Stimson, *Rise of the Labor Movement*, chaps. 20–22; Michael Kazin, *Barons of Labor: The San Francisco Building Trades and Union Power in the Progressive Era* (Urbana: University of Illinois Press, 1989), 204–208; Herbert Shapiro, "The McNamara Case: A Window on Class Antagonism in the Progressive Era," *Southern California Quarterly* 70, no. 2 (Spring 1988): 69–89; James Kraft, "The Fall of Job Harriman's Socialist Party: Violence, Gender, and Politics in Los Angeles, 1911," *Southern California Quarterly* 70, no. 1 (Winter 1988): 43–57; and Fine, *"Without Blare of Trumpets,"* 84–129.

50. Stimson, *Rise of the Labor Movement*, 334–335; Clark, "The Limits of Liberty," 454–456.

51. Kraft, "The Fall of Job Harriman's Socialist Party," 53–54.

52. Johnson, "A Serpent in the Garden," 490–491.

53. For the career of the McNamara brothers, see Fine, *"Without Blare of Trumpets,"* chaps. 4–5; and Philip S. Foner, *History of the Labor Movement in the United States*, vol. 5, *The AFL in the Progressive Era, 1910–1915* (New York: International Publishers, 1980), chap. 7.

54. Johnson, "A Serpent in the Garden," 501.

55. Quoted in Knox Mellon, "Job Harriman: The Early and Middle Years, 1861–1912" (PhD diss., Claremont Graduate School, 1972), 102.

56. Dennis McDougal, *Privileged Son: Otis Chandler and the Rise and Fall of the L.A. Times Dynasty* (Cambridge, Mass.: Perseus, 2001), 47.

57. Quoted in Kraft, "The Fall of Job Harriman's Socialist Party," 53.

58. Ibid.

59. Bruce M. Stave, ed., *Socialism and the Cities* (Port Washington, N.Y.: Kennikat Press, 1975), 4–5.

60. Quoted in Kraft, "The Fall of Job Harriman's Socialist Party," 54. See also Jane Apostol, "Why Women Should Not Have the Vote: Anti-Suffrage Views in the Southland in 1911," *Southern California Quarterly* 70, no. 2 (Spring 1988): 29–42.

61. *Los Angeles Citizen*, November 2, 1911, 7.

62. Johnson, "A Serpent in the Garden," 497; Eileen V. Wallis, *Earning Power: Women and Work in Los Angeles, 1880–1930* (Reno: University of Nevada Press, 2010), 96–97. See also Gayle Gullett, *Becoming Citizens: The Emergence and Development of the California Women's Movement, 1880–1911* (Urbana: University of Illinois

Press, 2000), 42–43; and Daniel Johnson, "'No Make-Believe Class Struggle': The Socialist Municipal Campaign in Los Angeles, 1911," *Labor History* 41, no. 1 (February 2000): 41.

63. For more on this point, see James Weinstein, *The Decline of Socialism in America, 1912–1925* (New York: Monthly Review Press, 1967), 107–108, 329–331.

64. *California Social Democrat*, December 14, 1911, 2.

65. Quoted in Johnson, "A Serpent in the Garden," 452–456.

66. Clark, "The Limits of Liberty," 456.

67. Fine, *"Without Blare of Trumpets,"* 95.

68. Clark, "The Limits of Liberty," 458–459.

69. Quoted in ibid., 460.

70. Ibid.

71. The *Los Angeles Times* poured out a stream of invective against the various skilled and manufacturing workers who participated in the 1910–1911 strike wave. Otis was particularly upset with the labor organizers from San Francisco who came down to L.A. to help. On June 22, 1910, for example, he penned an editorial stating: "These are days of common peril in Los Angeles. A foreign foe is at the gates and threatens all alike. . . . The call comes to drop all little disputes and devote all attention to the enemy" (*Los Angeles Times*, June 22, 1910, 8).

72. *Los Angeles Citizen*, December 14, 1910, 7.

73. Stimson, *Rise of the Labor Movement*, 349–350.

74. *Los Angeles Times*, August 11, 1911, 6; February 9, 1912, 10.

75. *Los Angeles Citizen*, January 19, 1912, 4. See also *Proceedings of the Thirteenth Annual Convention of the California State Federation of Labor*, San Diego, October 1912, 74.

76. Quoted in *Proceedings of the Thirteenth Annual Convention*, 75.

77. For a brief overview of the labor legislation passed by the first Wilson administration between 1913 and 1916, see Foster Rhea Dulles and Melvyn Dubofsky, *Labor in America: A History*, 4th ed. (Arlington Heights, Ill.: Harlan Davidson, 1984), 194–196.

78. Richard Coke Lower, *A Bloc of One: The Political Career of Hiram Johnson* (Stanford, Calif.: Stanford University Press, 1993), 33–34.

79. Michael Paul Rogin and John L. Shover, *Political Change in California: Critical Elections and Social Movements, 1890–1966* (Westport, Conn.: Greenwood, 1970), 80.

80. On November 24, 1911, AFL president Samuel Gompers issued a statement saying that while he urged AFL members to send money to help finance Job Harriman's 1911 mayoral campaign, this appeal "was in no way to be construed as indorsement [*sic*] of the socialist ticket or its principles." See Peter J. Albert and Grace Palladino, eds., *The Samuel Gompers Papers*, vol. 8, *Progress and Reaction in the Age of Reform, 1909–1913* (Urbana: University of Illinois Press, 2001), 291.

81. *Los Angeles Citizen*, April 4, 1913, 4.

82. *Los Angeles Times*, May 8, 1913, 2:4.

83. For the week ending April 23, 1913, the Union Labor Club, which backed Harriman in the mayoral election, raised only $185 in political contributions from fourteen unions. The total number of unions in the Central Labor Council at this time was sixty-seven. If that week's total was typical, it meant that the city's unions contributed less than $2,000 during the course of the five-week primary campaign. See *Los Angeles Citizen*, April 25, 1913, 5.

84. Greenstein, Lennon, and Rolfe, *Bread and Hyacinths*, 85–86.

85. Stimson, *Rise of the Labor Movement*, 118; *Los Angeles Citizen*, July 3, 1914, 3; Ralph Edward Shaffer, "A History of the Socialist Party of California" (Charles E. Young Research Library, University of California, Los Angeles), 150.

86. Louis B. Perry and Richard S. Perry, *A History of the Los Angeles Labor Movement, 1911–1941* (Berkeley: University of California Press, 1963), 51.

87. *Los Angeles Citizen*, February 17, 1914, 2; March 14, 1914, 3.

88. Ibid., January 5, 1914, 1.

CHAPTER THREE

1. Robert Gottlieb and Irene Wolt, *Thinking Big: The Story of the Los Angeles Times, Its Publishers, and Their Influence on Southern California* (New York: Putnam, 1977), chaps. 8–9.

2. Bruce Nelson, *Workers on the Waterfront: Seamen, Longshoremen, and Unionism in the 1930s* (Urbana: University of Illinois Press, 1988), chaps. 1–2.

3. Ibid.

4. The Magonistas derived their name from their support of two brothers, Ricardo and Enrique Magón, who helped to found the Partido Liberal Mexicano, one of a number of groups seeking to overthrow the dictatorship of Mexican president Porfirio Díaz. They edited and distributed *Regeneración*, the PLM's official journal. See Colin M. MacLachlan, *Anarchism and the Mexican Revolution: The Political Trials of Ricardo Flores Magón in the United States* (Berkeley: University of California Press, 1991), passim.

5. For a discussion of the concepts of syndicalism and anarchism, see David Montgomery, *Workers' Control in America: Studies in the History of Work, Technology, and Labor Struggles* (Cambridge: Cambridge University Press, 1979), chap. 4.

6. Magón, Haywood, and Goldman were all members of the IWW. See also Mark Wild, *Street Meeting: Multiethnic Neighborhoods in Early Twentieth-Century Los Angeles* (Berkeley: University of California Press, 2005), chap. 6.

7. John Mason Hart, "The Evolution of the Mexican and Mexican-American Working Classes," in *Border Crossings: Mexican and Mexican-American Workers*, ed. John Mason Hart (Wilmington, Del.: Scholarly Resources, 1998), 16–17.

8. For a study of the ideology of the IWW locals in the metal mining states of the American West, see Melvyn Dubofsky, *We Shall Be All: A History of the Industrial Workers of the World* (Chicago: Quadrangle Books, 1969), chap. 2.

9. Peter Gerhard, "The Socialist Invasion of Baja California, 1911," *Pacific Historical Review* 15, no. 3 (September 1946): 295.

10. Robert E. Ireland, "The Radical Community: Mexican and American Radicalism, 1900–1910," *Journal of Mexican American History* 2, no. 1 (Fall 1971): 26; Devra Anne Weber, "'Leaving Trails of Powder': Journeys of Ferdinand Palomarez, Traveling Organizer and Propagandist of the Partido Liberal Mexicano" (University of California, Riverside, 2004), 16.

11. Weber, "'Leaving Trails of Powder,'" 20.

12. Ibid.

13. Ibid., 12–16.

14. Paul Greenstein, Nigey Lennon, and Lionel Rolfe, *Bread and Hyacinths: The Rise and Fall of Utopian Los Angeles* (Los Angeles: California Classics, 1992), 44.

15. Ibid.; Edward J. Escobar, *Race, Police, and the Making of a Political Identity: Mexican Americans and the Los Angeles Police Department, 1900–1945* (Berkeley: University of California Press, 1999), 57–59.

16. Quoted in Greenstein, Lennon, and Rolfe, *Bread and Hyacinths*, 45.

17. Escobar, *Race, Police, and the Making of a Political Identity*, 60–61.

18. Ibid., 68.

19. For some speculative remarks on these topics, see George J. Sánchez, *Becoming Mexican American: Ethnicity, Culture, and Identity in Chicano Los Angeles, 1900–1945* (New York: Oxford University Press, 1993), chaps. 1–2.

20. Gottlieb and Wolt, *Thinking Big*, 165–167; Eugene Keith Chamberlain, "Mexican Colonization versus American Interests in Lower California," *Pacific Historical Review* 20, no. 1 (February 1951): 43–55.

21. Quoted in Gottlieb and Wolt, *Thinking Big*, 167–168.

22. Dennis McDougal, *Privileged Son: Otis Chandler and the Rise and Fall of the L.A. Times Dynasty* (Cambridge, Mass.: Perseus, 2001), 75.

23. Quoted in Gottlieb and Wolt, *Thinking Big*, 169.

24. Gerhard, "The Socialist Invasion of Baja California," 303–304; W. Dirk Raat, *Revoltosos: Mexico's Rebels in the United States, 1903–1923* (College Station: Texas A&M Press, 1981), 58; William David Estrada, *The Los Angeles Plaza: Sacred and Contested Space* (Austin: University of Texas Press, 2008), 139–140.

25. Quoted in Estrada, *The Los Angeles Plaza*, 142.

26. Marc Karson, *American Labor Unions and Politics, 1900–1918* (Carbondale: Southern Illinois University Press, 1958), 83–89.

27. Philip Taft, *The AF of L in the Time of Gompers* (New York: Harper and Row, 1957), 114.

28. The AFL's proscription of the IWW did not, however, prevent Los Angeles radicals from providing assistance to the Wobblies during the free speech fights and the strikes that erupted in Fresno, San Diego, and other places in 1908–1913. For

example, after Richard Ford and Hermann D. Suhr were arrested for murder during the Wheatland hop pickers' strike in August 1913, the statewide Socialist Party, with L.A. trade union Socialists playing a prominent part, provided attorneys and financial support for the defense of the accused. On the free speech fights, see Philip S. Foner, *History of the Labor Movement in the United States*, vol. 4 (New York: International Publishers, 1965), 267–270; and Ralph E. Shaffer, "Radicalism in California, 1869–1929" (microfilm, Charles E. Young Research Library, University of California, Los Angeles, 1962), 231–233.

29. David A. Shannon, *The Socialist Party of America: A History* (New York: Macmillan, 1955), 72.

30. *Los Angeles Social Democrat*, June 11, 1912, 4.

31. *Revolt*, July 1, 1912, 2 (Northern California Labor Archive, San Francisco State University).

32. Quoted in Raat, *Revoltosos*, 60.

33. Ibid., 59.

34. Ibid. In July 1912 Frank Wolfe, correspondent for the Socialist Party's national press service in Los Angeles, supported Harriman's opinion when he complained that the Magón brothers were "not socialists." See Shaffer, "Radicalism in California," 232.

35. Raat, *Revoltosos*, 59; Wild, *Street Meeting*, 161.

36. Shaffer, "Radicalism in California," 153; *Report of California Secretary of State on Elections* (Sacramento: State Printing Office, 1916), 33.

37. Raat, *Revoltosos*, 276–277.

38. Ibid., 277–290.

39. Quoted in Escobar, *Race, Police, and the Making of a Political Identity*, 73.

40. Ibid.

41. Ibid., 75.

42. For an analysis of the early stages of the Americanization movement, see John Higham, *Strangers in the Land: Patterns of American Nativism, 1860–1925* (New York: Atheneum, 1963), chap. 9.

43. Sánchez, *Becoming Mexican American*, 94–107. See also Frank Van Nuys, *Americanizing the West: Race, Immigrants, and Citizenship, 1890–1930* (Lawrence: University Press of Kansas, 2002), chap. 2.

44. Louis B. Perry and Richard S. Perry, *A History of the Los Angeles Labor Movement, 1911–1941* (Berkeley: University of California Press, 1963), 165.

45. For a history of San Pedro and its occupations, see W. W. Robinson, *San Pedro and Wilmington: A Calendar of Events in the Making of Two Cities and the Los Angeles Harbor* (Los Angeles: Title Guarantee and Trust, 1937); and Ella Ludwig, *History of the Harbor District of Los Angeles: Dating from Its Earliest History* (Los Angeles: Historic Record, 1927).

46. Quoted in Roy Church and Quentin Outram, *Strikes and Solidarity: Coalfield Conflict in Britain, 1889–1966* (Cambridge: Cambridge University Press, 1998), 262.

47. Herb Mills and David Wellman, "Contractually Sanctioned Job Action and Workers' Control: The Case of San Francisco Longshoremen," *Labor History* 28, no. 2 (Spring 1987): 172–174.

48. Nelson, *Workers on the Waterfront*, 60.

49. Mills and Wellman, "Contractually Sanctioned Job Action," 174. See also Charles P. Larrowe, *Shape-Up and Hiring Hall: A Comparison of Hiring Methods and Labor Relations on the New York and Seattle Waterfronts* (Berkeley: University of California Press, 1955).

50. Howard Kimeldorf, *Reds or Rackets? The Making of Radical and Conservative Unions on the Waterfront* (Berkeley: University of California Press, 1988), 28–29.

51. Ibid., 20–26; Nicholas P. Lovrich, *Yugoslavs and Italians in San Pedro: Political Culture and Civic Involvement* (Palo Alto, Calif.: Ragusan Press, 1977), 16–27.

52. Quoted in Kimeldorf, *Reds or Rackets?* 27.

53. Perry and Perry, *A History of the Los Angeles Labor Movement*, 165.

54. Ibid., 176.

55. Ibid., 166.

56. On the life of Harry Bridges and his role in the ILWU, see Charles P. Larrowe, *Harry Bridges: The Rise and Fall of Radical Labor in the United States* (Westport, Conn.: Lawrence Hill, 1972), passim.

57. For an overview of labor in World War I, see Foster Rhea Dulles and Melvyn Dubofsky, *Labor in America: A History*, 4th ed. (Arlington Heights, Ill.: Harlan Davidson, 1984), chap. 13.

58. Perry and Perry, *A History of the Los Angeles Labor Movement*, 106–108, 147–162; Lizabeth Cohen, *Making a New Deal: Industrial Workers in Chicago, 1919–1939* (Cambridge: Cambridge University Press, 1990), 74.

59. Perry and Perry, *A History of the Los Angeles Labor Movement*, 161–162; *California War Bulletin*, September 29, 1917, 14, box 5, World War I Collection, Special Collections, Charles E. Young Research Library, University of California, Los Angeles. For the policies of the National War Labor Board, see Valerie Jean Conner, *The National War Labor Board: Stability, Social Justice, and the Voluntary State in World War I* (Chapel Hill: University of North Carolina Press, 1983).

60. *California War Bulletin*, October 6, 1917, 3–4. It is noteworthy that in many cities labor frequently proposed the idea of an "industrial democracy" to counter the employers' emphasis on "industrial freedom," whereas in Los Angeles this issue was rarely raised. For a discussion of industrial democracy in and after World War I, see Joseph A. McCartin, *Labor's Great War: The Struggle for Industrial Democracy and the Origins of Modern American Labor Relations, 1912–1921* (Chapel Hill: University of North Carolina Press, 1997), especially the introduction.

61. Perry and Perry, *A History of the Los Angeles Labor Movement*, 170–173.

62. Thomas R. Clark, "The Limits of Liberty: Courts, Police, and Labor Unrest in California, 1890–1926" (PhD diss., University of California, Los Angeles, 1994), 564.

63. Maurine Weiner Greenwald, *Women, War, and Work: The Impact of World War I on Women Workers in the United States* (Westport, Conn.: Greenwood Press, 1980), chap. 5.

64. Perry and Perry, *A History of the Los Angeles Labor Movement*, 140–145.

65. William D. Friedricks, "Capital and Labor in Los Angeles: Henry E. Huntington vs. Organized Labor, 1900–1920," *Pacific Historical Review* 59, no. 3 (August 1990): 391.

66. Quoted in ibid.

67. Ibid., 373.

68. Clark, "The Limits of Liberty," 564–567; Friedricks, "Capital and Labor in Los Angeles," 393–395; Spencer Crump, *Ride the Big Red Cars: How Trolleys Helped Build Southern California* (Glendale, Calif.: Anglo-American Books, 1983), 136.

69. Perry and Perry, *A History of the Los Angeles Labor Movement*, 75–84.

70. M. Guy Bishop, "'Strong Voices and 100 Per Cent Patriotism': The Four-Minute Men of Los Angeles County, 1917–1918," *Southern California Quarterly* 77, no. 3 (Fall 1992): 199–214; *California War Bulletin*, September 29, 1917, 3.

71. Tom Sitton, *John Randolph Haynes: California Progressive* (Stanford, Calif.: Stanford University Press, 1992), 137.

72. See, for example, Gov. William D. Stephens, "Independence Day Address, July 4, 1918," in William D. Stephens, *California in the War: War Addresses, Proclamations, and Patriotic Messages* (Sacramento: California Historical Survey Commission, 1920), 35–38.

73. In November 1919, the *Los Angeles Times* printed no fewer than thirteen front-page articles with headlines such as "ALL FORCES OF LAW AND ORDER FOR SMASHING IWW'S, BOLSHEVIKS, AND OTHER ENEMIES OF GOVERNMENT." See Howard Abramowitz, "The Press and the Red Scare, 1919–1921," in *Popular Culture and Political Change in Modern America*, ed. Ronald Edsforth and Larry Bennett (Albany, N.Y.: SUNY Press, 1991), 70.

74. Errol Wayne Stevens, *Radical L.A.: From Coxey's Army to the Watts Riots, 1894–1965* (Norman: University of Oklahoma Press, 2009), 132–133.

75. Quoted in ibid., 134.

76. Roger Daniels, *Concentration Camp USA: Japanese Americans and World War II* (New York: Holt, Rinehart and Winston, 1971), 16–18.

77. Quoted in Douglas Flamming, *Bound for Freedom: Black Los Angeles in Jim Crow America* (Berkeley: University of California Press, 2005), 167.

78. Eldridge Foster Dowell, *A History of Criminal Syndicalism Legislation in the United States* (Baltimore: Johns Hopkins University Press, 1939), passim.

79. Stevens, *Radical L.A.*, 137.

80. Perry and Perry, *A History of the Los Angeles Labor Movement*, 176–180; Nelson, *Workers on the Waterfront*, 50–51.

81. The M&M originally requested five hundred special police, but that number was reduced to one hundred by the efforts of Socialist councilman Fred Wheeler. See Perry and Perry, *A History of the Los Angeles Labor Movement*, 177–178.

82. Ibid., 178–181; *San Pedro Pilot*, November 1, 1919, 8.

83. Perry and Perry, *A History of the Los Angeles Labor Movement*, 181–182.

84. For a discussion of the flimsy evidence used to convict IWW members in trials held in 1918 and 1920 in Los Angeles and Sacramento, see Dubofsky, *We Shall Be All*, 438–439.

85. Ibid., 351.

86. Nelson, *Workers on the Waterfront*, 60–61; Perry and Perry, *A History of the Los Angeles Labor Movement*, 182. For the influence of the IWW and the One Big Union movement on the growth of industrial unionism in the U.S. labor movement during the 1919 strike wave, see Marion D. Savage, *Industrial Unionism in America* (New York: Ronald Press, 1922); and David Montgomery, *The Fall of the House of Labor: The Workplace, the State, and American Labor Activism, 1865–1925* (Cambridge: Cambridge University Press, 1987), 425–430.

87. Quoted in Nelson Van Valen, "'Cleaning Up the Harbor': The Suppression of the IWW at San Pedro, 1922–1925," *Southern California Quarterly* 61, no. 2 (Spring 1984): 152.

88. Perry and Perry, *A History of the Los Angeles Labor Movement*, 184.

89. Ibid., 184–185.

90. Quoted in Van Valen, "'Cleaning Up the Harbor,'" 156.

91. Ibid., 156–157.

92. Quoted in ibid., 158.

93. Ibid., 164.

94. Hyman Weintraub, "The I.W.W. in California, 1905–1931" (MA thesis, University of California, Los Angeles, 1947), 236–246; Van Valen, "'Cleaning Up the Harbor,'" 156–158.

CHAPTER FOUR

1. W. W. Robinson, "The Southern California Real Estate Boom of the 1920s," in *A Southern California Historical Anthology*, ed. Doyce Nunis Jr. (Los Angeles: Historical Society of Southern California, 1984), 329–336.

2. On African Americans in the 1920s, see Douglas Flamming, *Bound for Freedom: Black Los Angeles in Jim Crow America* (Berkeley: University of California Press, 2005), chap. 6. On Asians and Mexicans, see Martin Schiesl and Mark M. Dodge, eds., *City of Promise: Race and Historical Change in Los Angeles* (Claremont, Calif.: Regina Books, 2006), chaps. 1–2.

3. Robinson, "The Southern California Real Estate Boom," 329–336.

4. Becky Nicolaides, *My Blue Heaven: Life and Politics in the Working-Class Suburbs of Los Angeles, 1920–1965* (Chicago: University of Chicago Press, 2002), 28–29.

5. Greg Hise, "Industry and Imaginative Geographies," in *Metropolis in the Making: Los Angeles in the 1920s*, ed. Tom Sitton and William Deverell (Berkeley: University of California Press, 2001), 20–21.

6. For an introduction to the history of the Hollywood movie industry, see Steven J. Ross, "How Hollywood Became Hollywood: Money, Politics, and Movies," in Sitton and Deverell, *Metropolis in the Making*, chap. 11. See also Michael Charles Nielsen, "Motion Picture Craft Workers and Craft Unions in Hollywood: The Studio Era, 1912–1948" (PhD diss., University of Illinois, 1985), passim. For a discussion of the rise of the "five big studios," see Mae D. Huettig, *Economic Control of the Motion Picture Industry: A Study in Industrial Organization* (Philadelphia: University of Pennsylvania Press, 1944), chap. 1.

7. Laurie Caroline Pintar, "Off-Screen Realities: A History of Labor Activism in Hollywood, 1933–1947" (PhD diss., University of Southern California, 1995), 10–12.

8. Quoted in ibid., 9.

9. An aerial photograph taken in 1921 contrasted the elegant mansions and cultivated fruit gardens that dominated the landscape at the western end of Hollywood Boulevard, near La Brea Avenue, with what it identified as "the flotsam and jetsam of Poverty Row." The accompanying text identified Poverty Row as the residential area near the corner of Sunset and Gower. "To the residents of Hollywood, this area was popularly called Gower Gulch." See Bruce Torrence, *Hollywood: The First Hundred Years* (Hollywood: Hollywood Chamber of Commerce, 1979), 87–89.

10. Nielsen, "Motion Picture Craft Workers," chaps. 3–4; John R. Cauble, "A Study of the International Alliance of Theatrical Stage Employees and Moving Picture Operators of the United States and Canada" (MA thesis, University of California, Los Angeles, 1964), passim.

11. Mike Nielsen and Gene Mailes, *Hollywood's Other Blacklist: Union Struggles in the Studio System* (London: British Film Institute, 1995), 3–6.

12. Ibid., 5–6; Nielsen, "Motion Picture Craft Workers," 63.

13. Nielsen, "Motion Picture Craft Workers," 63–64.

14. Hugh Lovell and Tasile Carter, *Collective Bargaining in the Motion Picture Industry: A Struggle for Stability* (Berkeley: Institute of Industrial Relations, 1955), 15.

15. Murray Ross, *Stars and Strikes: Unionization of Hollywood* (New York: Columbia University Press, 1941), 6–8.

16. Ibid.

17. Cauble, "A Study of the International Alliance of Theatrical Stage Employees," 137–139.

18. Quoted in Nielsen and Mailes, *Hollywood's Other Blacklist*, 6. Also see Nielsen, "Motion Picture Craft Workers," 107–110.

19. Louis B. Perry and Richard S. Perry, *A History of the Los Angeles Labor Movement, 1911–1941* (Berkeley: University of California Press, 1963), 322; Steven J. Ross, *Working-Class Hollywood: Silent Film and the Shaping of Class in America* (Princeton, N.J.: Princeton University Press, 1998), 131–132.

20. Quoted in Ross, *Working-Class Hollywood,* 133.

21. Ibid., 132–133; Nielsen, "Motion Picture Craft Workers," 78–79, 92–93.

22. Ross, *Stars and Strikes,* 8–12; Nielsen, "Motion Picture Craft Workers," 59–63, 85–88.

23. Nielsen, "Motion Picture Craft Workers," 80.

24. Lovell and Carter, *Collective Bargaining,* 15–16.

25. Ibid., 16–17; Nielsen, "Motion Picture Craft Workers," 59–63, 85–88.

26. For the impact of the red scare in Hollywood in the 1920s, see Robert Gottlieb and Irene Wolt, *Thinking Big: The Story of the* Los Angeles Times, *Its Publishers, and Their Influence on Southern California* (New York: Putnam, 1977), chap. 10. For the role of the Ku Klux Klan, see Flamming, *Bound for Freedom,* chap. 6.

27. Ross, *Working-Class Hollywood,* 93–94, 102.

28. Ibid., 137.

29. For the history of the AFL craft unions in downtown Los Angeles during the 1920s, see Perry and Perry, *A History of the Los Angeles Labor Movement,* chap. 6. For background, see Philip Taft, *The AF of L in the Time of Gompers* (New York: Harper and Row, 1957).

30. Quoted in Harold S. Roberts, *The Rubber Workers: Labor Organization and Collective Bargaining in the Rubber Industry* (New York: Harper Bros., 1944), 85.

31. For the development of the CIO in Los Angeles, see Chapter Six of this volume.

32. Nicolaides, *My Blue Heaven,* 76.

33. Tom Thienes, "Contributions toward the History of the City of South Gate," 6, manuscript written for the Works Progress Administration, 1942, Weaver Library Archives, South Gate, Calif.

34. Nicolaides, *My Blue Heaven,* 46–47, 102–104.

35. Mary-Ellen Bell Ray, *The City of Watts, California: 1907 to 1950* (Los Angeles: Rising Publishing, 1985), 8–9.

36. Ibid., 54–55.

37. Quoted in Mike Davis, "Sunshine and the Open Shop: Ford and Darwin in 1920s Los Angeles," in Sitton and Deverell, *Metropolis in the Making,* 117.

38. Quoted in Charles S. Johnson, "Industrial Survey of the Negro Population of Los Angeles, California," National Urban League, Los Angeles, 1926, 24.

39. Nicolaides, *My Blue Heaven,* 43. See also James N. Gregory, *American Exodus: The Dust Bowl Migration and Okie Culture in California* (New York: Oxford University Press, 1989), chap. 5.

40. Quoted in Flamming, *Bound for Freedom*, 198.

41. Although a direct connection cannot be drawn, it is likely that some of the new arrivals in South Gate from Texas and Oklahoma had participated in the so-called Klan wars then raging in their home states. In 1923 the anti-Klan governor of Oklahoma, John C. Walton, was nearly impeached by local supporters of the KKK. See Garin Burbank, *When Farmers Voted Red: The Gospel of Socialism in the Oklahoma Countryside, 1910–1924* (Westport, Conn.: Greenwood Press, 1976), chap. 8.

42. Nicolaides, *My Blue Heaven*, 165.

43. Quoted in *Watts News*, October 14, 1923, 2.

44. Flamming, *Bound for Freedom*, 210–211.

45. Gregory, *American Exodus*, chap. 7. See also Charles B. Spaulding's thesis on Bell Gardens entitled "The Development of Organization and Disorganization in the Social Life of a Rapidly Growing Working-Class Suburb within a Metropolitan District" (PhD diss., University of Southern California, 1939), 196–207.

46. Nicolaides, *My Blue Heaven*, 108–111.

47. Ibid., 176. It must be remembered, however, that Progressivism in California was largely a Republican Party phenomenon.

48. Burbank, *When Farmers Voted Red*, chap. 7.

49. Patricia Ray Adler, "Watts: From Suburb to Black Ghetto" (PhD diss., University of Southern California, 1977), 129.

50. John L. Shover, "The California Progressives and the 1924 Campaign," *California Historical Quarterly* 51, no. 1 (Spring 1972): 66–67.

51. Adler, "Watts: From Suburb to Black Ghetto," 190–191.

52. Nicolaides, *My Blue Heaven*, 177; Adler, "Watts: From Suburb to Black Ghetto," 189; Daniel P. Melcher, "The Challenge to Normalcy: The 1924 Election in California," *Southern California Quarterly* 60, no. 1 (Summer 1978): 155–182.

53. Quoted in Rosalie R. Wride, "A History of the Long Beach Oil Fields" (MA thesis, Occidental College, 1949), 34. The Shell oil gusher of June 1921 was not the first one to spur the Southern California oil boom; previous strikes had been made in Huntington Beach and Santa Fe Springs. But the Signal Hill discovery was the most famous, and it inspired Upton Sinclair (whose wife, Mary Craig, owned oil property in Long Beach) to write one of his most famous muckraking novels, *Oil!* (1926), which described the wealth, excitement, and political corruption that accompanied the rise of the oil industry. See Jules Tygiel's foreword in the paperback edition of Sinclair's *Oil!* (Berkeley: University of California Press, 1997), v–xi; and Lauren Coodley, ed., *The Land of Orange Groves and Jails: Upton Sinclair's California* (Berkeley: Heyday Books, 2004), passim.

54. For general accounts of the early history of the oil industry in Signal Hill and its impact on nearby Long Beach, see Ken Davis, *Signal Hill* (Charleston, S.C.: Arcadia Publishing, 2006); *Signal Hill: The "Magic Mound"* (published by City of Signal

Hill); and Larry L. Meyer and Patricia Kalayjian, *Long Beach: Fortune's Harbor* (Tulsa, Okla.: Continental Heritage Press, 1983), 23.

55. California State Department of Mines, *Report of Oil and Gas Division* (Sacramento: State Printing Office, 1929), 134.

56. Jonathan Booth, interview by Colleen Fliedner, 1982, Oral History of Signal Hill Oil Workers, Virtual Oral/Aural History Archive, California State University, Long Beach (VOAHA/CSULB).

57. Ibid. For further insight into the escalation of land prices set off by the oil boom in Signal Hill and the profits that were made by ordinary citizens, see Walker A. Tompkins, *The Little Giant of Signal Hill: An Adventure in American Enterprise* (Englewood Cliffs, N.J.: Prentice-Hall, 1964).

58. A list of twenty-five small-scale oil well owners in the 1920s and 1930s, several of whom were newcomers to Signal Hill, is provided in Wride, "A History of the Long Beach Oil Fields," appendix E.

59. The largest houses in Signal Hill, where most of the major oil lease owners and company managers lived, were located on large lots on Crescent and Panorama streets and on Signal Hill Drive, which commanded excellent views of the Pacific Ocean. By contrast, most of the houses on California, Orange, and Walnut streets, where large numbers of oil workers lived, were smaller and much less pretentious, sometimes being little more than wooden shacks. See *Signal Hill: The "Magic Mound,"* 9–10; Julie Bendzick-Sin, "The Black Gold Rush Begins," *Star-Tribune* (Signal Hill), November 9, 1990, 2; and Security Trust and Savings Bank, Chart of Signal Hill Oil Field, October 1922, Signal Hill Public Library Archives.

60. California Bureau of Labor Statistics, *Thirty-fourth Annual Report* (Sacramento: State Printing Office, 1924), 32–33.

61. *Signal Hill Beacon*, October 2, 1925, 1. For a more detailed account of work processes in the oil industry and the changing character of oil well technology, see Nancy Lynn Quam-Wickham, "Petroleocrats and Proletarians: Work, Class, and Politics in the California Oil Industry, 1917–1925" (PhD diss., University of California, Berkeley, 1994), chaps. 1–2.

62. Gerald White, *Formative Years in the Far West: A History of the Standard Oil Company and Predecessors through 1919* (New York: Appleton Century-Crofts, 1962), chap. 20; Quam-Wickham, "Petroleocrats and Proletarians," 41–52, 69–76.

63. The Central Labor Council of Long Beach was run by a small group of carpenters, printers, and other conservative tradesmen who followed the narrow, "pure and simple" trade unionism philosophy of the AFL. Long Beach in the 1920s was also quite heavily influenced by recently arrived rural migrants from Iowa and other midwestern states who supported the Prohibition movement and the Ku Klux Klan. See Robert Dewitt Morgan, "History of Organized Labor in Long Beach" (MA thesis, California State University, Long Beach, 1940).

64. Quam-Wickham, "Petroleocrats and Proletarians," 83–98.

65. Joy Elliott, interview by Kaye Briegel, 1989; Virginia Maxfield, interview by Kaye Briegel, 1989; both in Oral History of Signal Hill Oil Workers, VOAHA/CSULB.

66. Harvey O'Connor, *History of the Oil Workers International Union—CIO* (Denver: OWIU, 1950), 9–12.

67. Quam-Wickham, "Petroleocrats and Proletarians," 165, 173–174.

68. *Los Angeles Times*, December 20, 1917, 6.

69. O'Connor, *History of the Oil Workers International Union*, 12; Quam-Wickham, "Petroleocrats and Proletarians," 180.

70. O'Connor, *History of the Oil Workers International Union*, 13 14.

71. *Proceedings of the Thirty-ninth Annual Convention of the American Federation of Labor*, Atlantic City, June 1919, 128–129.

72. Quam-Wickham, "Petroleocrats and Proletarians," 182–183; *Western Oil News* 1, no. 49 (January 6, 1922): 1; *Signal Hill Beacon*, October 2, 1925, 3.

73. O'Connor, *History of the Oil Workers International Union*, 18–25; *Proceedings of the Forty-first Annual Convention of the American Federation of Labor*, Denver, 1921, 446, 469–470.

74. Quoted in *Proceedings, Forty-second Annual Convention of the American Federation of Labor*, Cincinnati, June 1922, 453–454.

75. *International Oil Worker*, July 23, 1925, 2.

76. Ibid., September 17, 1925, 1.

77. The best overall descriptions of the rise of the citrus industry in Southern California in the 1920s are found in Gilbert G. Gonzáles, *Labor and Community: Mexican Citrus Worker Villages in a Southern California County, 1900–1950* (Urbana: University of Illinois Press, 1994), passim; and Matt Garcia, *A World of Its Own: Race, Labor, and Citrus in the Making of Greater Los Angeles, 1900–1970* (Chapel Hill: University of North Carolina Press, 2001). See also the symposium entitled "Citriculture and Southern California," in *California History* 74, no. 1 (Spring 1995); and David Vaught, *Cultivating California: Growers, Specialty Crops, and Labor, 1875–1920* (Baltimore: Johns Hopkins University Press, 1999).

78. Carey McWilliams, *Factories in the Field: The Story of Migratory Farm Labor in California* (Salt Lake City: Peregrine Publishers, 1971), chap. 6.

79. Ibid., ix.

80. For a discussion of the size of the ranches in the San Gabriel Valley and whether they could be considered family farms, see the essays by Ronald Tobey, Charles Wetherell, H. Vincent Moses, Anthea M. Hartig, and Michael C. Steiner in the *California History* symposium "Citriculture and Southern California," 6–45, 100–118; and David Vaught, "Factories in the Field Revisited," *Pacific Historical Review* 66, no. 2 (May 1997): 149–184.

81. Quoted in the La Follette Committee hearings: U.S. Senate, "The Disadvantaged Status of Unorganized Labor in California's Industrialized Agriculture," *Violations of Free Speech and the Rights of Labor: Report of the Committee on Education and Labor*, pt. 3, 286 (77th Cong., 2nd sess.) (Washington, D.C.: Government Printing Office, 1942).

82. Quoted in ibid. These steps in the citrus harvesting process are described in Gonzáles, *Labor and Community*, chap. 2.

83. U.S. Senate, "Employers Associations and Their Labor Policies in California's Industrialized Agriculture," *Violations of Free Speech and the Rights of Labor*, pt. 4, 538–547; Charles Collins Teague, "A Memorial," California Fruit Growers Exchange, 1950, Clark Memorial Library, Los Angeles.

84. Gonzales, *Labor and Community*, 27.

85. Paul Garland Williamson, "Labor in the California Citrus Industry" (MA thesis, University of California, Berkeley, 1946), 95. Matt Garcia (*A World of Its Own*, 38) argues that the Mexicans, Filipinos, and Sikhs who worked in citrus in the 1920s were part of a dual labor market system in which white fruit pickers were paid more for the same work.

86. Gonzáles, *Labor and Community*, 36–42.

87. A brief description of the Arbol Verde *colonia* can be found in Garcia, *A World of Its Own*, 70–74.

88. Ibid. See also Helen O'Brien, "The Mexican Colony: A Study of Cultural Change" (Pomona College, 1932), 23–24; and Mary C. Sauter, "Arbol Verde: Cultural Conflict and Accommodation in a California Mexican Community" (MA thesis, Pomona College, 1961), 242; both papers found in Special Collections, Honnold/Mudd Library, Claremont, Calif.

89. Garcia, *A World of Its Own*, 74–75.

90. Perry and Perry, *A History of the Los Angeles Labor Movement*, 196.

91. Ibid., 197.

92. Ibid., 208–210; John Laslett and Mary Tyler, *The ILGWU in Los Angeles, 1907–1988* (Inglewood, Calif.: Ten Star Press, 1989), chap. 4.

93. Perry and Perry, *A History of the Los Angeles Labor Movement*, 203–206.

94. Quoted in Irving Bernstein, *The Lean Years: A History of the American Worker, 1920–1933* (Baltimore: Penguin Books, 1960), 155. See also Robert W. Dunn, *The Americanization of Labor: The Employers' Offensive against the Trade Unions* (New York: International Publishers, 1927), 17–18.

95. Quoted in *Los Angeles Times*, January 24, 1924, 4.

96. Selig Perlman, *A Theory of the Labor Movement* (New York, Augustus M. Kelley, 1966), chap. 7. Perlman's theory is now seen, in many ways correctly, as misleading and out of date because of its narrow focus on "job consciousness" as the sole "realistic" philosophy of the U.S. labor movement. But the merit of some of his insights

should be recognized nonetheless. See John Laslett, "The American Tradition of Labor Theory, And Its Relevance to the Contemporary Working Class," in *Theories of the Labor Movement*, ed. Simeon Larson and Bruce Nissen (Detroit: Wayne State University Press, 1987), 359–378.

97. "General Industrial Report," Industrial Department, Los Angeles Chamber of Commerce, 1929, Los Angeles.

98. Ibid.

99. Cited in Bernstein, *The Lean Years*, 161.

100. Quoted in John C. Clifford, "The Economic Boom in California in the 1920s" (PhD diss., University of California, Berkeley, 1971), 247.

CHAPTER FIVE

1. A good overview of Upton Sinclair's EPIC program is found in James N. Gregory, "Introduction," in *I, Candidate for Governor, and How I Got Licked*, by Upton Sinclair (1934; repr., Berkeley: University of California Press, 1994).

2. Errol Wayne Stevens, *Radical L.A.: From Coxey's Army to the Watts Riots, 1894–1965* (Norman: University of Oklahoma Press, 2009), 189.

3. Ibid. In 1946 a retrospective study concluded that "so far as manufacturing activity in the aggregate is concerned, there is virtually no difference between the impact of the Great Depression upon the California economy and upon the national economy" (Frank L. Kidner, *California Business Cycles* [Berkeley: University of California Press, 1946], 56). For a comparative study of the Depression in L.A., San Francisco, Seattle, and Portland, see William H. Mullins, *The Depression and the Urban West Coast, 1929–1933* (Bloomington: Indiana University Press, 1991).

4. Stevens, *Radical L.A.*, 189.

5. Becky Nicolaides, *My Blue Heaven: Life and Politics in the Working-Class Suburbs of Los Angeles, 1920–1965* (Chicago: University of Chicago Press, 2002), 58.

6. Ibid.

7. *Proceedings of the Thirty-third Annual Convention of the California State Federation of Labor*, Modesto, 1932, 16–17.

8. Quoted in Leonard Leader, "Los Angeles and the Great Depression" (PhD diss., University of California, Los Angeles, 1972), 17.

9. Stevens, *Radical L.A.*, 189–190.

10. Quoted in Mullins, *The Depression and the Urban West Coast*, 124.

11. *Los Angeles Times*, February 14, 1931, 8.

12. Kevin Starr, *Endangered Dreams: The Great Depression in California* (New York: Oxford University Press, 1996), 67–83, 192–194.

13. The main ally of CAWIU was the Unión Trabajadores del Valle Imperial, a Mexican union based on local *mutualistas*, which was supported by unions in Mexico but opposed by the U.S. Immigration Service and the local Mexican consulates. Eugene

Dennis and Dorothy Healey, as well as other young radicals who later became major figures in the California Communist Party, were also involved in this campaign. Note that the Mexican strike leaders, some of whom were veterans of the Mexican Revolution, often knew more about strike tactics than the Anglo leaders of CAWIU. According to Dorothy Healey, the response of the Mexicans to the involvement of the Communists was: "Of course we're for the revolution. When the barricades are ready, we'll be there with you, but don't bother us with meetings all the time. We know what to do, we know who the enemy is!" (Dorothy Healey and Maurice Isserman, *Dorothy Healey Remembers: A Life in the American Communist Party* [New York: Oxford University Press, 1990], 45–46). See Mark Reisler, *By the Sweat of Their Brow: Mexican Immigrant Labor in the United States, 1900–1940* (Westport, Conn.: Greenwood Press, 1976), 229–231; and Peggy Dennis, *The Autobiography of an American Communist: A Personal View of a Political Life, 1925–1975* (Westport, Conn: Lawrence Hill, 1977), 44–48.

14. Reisler, *By the Sweat of Their Brow*, 283; Starr, *Endangered Dreams*, chap. 6.

15. Frank Donner, *Protectors of Privilege: Red Squads and Police Repression in Urban America* (Berkeley: University of California Press, 1990), 61.

16. Ibid., 60–63; Mark Wild, *Street Meeting: Multiethnic Neighborhoods in Early Twentieth-Century Los Angeles* (Berkeley: University of California Press, 2005), 184–192.

17. George Sánchez, *Becoming Mexican American: Ethnicity, Culture, and Identity in Chicano Los Angeles, 1900–1945* (New York: Oxford University Press, 1993), 211. In 1937–1938 President Lázaro Cárdenas expropriated thousands of acres of land on the Mexican side of the border owned by the Colorado River Land Company, an outgrowth of the C&M ranch, the property that had been owned before World War I by General Otis and Harry Chandler of the *Los Angeles Times*. Some of the land was used to establish agricultural colonies for returning Mexicans who had been repatriated from Los Angeles during the Depression. See Robert Gottlieb and Irene Wolt, *Thinking Big: The Story of the* Los Angeles Times, *Its Publishers, and Their Influence on Southern California* (New York: Putnam, 1977), 178–180; and Benny J. Andres, "Invisible Borders: Repatriation and Colonization of Mexican Migrant Workers along the California Borderlands during the 1930s," *California History* 88, no. 4 (2011): 5–21.

18. Abraham Hoffman, *Unwanted Mexican Americans in the Great Depression: Repatriation Pressures, 1929–1939* (Tucson: University of Arizona Press, 1976), 28. In 1929–1930 Mexicans made up one-quarter of all L.A. residents on relief, accounting for a substantial proportion of the budget of the county welfare department. In 1931–1932, however, the repatriation scheme reduced the number of Mexicans on relief by half. See Zaragosa Vargas, *Labor Rights Are Civil Rights: Mexican American Workers in Twentieth-Century America* (Princeton, N.J.: Princeton University Press, 2005), 45.

19. Quoted in William Deverell, *Whitewashed Adobe: The Rise of Los Angeles and the Remaking of Its Mexican Past* (Berkeley: University of California Press, 2004), 121.

20. Jean Bruce Poole and Tevvy Ball, *El Pueblo: The Historic Heart of Los Angeles* (Los Angeles: Getty Conservation Institute, 2002), 73.

21. Ibid., 75–77. See also Shifra M. Goldman, "Siqueiros and Three Early Murals in Los Angeles," in *Dimensions of the Americas: Art and Social Change in Latin America and the United States*, ed. Shifra M. Goldman (Chicago: University of Chicago Press, 1994), 229–231.

22. Poole and Ball, *El Pueblo*, 74–75.

23. David A. Shannon, *The Socialist Party of America: A History* (New York: Macmillan, 1955), 324. For the negative impact on the Socialists of Sinclair's switch from the Socialist Party to the Democratic Party, see Leonard Leader, "Upton Sinclair's EPIC Switch: A Dilemma for American Socialists," *Southern California Quarterly* 62, no. 4 (Winter 1980): 278–294.

24. Karl G. Yoneda, *Ganbatte: Sixty-Year Struggle of a Kibei Worker* (Los Angeles: UCLA Asian American Studies Center, 1983), 41. See also Scott Kurashige, *The Shifting Grounds of Race: Black and Japanese Americans in the Making of Multiethnic Los Angeles* (Princeton, N.J.: Princeton University Press, 2008), 77–79.

25. Harvey Klehr, *The Heyday of American Communism: The Depression Decade* (New York: Basic Books, 1984), chap. 13. For a more detailed account of the Popular Front in America, see Michael Denning, *The Cultural Front: The Laboring of American Culture in the Twentieth Century* (New York: Verso, 1997).

26. Quoted in Wild, *Street Meeting*, 181.

27. Ibid., 182; Dan Carter, *Scottsboro: A Tragedy of the American South* (Baton Rouge: Louisiana State University Press, 1969); Charles H. Martin, "The International Labor Defense and Black America," *Labor History* 26, no. 2 (Spring 1985): 165–194.

28. Wild, *Street Meeting*, 180.

29. Quoted in *Abstract of Hearings on Unemployment before the California State Unemployment Commission, April and May 1932* (San Francisco, 1932), 190–191; Wild, *Street Meeting*, 183. For a review of monetary relief provided to the unemployed from city, state, and federal sources, see Leader, "Los Angeles and the Great Depression," chap. 4; and Roy Rosenzweig, "Organizing the Unemployed: The Early Years of the Great Depression, 1929–1933," *Radical America* 10, no. 4 (July-August 1976): 42–43.

30. Michael Furmanovsky, "Labor Upsurge of 1934 and the Limitations of Red Unionism" (University of California, Los Angeles, 1988), 23–24.

31. Klehr, *Heyday of American Communism*, 90–91.

32. Healey and Isserman, *Dorothy Healey Remembers*, 41; Peggy Dennis, *Autobiography of an American Communist*, chap. 2; Ben Dobbs, "Democracy and the American Communist Movement," 61–65, interview by Michael Furmanovsky, 1987, transcript, Center for Oral History Research, Special Collections, Charles E. Young Research Library, University of California, Los Angeles.

33. Wild, *Street Meeting*, 185–189; Donner, *Protectors of Privilege*, 59–93.

34. Dennis, *Autobiography of an American Communist*, 48.

35. Mullins, *The Depression and the Urban West Coast*, 143.

36. Pauline V. Young, "The New Poor," *Sociology and Social Research* 17, no. 3 (January-February 1933): 234–242; Melvyn J. Vincent, "Relief and Resultant Attitudes," *Sociology and Social Research* 20, no. 1 (September-October 1935): 28–29. For two later studies, which take opposing views of the matter, see Staughton Lynd, "The Possibility of Radicalism in the Early 1930s: The Case of Steel," *Radical America* 6, no. 6 (November-December 1972): 37–64; and Sidney Verba and Kay Lehman Schlozman, "Unemployment, Class Consciousness, and Radical Politics: What Didn't Happen in the Thirties," *Journal of Politics* 39, no. 3 (May 1977): 291–323.

37. Nicolaides, *My Blue Heaven*, 168.

38. *Los Angeles Citizen*, November 4, 1930, 2.

39. The most detailed source of information about Southern California's self-help cooperatives in the 1930s is Clark H. Kerr's massive, five-volume doctoral dissertation on the topic, which, surprisingly, he never published. See Kerr, "Productive Enterprises of the Unemployed, 1931–1938" (PhD diss., University of California, Berkeley, 1939).

40. Leader, "Los Angeles and the Great Depression," chap. 6; Kerr, "Productive Enterprises," chaps. 16, 18.

41. Kerr, "Productive Enterprises," 646–658.

42. Ibid., 461–462.

43. Ibid., 457–461.

44. Constantine Panunzio et al., *Self-Help Cooperatives in Los Angeles* (Berkeley: University of California Press, 1939), 65.

45. For a further summary of federal relief programs in the New Deal, see Irving Bernstein, *A Caring Society: The New Deal, the Worker, and the Great Depression* (Boston: Houghton Mifflin, 1985), chaps. 2–3.

46. Leader, "Los Angeles and the Great Depression," 116; Kerr, "Productive Enterprises," chaps. 37–38.

47. Upton Sinclair, *I, Candidate for Governor, and How I Got Licked* (1934; repr., Berkeley: University of California Press, 1994), 5–6.

48. Gregory, "Introduction," vi.

49. This description of Sinclair's EPIC plan is based on Starr, *Endangered Dreams*, 131–132; Clarence Fredric McIntosh, "Upton Sinclair and the EPIC Movement, 1933–1936" (PhD diss., Stanford University, 1955), 82–83; and the revised EPIC plan Sinclair himself published in 1935, which is reproduced in the 1994 reprint of *I, Candidate for Governor*, appendix 2.

50. Sinclair's *I, Governor of California: And How I Ended Poverty; A True Story of the Future* is summarized in Gregory, "Introduction," vi.

51. Carey McWilliams, *Southern California: An Island on the Land* (Salt Lake City: Peregrine Smith Books, 1973), 296–299.

52. Gregory, "Introduction," viii–ix.

53. Michael Paul Rogin and John L. Shover, *Political Change in California: Critical Elections and Social Movements, 1890–1966* (Westport, Conn.: Greenwood, 1970), 134.

54. Nicolaides, *My Blue Heaven*, 147, 175.

55. Leader, "Los Angeles and the Great Depression," chap. 6. For a detailed history of California's utopian movements, see Robert V. Hine, *California's Utopian Colonies* (New Haven, Conn.: Yale University Press, 1966).

56. Starr, *Endangered Dreams*, 139.

57. Gregory, "Introduction," vii in, *Los Angeles Times,* August 30, 1934, 5; *Statement of the Vote: Primary Election in California, August 28, 1934* (Sacramento: State Printing Office, 1934), 39–45.

58. Quoted in Gregory, "Introduction," vii–ix.

59. James N. Gregory, "California's EPIC Turn" (University of Washington, 2004), 21–22; *Los Angeles Times*, August 30, 1934, 11.

60. *EPIC News*, August 4, 1923, 9.

61. Ibid., September 14, 1934, 11; September 28, 1934, 6; October 6, 1934, 2.

62. Richard Norman Baisden, "Labor Unions in Los Angeles Politics" (PhD diss., University of Chicago, 1958), 146.

63. Ibid., 147–148.

64. Douglas Flamming, "Becoming Democrats: Liberal Politics and the African American Community in Los Angeles, 1930–1965," in *Seeking El Dorado: African Americans in California*, ed. Lawrence B. de Graaf, Kevin Mulroy, and Quintard Taylor (Seattle: University of Washington Press; Los Angeles: Autry Museum of Western Heritage, 2001), 284–288.

65. *Proceedings of the Thirty-sixth Annual Convention of the California State Federation of Labor*, Sacramento, 1935, 11.

66. *Los Angeles Citizen*, October 30, 1936, 1.

67. Ibid., August 11, 1936, 2; August 16, 1936, 2. See also *Statement of the Vote at General Election Held On November 3, 1936, in the State of California* (Sacramento: State Printing Office, 1936), 33–35.

68. Rogin and Shover, *Political Change in California*, 138. See also Robert Joseph Pitchell, "Twentieth Century California Voting Behavior" (PhD diss., University of California, Berkeley, 1955), 288–295.

69. Robert E. Burke, *Olson's New Deal for California* (Westport, Conn.: Greenwood, 1982), 32–33.

70. Tom Sitton, *Los Angeles Transformed: Fletcher Bowron's Urban Reform Revival, 1938–1953* (Albuquerque: University of New Mexico Press, 2005), 32–38.

71. Burke, *Olson's New Deal*, 61–77, 226–229.

72. Milton Lawrence Culver, "The Island, the Oasis, and the City: Santa Catalina, Palm Springs, Los Angeles, and Southern California's Shaping of American Life and Leisure" (PhD diss., University of California, Los Angeles, 2004), 335–338.

73. Ibid., 344–345.

74. In 1926 white racists burned down the Pacific Beach Club, a resort building for African Americans, which black entrepreneurs were in the process of constructing near the ocean in Huntington Beach. See Daniel Cady, "'A Place of Our Very Own': The Pacific Beach Club, African Americans, and Incendiary White Southerners" (Huntington Library, 2005), 32–37.

75. Culver, "The Island," 348–351.

76. Phoebe S. Kropp, "Citizens of the Past? Olvera Street and the Construction of Race and Memory in 1930s Los Angeles," *Radical History Review*, no. 81 (Fall 2001): 35–36.

77. Quoted in ibid., 37. For further analysis of Anglo romanticization of L.A.'s Spanish fantasy past, see McWilliams, *Southern California*, chap. 4; and William Deverell, "Privileging the Mission over the Mexican: The Rise of Regional Consciousness in Southern California," in *Many Wests: Place, Culture, and Regional Identity*, ed. David M. Wrobel and Michael C. Steiner (Lawrence: University Press of Kansas, 1997), 114–132.

78. John Modell, *The Economics and Politics of Racial Accommodation: The Japanese of Los Angeles, 1900–1942* (Urbana: University of Illinois Press, 1977), chap. 3.

79. Lon Kurashige, "The Problem of Biculturalism: Japanese American Identity and Festival before World War II," *Journal of American History* 86, no. 4 (March 2000): 1632.

80. Ibid., 1642–1643.

81. On the lack of progress on civil rights during the 1930s, see Alexander Tsesis, *We Shall Overcome: A History of Civil Rights and the Law* (New Haven, Conn.: Yale University Press, 2008), chap. 8.

82. On the growth of anti-Japanese prejudice in the late 1930s, see Roger Daniels, *Concentration Camp USA: Japanese Americans and World War II* (New York: Holt, Rinehart and Winston, 1971), chaps. 1–2.

83. Pitchell, "Twentieth Century California Voting Behavior," 290.

84. Lizabeth Cohen, *Making a New Deal: Industrial Workers in Chicago, 1919–1939* (Cambridge: Cambridge University Press, 1990), 254–255.

85. Thomas J. Sitton, "Urban Politics and Reform in New Deal Los Angeles: The Recall of Mayor Frank L. Shaw" (PhD diss., University of California, Riverside, 1983), 51.

86. Quoted in Robert W. Kenny, "My First Forty Years in California Politics, 1922–1962," 134, interview by Doyce B. Nunis, 1961, transcript, Center for Oral History Research, UCLA. The inclusion of New York Mayor Fiorello LaGuardia's name

on the committee is significant because he was a Republican. Just after he became mayor, Bowron announced: "Although I am a Republican, I am a New Deal Republican and have supported President Roosevelt. I am going to give Los Angeles a New Deal" (Sitton, *Los Angeles Transformed*, 31–32).

87. Quoted in Baisden, "Labor Unions in Los Angeles Politics," 130.

88. Lyle W. Dorsett, *Franklin D. Roosevelt and the City Bosses* (Port Washington, N.Y.: Kennikat Press, 1977), 94–97.

89. J. David Greenstone, *Labor in American Politics* (New York: Knopf, 1969), 147.

90. Douglas Flamming, *Bound for Freedom: Black Los Angeles in Jim Crow America* (Berkeley: University of California Press, 2005), 302–304; Dennis, *Autobiography of an American Communist*, 61–64; Dobbs, "Democracy and the American Communist Movement," 72–79; Healey and Isserman, *Dorothy Healey Remembers*, 40–67; Larry Ceplair and Steven Englund, *The Inquisition in Hollywood: Politics in the Film Community, 1930–1960* (Berkeley: University of California Press, 1983), 54–78; Steve Murdock, "California Communists—Their Years of Power," *Science and Society* 34, no. 4 (Winter 1970): 481–484; Michael Furmanovsky, "Notes for a Dissertation Prospectus" (University of California, Los Angeles, 1988). I arrived at the membership figure of two thousand by halving Harvey Klehr's overall California membership figure of six thousand for the year 1938 and by taking into account the more conservative figure of fifteen hundred given by Los Angeles CP functionary J. Thorne in his report to the Los Angeles County party convention in December 1937. See Klehr, *Heyday of American Communism*, 270. Thorne's report is contained in the Communist Party Vertical File, Southern California Library for Social Studies and Research, Los Angeles.

91. Quoted in Ceplair and Englund, *Inquisition in Hollywood*, 58.

92. Klehr, *Heyday of American Communism*, 271.

93. Louis B. Perry and Richard S. Perry, *A History of the Los Angeles Labor Movement, 1911–1941* (Berkeley: University of California Press, 1963), chaps. 11–13; Vicki L. Ruiz, *Cannery Women, Cannery Lives: Mexican Women, Unionization, and the California Food Processing Industry, 1930–1950* (Albuquerque: University of New Mexico Press, 1987), passim; Harvey O'Connor, *History of the Oil Workers International Union—CIO* (Denver: OWIU, 1950), 428–438.

94. Nicolaides, *My Blue Heaven*, 46–50; Myrna Cherkoss Donahoe, "Workers' Response to Plant Closures: The Cases of Steel and Auto in Southeast Los Angeles, 1935–1986" (PhD diss., University of California, Irvine, 1987), 30.

95. Bruce M. Stave, "Chicago and the New Deal," in *The New Deal: The State and Local Levels*, ed. John Braeman, Robert Bremmer, and David Brody (Columbus: Ohio State University Press, 1975), 399.

96. Nelson Lichtenstein, *Labor's War at Home: The CIO in World War II* (Cambridge: Cambridge University Press, 1982), 18–19; Frank Cormier and William S. Eaton, *Reuther* (Englewood Cliffs, N.J.: Prentice-Hall, 1969), 123–124.

97. Donahoe, "Workers' Response to Plant Closures," 21–22; Irving Howe and B. J. Widick, *The UAW and Walter Reuther* (New York: Random House, 1949), 116–117.

98. Ruth Milkman, *L.A. Story: Immigrant Workers and the Future of the U.S. Labor Movement* (New York: Russell Sage Foundation, 2006), 38; William B. Elconin, "The UE in Southern California," 131–132, interview by Myrna C. Donahoe, 1988, transcript, Center for Oral History Research, UCLA.

99. Baisden "Labor Unions in Los Angeles Politics," 155–156.

100. Quoted in ibid., 158.

101. Quoted in Ruth L. Horowitz, *Political Ideologies of Organized Labor: The New Deal Era* (New Brunswick, N.J.: Transaction Books, 1978), 212–213.

102. Baisden, "Labor Unions in Los Angeles Politics," 155–160, 179; Burke, *Olson's New Deal*, 131; *Western Worker*, October 12, 1936, 2, and October 15, 1936, 8; James L. Daugherty, "Utility Workers, the UE, and the CIO," 89, interview by Myrna C. Donahoe, 1988, transcript, Center for Oral History Research, UCLA. For another negative view of the LNPL, see Dobbs, "Democracy and the American Communist Movement," 142. Dorothy Healey had a more positive view of the LNPL in the 1936 election, saying that it proved effective in "getting union members to the polls." But even if this was true, it could not have compensated for the relatively small number of CIO members available to vote. See Healey and Isserman, *Dorothy Healey Remembers*, 76.

CHAPTER SIX

1. *Los Angeles Citizen*, June 15, 1934, 1.

2. Louis B. Perry and Richard S. Perry, *A History of the Los Angeles Labor Movement, 1911–1941* (Berkeley: University of California Press, 1963), 244–266.

3. Quoted in U.S. Senate, "Employers Associations and Collective Bargaining in California," *Violations of Free Speech and the Rights of Labor: Report of the Committee on Education and Labor*, pt. 2, 128 (77th Cong., 2nd sess., no. 1150) (Washington, D.C.: Government Printing Office, 1942).

4. Perry and Perry, *A History of the Los Angeles Labor Movement*, 311–312.

5. Ibid., chap. 15.

6. Ibid., chap. 11.

7. On the 1933–1934 labor upsurge, see, for example, James R. Green, *The World of the Worker: Labor in Twentieth-Century America* (Urbana: University of Illinois Press, 1998), 140–142.

8. Zaragosa Vargas, *Labor Rights Are Civil Rights: Mexican American Workers in Twentieth-Century America* (Princeton, N.J.: Princeton University Press, 2005), 63–71.

9. For biographical information about Rose Pesotta, see Pesotta, *Bread upon the Waters* (New York: Dodd, Mead, 1944); and Elaine Leeder, *The Gentle General: Rose Pesotta, Anarchist and Labor Organizer* (Albany, N.Y.: SUNY Press, 1993).

10. For a discussion of the emergence of feminist ideas in the ILGWU and the difficulties leaders such as Fannia Cohen experienced in trying to implement them, see Nancy MacLean, "The Culture of Resistance: Female Institution Building in the International Ladies Garment Workers Union, 1905–1925," Michigan Occasional Paper no. 21 (Ann Arbor: Women's Studies Program, University of Michigan, 1982).

11. John H. M. Laslett, "Gender, Class, or Ethno-Cultural Struggle? The Problematic Relationship between Rose Pesotta and the Los Angeles ILGWU," *California History* 72, no. 1 (Spring 1993): 197. For other accounts of the 1933 dressmakers strike, see George Sánchez, *Becoming Mexican American: Ethnicity, Culture, and Identity in Chicano Los Angeles* (New York: Oxford University Press, 1993), 232–234; and Douglas Monroy, "La Costura en Los Angeles, 1933–1939: The ILGWU and the Politics of Domination," in *Mexican Women in the United States: Struggles Past and Present*, ed. Magdalena Mora and Adelaida R. Del Castillo (Los Angeles: UCLA Chicano Studies Research Center, 1980), 177–191.

12. Quoted in Laslett, "Gender, Class, or Ethno-Cultural Struggle?" 197.

13. Ibid.

14. Ibid., 198–199.

15. Ibid., 201–202.

16. Quoted in ibid., 201.

17. Ibid.

18. Ibid., 206.

19. Pesotta, *Bread upon the Waters*, 26.

20. Cletus E. Daniel, *Bitter Harvest: A History of California Farmworkers, 1870–1941* (Berkeley: University of California Press, 1982), chap. 5.

21. This narrative of the El Monte strike is based on the account in Daniel, *Bitter Harvest*, 146–149. See also Ronald Lopez, "The El Monte Berry Strike of 1933," *Aztlan* 1, no. 10 (1970): 101–122; Charles B. Spaulding, "The Mexican Strike at El Monte, California," *Sociology and Social Research* 18, no. 6 (July-August 1934): 571–580.

22. Daniel, *Bitter Harvest*, 147–148.

23. Ibid., 148.

24. Ibid., 149.

25. Ibid.

26. Quoted in ibid., 106.

27. Ibid., 153–155.

28. Quoted in Sánchez, *Becoming Mexican American*, 238. See also Vicki L. Ruiz, *Cannery Women, Cannery Lives: Mexican Women, Unionization, and the California Food Processing Industry, 1930–1950* (Albuquerque: University of New Mexico Press, 1987), 75–76.

29. Ruiz, *Cannery Women*, 75–76.

30. On Dorothy Healey, see Dorothy Healey and Maurice Isserman, *Dorothy*

Healey Remembers: A Life in the American Communist Party (New York: Oxford University Press, 1990), passim. On Luisa Moreno, see Carlos Larralde and Richard Griswold del Castillo, "Luisa Moreno: A Hispanic Civil Rights Leader in San Diego," *Journal of San Diego History* 41, no. 4 (Fall 1995): 67–84; Vicki L. Ruiz, "Una Mujer Sin Fronteras: Luisa Moreno and Latina Labor Activism," *Pacific Historical Review* 73, no. 1 (February 2004): 1–20.

31. Ruiz, *Cannery Women*, 74–77; Vargas, *Labor Rights Are Civil Rights*, 151–153.

32. Quoted in Ruiz, *Cannery Women*, 97.

33. Sánchez, *Becoming Mexican American*, 239.

34. Vargas, *Labor Rights Are Civil Rights*, 185–186.

35. Perry and Perry, *A History of the Los Angeles Labor Movement*, 365–367

36. Ibid., 366–367.

37. Peter "Pete" Grassi, interview by Norman Fainsod, February 14, 1984, transcript, 3–4, 15–16, ILWU Local 13 Oral History Project, Urban Archives Center, Oviatt Library, California State University, Northridge. See also Henry P. Sitka, *San Pedro: A Pictorial History* (San Pedro: San Pedro Historical Society, 1981), 86. The main foreign-language groups in San Pedro at this time were Italians, Scandinavians, Greeks, Yugoslavs, Mexicans, and Japanese. Most of the Japanese lived in the fishing neighborhood of Terminal Island. Among the several hundred Mexicans living in San Pedro in 1934 were twenty-one with the name Rodríguez, nine of whom were laborers; twenty-nine named Sánchez, three of whom were longshoremen; and thirty with the name López, three of whom were cannery workers and one of whom was a longshoreman. The Scandinavians in San Pedro were better off: of the sixteen inhabitants with the surname Jensen, two were seamen and two were longshoremen, while the other three were listed as a machinist, a boilermaker, and a master mariner. See *San Pedro and Wilmington City Directory and Buyers Guide* (Los Angeles: Los Angeles Directory Co., 1934), 214, 218, 234, 309; and Nicholas P. Lovrich Jr., *Yugoslavs and Italians in San Pedro: Political Culture and Civic Involvement* (Palo Alto, Calif.: Ragusan Press, 1977), passim.

38. Minutes of Executive Board, May 12, 1934, series 1, box 1, ILWU Local 13 Collection, Oviatt Library, California State University, Northridge.

39. Alfred Langley, interview by Tony Salcido, 1993, transcript, 16, ILWU Local 13 Oral History Project.

40. Quoted in *San Pedro News-Pilot*, May 15, 1934, 2.

41. Perry and Perry, *A History of the Los Angeles Labor Movement*, 369.

42. Minutes of Executive Board, June 14, 1934, 13, series 1, box 1, ILWU Local 13 Collection; Langley interview, 14.

43. Perry and Perry, *A History of the Los Angeles Labor Movement*, 368; *Los Angeles Citizen*, June 22, 1934, 1.

44. Perry and Perry, *A History of the Los Angeles Labor Movement*, 370–373.

45. Ibid., 369–373.

46. Bruce Nelson, *Workers on the Waterfront: Seamen, Longshoremen, and Unionism in the 1930s* (Urbana: University of Illinois Press, 1988), 238–239.

47. The fragmented character of trade unionism among the employees in the Los Angeles furniture industry is discussed in Luis Arroyo, "Industrial Unionism and the Los Angeles Furniture Industry, 1918–1954" (PhD diss., University of California, Los Angeles, 1979), chap. 1. For the role of the Southern California Furniture Manufacturers Association in preserving the open shop, see Arroyo, "Industrial Unionism," 83; and U.S. Senate, "Employers Associations and Collective Bargaining in California," 66:796–798 (La Follette Committee).

48. "Addenda on Furniture Industry," WPA Report, 13–14, box 155, Ephemera, Collection 200, Special Collections, Charles E. Young Research Library, University of California, Los Angeles.

49. Quoted in Sánchez, *Becoming Mexican American*, 241.

50. Quoted in *Los Angeles Citizen*, June 14, 1937, 4. As in other industries, employers in the furniture industry preferred dealing with the AFL rather than the CIO. According to Luis Arroyo, AFL Furniture Workers Locals 15 and 1561 "were aided by some employers who would fire any of their employees who were affiliated with CIO Local No. 576." See Luis Leobardo Arroyo, "Chicano Participation in Organized Labor: The CIO in Los Angeles, 1938–1950, An Extended Research Note," *Aztlan* 6, no. 2 (Summer 1975): 285.

51. Perry and Perry, *A History of the Los Angeles Labor Movement*, 416.

52. William Seligman, "For an Independent Trade Union Movement," 249, interview by Michael Furmanovsky, 1985, transcript, Center for Oral History Research, Special Collections, Charles E. Young Research Library, University of California, Los Angeles.

53. Quoted in ibid., 190.

54. John Laslett and Mary Tyler, *The ILGWU in Los Angeles, 1907–1988* (Inglewood, Calif.: Ten Star Press, 1989), 43.

55. Perry and Perry, *A History of the Los Angeles Labor Movement*, 423.

56. Ibid.

57. *Los Angeles Citizen*, February 29, 1938, 4; David F. Selvin, *Sky Full of Storm: A Brief History of California Labor* (San Francisco: California Historical Society, 1975), 55.

58. Leaflet in Healey (Shevy Healey) Papers, folder 2, box 1, Southern California Library for Social Studies and Research, Los Angeles.

59. James L. Daugherty, "Utility Workers, the UE, and the CIO," 88–90, interview by Myrna C. Donahoe, 1988, transcript, Center for Oral History Research, UCLA. See also Sarah Cooper, "On the Archival Trail of the CIO and Hollywood's Labor Wars," *California History* 75, no. 1 (Spring 1996): 34–39.

60. Cooper, "On the Archival Trail," 38–39.

61. Douglas Monroy, *Rebirth: Mexican Los Angeles from the Great Migration to the Great Depression* (Berkeley: University of California Press, 1999), 251.

62. "Report on Election of Officers," folder 16, box 7, Philip Marshall Connelly Papers, Collection of Los Angeles CIO Industrial Union Council Records (Collection 2015), Special Collections, Charles E. Young Research Library, University of California, Los Angeles.

63. *Labor Herald*, April 26, 1939, 4.

64. Douglas Flamming, *Bound for Freedom: Black Los Angeles in Jim Crow America* (Berkeley: University of California Press, 2005), 300. See also Alonzo Nelson Smith, "Black Employment in the Los Angeles Area, 1938–1948" (PhD diss., University of California, Los Angeles, 1978), 166.

65. Flamming, *Bound for Freedom*, 355–359.

66. Quoted in Sánchez, *Becoming Mexican American*, 247.

67. David Oberweiser Jr., "The CIO: A Vanguard for Civil Rights in Southern California, 1940–1946," in *American Labor in the Era of World War II*, ed. Sally M. Miller and Daniel A. Cornford (Westport, Conn.: Praeger, 1995), 201–202.

68. Sánchez, *Becoming Mexican American*, 250.

69. Vargas, *Labor Rights Are Civil Rights*, 186.

70. Natalia Molina, *Fit to Be Citizens? Public Health and Race in Los Angeles, 1879–1939* (Berkeley: University of California Press, 2006), 172.

71. In 1989, historian Gary Gerstle proposed a reworking of the definition of "Americanism" to include the concept of "working-class Americanism"—the idea that embracing trade union goals is a valid means of asserting workers' aspirations for full U.S. citizenship. Although the idea can easily be exaggerated, it provides a valid way of linking second-generation immigrants' desires for both union membership and U.S. identity in the 1930s. See Gerstle, *Working-Class Americanism: The Politics of Labor in a Textile City, 1914–1960* (Cambridge: Cambridge University Press, 1989), 8–15, 331–336.

72. *Labor Herald*, July 18, 1939, 4.

73. Perry and Perry, *A History of the Los Angeles Labor Movement*, 409–417. One of the bitterest conflicts, which was attended by much violence, was between the Teamsters and the ILWU, who battled over the right to organize the city's warehouse employees. Chapter Seven describes this fight; see also Perry and Perry, *A History of the Los Angeles Labor Movement*, 469–476; and Arroyo, "Chicano Participation in Organized Labor," 280–283.

74. Harvey Klehr, *The Heyday of American Communism: The Depression Decade* (New York: Basic Books, 1984), 270–272. See also Healey and Isserman, *Dorothy Healey Remembers*, 118–123; and Michael Furmanovsky, "Labor Upsurge of 1934 and the Limitations of Red Unionism" (University of California, Los Angeles, 1988), 81.

75. Klehr, *Heyday of American Communism*, 272.

76. In his first report as president of the ILWU in 1937, Harry Bridges proposed that the provisions in the union bylaws regarding the election and recall of officers be strengthened so as to make it easier for rank-and-file union members "to immediately suspend or remove any officials using or attempting to use his authority to exercise dictatorial . . . control" (Bridges quoted in Charles P. Larrowe, *Harry Bridges: The Rise and Fall of Radical Labor in the United States* [Westport, Conn.: Lawrence Hill, 1972], 126).

77. Perry and Perry, *A History of the Los Angeles Labor Movement*, 444; "Articles Excerpted from the *Los Angeles Examiner*, August 4–18, 1938," Register of the California CIO Council, Union Research and Information Service Records, 1935–1956, mss 013, box 1/18, Southern California Library for Social Studies and Research, Los Angeles; folder 1, box 1, Connelly Papers.

78. Folder 1, box 1, Connelly Papers.

79. For more detail on why the CIO broke away from the AFL, see Robert H. Zieger, *The CIO, 1935–1955* (Chapel Hill: University of North Carolina Press, 1995), chaps. 1–3.

80. See Donald H. Grubbs, *Cry from the Cotton: The Southern Tenant Farmers' Union and the New Deal* (Chapel Hill: University of North Carolina Press, 1971).

81. Quoted in Monroy, *Rebirth*, 163.

82. *Los Angeles Citizen*, August 4, 1937, 4.

83. Peter Friedlander, *Emergence of a UAW Local, 1936–1939: A Study in Class and Culture* (Pittsburgh: University of Pittsburgh Press, 1975), chap. 7. See also Thomas Gobel, "Becoming American: Ethnic Workers and the Rise of the CIO," *Labor History* 29, no. 2 (Spring 1988): 173–198.

CHAPTER SEVEN

1. Becky Nicolaides, *My Blue Heaven: Life and Politics in the Working-Class Suburbs of Los Angeles, 1920–1965* (Chicago: University of Chicago Press, 2002), 82.

2. Harold M. Levinson, *Collective Bargaining in the Steel Industry: Pattern Setter or Pattern Follower?* (Ann Arbor: University of Michigan Press, 1962), 2–3.

3. Further details about the struggle between the Los Angeles unions and the Merchants and Manufacturers Association and its allies in the 1930s can be found in the letters, memos, and reports collected as evidence for Senator Robert M. La Follette's Senate hearings on labor rights and free speech. See U.S. Senate, "Supplementary Exhibits on Los Angeles Chamber of Commerce and Merchants and Manufacturers Association," *Hearings before the Committee on Education and Labor, Subcommittee Investigating Violations of Free Speech and the Rights of Labor*, pt. 63, 76th Cong., 2nd sess. (Washington, D.C.: Government Printing Office, 1940).

4. *Los Angeles Citizen*, March 12, 1937, 8; April 4, 1937, 3.

5. Quoted in U.S. Senate, "Supplementary Exhibits," 22985.

6. Louis B. Perry and Richard S. Perry, *A History of the Los Angeles Labor Move-*

ment, 1911–1941 (Berkeley: University of California Press, 1963), 461–463; Luis Arroyo, "Industrial Unionism and the Los Angeles Furniture Industry, 1918–1954" (PhD diss., University of California, Los Angeles, 1979), chap. 3.

7. Quoted in "The Story of the Pot and the Kettle," circular of UFWA Local 576, December 4, 1939, 6, mss. 013, California CIO Council, Register, Union Research and Information Service Records, 1935–1956, Southern California Library for Social Studies and Research, Los Angeles.

8. Ibid.

9. Perry and Perry, *A History of the Los Angeles Labor Movement*, 463.

10. Ibid., 463–464.

11. Robert D. Parmet, *The Master of Seventh Avenue: David Dubinsky and the American Labor Movement* (New York: New York University Press, 2005), 283–285.

12. Perry and Perry, *A History of the Los Angeles Labor Movement*, 469–470. See also Harvey Schwartz, *The March Inland: Origins of the ILWU Warehouse Division, 1934–1938* (Los Angeles: UCLA Institute of Industrial Relations, 1978), passim.

13. Perry and Perry, *A History of the Los Angeles Labor Movement*, 470–472. See also Mario T. García, *Memories of Chicano History: The Life and Narrative of Bert Corona* (Berkeley: University of California Press, 1994), chap. 5.

14. Quoted in *Los Angeles Citizen*, June 28, 1913, 4.

15. Perry and Perry, *A History of the Los Angeles Labor Movement*, 426–430; Errol Wayne Stevens, *Radical L.A.: From Coxey's Army to the Watts Riots, 1894–1965* (Norman: University of Oklahoma Press, 2009), 236–237; Robert Gottlieb and Irene Wolt, *Thinking Big: The Story of the* Los Angeles Times, *Its Publishers, and Their Influence on Southern California* (New York: Putnam, 1977), 214–219.

16. Stevens, *Radical L.A.*, 238–243; Perry and Perry, *A History of the Los Angeles Labor Movement*, 433–438. Also see *Los Angeles Citizen*, December 3, 1937, 1; December 24, 1937, 12; January 14, 1938, 1, 8; November 11, 1938, 1.

17. Perry and Perry, *A History of the Los Angeles Labor Movement*, 517–518; John Allard, "Organizing the United Auto Workers in Los Angeles," 18–19, interview by Michael Furmanovsky, 1986, transcript, Center for Oral History Research, Special Collections, Charles E. Young Research Library, University of California, Los Angeles.

18. U.S. Senate, "Employers Associations and Collective Bargaining in California," *Violations of Free Speech and the Rights of Labor: Report of the Committee on Education and Labor*, pt. 2, 77th Cong., 2nd sess., no. 1150 (Washington, D.C.: Government Printing Office, 1942), 214.

19. Allard, "Organizing the United Auto Workers," 14.

20. Quoted in ibid., 16.

21. U.S. Senate, "Employers Associations and Collective Bargaining in California" (77th Cong., 2nd sess.), 214.

22. Quoted in ibid., 21057.

23. Perry and Perry, *A History of the Los Angeles Labor Movement*, 519.

24. Gottlieb and Wolt, *Thinking Big*, 188, 200, 219–221; Stevens, *Radical L.A.*, 139–140.

25. Perry and Perry, *A History of the Los Angeles Labor Movement*, 518–519; U.S. Senate, "Employers Associations and Collective Bargaining in California," *Report of the Committee on Education and Labor, Subcommittee Investigating Violations of Free Speech and the Rights of Labor,* 78th Cong., 2nd sess. (Washington, D.C.: Government Printing Office, 1944), 21098–21099.

26. For introductions to the rise of the aircraft industry in Los Angeles, see James Richard Wilburn, "Social and Economic Aspects of the Aircraft Industry in Metropolitan Los Angeles during World War II" (PhD diss., University of California, Los Angeles, 1971), chap. 1; and Greg Hise, *Magnetic Los Angeles: Planning the Twentieth-Century Metropolis* (Baltimore: Johns Hopkins University Press, 1997), chap. 4.

27. Wilburn, "Social and Economic Aspects of the Aircraft Industry," 121–135.

28. At the time the Second World War broke out, in September 1939, Douglas employed 7,589 airplane workers. By 1944, Douglas Aircraft had expanded to six major production plants employing 160,000 workers in both Northern and Southern California. See Arthur C. Verge, *Paradise Transformed: Los Angeles during the Second World War* (Dubuque, Iowa: Kendall Hunt, 1993), 97.

29. Perry and Perry, *A History of the Los Angeles Labor Movement*, 447–453.

30. *Los Angeles Times,* February 28, 1937, 2; U.S. Senate. "Employers Associations and Collective Bargaining in California" (78th Cong., 2nd sess.), 23442–23450.

31. Quoted in *Los Angeles Times,* March 3, 1937, 2.

32. *Los Angeles Citizen,* February 26, 1937, 5; March 5, 1937, 4.

33. *Los Angeles Times,* March 3, 1937, 2.

34. *Los Angeles Citizen,* March 12, 1937, 2.

35. Perry and Perry, *A History of the Los Angeles Labor Movement*, chap. 13.

36. Harvey O'Connor, *History of the Oil Workers International Union–CIO* (Denver: OWIU, 1950), 26; "Job Analysis" (list of workers employed by Long Beach Oil Development Co., 1940), folder 10, box 34, Oil, Chemical, and Atomic Workers International Union (OCAW), Local 128 Collection, Western Historical Collections, University of Colorado, Boulder.

37. "Audit Balance of District 1 Locals, Sept. 30, 1930," folder 3, box 29, OCAW Local 128 Collection; "History of Oil Workers Local #128," typescript, folder 29, box 42, OCAW Local 128 Collection.

38. Upton Sinclair, *Oil!* (Berkeley: University of California Press, 1997), 83.

39. O'Connor, *History of the Oil Workers International Union*, 28.

40. U.S. Senate, "Supplementary Exhibits," 23518.

41. Quoted in ibid., 23529.

42. Ibid., 23522–23531.

43. When representatives of the Oil Workers Union went to Washington to discuss the Petroleum Code, the American Petroleum Institute introduced a draft of the code without NIRA's Section 7a attached to it. The absence of Section 7a would have prevented the oil workers from forming a union. See O'Connor, *History of the Oil Workers International Union*, 30.

44. *Proceedings, Fifty-fifth Annual Convention of the American Federation of Labor*, Atlantic City, 1935, 825–827.

45. "History of the Oil Workers International Union," typescript, folder 19, box 42, OCAW Local 128 Collection.

46. Kendall Beaton, *Enterprise in Oil: A History of Shell in the United States* (New York: Appleton-Century-Crofts, 1957), 489.

47. O'Connor, *History of the Oil Workers International Union*, 253–254; "History of Oil Workers Local #128," 9–10, OCAW Local 128 Collection.

48. O'Connor, *History of the Oil Workers International Union*, 47; Harvey Levenstein, *Communism, Anticommunism, and the CIO* (Westport, Conn.: Greenwood Press, 1981), chap. 3; Judith Stepan-Norris and Maurice Zeitlin, *Left Out: Reds and America's Industrial Unions* (Cambridge: Cambridge University Press, 2003), 164.

49. "History of Oil Workers Local #128," 11–12, OCAW Local 128 Collection.

50. Donald Garnel, *The Rise of Teamster Power in the West* (Berkeley: University of California Press, 1972), 164.

51. Ruth Milkman, *L.A. Story: Immigrant Workers and the Future of the U.S. Labor Movement* (New York: Russell Sage Foundation, 2006), 104–106.

52. Garnel, *The Rise of Teamster Power*, 72–75, 141–143.

53. Quoted in ibid., 155. The Intelligence Bureau of the LAPD in downtown Los Angeles received numerous complaints from warehouse companies operating out of San Pedro Harbor about threatening behavior by members of Teamsters Local 692, who stopped nonunion truckers at the harbor gates and threatened them with violence if they did not become members of the union. See U.S. Senate, "Supplementary Exhibits," 23535–23557.

54. Garnel, *The Rise of Teamster Power*, 163.

55. The most straightforward account of the Browne-Bioff period in IATSE's history and its ramifications for Hollywood's studio employees can be found in Michael Charles Nielsen, "Motion Picture Craft Workers and Craft Unions in Hollywood: The Studio Era, 1912–1948" (PhD diss., University of Illinois, 1985), chap. 6.

56. Perry and Perry, *A History of the Los Angeles Labor Movement*, chap. 9.

57. Ibid.

58. Quoted in Laurie Caroline Pintar, "Herbert K. Sorrell as the Grade-B Hero: Militancy and Masculinity in the Studios," *Labor History* 37, no. 3 (Summer 1996): 400.

59. The "iron law of oligarchy" refers to the argument made by prominent French

sociologist Robert Michels that, with the passage of time, large-scale organizations such as trade unions and political parties inevitably develop authoritarian, bureaucratic structures. See Robert Michels, *Political Parties: A Sociological Study of the Oligarchical Tendencies of Modern Democracy* (New York: Free Press, 1962), passim.

60. Nielsen, "Motion Picture Craft Workers," 210–209.

61. David Witwer, *Shadow of the Racketeer: Scandal in Organized Labor* (Urbana: University of Illinois Press, 2009), 10–13.

62. Milkman, *L.A. Story*, 52–59. See also Paul Bullock, *Building California: The Story of the Carpenters Union* (Los Angeles: UCLA Center for Labor Research and Education, 1982), 112–114, 141–147; and Cornelius J. Haggerty, "Labor, Los Angeles, and the Legislature," *Labor Leaders View the Warren Era*, 23–25, interview by Amelia R. Fry, 1976, Earl Warren Oral History Project, Bancroft Library, University of California, Berkeley.

63. Robert Zieger, *The CIO, 1935–1955* (Chapel Hill: University of North Carolina Press, 1995), 34–39; *Southern California Business* 37, no. 2 (April 1939): 14–16.

64. Brophy quoted in *Labor Herald*, August 25, 1938, 3.

65. Christopher Tomlins, "AFL Unions in the 1930s: Their Performance in Historical Perspective," *Journal of American History* 65, no. 4 (March 1979): 1023.

66. *Los Angeles Citizen*, June 14, 1939, 5; Lizabeth Cohen, *Making a New Deal: Industrial Workers in Chicago, 1919–1939* (Cambridge: Cambridge University Press, 1990), 311.

67. Van Dusen Kennedy, *Nonfactory Unionism and Labor Relations* (Berkeley: Institute of Labor Relations, 1955), 6.

68. Mark Perlman, *The Machinists: A New Study in American Trade Unionism* (Cambridge, Mass.: Harvard University Press, 1962), 8–84, 132–142; see also Tomlins, "AFL Unions in the 1930s," 1027–1034.

69. Industrial Department, Los Angeles Chamber of Commerce, "Economic Background to Los Angeles County," in *Eight Studies on the Industrial Development of Los Angeles County* (Los Angeles: Los Angeles Chamber of Commerce, n.d.), 6.

70. Perry and Perry, *A History of the Los Angeles Labor Movement*, chap. 15; Verge, *Paradise Transformed*, 2–3.

71. Quoted in U.S. Senate, "A Study of Labor Policies of Employers Associations in the Los Angeles Area, 1935–39," *Violations of Free Speech and the Rights of Labor: Report of the Committee on Education and Labor*, pt. 6, 78th Cong., 1st sess. (Washington, D.C.: Government Printing Office, 1942), 44.

72. Despite the difficulties Democratic Governor Olson experienced in 1939–1941, during the course of the 1930s the California state legislature in Sacramento passed many of the same labor laws at the state level as the Roosevelt administration did in Washington, including favorable laws on unemployment insurance, public relief, and organizing rights. See Robert E. Burke, *Olson's New Deal for California*

(Westport, Conn.: Greenwood Press, 1982; originally pub. 1953), chap. 5; Philip Taft, *Labor Politics American Style: The California State Federation of Labor* (Cambridge, Mass.: Harvard University Press, 1968), 86–87, 111–115.

73. Quoted in Wilburn, "Social and Economic Aspects of the Aircraft Industry," 34.

74. U.S. Senate, "Supplementary Exhibits," 792–793.

75. Ibid., 916–919. See also Gottlieb and Wolt, *Thinking Big*, 217–218.

76. Quoted in Gene B. Tipton, "The Labor Movement in the Los Angeles Area during the 1940s" (PhD diss., University of California, Los Angeles, 1953), 241.

77. *Business Week*, December 13, 1941, 19.

CHAPTER EIGHT

1. For general introductions to the impact of World War II on Southern California, see Roger W. Lotchin, *The Bad City in the Good War: San Francisco, Los Angeles, Oakland, and San Diego* (Bloomington: Indiana University Press, 2003); Gerald R. Nash, *World War II and the West: Reshaping the Economy* (Lincoln: University of Nebraska Press, 1990); and Arthur C. Verge, *Paradise Transformed: Los Angeles during the Second World War* (Dubuque, Iowa: Kendall Hunt, 1993).

2. Lotchin, *The Bad City*, 159.

3. Arthur C. Verge, "The Impact of the Second World War on Los Angeles," *Pacific Historical Review* 63, no. 3 (August 1994): 292–293.

4. This debate is covered by Don Parson in his *Making a Better World: Public Housing, the Red Scare, and the Direction of Modern Los Angeles* (Minneapolis: University of Minnesota Press, 2005), chap. 2.

5. Verge, *Paradise Transformed*, 87.

6. U.S. Census Bureau, "Wartime Changes in Population and Family Characteristics: Los Angeles Congested Production Area," Series CA-2, no. 5 (Washington, D.C.: Government Printing Office, 1944), 1–9. For the "southernization" of Southern California in the 1930s and 1940s, see James R. Gregory, *American Exodus: The Dust Bowl Migration and Okie Culture in California* (New York: Oxford University Press, 1989), chaps. 4–5.

7. Quoted in U.S. Census Bureau, "Wartime Changes in Population," 5.

8. For the shipbuilding and aircraft industries in Long Beach during World War II, see Stephen T. Sato, *San Pedro Bay Area: Featuring Long Beach, San Pedro, and Wilmington* (Chatsworth, Calif.: Windsor Publications, 1990), 53–55.

9. Greg Hise, *Magnetic Los Angeles: Planning the Twentieth-Century Metropolis* (Baltimore: Johns Hopkins University Press, 1997), 142.

10. U.S. Census Bureau, "Wartime Changes in Population," 6–7.

11. Quoted in Verge, *Paradise Transformed*, 109–110.

12. Quoted in Parson, *Making a Better World*, 65.

13. Ibid., 40.

14. Ibid., 56.

15. Quoted in ibid., 65.

16. Lotchin, *The Bad City,* 134. Historian Peter La Chapelle even suggests that "eugenics and race talk allowed native white Californians to create myths that downplayed the status of white Dust Bowlers to such an extent that migrants were subjected to the forms of harassment typically faced by racial minority groups" (*Proud to Be an Okie: Cultural Politics, Country Music, and Migration to Southern California* [Berkeley: University of California Press, 2007], 23).

17. La Chapelle, *Proud to Be an Okie,* 67–73.

18. Because the FEPC paid scant attention to the employment needs of Mexican workers, the Industrial Council of the CIO and Mexican American civil rights groups scheduled a conference to discuss the matter on December 7, 1941, but its efforts were stymied by the attack on Pearl Harbor that same day. See David Oberweiser, "The CIO: A Vanguard for Civil Rights in Southern California, 1940–46," in *American Labor in the Era of World War II,* ed. Sally M. Miller and Daniel A. Cornford (Westport, Conn.: Praeger, 1995), 203.

19. Verge, *Paradise Transformed,* 58.

20. Zaragosa Vargas, *Labor Rights Are Civil Rights: Mexican American Workers in Twentieth-Century America* (Princeton, N.J.: Princeton University Press, 2005), 192–198; Eduardo Obregón Pagán, *Murder at the Sleepy Lagoon: Zoot Suits, Race, and Riot in Wartime L.A.* (Chapel Hill: University of North Carolina Press, 2003), passim.

21. Lotchin, *The Bad City,* 128–130; Josh Sides, *L.A. City Limits: African American Los Angeles from the Great Depression to the Present* (Berkeley: University of California Press, 2003), 42–48.

22. Quoted in Sides, *L.A. City Limits,* 50–51.

23. Quoted in Regina Freer, "L.A. Race Woman: Charlotta Bass and the Complexities of Black Political Development in Los Angeles," *American Quarterly* 56, no. 3 (September 2004): 617.

24. Alonzo Nelson Smith, "Black Employment in the Los Angeles Area, 1938–1948" (PhD diss., University of California, Los Angeles, 1978), 219–222.

25. James Richard Wilburn, "Social and Economic Aspects of the Aircraft Industry in Metropolitan Los Angeles during World War II" (PhD diss., University of California, Los Angeles 1971), 91–92.

26. Quoted in Alonzo N. Smith, "Blacks and the Los Angeles Municipal Transit System, 1941–1945," *Urbanism Past and Present* 6, no. 2 (Winter/Spring 1980–1981): 29.

27. Ibid., 28–30.

28. Quoted in Verge, *Paradise Transformed,* 47.

29. Smith, "Black Employment in the Los Angeles Area," 98.

30. Lotchin, *The Bad City,* 3–5.

31. Kevin Allen Leonard, "Federal Power and Racial Politics in Los Angeles dur-

ing World War II," in *Power and Place in the North American West*, ed. Richard White and John M. Findlay (Seattle: University of Washington Press, 1999), 92–98. For further details on the role of the FEPC, see Louis Ruchames, *Race, Jobs, and Politics: The Story of FEPC* (New York: Columbia University Press, 1953); and Merl E. Reed, *Seedtime for the Modern Civil Rights Movement: The President's Commission on Fair Employment Practices, 1941–1946* (Baton Rouge: Louisiana State University Press, 1991).

32. Quoted in Sides, *L.A. City Limits*, 61–62.

33. Josh Sides, "Battle on the Home Front: African American Shipyard Workers in World War II Los Angeles," *California History* 75, no. 3 (Fall 1996): 247–249.

34. Quoted in ibid., 249.

35. Ibid., 249 256; Charles Wollenberg, "*James vs. Marinship:* Trouble on the New Black Frontier," *California History* 60, no. 3 (Fall 1981): 262–279.

36. David Fine, *Imagining Los Angeles: A City in Fiction* (Albuquerque: University of New Mexico Press, 2000), 198.

37. Chester B. Himes, *If He Hollers, Let Him Go* (Garden City, N.Y.: Doubleday, 1946).

38. Ibid. For scholarly discussions of Himes's novels, see Gilbert H. Muller, *Chester Himes* (Boston: Twayne Publishers, 1989); and Stephen F. Milliken, *Chester Himes: A Critical Appraisal* (Columbia: University of Missouri Press, 1976).

39. Quoted in Himes, *If He Hollers*, 24.

40. Ibid., 33.

41. Quoted in ibid., 47.

42. Ibid., 73.

43. Ibid., chaps. 20–22.

44. Quoted in Eileen Boris, "'You Wouldn't Want One of 'Em Dancing with Your Wife': Racialized Bodies on the Job in World War II," *American Quarterly* 50, no. 1 (March 1998): 94.

45. Quoted in *Los Angeles Times*, January 24, 1942, 8.

46. *Labor in California, 1943–1944* (San Francisco: State of California, Department of Industrial Relations, 1945), 46–47; Stanley Ward, "Wartime Expansion of the California Airframe Industry," *Monthly Labor Review* 61, no. 4 (October 1945): 723.

47. In her study of World War II propaganda promoting the recruitment of female war workers, Maureen Honey focuses on the magazines *True Story* and the *Saturday Evening Post* and argues that the message sent was biased toward a middle-class image of women. See Honey, *Creating Rosie the Riveter: Class, Gender, and Propaganda during World War II* (Amherst: University of Massachusetts Press, 1984), passim.

48. Alice Kessler-Harris, "'Rosie the Riveter': Who Was She?" *Labor History* 24, no. 2 (Spring 1983): 249–250.

49. *The Life and Times of Rosie the Riveter*, DVD, directed by Connie Field (Berke-

ley, Calif: Clarity Films, 1980), http://www.clarityfilms.org, also available at the Instructional Media Library, University of California, Los Angeles.

50. Kessler-Harris, "'Rosie the Riveter,'" 251.

51. Quoted in Sherna Berger Gluck, *Rosie the Riveter Revisited: Women, the War, and Social Change* (New York: New American Library, 1987), 209.

52. Ibid., 38.

53. *The Life and Times of Rosie the Riveter* (film); Deborah Scott Hirshfield, "Women Shipyard Workers in the Second World War: A Note," *International History Review* 11, no. 2 (May 1989): 478–485.

54. Quoted in D'Ann Campbell, *Women at War with America: Private Lives in a Patriotic Era* (Cambridge, Mass.: Harvard University Press, 1984), 125. One of the managers at Vultee, which was the first aircraft factory to employ women, calculated that every time a woman walked through the plant, the male employees were so distracted that the company lost $250 in decreased productivity (*Los Angeles Times*, February 3, 1942, 3).

55. *Lockheed-Vega Star*, May 28, 1943, 7.

56. *Labor Herald*, September 14, 1943, 4.

57. Lotchin, *The Bad City*, 76; *Handbook of California Labor Statistics, 1940–1950* (San Francisco: State of California, Department of Industrial Relations, 1951), 71.

58. Gluck, *Rosie the Riveter Revisited*, 265.

59. Ibid.

60. Quoted in Campbell, *Women at War with America*, 134.

61. Gluck, *Rosie the Riveter Revisited*, 264.

62. Quoted in *Lockheed-Vega Star*, January 14, 1944, 7.

63. For an excellent study of the automobile and electrical industries that discusses the ambivalence of male trade unionists toward women workers in this period, see Ruth Milkman, *Gender at Work: The Dynamics of Job Segregation by Sex during World War II* (Urbana: University of Illinois Press, 1987).

64. However, Ruth Milkman points out that employers and male trade union leaders had somewhat different motives for confining women workers to the lower half of the dual labor market. Capitalist employers did so mainly to maximize their profits, whereas male union leaders did so in order to prevent women from challenging the prerogatives of male dominance at the workplace. See Campbell, *Women at War with America*, 155–157; Milkman, *Gender at Work*, 4–11; and Heidi Hartmann, "Capitalism, Patriarchy, and Job Segregation by Sex," in *Women and the Workplace: The Implications of Occupational Segregation*, ed. Martha Blaxall and Barbara Reagan (Chicago: University of Chicago Press, 1976), 137–169.

65. For an interesting analysis of this threat, see Boris, "'You Wouldn't Want One of 'Em Dancing with Your Wife,'" 77–98.

66. Quoted in Sides, *L.A. City Limits*, 69.

67. Ibid. The impact of this decision on the admission of black women into the Boilermakers Union is unclear. In August 1942, the union approved the admission of women by a national referendum vote, but local unions "in critical defense areas" opposed it. I have been unable to ascertain whether Los Angeles Lodge 92 was one of those local unions. See Campbell, *Women at War with America*, 144; William H. Harris, "Federal Intervention in Union Discrimination: FEPC and West Coast Shipyards during World War II," *Labor History* 22, no. 3 (Summer 1981): 325–348; and Wollenberg, "*James vs. Marinship*," 262–279.

68. Sides, "Battle on the Home Front," 255.

69. Bruce Nelson, "The 'Lords of the Docks' Reconsidered: Race Relations among West Coast Longshoremen, 1933–1961," in *Waterfront Workers: New Perspectives on Race and Class*, ed. Calvin Winslow (Urbana: University of Illinois Press, 1998), 158–160. See also Moon-Kie Jung, *Reworking Race: The Making of Hawaii's Interracial Labor Movement* (New York: Columbia University Press, 2006).

70. Quoted in Nelson, "The 'Lords of the Docks' Reconsidered," 159.

71. Ibid., 168–169. See also Lester Rubin, *The Negro in the Longshore Industry*, Racial Policies of American Industry Report no. 26 (Philadelphia: University of Pennsylvania Press, 1974), 142–144.

72. See, for example, Herbert Hill's analysis of the contradiction between the CIO's declarations in favor of racial equality and the practice of racial discrimination by many of its local affiliates: Hill, "The Problem of Race in American Labor History," *Reviews in American History* 24, no. 2 (June 1996): 189–208.

73. Nelson, "The 'Lords of the Docks' Reconsidered," 174.

74. Campbell, *Women at War with America*, 141; Hirshfield, "Women Shipyard Workers," 478–483.

75. *Los Angeles Times*, April 14, 1944, 8. On the NLRB elections at the Douglas plant in Santa Monica, see Wilburn, "Social and Economic Aspects of the Aircraft Industry," 128–129.

76. *American Aeronaut*, October 21, 1944, 2.

77. Quoted in Campbell, *Women at War with America*, 147.

78. Karen Tucker Anderson, "Last Hired, First Fired: Black Women Workers during World War II," *Journal of American History*, vol. 69, no. 2 (June 1982): 87.

79. *The Life and Times of Rosie the Riveter* (film).

80. Bernice Anita Reed, "Accommodation between Negro and White Employees in a West Coast Aircraft Industry during World War II, 1942–1944," *Social Forces* 16, no. 1 (October 1947): 76–84.

81. Quoted in ibid., 77.

82. Quoted in ibid., 81.

83. For a general introduction to the attitude of U.S. labor toward federal labor policy in World War II, see Nelson Lichtenstein, *Labor's War at Home: The CIO in*

World War II (Cambridge: Cambridge University Press, 1982), chaps. 3–4. For the AFL, see Andrew E. Kersten, *Labor's Home Front: The American Federation of Labor during World War II* (New York: New York University Press, 2006).

84. Lichtenstein, *Labor's War at Home*, 60–61.

85. On June 3, 1941, President Roosevelt asked Congress to pass legislation to keep open those defense plants that were threatened by strike activity. See ibid., 61.

86. *Los Angeles Times*, June 7, 1941, 2; Wyndham Mortimer, "Reflections of a Labor Organizer," 165–170, interview by Elizabeth I. Dixon, 1967, transcript, Center for Oral History Research, Special Collections, Charles E. Young Research Library, University of California, Los Angeles.

87. James Prickett, "Communist Conspiracy or Wage Dispute? The 1941 Strike at North American Aviation," *Pacific Historical Review* 50, no. 2 (May 1981): 226. Mortimer was understandably angered by his abrupt dismissal, particularly since Frankenstein had until a few days previous been a strong supporter of the strike. For Mortimer's reactions to the crisis, see Mortimer, "Reflections of a Labor Organizer," 168–197; and Wyndham Mortimer, *Organize! My Life as a Union Man* (Boston: Beacon Press, 1971), chap. 2.

88. Quoted in Lichtenstein, *Labor's War at Home*, 62.

89. Buzzell declared that Frankenstein had "confirmed our [the AFL's] charge that the North American strike was the action of a radical, un-American minority." The charge that the strike was Communist-inspired faded when, on June 21, 1941, Germany invaded the Soviet Union, thereby causing the Communist Party nationwide to reverse its policy and give whole-hearted support to the U.S. defense effort. For Buzzell's views, see *Los Angeles Times*, June 9, 1941, 4.

90. Mortimer, "Reflections of a Labor Organizer," 165–168; John Allard, "Organizing the United Auto Workers in Los Angeles," 39–45, interview by Michael Furmanovsky, 1986, transcript, Center for Oral History Research, UCLA; Tom Sitton, *Los Angeles Transformed: Fletcher Bowron's Urban Reform Revival, 1938–1953* (Albuquerque: University of New Mexico Press, 2005), 57.

91. Lichtenstein, *Labor's War at Home*, 65–66; Allard, "Organizing the United Auto Workers in Los Angeles," 44–48.

92. Lichtenstein, *Labor's War at Home*, 66.

93. Ibid., 79–80; Foster Rhea Dulles and Melvyn Dubofsky, *Labor in America: A History*, 4th ed. (Arlington Heights, Ill.: Harlan Davidson, 1984), 323. For the "Little Steel formula," see Robert H. Zieger, *The CIO, 1935–1955* (Chapel Hill: University of North Carolina Press, 1995), 168–169.

94. Gene B. Tipton, "The Labor Movement in the Los Angeles Area during the 1940s" (PhD diss., University of California, Los Angeles, 1953), 368–370.

95. *CIO News*, June 23, 1941, 3; *Labor Herald*, May 15, 1942, 1, and June 28, 1941, 2; *Los Angeles Citizen*, September 14, 1945, 7; *Los Angeles Times*, May 1, 1941, 5.

96. *Union Labor in California, 1945* (San Francisco: State of California, Department of Industrial Relations, 1946), 8.

97. Tipton, "The Labor Movement in the Los Angeles Area," 54–58.

98. Ibid., 12–18.

99. Ibid., 18–20.

100. AFL president William Green appointed an interim administrator, Paul J. Smith, to enquire into Buzzell's conduct and take over temporary control of the AFL's Central Labor Council. The inquiry found not only that Buzzell had failed to cooperate with the Labor Victory Committee but also that he had embezzled council funds for his personal use. See Richard Norman Baisden, "Labor Unions in Los Angeles Politics" (PhD diss., University of Chicago, 1958), 241–249.

101. Joel Seidman, *American Labor from Defense to Reconversion* (Chicago: University of Chicago Press, 1953), 188, 200–204.

102. Sitton, *Los Angeles Transformed*, 56–58; Fred Carver to Philip Connelly, April 11, 1945, folder 6, box 3, Philip Marshall Connelly Papers (Collection 2015), Special Collections, Charles E. Young Research Library, University of California, Los Angeles.

103. Verge, *Paradise Transformed*, 140.

104. Quoted in Kevin Allen Leonard, "'Brothers under the Skin?': African Americans, Mexican Americans, and World War II," in *The Way We Really Were: The Golden State in the Second Great War*, ed. Roger W. Lotchin (Urbana: University of Illinois Press, 2000), 194.

105. Quoted in ibid., 200.

106. Quoted in ibid., 194.

107. Sides, *L.A. City Limits*, 139–147; Daniel Hurewitz, *Bohemian Los Angeles and the Making of Modern Politics* (Berkeley: University of California Press, 2007), 217–218. For a full-length study of the Civil Rights Congress, see Gerald Horne, *Communist Front?: The Civil Rights Congress, 1946–1956* (Madison, N.J.: Fairleigh Dickinson University Press, 1988).

108. Shelton Stromquist, ed., *Labor's Cold War: Local Politics in a Global Context* (Urbana: University of Illinois Press, 2008), 6.

109. Quoted in Hurewitz, *Bohemian Los Angeles*, 224.

110. Verge, *Paradise Transformed*, 141.

111. For a study of the ambivalence, and frequent hostility, of male trade union leaders toward women workers with regard to wage levels, seniority rights, electoral office, and the definition of "women's work," see Milkman, *Gender at Work*, chaps. 5–6.

112. Quoted in Karen Tucker Anderson, "Last Hired, First Fired," 95.

113. Ibid.; Campbell, *Women at War with America*, 240.

114. Alice Kessler-Harris, *Out to Work: A History of Wage-Earning Women in the United States* (New York: Oxford University Press, 1982), 236.

115. *Los Angeles Examiner,* February 28, 1944, 4.

116. See, for example, Milkman, *Gender at Work,* passim; Gluck, *Rosie the Riveter Revisited,* 267; and J. E. Trey, "Women in the War Economy—World War II," *Review of Radical Political Economics,* no. 4 (July 1972): 40–57.

117. Milkman, *Gender at Work,* chap. 7.

118. Leonard, "'Brothers under the Skin?'" 204.

119. Kenneth C. Burt, "The Fight for Fair Employment and the Shifting Alliances among Latinos and Labor in Cold War Los Angeles," in Stromquist, *Labor's Cold War,* 84–87.

120. Tipton, "The Labor Movement in the Los Angeles Area," 370. In her calculations, Ruth Milkman puts the number at only 252,396. The difference appears to be explained by the fact that Tipton's figures were for L.A. County, whereas Milkman's were for the city. See Milkman, *L.A. Story: Immigrant Workers and the Future of the U.S. Labor Movement* (New York: Russell Sage Foundation, 2006), appendix A.

121. Lichtenstein, *Labor's War at Home,* 221.

122. Scott Greer, *Last Man In: Racial Access to Union Power* (Glencoe, Ill.: Free Press, 1959), 20–40, 172–174.

CHAPTER NINE

1. Kevin Starr provides a good summary of these events in his *Embattled Dreams: California in War and Peace, 1940–1950* (New York: Oxford University Press, 2002), chap. 10. See also Kevin J. Fernlund, ed., *The Cold War American West, 1945–1989* (Albuquerque: University of New Mexico Press, 1998), passim.

2. For evidence about the consumer boom, see Lizabeth Cohen, *A Consumers' Republic: The Politics of Mass Consumption in Postwar America* (New York: Knopf, 2003).

3. For discussions of this cultural shift, see Lisa McGirr, *Suburban Warriors: The Origins of the New American Right* (Princeton, N.J.: Princeton University Press, 2001); and Kurt Schuparra, *Triumph of the Right: The Rise of the California Conservative Movement, 1945–1966* (Armonk, N.Y.: M. E. Sharpe, 1998).

4. James R. Green, *The World of the Worker: Labor in Twentieth-Century America* (Urbana: University of Illinois Press, 1998), 193–195; Foster Rhea Dulles and Melvyn Dubofsky, *Labor in America: A History,* 4th ed. (Arlington Heights, Ill.: Harlan Davidson, 1984), 334–340.

5. The best account of the Hollywood strike and lockout is provided in Gerald Horne, *Class Struggle in Hollywood, 1930–1950: Moguls, Mobsters, Stars, Reds, and Trade Unionists* (Austin: University of Texas Press, 2001), passim.

6. Ibid., 6.

7. Further details of the Hollywood strike can be found in Michael Charles Nielsen, "Motion Picture Craft Workers and Craft Unions in Hollywood: The Studio

Era, 1912–1948" (PhD diss., University of Illinois, 1985), chap. 7. For other accounts, see Hugh Lovell and Tasile Carter, *Collective Bargaining in the Motion Picture Industry: A Struggle for Stability* (Berkeley: Institute of Industrial Relations, 1955), 14–26; and Mike Nielsen and Gene Mailes, *Hollywood's Other Blacklist: Union Struggles in the Studio System* (London: British Film Institute, 1995), chaps. 5–8.

8. Quoted in Horne, *Class Struggle in Hollywood*, 167–175.

9. After the Hollywood strike was over, Ed Gibbons, press agent for IATSE, charged Herbert Sorrell, president of the Conference of Studio Unions, with being a covert member of the Communist Party, even though there was no real evidence to prove it. Sorrell was tried and convicted by a committee of the AFL Central Labor Council and expelled as a delegate from its meetings, as well as from his own Painters Union local. See Nielsen, "Motion Picture Craft Workers," 317–318; and Nielsen and Mailes, *Hollywood's Other Blacklist*, 166–167.

10. For the details of Roy Brewer's career, see Nielsen and Mailes, *Hollywood's Other Blacklist*, xii, 101. David Witwer argues that union corruption, such as that manifested by IATSE, helped precipitate the overall decline of the U.S. labor movement (*Shadow of the Racketeer: Scandal in Organized Labor* [Urbana: University of Illinois Press, 2009], 8–11). Whether IATSE's prominent role in Hollywood played a special role in weakening the L.A. unions is so far unclear.

11. Quoted in Nielsen, "Motion Picture Craft Workers," 296.

12. Ibid., 299–300.

13. In her imaginative study of the cartoons printed during the strike by *Picket Line*, a CSU publication, Laurie Caroline Pintar made use of Sorrell's former career as a boxer to reflect on the role of masculinity, gender, and race in the conflict. In addition to reproducing photos of attractive women doing picket duty, the *Picket Line* cartoons showed the male picketers as highly masculine figures—but also, in line with the racial composition of the studios' labor force, as exclusively white. See Pintar, "Herbert K. Sorrell as the Grade-B Hero: Militancy and Masculinity in the Studios," *Labor History* 37, no. 3 (Summer 1996): 392–416; and Pintar, "Off-Screen Realities: A History of Labor Activism in Hollywood, 1933–1947" (PhD diss., University of Southern California, 1955), chap. 5.

14. *Los Angeles Times*, October 6, 1945, 4.

15. Nielsen, "Motion Picture Craft Workers," 306–324; Horne, *Class Struggle in Hollywood*, 180–190.

16. Quoted in Nielsen, "Motion Picture Craft Workers," 341.

17. Quoted in Horne, *Class Struggle in Hollywood*, 4. In an interview, Father George H. Dunne, a liberal Catholic priest who was a CSU supporter and was disciplined by the Catholic Church in Los Angeles for giving evidence before a congressional hearing on the strike, stated that Reagan may have known about the collusion between IATSE and the studio heads and also noted that Reagan "interpreted every-

thing [in the dispute] in terms of the Communist threat." See George H. Dunne, "Christian Advocacy and Labor Strife in Hollywood," 28–30, 37–45, interview by Mitch Tuchman, 1981, transcript, Center for Oral History Research, Special Collections, Charles E. Young Research Library, University of California, Los Angeles. See also Dunne, *Hollywood Labor Dispute: A Study in Immorality* (Los Angeles: Conference Publishing, 1950).

18. Steven J. Ross, *Working-Class Hollywood: Silent Film and the Shaping of Class in America* (Princeton, N.J.: Princeton University Press, 1998), 244. See also David F. Prindle, *The Politics of Glamour: Ideology and Democracy in the Screen Actors Guild* (Madison: University of Wisconsin Press, 1988); and Lary May, *Screening Out the Past: The Birth of Mass Culture and the Motion Picture Industry* (Chicago: University of Chicago Press, 1980).

19. Michael Denning, *The Cultural Front: The Laboring of American Culture in the Twentieth Century* (London: Verso, 1997), chap 1.

20. Quoted in Horne, *Class Struggle in Hollywood*, 75.

21. For a summary of the General Motors strike, see Green, *The World of the Worker*, 154–155.

22. Quoted in Becky Nicolaides, *My Blue Heaven: Life and Politics in the Working-Class Suburbs of Los Angeles, 1920–1965* (Chicago: University of Chicago Press, 2002), 235.

23. Ibid.

24. Quoted in ibid., 238.

25. Ibid.

26. Ibid., 237–238.

27. For a discussion of the rise of business unionism and its consequences, see Green, *The World of the Worker*, chap. 6.

28. Nicolaides, *My Blue Heaven*, 250.

29. For a discussion of the consciousness raising role of labor-focused cultural events, see Roy Rosenzweig, *Eight Hours for What We Will: Workers and Leisure in an Industrial City, 1870–1920* (New York: Cambridge University Press, 1983).

30. Nicolaides, *My Blue Heaven*, 251–252.

31. Ibid., 252–253.

32. Ibid., chap. 7.

33. Green, *The World of the Worker*, 187.

34. Ibid., 186–188.

35. Philip Taft, *The AF of L from the Death of Gompers to the Merger* (New York: Harper, 1959), chap. 19.

36. For changes in the political opinions of Walter Reuther, see Nelson Lichtenstein, *The Most Dangerous Man in Detroit: Walter Reuther and the Fate of American Labor* (New York: Basic Books, 1995), chaps. 12–13.

37. Robert H. Zieger, *The CIO, 1935–1955* (Chapel Hill: University of North Carolina Press, 1995), 246–248, 279–280.

38. Quoted in Dorothy Healey and Maurice Isserman, *Dorothy Healey Remembers: A Life in the American Communist Party* (New York: Oxford University Press, 1990), 125–126.

39. Zieger, *The CIO*, 253–256. For a more detailed study of the CIO's relations with the Communist-influenced unions in its ranks and their expulsion in 1950, see Harvey A. Levenstein, *Communism, Anticommunism, and the CIO* (Westport, Conn.: Greenwood Press, 1981), passim.

40. Zieger, *The CIO*, 266–275. Henry Wallace was a somewhat naive, idealistic New Dealer who sought to continue the U.S.–Soviet World War II alliance and broke with President Truman over Cold War foreign policy. See Karl M. Schmidt, *Henry A. Wallace: Quixotic Crusade, 1948* (Binghamton, N.Y.: Syracuse University Press, 1960), passim.

41. Zieger, *The CIO*, 250–253.

42. Ben Dobbs, "Democracy and the American Communist Movement," 339–340, interview by Michael Furmanovsky, 1987, transcript, Center for Oral History Research, UCLA.

43. Quoted in John Allard, "Organizing the United Auto Workers in Los Angeles," 78, interview by Michael Furmanovsky, 1986, transcript, Center for Oral History Research, UCLA.

44. Ibid., 81.

45. Quoted in Schmidt, *Henry A. Wallace*, 260.

46. Allard, "Organizing the United Auto Workers," 88.

47. See, for example, Roger Keeran, *The Communist Party and the Auto Workers Unions* (Bloomington: Indiana University Press, 1980), 280–284; and Lichtenstein, *The Most Dangerous Man in Detroit*, 266–270.

48. Quoted in Allard, "Organizing the United Auto Workers," 91.

49. Virgil Collins, interview by Becky Nicolaides, August 25, 1991, Laguna Hills, Calif., 6. I am grateful to Becky Nicolaides for providing me with this material.

50. In 1947, Guatemalan-born Luisa Moreno gave up her organizing activities on behalf of Mexican cigarmakers, garment workers, and cannery workers in Southern California to devote herself to her family in San Diego. However, in August 1949 the federal government issued an order to deport her back to Guatemala, calling her a "dangerous alien." After a fifteen-month fight to remain in the United States, Moreno voluntarily accepted deportation in November 1950. See Jeffrey M. Garcilazo, "McCarthyism, Mexican Americans, and the Los Angeles Committee for the Protection of the Foreign-Born, 1950–1954," *Western Historical Quarterly* 32, no. 3 (Autumn 2001): 278–279.

51. Quoted in Robert Justin Goldstein, *Political Repression in Modern America, 1870 to the Present* (Cambridge, Mass.: Schenkman, 1978), 245.

52. Healey and Isserman, *Dorothy Healey Remembers*, 145–146.

53. "FBI Report, 7/15/1949," file 2, box 4, Dorothy Healey Papers, Special Collections, Charles E. Young Research Library, University of California, Los Angeles; Healey and Isserman, *Dorothy Healey Remembers*, 146.

54. Scott Kurashige, *The Shifting Grounds of Race: Black and Japanese Americans in the Making of Multiethnic Los Angeles* (Princeton, N.J.: Princeton University Press, 2008), 213.

55. For the impact of the Khrushchev revelations and the emergence of the New Left, see Joseph Starobin, *American Communism in Crisis, 1943–1957* (Cambridge, Mass.: Harvard University Press, 1972), chap. 10; and Milton Cantor, *The Divided Left: American Radicalism, 1900–1975* (New York: Hill and Wang, 1978), chap. 10.

56. Garcilazo, "McCarthyism, Mexican Americans," 278–282. See also Juan Ramon Garcia, *Operation Wetback: The Mass Deportation of Mexican Undocumented Workers in 1954* (Westport, Conn.: Greenwood Press, 1980), passim.

57. Quoted in *Los Angeles Daily News*, February 14, 1951, 3.

58. Ibid.

59. Garcilazo, "McCarthyism, Mexican Americans," 276–289.

60. Garcia, *Operation Wetback*, 197.

61. Quoted in Garcilazo, "McCarthyism, Mexican Americans," 293.

62. Rob Kling, Spencer Olin, and Mark Poster, eds., *Postsuburban California: The Transformation of Orange County since World War II* (Berkeley: University of California Press, 1991), 231–232. See also Laura R. Barraclough, *Making the San Fernando Valley: Rural Landscapes, Urban Development, and White Privilege* (Athens: University of Georgia Press, 2011).

63. Tom Sitton, *Los Angeles Transformed: Fletcher Bowron's Urban Reform Revival, 1938–1953* (Albuquerque: University of New Mexico Press, 2005), 93–125.

64. Kenneth C. Burt, *The Search for a Civic Voice: California Latino Politics* (Claremont, Calif.: Regina Books, 2007), chap. 3.

65. For an account of the contribution of Mexican Americans to the revival of the civil rights movement in Los Angeles after World War II, see Kenneth C. Burt, "Latino Empowerment in Los Angeles: Postwar Dreams and Cold War Fears, 1948–1952," in *Labor's Heritage* 8, no. 1 (Summer 1996): 4–26.

66. Burt, *The Search for a Civic Voice*, 63–84; P. David Finks, *The Radical Vision of Saul Alinsky* (New York: Paulist Press, 1984), 35–40.

67. George Sánchez, "'What's Good for Boyle Heights Is Good for the Jews': Creating Multiracialism on the Eastside during the 1950s," *American Quarterly* 56, no. 3 (September 2004): 633–645; Neil C. Sandberg, *Jewish Life in Los Angeles: A Window to Tomorrow* (Lanham, Md.: University Press of America, 1986), chap. 2; Japanese American National Museum, *Images of America: Los Angeles's Boyle Heights* (Los Angeles: Japanese American National Museum, 2005), passim. See also Kather-

ine Underwood, "Process and Politics: Multiracial Electoral Coalition Building and Representation in Los Angeles' Ninth District, 1949–1962" (PhD diss., University of California, San Diego, 1992), 69–70.

68. Quoted in "Community Services Organization," pamphlet, folder 2, box 9, Edward Roybal Papers, Special Collections, Charles E. Young Research Library, University of California, Los Angeles.

69. Burt, *The Search for a Civic Voice*, 63–64.

70. Officials of the CSO frequently appealed for money to local leaders of the United Steelworkers, the Retail Clerks, the ILGWU, and other non-Communist unions. Another sign of the CSO's close links with organized labor was the logo used in a pamphlet issued by the Boyle Heights office of the CSO in 1953. It read, "A Proven formula for Success: CSO + LABOR = A Better Community." See letters from Anthony P. Rios and Edward Roybal dated June 5, 1951, and August 28, 1953, folder 4, box 9, Edward Roybal Papers.

71. Kenneth C. Burt, "The Battle for Standard Coil: The United Electrical Workers, the Community Services Organization, and the Catholic Church in Latino East Los Angeles," in *American Labor and the Cold War: Grassroots Politics and Postwar Political Culture*, ed. Robert W. Cherny, William Issel, and Kieran Walsh Taylor (New Brunswick, N.J.: Rutgers University Press, 2004), 128.

72. Ibid., 133. For more on the expulsion of the United Electrical Workers from the CIO and the conflict between rival unions to take over its members, see Ronald L. Filippelli and Mark D. McColloch, *Cold War in the Working Class: The Rise and Decline of the United Electrical Workers* (Albany, N.Y.: SUNY Press, 1995).

73. Burt, "The Battle for Standard Coil," 127.

74. Mexican American women in Boyle Heights also played an important role in registering voters and getting them out on election day. See Margaret Rose, "Gender and Civic Activism in Mexican American Barrios in California: The Community Services Organization, 1947–1962," in *Not June Cleaver: Women and Gender in Postwar America, 1945–1960*, ed. Joanne Meyerowitz (Philadelphia: Temple University Press, 1994), 177–188.

75. Underwood, "Process and Politics," 104; Ellen Schrecker, *Many Are the Crimes: McCarthyism in America* (Princeton, N.J.: Princeton University Press, 1998), chap. 3.

76. Don Parson, "'The Darling of the Town's Neo-Fascists': The Bombastic Political Career of Councilman Edward Davenport," *Southern California Quarterly* 81, no. 4 (Winter 1999): 477.

77. Quoted in ibid., 478.

78. Ibid.

79. Quoted in Underwood, "Process and Politics," 180n.11.

80. Ibid., 181.

81. Quoted in Parson, "'The Darling of the Town's Neo-Fascists,'" 480.

82. Quoted in ibid., 481.

83. Ibid., 93.

84. Sitton, *Los Angeles Transformed*, 114–115, 154–156; Underwood, "Process and Politics," 184–189; Richard O. Davies, *Housing Reform during the Truman Administration* (Columbia: University of Missouri Press, 1966), 31–32, 87–94.

85. Don Parson, *Making a Better World: Public Housing, the Red Scare, and the Direction of Modern Los Angeles* (Minneapolis: University of Minnesota Press, 2005), 76–102.

86. Ibid., chap. 5.

87. Quoted in ibid., 183.

88. Ibid., 114–117.

89. Ibid., 117–125.

90. Quoted in ibid., 118.

91. Ibid., 124–126.

92. Ibid., 127–128.

93. Ibid., 129. See also Daniel Martinez HoSang, *Racial Propositions: Ballot Initiatives and the Making of Postwar California* (Berkeley: University of California Press, 2010), passim.

94. Eric Avila, *Popular Culture in the Age of White Flight: Fear and Fantasy in Suburban Los Angeles* (Berkeley: University of California Press, 2004), chap. 2.

95. By the early 1960s, of the 334,916 African Americans living in Los Angeles, 93.7 percent lived in the Central Avenue district. Between 1950 and 1960, the percentage of Latinos living in East L.A. rose from 29.4 percent to 51.5 percent. See Los Angeles County Commission on Human Relations, *Population and Housing in L.A. County* (Berkeley: Institute of Governmental Studies, 1963), 3.

96. Parson, *Making a Better World*, 167–168.

97. For more on Richard Neutra's design for the Elysian Park Heights public housing project, see Thomas Hines, "Housing, Baseball, and Creeping Socialism: The Battle of Chavez Ravine, Los Angeles, 1949–1959," *Journal of Urban History* 8, no. 2 (February 1982): 123–148.

98. Parson, *Making a Better World*, 167–180; Avila, *Popular Culture*, 157.

99. Quoted in Don Normark, *Chavez Ravine, 1949: A Los Angeles Story* (San Francisco: Chronicle Books, 1999), 63.

100. Ibid.

101. Parson, *Making a Better World*, 174–180. For a broader analysis of the effects of the Cold War in undermining the New Deal order, see Steve Fraser and Gary Gerstle, eds., *The Rise and Fall of the New Deal Order, 1930–1980* (Princeton, N.J.: Princeton University Press, 1989), pt. 2.

102. For a general account of the rise of the conservative movement in Southern California, see McGirr, *Suburban Warriors*, passim.

103. Schuparra, *Triumph of the Right*, chap. 4.

104. Quoted in Kevin Roderick, *The San Fernando Valley: America's Suburb* (Los Angeles: Los Angeles Times Books, 2001), 147.

105. McGirr, *Suburban Warriors*, 25–27. See also Roderick, *The San Fernando Valley*, 133–135; and Michael Welsh, "The Legacy of Containment: The Military-Industrial Complex in the American West," in Fernlund, *The Cold War American West*, 87–100.

106. Quoted in Nicolaides, *My Blue Heaven*, 271. See also Avila, *Popular Culture*, chap. 4; and Richard Francaviglia, "Main Street, USA: A Comparison/Contrast of Streetscapes in Disneyland and Walt Disney World," *Journal of Popular Culture* 15 (Summer 1981): 141–156.

107. Totton J. Anderson and Eugene C. Lee, "The 1964 Election in California," *Western Political Quarterly* 18, no. 2, pt. 2 (June 1965): 456–457.

108. Ibid., 458.

109. Quotes taken from Robert Mason, *Richard Nixon and the Quest for a New Majority* (Chapel Hill: University of North Carolina Press, 2004), chap. 5.

110. Nicolaides, *My Blue Heaven*, 327.

111. For the founding and development of the Jewish–African American political coalition in Los Angeles, see Raphael Sonenshein, *Politics in Black and White: Race and Power in Los Angeles* (Princeton, N.J.: Princeton University Press, 1993), especially chaps. 5–8. See also Karen M. Kaufmann, *The Urban Voter: Group Conflict and Mayoral Voting Behavior in American Cities* (Ann Arbor: University of Michigan Press, 2004), chap. 4.

CHAPTER TEN

1. Harvard Sitkoff, *The Struggle for Black Equality, 1954–1980* (New York: Hill and Wang, 1981), 200–201. For more detailed accounts of the Watts uprising and its consequences, see Gerald Horne, *Fire This Time: The Watts Uprising and the 1960s* (Charlottesville: University of Virginia Press, 1995); and Paul Bullock, ed., *Watts: The Aftermath—An Inside View of the Ghetto by the People of Watts* (New York: Grove Press, 1969).

2. Sitkoff, *The Struggle for Black Equality*, 201; Gordon DeMarco, *A Short History of Los Angeles* (San Francisco: Lexikos Publishing, 1987), 165–166.

3. Horne, *Fire This Time*, 81–82.

4. Raphael J. Sonenshein, *Politics in Black and White: Race and Power in Los Angeles* (Princeton, N.J.: Princeton University Press, 1993), chaps. 7–11.

5. Ibid., chap. 7.

6. Steven P. Erie, *Globalizing L.A.: Trade, Infrastructure, and Regional Development* (Stanford, Calif.: Stanford University Press, 2004), chap. 1.

7. For an analysis of how ethno-racial conflict turned many white working-class voters into "Reagan Democrats," see Stanley B. Greenberg, *Middle Class Dreams: The*

Politics and Power of the New American Majority (New Haven, Conn.: Yale University Press, 1996), chap. 5.

8. For a provocative discussion of the race-class-gender paradigm, see Michael Omi and Howard Winant, *Racial Formation in the United States: From the 1960s to the Present* (New York: Routledge and Kegan Paul, 1986), 29–35. See also Ava Baron, ed., *Work Engendered: Toward a New History of American Labor* (Ithaca, N.Y.: Cornell University Press, 1991), chap. 1.

9. Governor's Commission on the Los Angeles Race Riots, *Violence in the City: An End or a Beginning? A Report* (Los Angeles: Governor's Commission, 1965), 1:7–8.

10. Excerpt from *Business Week*, March 25, 1967, file 1, box 2, Debbie Louis Collection on Civil Rights, 1949–1991, Special Collections, Charles E. Young Research Library, University of California, Los Angeles.

11. Quoted from Clara James, "The South Side Citizens Defense Committee," in *The West in the History of the Nation: A Reader*, ed. William E. Deverell and Anne F. Hyde (Boston: Bedford/St. Martin's Press, 2000), 2:237. For a more extended case study of white flight, see Kevin M. Kruse, *White Flight: Atlanta and the Making of Modern Conservatism* (Princeton, N.J.: Princeton University Press, 2005), passim.

12. Bullock, *Watts: The Aftermath*, 51; organizations listed in pamphlet published by the Watts Labor Community Action Committee, appendix 1, Los Angeles, 1969, Debbie Louis Collection on Civil Rights.

13. Watts Labor Community Action Committee pamphlet, back page.

14. Robert Bauman, *Race and the War on Poverty: From Watts to East L.A.* (Norman: University of Oklahoma Press, 2008), 71–72.

15. Paul Schrade, "UAW Workplace and Community Action," 2: 338–362, interview by Thomas J. Connors, 1989–1990, transcript, Center for Oral History Research, Special Collections, Charles E. Young Research Library, University of California, Los Angeles.

16. Paul Schrade to Virgil Collins, April 13, 1972, folder 20, box 1, series 11, Virgil Collins Collection, Walter P. Reuther Library, Wayne State University, Detroit; *Los Angeles Times*, April 3, 1972, 4.

17. Excerpt from *Business Week*, March 25, 1967, file 1, box 2, Debbie Louis Collection on Civil Rights.

18. Watts Labor Community Action Committee pamphlet, 3.

19. Bauman, *Race and the War on Poverty*, 95–100, John R. Chavez, *Eastside Landmark: A History of the East Los Angeles Community Union, 1968–1993* (Stanford, Calif.: Stanford University Press, 1998), 57–64.

20. Quoted in Chavez, *Eastside Landmark*, 63.

21. Ibid.

22. August Meier and Elliott Rudwick, *CORE: A Study in the Civil Rights Movement, 1942–1968* (Urbana: University of Illinois Press, 1975), 110.

23. *Los Angeles Times*, June 17, 1963, 5.

24. Meier and Rudwick, *CORE*, 110.

25. During this "shop in," civil rights activists incapacitated the Thriftimart store by flooding it with volunteers who monopolized the shopping carts but purchased only one item each. See Rev. H. Hartford Brookins to UCRC members, July 13, 1963, folder 4, box 57, UAW Region 6 Collection, Walter P. Reuther Library.

26. Quoted in CORE, "Membership Bulletin," December 1963, file 7, box 12, Debbie Louis Collection on Civil Rights.

27. Ibid., March 1964.

28. Scott Kurashige, *The Shifting Grounds of Race: Black and Japanese Americans in the Making of Multiethnic Los Angeles* (Princeton, N.J.: Princeton University Press, 2008), 272.

29. U.S. Census Bureau, *Census of Population, 1960* (Washington, D.C.: Government Printing Office, 1960), reports PD (3), PC (2)–ID; Fred Romero, "Chicanos and Occupational Mobility," in *Minorities in the Labor Market*, ed. Paul Bullock (Los Angeles: Institute of Industrial Relations, UCLA, 1977), 69.

30. Paul Bullock, *Aspiration vs. Opportunity: "Careers" in the Inner City*, Policy Papers in Human Resources and Industrial Relations, no. 20 (Ann Arbor: Institute of Labor and Industrial Relations, University of Michigan–Wayne State University, 1973), 12.

31. Ibid., chap. 2; Horne, *Fire This Time*, 11–12, 190.

32. Bullock, *Aspiration vs. Opportunity*, 256n.32.

33. Martin Schiesl, "Behind the Badge: The Police and Social Discontent in Los Angeles since 1950," in *20th Century Los Angeles: Power, Promotion, and Social Conflict*, ed. Norman M. Klein and Martin J. Schiesl (Claremont, Calif.: Regina Books, 1990), 166–168.

34. Quoted in Bullock, *Aspiration vs. Opportunity*, 153.

35. Arthur M. Ross and Herbert Hill, eds., *Employment, Race, and Poverty* (New York: Harcourt, Brace and World, 1967), 426–427.

36. For details of this agreement, see Paul T. Hartman, *Collective Bargaining and Productivity: The Longshore Mechanization Agreement* (Berkeley: University of California Press, 1969).

37. Excerpt from Los Angeles newspaper, name and date unknown, folder 6, box 12, Debbie Louis Collection on Civil Rights.

38. Ibid.

39. Los Angeles CORE, "We Charge Genocide," folder 6, box 12, Debbie Louis Collection on Civil Rights.

40. Edna Bonacich and Jake B. Wilson, *Getting the Goods: Ports, Labor, and the Logistics Revolution* (Ithaca, N.Y.: Cornell University Press, 2008), 188–189.

41. Nancy F. Gabin, *Feminism in the Labor Movement: Women and the United Auto*

Workers, 1935–1975 (Ithaca, N.Y.: Cornell University Press, 1990), 218–219. See also Nancy MacLean, *Freedom Is Not Enough: The Opening of the American Workplace* (Cambridge, Mass.: Harvard University Press, 2006), chap. 4

42. Gabin, *Feminism in the Labor Movement*, 191–192.

43. Lorenzo H. Traylor, Director, Los Angeles EEOC Office, to Sal Astorga, President, UAW Local 216, August 9, 1972, plus attachments, folder 4, box 39, UAW Local 216 Collection, Walter P. Reuther Library, Wayne State University.

44. William L. Oliver to Irving Bluestone et al., November 22, 1974, folder 4, box 39, UAW Local 216 Collection.

45. Quoted in Kathy Seal, "Charge of Discrimination," folder 4, box 39, UAW Local 216 Collection.

46. Quoted in Alfred P. Rowley, "Charge of Discrimination," folder 4, box 39, UAW Local 216 Collection.

47. For details of the Philadelphia and hometown plans, see Herbert Hill, "Labor Union Control of Job Training: A Critical Analysis of Apprenticeship Outreach Programs and the Hometown Plan," Occasional Papers, vol. 2, no. 1 (Washington, D.C.: Howard University, Institute for Urban Affairs and Research, 1974), passim.

48. Quoted in ibid., 97.

49. Quoted in Paul Bullock, *Building California: The Story of the Carpenters Union* (Los Angeles: UCLA Center for Labor Research and Education, Institute for Industrial Relations, 1982), 336.

50. Ibid.

51. For the initial formulation of the dual labor market theory, see Edna Bonacich, "A Theory of Ethnic Antagonism: The Split Labor Market," *American Sociological Review* 37, no. 5 (October 1972): 547–559.

52. David M. Gordon, Richard Edwards, and Michael Reich, *Segmented Work, Divided Workers: The Historical Transformation of Labor in the United States* (Cambridge: Cambridge University Press, 1982), chap. 5.

53. For this and other criticisms of split labor market theory, see Omi and Winant, *Racial Formation in the United States*, passim.

54. Bernard E. Anderson, "Economic Trends and Economic Opportunity for the Black Community," in Bullock, *Minorities in the Labor Market*, 20.

55. Romero, "Chicanos and Occupational Mobility," 79.

56. Amado Y. Cabezas, "Evidence for the Low Mobility of Asian Americans in the Labor Market," in Bullock, *Minorities in the Labor Market*, 46.

57. Ibid., 63.

58. For an account of the East L.A. "blowouts," see Ernesto Chávez, *"¡Mi Raza Primero!" (My People First!): Nationalism, Identity, and Insurgency in the Chicano Movement in Los Angeles, 1966–1978* (Berkeley: University of California Press, 2002), chaps. 1–2.

59. Shifra M. Goldman and Tomás Ybarra-Frausto, eds., *Arte Chicano: A Comprehensive Annotated Bibliography of Chicano Art, 1965–1981* (Berkeley: Chicano Studies Library Publication Unit, University of California, 1985), 35.

60. Quoted in Donald Glen Cooper, "The Controversy over Desegregation in the Los Angeles Unified School District, 1962–1981" (PhD diss., University of Southern California, 1991), 62.

61. David Lopez-Lee, *School Desegregation in the Los Angeles School District: A Staff Report Prepared for the Hearing of the U.S. Commission on Civil Rights in Los Angeles, California, December 1976* (Washington, D.C.: Office for Civil Rights, HEW, 1976), 53. See also John Caughey, *To Kill a Child's Spirit: The Tragedy of School Segregation in Los Angeles* (Itasca, Ill.: F. E. Peacock Publishers, 1973), chap. 1, and Henry J. Gutierrez, "Racial Politics in Los Angeles: Black and Mexican American Challenges to Unequal Education in the 1960s," *Southern California Quarterly* 78, no. 1 (Spring 1996): 31–43.

62. Jeanne Theoharis, "'Alabama on Avalon': Rethinking the Watts Uprising and the Character of Black Protest in Los Angeles," in *The Black Power Movement: Rethinking the Civil Rights–Black Power Era*, ed. Peniel F. Joseph (London: Routledge, 2006), 42–45.

63. Ibid., 42.

64. Quoted in Becky Nicolaides, *My Blue Heaven: Life and Politics in the Working-Class Suburbs of Los Angeles, 1920–1965* (Chicago: University of Chicago Press, 2002), 301.

65. Quoted in *Hearings before United States Commission on Civil Rights, Los Angeles, 1960* (Washington, D.C.: Government Printing Office, 1960), 412.

66. Edward W. Soja, "Los Angeles, 1965–1992: From Crisis-Generated Restructuring to Restructuring-Generated Crisis," in *The City: Los Angeles and Urban Theory at the End of the Twentieth Century*, ed. Allen J. Scott and Edward W. Soja (Berkeley: University of California Press, 1996), 434–439.

67. Quoted in Philip J. Ethington, "Segregated Diversity: Race-Ethnicity, Space, and Political Fragmentation in Los Angeles County, 1940–1994," Final Report to John Randolph Haynes and Dora Haynes Foundation, 2000, 40.

68. Raymond W. Wolfinger and Fred I. Greenstein, "The Repeal of Fair Housing in California: An Analysis of Referendum Voting," *American Political Science Review* 62, no. 3 (September 1968): 753–759.

69. Ethington, "Segregated Diversity," 42.

70. Attorney General Stanley Mosk to President of California Real Estate Association, June 14, 1964, folder 3–12, box 3, Max Mont Collection, 1941–1980, Urban Archives Center, Oviatt Library, California State University, Northridge.

71. Quoted in "Circular from L.A. County Federation of Labor," August 14, 1964, file 2–8, box 2, Max Mont Collection.

72. "Report on Operations of NAACP Headquarters for 'No on Proposition 14,'" November 12, 1964, file 4–3, box 3, Max Mont Collection; Schrade, "UAW Workplace and Community Action," 2:353–354.

73. "Statement of Congress of Racial Equality Regarding Housing in L.A. County," file 14, box 12, Debbie Louis Collection on Civil Rights.

74. Quoted in *South Side Press*, August 11, 1964, 2.

75. Ibid., November 7, 1964, 3; Nicolaides, *My Blue Heaven*, 313.

76. Sonenshein, *Politics in Black and White*, 69–70.

77. Ethington, "Segregated Diversity," 42.

78. *Los Angeles Times*, March 17, 1968, 4; Chávez, *"¡Mi Raza Primero!" (My People First!)*, 45–46. See also Laura Pulido, *Black, Brown, Yellow, and Left: Radical Activism in Los Angeles* (Berkeley: University of California Press, 2006), 115–117.

79. Chávez, *"¡Mi Raza Primero!" (My People First!)*, chap. 3.

80. Robert Bauman, "The Black Power and Chicano Movements in the Poverty Wars in Los Angeles," *Journal of Urban History* 33, no. 2 (January 2007): 277–295. See also J. David Greenstone and Paul E. Peterson, *Race and Authority in Urban Politics: Community Participation and the War on Poverty* (New York: Russell Sage Foundation, 1973), 29–34.

81. Quoted in "Learn, Baby, Learn," pamphlet issued by Operation Bootstrap, file 1, box 7, Debbie Louis Collection on Civil Rights.

82. Meier and Rudwick, *CORE*, 310.

83. Quoted in William L. Van Deburg, ed., *Modern Black Nationalism: From Marcus Garvey to Louis Farrakhan* (New York: New York University Press, 1997), 175. In 1968 Roy Innis, CORE's national director, wrote an article in which he articulated the case for Black Power. The American constitutional system, he wrote, was designed by and for a white population whose interests differed from those of African Americans. "A crucial weakness has been the lack of control by black people over the institutions that surround them." The result was that black enclaves in U.S. society, like Harlem or Watts, had become "colonial appendages" that were humiliatingly dependent on white largesse. Innis did not specify what form Black Power should take, but he called for far-reaching changes that would enable African American communities to control their own destinies. See Roy Innis, "New Social Contract," in Van Deburg, *Modern Black Nationalism*, 176–181.

84. One of the practical consequences of the rise of nationalist influence was that, as the East L.A. community grew larger and more influential in the 1970s, one of its leaders, Esteban Torres, made an unsuccessful attempt to have the area incorporated as a separate city. See Bauman, *Race and the War on Poverty*, 81, 98–101; and Chavez, *Eastside Landmark*, chaps. 3–4.

85. Quoted in Pulido, *Black, Brown, Yellow, and Left*, 143.

86. Judson L. Jeffries and Malcolm Foley, "To Live and Die in L.A.," in *Comrades:*

A Local History of the Black Panther Party, ed. Judson L. Jeffries (Bloomington: Indiana University Press, 2007), 255–290.

87. Fred Moten, *In the Break: The Aesthetics of the Black Radical Tradition* (Minneapolis: University of Minnesota Press, 2003); Richard Griswold del Castillo, Teresa McKenna, and Yvonne Yarbro-Bejaran, eds., *Chicano Art: Resistance and Affirmation, 1965–1985* (Los Angeles: Wight Art Gallery, University of California, Los Angeles, 1991); Shifra Goldman, ed., *Dimensions of the Americas: Art and Social Change in Latin America and the United States* (Chicago: University of Chicago Press, 1994), 10–24.

88. Dan La Botz, *Cesar Chavez and La Causa* (New York: Pearson Longman, 2006), chaps. 3–5.

89. Vernon M. Briggs Jr., Walter Fogel, and Fred H. Schmidt, *The Chicano Worker* (Austin: University of Texas Press, 1977), chap. 5.

90. "Biographical Notes on Max Mont," *Descriptive Finding Guide for the Max Mont Collection*, Max Mont Collection; *Los Angeles Times*, July 8, 1973, 3, 26.

91. *Los Angeles Citizen*, July 17, 1973, 4.

92. La Botz, *Cesar Chavez and La Causa*, 130–131; José-Antonio Orosco, *Cesar Chavez and the Common Sense of Nonviolence* (Albuquerque: University of New Mexico Press, 2008), 77–85. See also Frederick J. Dalton, *The Moral Vision of Cesar Chavez* (Maryknoll, N.Y.: Orbis Books, 2003), passim.

93. Kenneth C. Burt, *The Search for a Civic Voice: California Latino Politics* (Claremont, Calif.: Regina Books, 2007), 291–293, 300.

94. Randy Shaw, *Beyond the Fields: Cesar Chavez, the UFW, and the Struggle for Justice in the 21st Century* (Berkeley: University of California Press, 2008), passim.

95. Margaret Rose, "César Chávez and Dolores Huerta: Partners in 'La Causa,'" in *César Chávez: A Brief Biography with Documents*, ed. Richard W. Etulain (New York: Bedford/St. Martin's Press, 2002), 98–101. See also Ruth Carranza, "From the Fields into the History Books," *Intercambios Femenilas* 3 (Winter 1989): 14–28.

96. Margaret Rose, "Women in the United Farm Workers: A Study of Chicana and Mexicana Participation in a Labor Union, 1950–1980" (PhD diss., University of California, Los Angeles, 1988), chap. 6.

97. Margaret Rose, "From the Fields to the Picket Line: Huelga Women and the Boycott, 1965–1975," *Labor History* 31, no. 3 (Summer 1990): 271–282; Jean Murphy, "Unsung Heroine of La Causa," *Regeneración* 1 (1971): 8–12.

98. Quoted in Rose, "Women in the United Farm Workers," 274.

99. Quoted in Alexander Tsesis, *We Shall Overcome: A History of Civil Rights and the Law* (New Haven, Conn.: Yale University Press, 2008), 289.

100. Quoted in MacLean, *Freedom Is Not Enough*, 203–204.

101. Sonenshein, *Politics in Black and White*, 55–63. See also Raphael J. Sonenshein, "The Dynamics of Biracial Coalitions: Crossover Politics in Los Angeles," *Western Political Quarterly* 42, no. 2 (June 1989): 336–340.

102. Sonenshein, *Politics in Black and White*, chap. 4; Thomas Bradley, "The Impossible Dream," 28–94, interview by Bernard Galm, 1984, transcript, Center for Oral History Research, UCLA.

103. Bradley, "The Impossible Dream," 153.

104. Rufus P. Browning, Dale Rogers Marshall, and David H. Tabb, *Protest Is Not Enough: The Struggle of Blacks and Hispanics for Equality in Urban Politics* (Berkeley: University of California Press, 1984), chap. 1; Raphael J. Sonenshein, "Biracial Coalition Politics in Los Angeles," *PS* 19, no. 3 (Summer 1986): 582–590. See also James A. Regalado, "Latino Representation in Los Angeles," in *Latino Empowerment: Progress, Problems, and Prospects*, ed. Roberto E. Villarreal, Norma G. Hernandez, and Howard D. Neighbor (Westport, Conn.; Greenwood Press, 1988), 91–104.

105. Sonenshein, *Politics in Black and White*, 70–75; Bradley, "The Impossible Dream," 94–96.

106. Bradley, "The Impossible Dream," 94–95.

107. *Los Angeles Citizen*, June 1, 1973, 4.

108. *Los Angeles Times*, June 2, 1973, 5. On the leftward shift of the *Los Angeles Times*, see Robert W. Gottlieb and Irene Wolt, *Thinking Big: The Story of the Los Angeles Times, Its Publishers, and Their Influence on Southern California* (New York: Putnam, 1977), chaps. 30–34; and Karen M. Kaufmann, *The Urban Voter: Group Conflict and Mayoral Voting Behavior in American Cities* (Ann Arbor: University of Michigan Press, 2004), chap. 3.

109. Sonenshein, *Politics in Black and White*, 148–149, 155–161. Bradley's administration also appointed several African Americans to the police commission, which somewhat improved the commission's relations with the African American community. But it was unable to reduce the number of police shootings. See Peter K. Eisinger, "Black Mayors and the Politics of Racial Economic Advancement," in *Culture, Ethnicity, and Identity: Current Issues in Research*, ed. William C. McCready (New York: Academic Press, 1983), 95–109.

110. Thomas J. Sugrue, *Sweet Land of Liberty: The Forgotten Struggle for Civil Rights in the North* (New York: Random House, 2008), 505–507; Pulido, *Black, Brown, Yellow, and Left*, 45–56.

111. Ruth Milkman, *L.A. Story: Immigrant Workers and the Future of the U.S. Labor Movement* (New York: Russell Sage Foundation, 2006), chap. 3.

112. Bradley, "The Impossible Dream," 193–194.

113. Bullock, *Watts: The Aftermath*, 7–18.

114. California Legislature, Joint Committee on the State's Economy, *Transcript of Hearing on Problems and Opportunities for Job Development in Urban Areas of Persistent High Unemployment, Carson, Calif., July 22, 1982* (Sacramento: State Printing Office, 1982), 29, 50, 59, 111.

115. Mike Davis, "'Chinatown,' Part Two? The 'Internationalization' of Downtown Los Angeles," *New Left Review*, no. 164 (July/August 1987): 8.

116. *Los Angeles Times*, May 14, 1980, 7; James A. Regalado, ed., "Minority Political Empowerment: The Changing Face of California?" (Edmund G. Brown Institute of Public Affairs, California State University, Los Angeles, 1991), 12–13.

117. Davis, "'Chinatown,' Part Two?" 13–14; Sonenshein, "The Dynamics of Biracial Coalitions," 346–347; Kaufmann, *The Urban Voter*, chap. 4.

118. For an introduction to the economic crisis of the 1970s and 1980s in Los Angeles, see Scott and Soja, *The City*, chap. 14.

CHAPTER ELEVEN

1. Quoted by Jefferson Cowie in his "'Vigorously Left, Right, and Center': The Crosscurrents of Working-Class America in the 1970s," in *America in the Seventies*, ed. Beth Bailey and David Farber (Lawrence: University of Kansas Press, 2004), 75.

2. Ibid., 75–76.

3. A good introduction to the restructuring crisis can be found in Edward Soja, Rebecca Morales, and Goetz Wolff, "Urban Restructuring: An Analysis of Social and Spatial Change in Los Angeles," *Economic Geography* 59, no. 4 (October 1983): esp. 217–222.

4. On the influx of Pacific Rim immigrants in the 1970s and 1980s, see Marta López-Garza and David R. Diaz, eds., *Asian and Latino Immigrants in a Restructuring Economy: The Metamorphosis of Southern California* (Stanford, Calif.: Stanford University Press, 2002), chaps. 3–5, 15–18; and Leo R. Chavez, *Shadowed Lives: Undocumented Immigrants in American Society* (Fort Worth: Harcourt, Brace Jovanovich, 1991).

5. Allen J. Scott, *Technopolis: High-Technology Industry and Regional Development in Southern California* (Berkeley: University of California Press, 1993), passim.

6. Paul Ong and Evelyn Blumenberg, "Income and Racial Inequality in Los Angeles," in *The City: Los Angeles and Urban Theory at the End of the Twentieth Century*, ed. Allen J. Scott and Edward W. Soja (Berkeley: University of California Press, 1996), 311–335.

7. Quoted in Thomas B. Edsall and Mary D. Edsall, *Chain Reaction: The Impact of Race, Rights, and Taxes on American Politics* (New York: Norton, 1991), 200. See also Kenneth D. Durr, *Behind the Backlash: White Working-Class Politics in Baltimore, 1940–1980* (Chapel Hill: University of North Carolina Press, 2003); and William Kleinknecht, *The Man Who Sold the World: Ronald Reagan and the Betrayal of Main Street America* (New York: Nation Books, 2009).

8. Myrna Cherkoss Donahoe, "Workers' Response to Plant Closures: The Cases of Steel and Auto in Southeast Los Angeles, 1935–1986" (PhD diss., University of California, Irvine, 1987), chaps. 7–8.

9. Mike Davis, *City of Quartz: Excavating the Future in Los Angeles* (New York: Vintage, 1992), chap. 9.

10. Myrna C. Donahoe, "Economic Restructuring and Labor Organizing in Southwest Los Angeles, 1935–2001," in *Latino Los Angeles: Transformations, Communities, and Activism*, ed. Enrique C. Ochoa and Gilda L. Ochoa (Tucson: University of Arizona Press, 2005), 98–99.

11. Quoted in William Serrin, *The Company and the Union: The "Civilized Relationship" of the General Motors Corporation and the United Automobile Workers* (New York: Knopf, 1973), 118. Closing the automobile assembly plants also involved shutting down most of the twenty or so auto parts suppliers in Los Angeles who produced wheels, batteries, and other ancillary equipment for the Big Three auto manufacturers. In the late 1970s some of these auto parts companies began employing undocumented immigrants from Mexico at wages significantly lower than those paid to UAW members in order to reduce their costs. See Rebecca Morales, "Transitional Labor: Undocumented Workers in the Los Angeles Automobile Industry," Working Paper no. 7, Graduate School of Architecture and Urban Planning, University of California, Los Angeles, 1983.

12. Eric Mann, *Taking On General Motors: A Case Study of the UAW Campaign to Keep GM Van Nuys Open* (Los Angeles: UCLA Center for Labor Research and Education, Institute of Industrial Relations, 1987), 116–118.

13. Quoted in ibid., 118.

14. Quoted in ibid., 103. For background information on the closing of the Van Nuys plant, see Craig A. Zabala, "Collective Bargaining at UAW Local 645, General Motors Assembly Division, Van Nuys, California, 1976–1982," 2 vols. (PhD diss., University of California, Los Angeles, 1983).

15. Donahoe, "Economic Restructuring," 86–87.

16. Quoted in Eric Mann, "Keeping GM Van Nuys Open," *Labor Research Review* 1, no. 9 (Spring 1986): 40.

17. Ibid., 40–41.

18. Quoted in ibid., 36.

19. Ibid.

20. Ibid., 41–45; Kim Moody, *An Injury to All: The Decline of American Unionism* (New York: Verso, 1988), chap. 8.

21. Soja, Morales, and Wolff, "Urban Restructuring," 223–226.

22. Susan Faludi, *Stiffed: The Betrayal of the American Man* (New York: Morrow, 1999), chap. 2.

23. Ibid., 60.

24. Quoted in ibid., 58.

25. Quoted in ibid., 63.

26. Quoted in ibid., 76.

27. Quoted in ibid., 65–68.

28. Quoted in ibid., 90.

29. Beth Bailey, "She 'Can Bring Home the Bacon': Negotiating Gender in the 1970s," in Bailey and Farber, *America in the Seventies*, 109.

30. The 1992 L.A. County Aerospace Task Force report is quoted in *Los Angeles Times*, March 17, 1992, D2.

31. *Los Angeles Times*, July 27, 1997, D12.

32. Brigid O'Farrell and Suzanne Moore, "Unions, Hard Hats, and Women Workers," in *Women and Unions: Forging a Partnership*, ed. Dorothy Sue Cobble (Ithaca, N.Y.: ILR Press, 1993), chap. 3.

33. Dean Baker, *The United States since 1980* (Cambridge: Cambridge University Press, 2007), 73–74.

34. Quoted in Faludi, *Stiffed*, 87.

35. *Latinos and Housing in Los Angeles County*, Report of L.A. County Housing Commission, 1980, 14–15.

36. Quoted in Mike Davis, "'Chinatown,' Part Two? The 'Internationalization' of Downtown Los Angeles," *New Left Review*, no. 164 (July/August 1987): 21.

37. Donahoe, "Economic Restructuring," 95–96, 99–100.

38. Mike Davis, "The New Industrial Peonage," *Heritage* (newsletter of Southern California Library for Social Studies and Research) (Summer 1991): 8.

39. Ong and Blumenberg, "Income and Racial Inequality," 319–320.

40. Ibid., 322–323. See also Soja, Morales, and Wolff, "Urban Restructuring," 217–222.

41. James Allen and Eugene Turner, eds., *The Ethnic Quilt: Population Diversity in Southern California* (Northridge: Center for Geographical Studies, California State University, Northridge, 1997), 206–207.

42. Ong and Blumenberg, "Income and Racial Inequality," 324–327. On fears about the rise of a new underclass, see Roger Waldinger, "Up from Poverty? 'Race,' Immigration, and the Fate of Low-Skilled Workers," in *Strangers at the Gates: New Immigrants in Urban America*, ed. Roger Waldinger (Berkeley: University of California Press, 2001), chap. 3.

43. Donahoe, "Workers' Response to Plant Closures," 96; Mike Davis, *Magical Urbanism: Latinos Reinvent the U.S. City* (New York: Verso, 2001), 53–59.

44. Allen and Turner, *The Ethnic Quilt*, 211–212.

45. Philip Shapira, "The Crumbling of Smokestack California: A Case Study in Industrial Restructuring and the Reorganization of Work," Working Paper no. 437, Institute of Urban and Regional Development, University of California, Berkeley, 1984, 14–15.

46. Scott, *Technopolis*, 180–186.

47. Quoted in ibid., 179.

48. Ibid., 138–153.

49. David Naguib Pellow and Lisa Sun-Hee Park, *The Silicon Valley of Dreams: Environmental Injustice, Immigrant Workers, and the High-Tech Global Economy* (New York: New York University Press, 2002), 194. Pellow and Park describe the campaign against toxic pollution in chapters 4–5.

50. Scott, *Technopolis*, 179–184.

51. M. Patricia Fernandez-Kelly and Anna M. Garcia, "Invisible amidst the Glitter: Hispanic Women in the Southern California Electronics Industry," in *The Worth of Women's Work: A Qualitative Synthesis*, ed. Anne Statham, Eleanor M. Miller, and Hans O. Mauksch (Albany: State University of New York Press, 1988), 282.

52. Quoted in Gilbert G. Gonzalez and Raul A. Fernandez, *A Century of Chicano History: Empire, Nations, and Migration* (New York: Routledge, 2003), 142–143.

53. Quoted in Davis, *Magical Urbanism*, 35. See also Emilio Pradilla Cobos, "The Limits of the Mexican *Maquiladora* Industry," *Review of Radical Political Economics*, vol. 25, no. 4 (1993): 91–108.

54. Quoted in Gay Young, "Women, Border Industrialization Program, and Human Rights," Center for Inter-American and Border Studies, University of Texas, El Paso, 1984, 17–18.

55. Fernandez-Kelly and Garcia, "Invisible amidst the Glitter," 265–290.

56. Ibid., 277.

57. Scott, *Technopolis*, 183–185.

58. Quoted in David Bacon, *Organizing Silicon Valley's High Tech Workers*, pt. 2: "The Development of the High Tech Workforce," http://dbacon.igc.org/Unions/04hitec2.htm.

59. Quoted in ibid., pt. 7: "Electronics Companies Press for Political Changes," http://dbacon.igc.org/Unions/04hitec7.htm.

60. Ibid.

61. At one point, Linda, a Latina organizer in Northern California, reported the following: "Sure, the big [union] guys say they're interested in high-tech, but they give us only two or three organizers and a shoestring budget, and there's a couple hundred thousand workers out there. If this was steel, or auto, or any of the other traditional men's jobs, they'd give us a lot more attention." See Karen Hossfeld, "Why Aren't High-Tech Workers Organized? Lessons in Gender, Race, and Nationality from Silicon Valley," in *Working People of California*, ed. Daniel Cornford (Berkeley: University of California Press, 1995), 409–410, 417–418.

62. Ibid., 425.

63. John Laslett and Mary Tyler, *The ILGWU in Los Angeles, 1907–1988* (Inglewood, Calif.: Ten Star Press, 1989), 102–103.

64. Steve Babson, *The Unfinished Struggle: Turning Points in American Labor, 1877–Present* (Lanham, Md.: Rowman and Littlefield, 1999), chap. 5.

65. Moody, *An Injury to All*, 128–133. See also G. William Domhoff, *Who Rules America Now? A View for the 1980s*, 2nd ed. (Englewood Cliffs, N.J.: Prentice-Hall, 1983), chaps. 2–3.

66. Moody, *An Injury to All*, 129–130; Howard Jarvis, with Robert Pack, *I'm Mad as Hell: The Exclusive Story of the Tax Revolt and Its Leader* (New York: New York Times Books, 1979), passim.

67. Moody, *An Injury to All*, 132–135; Elizabeth Goodridge, "The Gipper's Winning Coalition: How Ronald Reagan Made Republicans out of Working Democrats," *U.S. News and World Report*, February 18, 2008, 14–23.

68. *Southern California Business* 42, no. 23 (June 7, 1978): 2; ibid., 42, no. 26 (July 12, 1978): 2–3.

69. Quoted in ibid., 42, no. 32 (August 4, 1978): 2.

70. Craig Zabala, "Sabotage in an Automobile Assembly Plant: Worker Voice on the Shopfloor," in *Autowork*, ed. Robert Asher and Ronald Edsforth (Albany: State University of New York Press, 1995), 219–225.

71. Moody, *An Injury to All*, 133–134; Jefferson Cowie, "'A One-Sided Class War': Rethinking Doug Fraser's 1978 Resignation from the Labor-Management Group," *Labor History* 44, no. 3 (August 2003): 307.

72. Quoted in Cowie, "'A One-Sided Class War,'" 310.

73. Moody, *An Injury to All*, 223. See also Mark Levitan, "The UAW, the Progressive Alliance, and the Paralysis of Social Unionism," *Changes* (July–August 1979): 23–24.

74. Babson, *The Unfinished Struggle*, 155–161.

75. Shapira, "The Crumbling of Smokestack California," 8.

76. Quoted in Thomas Byrne Edsall, *The New Politics of Inequality* (New York: Norton, 1984), 151.

77. Donahoe, "Workers' Response to Plant Closures," chap. 6.

78. Quoted in Serrin, *The Company and the Union*, 204.

79. Quoted in Dan La Botz, *Rank-and-File Rebellion: Teamsters for a Democratic Union* (London: Verso, 1990), 158.

80. Ibid., 152–158.

81. Donahoe, "Workers' Response to Plant Closures," 260.

82. Ed Sadlowski, director of District 31 in Chicago, the United Steelworkers' largest district, led the reform movement that sought to halt the union's decline by reversing the class collaborationist policies of the national leadership and pressuring the steel companies to invest sufficient resources in the aging steel plants to modernize them instead of selling off unprofitable factories. See Moody, *An Injury to All*, 224–229; Philip W. Nyden, *Steelworkers Rank-and-File: The Political Economy of a Union Reform Movement* (New York: Praeger, 1984), passim; and Staughton Lynd, *The Fight against Shutdowns: Youngstown's Steel Mill Closings* (San Pedro, Calif.: Singlejack Books, 1982).

83. Donahoe, "Workers' Response to Plant Closures," 259–260.

84. Quoted in La Botz, *Rank-and-File Rebellion*, 158.

85. *Los Angeles Times*, November 12, 1981, B7.

86. Quoted in Ruth Milkman, *L.A. Story: Immigrant Workers and the Future of the U.S. Labor Movement* (New York: Russell Sage Foundation, 2006), 99. See also Michael H. Belzer, "The Motor Carrier Industry: Truckers and Teamsters under Siege," in *Contemporary Collective Bargaining in the Private Sector*, ed. Paula B. Voos (Madison: Industrial Relations Research Association, University of Wisconsin, 1994), 258–260.

87. Milkman, *L.A. Story*, 85. See also Charles R. Perry, *Deregulation and the Decline of the Unionized Trucking Industry* (Philadelphia. Industrial Research Unit, Wharton School, University of Pennsylvania, 1986).

88. Milkman, *L.A. Story*, 92–97; Grace Palladino, *Skilled Hands, Strong Spirits: A Century of Building Trades History* (Ithaca, N.Y.: Cornell University Press, 2005), 185–188.

89. Laslett and Tyler, *The ILGWU in Los Angeles*, 92.

90. Ibid., 94–95.

91. Milkman, *L.A. Story*, 101–104. Tensions between Latinos and African Americans in Los Angeles increased in this period for other reasons as well, including neighborhood competition for low-income housing, conflict over the benefits to be gained from affirmative action and political redistricting, and access to patronage jobs at city hall. In minority neighborhoods with high unemployment rates and large numbers of high school dropouts, these tensions also contributed to the rapid growth in race-based gangs and to bloody confrontations between them over territory and control if the drug trade. See Earl Ofari Hutchinson, *The Latino Challenge to Black America: Towards a Conversation between African Americans and Hispanics* (Los Angeles: Middle Passage Books, 2007); James Diego Vigil, *The Projects: Gang and Non-Gang Families in East Los Angeles* (Austin: University of Texas Press, 2007); and Rufus P. Browning, Dale Rogers Marshall, and David H. Tabb, *Protest Is Not Enough: The Struggle of Blacks and Hispanics for Equality in Urban Politics* (Berkeley: University of California Press, 1984).

92. Quoted in Milkman, *L.A. Story*, 103. See also Cynthia Cranford, "Gender and Citizenship in the Restructuring of Janitorial Work in Los Angeles," *Gender Issues*, vol. 16, no. 4 (Fall 1998): 25–51.

93. Harvey Swados, "West-Coast Waterfront—The End of an Era," *Dissent* 8, no. 4 (Autumn 1961): 448–460.

94. Quoted in Paul T. Hartman, *Collective Bargaining and Productivity: The Longshore Mechanization Agreement* (Berkeley: University of California Press, 1969), 87–88.

95. Ibid., 112–118. See also J. R. Whittaker, *Containerization* (Washington, D.C.: Hemisphere Publishing, 1975), passim.

96. Nelson Lichtenstein cites this statement by Stephen Cohen and John Zysman: "Services are complements to manufacturing, not substitutes or successors." Lichtenstein then offers this distinction in an example from the computer industry: "A new program costs but pennies to manufacture, but tens of thousands of man- and woman-hours to create, de-bug, install, and market." See Lichtenstein, *State of the Union: A Century of American Labor* (Princeton, N.J.: Princeton University Press, 2002), 221–222.

97. Quoted in Milkman, *L.A. Story*, 80.

98. Michael Goldfield, *The Decline of Organized Labor in the United States* (Chicago: University of Chicago Press, 1987), 191–192.

99. Carol A. Vendrillo, "Collective Bargaining in California's Public Sector," in *Collective Bargaining in the Public Sector. The Experience of Eight States*, ed. Joyce M. Najita and James L. Stern (Armonk, N.Y.: M. E. Sharpe, 2001), 89–101.

100. Christina Vasquez, who at the time was one of the newly appointed Latina organizers in the ILGWU, recalled: "The County Federation of Labor at that time was busy blaming immigrants for the decline of the unions and falling wages. . . . One time, we brought a group of Latino workers to an L.A. County membership meeting. The union people were asking racist questions like, 'Where's your green card?' ' You're not supposed to be here.' 'You're working for lower wages'" (quoted in Ruth Milkman and Kent Wong, *Voices from the Front Lines: Organizing Immigrant Workers in Los Angeles* [Los Angeles: UCLA Center for Labor Research and Education, 2000], 7–8). See also Laslett and Tyler, *The ILGWU in Los Angeles*, chap. 17.

101. Milkman, *L.A. Story*, chap. 3.

102. Richard W. Etulain, ed., *César Chávez: A Brief Biography with Documents* (Boston: Bedford/St. Martin's Press, 2002), 18.

103. For a discussion of the relationship between "occupational niches" and job competition, see Allen and Turner, *The Ethnic Quilt*, 215–222.

104. See, for example, *Citizen's Advocate*, May 19, 1979, 7.

105. Quoted in *Report of Los Angeles Human Relations Commission*, Los Angeles, 1979, 24.

106. Quoted in *Los Angeles Times*, September 11, 1983, 14.

107. A good summary of IRCA's provisions can be found in Michael LeMay and Elliott Robert Barkan, eds., *U.S. Immigration and Naturalization Laws and Issues: A Documentary History* (Westport, Conn.: Greenwood Press, 1999), 282–287.

108. Lawrence H. Fuchs, "The Reaction of Black Americans to Immigration," in *Immigration Reconsidered: History, Sociology, and Politics*, ed. Virginia Yans-McLaughlin (New York: Oxford University Press, 1990), 300.

109. Quoted in *Los Angeles Times*, special edition reprint, November 14–30, 1993, 8.

110. Melvin L. Oliver, James H. Johnson Jr., and Walter C. Farrell Jr., "The Causes of the 1992 Los Angeles Civil Disorders," in *Reading Rodney King, Reading Urban Uprising*, ed. Robert Gooding-Williams (New York: Routledge, 1993), 114–115.

111. David O. Sears, "Urban Rioting in Los Angeles: A Comparison of 1965 with 1992," in Mark Baldassare, *The Los Angeles Riots: Lessons for the Urban Future* (Boulder, Colo.: Westview Press, 1994), 242.

112. Supplement to *Statement of Vote, General Election November 6, 1984* (Sacramento, 1985), 20–21.

113. In the November 1994 election, 67 percent of white California voters voted for Proposition 187, while 23 percent of Latino voters supported it. See Rodolpho F. Acuna, *Anything But Mexican: Chicanos in Contemporary Los Angeles* (New York: Verso, 1995), 156–160.

114. *Los Angeles Times*, August 12, 1994, 4.

115. Acuna, *Anything But Mexican*, 158.

116. Quoted in Kevin Johnson, "The New Nativism: Something Old, Something New, Something Borrowed, Something Blue," in *Immigrants Out! The New Nativism and the Anti-Immigrant Impulse in the United States*, ed. Juan F. Perea (New York: New York University Press, 1996), 178–179.

117. Kenneth C. Burt, *The Search for a Civic Voice: California Latino Politics* (Claremont, Calif.: Regina Books, 2007), 323.

118. Acuna, *Anything But Mexican*, 158–159; Robert Gottlieb, Mark Vallianatos, Regina M. Freer, and Peter Dreier, *The Next Los Angeles: The Struggle for a Livable City* (Berkeley: University of California Press, 2005), 156–157; Jean Stefanic, "Funding the Nativist Agenda," in Perea, *Immigrants Out!* 128.

119. Quoted in *Los Angeles Times*, November 4, 1994, D4.

120. Ibid.

121. Acuna, *Anything But Mexican*, 160.

122. Some observers believed that the display of Mexican flags alongside U.S. ones on this march helped to depress the "No" vote on Proposition 187 because it suggested disloyalty on the part of the marchers. See Acuna, *Anything But Mexican*, 158–159; and Ralph Armbruster, Kim Geron, and Edna Bonacich, "The Assault on California's Latino Immigrants: The Politics of Proposition 187," *International Journal of Urban and Regional Research* 19, no. 4 (December 1995): 662.

123. Harry P. Pachon, "Latino Politics in the Golden State: Ready for the 21st Century?" in *Racial and Ethnic Politics in California*, vol. 2, ed. Michael B. Preston, Bruce E. Cain, and Sandra Bass (Berkeley: Institute of Governmental Studies, University of California, Berkeley, 1998), 418–420.

124. Ibid., 420.

125. Gottlieb, Vallianatos, Freer, and Dreier, *The Next Los Angeles*, 159.

126. Gregory Rodriguez is quoted in Anthony York, "R.I.P. Prop. 187," *Salon News*, July 30 1999, http://www1.salon.com/news/feature/1999/07/30/immigration/index.html.

CHAPTER TWELVE

1. *Los Angeles Times*, March 14, 2006, B2.

2. Ibid.

3. Michael Schiavone, *Unions in Crisis? The Future of Organized Labor in America* (Westport, Conn.: Praeger, 2008), 59.

4. Roger Waldinger et al., "Justice for Janitors: Organizing in Difficult Times," *Dissent* 44, no. 1 (Winter 1997): 37–40. See also Roger Waldinger et al., "Helots No More: A Case Study of the Justice for Janitors Campaign in Los Angeles," Working Paper no. 15, Lewis Center for Regional Policy Studies, University of California, Los Angeles, 1996; and Catherine L. Fisk, Daniel J. B. Mitchell, and Christopher L. Erickson, "Union Representation of Immigrant Janitors in Southern California: Economic and Legal Challenges," in *Organizing Immigrants: The Challenge for Unions in Contemporary California*, ed. Ruth Milkman (Ithaca, N.Y.: ILR/Cornell University Press, 2000), 199–224.

5. Schiavone, *Unions in Crisis?* 46–49; Richard W. Hurd and William Rouse, "Progressive Union Organizing: The SEIU Justice for Janitors Campaign," *Review of Radical Political Economics* 21, no. 3 (October 1989): 70–75.

6. Carol Zabin, "Organizing Latino Workers in the Los Angeles Manufacturing Sector: The Case of American Racing Equipment," in Milkman, *Organizing Immigrants*, 150–168.

7. Ruth Milkman and Kent Wong, "Organizing the Wicked City: The 1992 Southern California Drywall Strike," in Milkman, *Organizing Immigrants*, 169–198.

8. Kim Geron, "The Local/Global Context of the Los Angeles Hotel-Tourism Industry," *Social Justice* 24, no. 2 (Summer 1997): 4–14; Lou Siegel, "LRR Voices: Local 11 Takes on L.A.," *Labor Research Review* 1, no. 20 (1993): 7–9; Thomas J. Adams, "Postwar Los Angeles and the Landscape of Modern Service Work," University of Chicago, 2008, 14–20.

9. Geron, "The Local/Global Context," 6–9.

10. Siegel, "LRR Voices: Local 11," 8; personal observation by the author at demonstration by HERE Local 814 in Santa Monica, April 4, 1993.

11. Vivien Rothstein, "Fighting for a Living Wage in Santa Monica," in *Teaching for Change: Popular Education and the Labor Movement*, ed. Linda Delp, Miranda Outman-Kramer, Susan J. Schurman, and Kent Wong (Los Angeles: UCLA Center for Labor Research and Education, 2002), 101–102.

12. Harold Meyerson, "A Clean Sweep: The SEIU's Organizing Drive for Janitors Shows How Unionization Can Raise Wages," *American Prospect* 11, no. 15 (June–July 2000): 25.

13. Ruth Milkman and Bongoh Kye, *The State of the Unions in 2008: A Profile of Union Membership in Los Angeles, California, and the Nation* (Los Angeles: UCLA Institute for Research on Labor and Employment, 2008), 2.

14. See, for example, press coverage of the giant immigrant rights march staged by the Latino community on May 1, 1986: *Los Angeles Times*, May 2, 1986, A1, 7–8.

15. For George Sánchez's views, see his book *Becoming Mexican American: Ethnicity, Culture, and Identity in Chicano Los Angeles, 1900–1945* (New York: Oxford University Press, 1993), passim.

16. Ruth Milkman, *L.A. Story: Immigrant Workers and the Future of the U.S. Labor Movement* (New York: Russell Sage Foundation, 2006), 33; Susan Bibler Coutin, "The Formation and Transformation of Salvadoran Community Organizations in Los Angeles," in *Latino Los Angeles: Transformations, Communities, and Activism*, ed. Enrique C. Ochoa and Gilda L. Ochoa (Tucson: University of Arizona Press, 2005), 151–177.

17. Kent Wong and Victor Narro, "Educating Immigrant Workers for Action," *Labor Studies Journal* 32, no. 1 (March 2007): 113–118.

18. Randy Shaw, *Beyond the Fields: Cesar Chavez, the UFW, and the Struggle for Justice in the 21st Century* (Berkeley: University of California Press, 2008), chap. 2.

19. Ibid.

20. John H. M. Laslett, "Playing Catch-Up: The Labor Movement in Los Angeles and San Francisco, 1985–2005," in *California Policy Options, 2008*, ed. Daniel J. B. Mitchell (Los Angeles: UCLA School of Public Affairs, 2008), 177.

21. Quotes taken from Héctor Delgado, *New Immigrants, Old Unions: Organizing Undocumented Workers in Los Angeles* (Philadelphia: Temple University Press, 1993), 61–63.

22. Ibid.

23. Robert Gottlieb, Mark Vallianatos, Regina M. Freer, and Peter Dreier, *The Next Los Angeles: The Struggle for a Livable City* (Berkeley: University of California Press, 2005), 95.

24. Ibid. I am indebted to Harold Meyerson for some of this information.

25. Ruth Milkman and Daisy Rooks, *California Union Membership: A Turn-of-the-Century Portrait* (Los Angeles: UCLA Institute for Research on Labor and Employment, 2003), 38.

26. Paul Johnston, "Public Sector Unionism," in *Crisis in the Public Sector: A Reader*, ed. Kenneth Fox et al. (New York: Monthly Review Press, 1982), 214–219.

27. Fox, *Crisis in the Public Sector*, chap. 1. See also Carol A. Vendrillo, "Collective Bargaining in California's Public Sector," in *Collective Bargaining in the Public Sector: The Experience of Eight States*, ed. Joyce M. Najita and James L. Stern (Armonk, N.Y.: M. E. Sharpe, 2001), 141.

28. Liz M. McNichol, "Fighting on Many Fronts: SEIU in Los Angeles," *Labor Research Review* 1, no. 15 (1990): 38.

29. Marjorie Murphy, *Blackboard Unions: The AFT and the NEA, 1900–1980* (Ithaca, N.Y.: Cornell University Press, 1990), chap. 13.

30. Quoted in *Voice of Local 399*, vol. 17, no. 4 (October/November 1993): 3, box 382, SEIU Collection, Walter P. Reuther Library, Wayne State University, Detroit.

31. *Voice of Local 399*, vol. 3, no. 2 (June/July 1979): 1–7, box 394, SEIU Collection.

32. Linda Delp and Katie Quan, "Homecare Worker Organizing in California: An Analysis of a Successful Strategy," *Labor Studies Journal* 27, no. 1 (Spring 2002): 1–23. See also Eileen Boris and Jennifer Klein, "Organizing Home Care: Low-Waged Workers in the Welfare State," *Politics and Society* 34, no. 1 (March 2006): 81–107.

33. Delp and Quan, "Homecare Worker Organizing," 4–13; Lola Smallwood Cuevas, Kent Wong, and Linda Delp, *Women's Work. Los Angeles Homecare Workers Revitalize the Labor Movement* (Los Angeles: UCLA Center for Labor Research and Education, 2009), 86–89.

34. Pierrette Hondagneu-Sotelo, *Doméstica: Immigrant Workers Cleaning and Caring in the Shadow of Affluence* (Berkeley: University of California Press, 2001), 221–229.

35. Wong and Narro, "Educating Immigrant Workers for Action," 115–116.

36. Cynthia Cranford, "Gender and Citizenship in the Restructuring of Janitorial Work in Los Angeles," *Gender Issues* 16, no. 4 (1998): 40.

37. Cynthia Jean Cranford, "Labor, Gender, and the Politics of Citizenship: Organizing Justice for Janitors in Los Angeles" (PhD diss., University of Southern California, 2001), 89.

38. Quoted in Cranford, "Gender and Citizenship," 186.

39. Ibid.

40. The living wage ordinance negotiated in 1997 for L.A. city employees was $7.25 an hour, plus family health benefits, or $8.50 an hour without the benefits. This was still insufficient to support a single mother with two children unless she had some other source of income. See David Reynolds, "Living Wage Campaigns as Social Movements: Experiences from Nine Cities," *Labor Studies Journal* 26, no. 2 (Summer 2001): 36.

41. Cranford, "Gender and Citizenship," 186.

42. Quoted in ibid., 187.

43. Kenneth C. Burt, *The Search for a Civic Voice: California Latino Politics* (Claremont, Calif.: Regina Books, 2007), 323–325.

44. Quoted in Larry Frank and Kent Wong, "Dynamic Political Mobilization: The Los Angeles County Federation of Labor," *Working U.S.A.: Journal of Labor and Society* 8, no. 2 (December 2004): 165.

45. Quoted in ibid., 164. See also Myrna Oliver, "Bill Robertson, 89; Labor Leader and Power Broker Helped Bring NFL's Raiders and Olympic Games to L.A.," *Los Angeles Times*, December 10, 2005, B4.

46. Frank and Wong, "Dynamic Political Mobilization," 168–169.

47. Kent Wong and Michael Viola, *Miguel Contreras: Legacy of a Labor Leader* (Los Angeles: UCLA Center for Labor Research and Education, 2009), passim.

48. Burt, *The Search for a Civic Voice*, 331–334.

49. Ruth Milkman and Kent Wong, "L.A. Confidential: An Interview with Miguel Contreras," *New Labor Forum*, no. 10 (Spring/Summer 2002): 56–57.

50. Quoted in ibid., 55.

51. Burt, *The Search for a Civic Voice*, 331–334.

52. Quoted in Milkman and Wong, " L.A. Confidential," 56.

53. Ibid.

54. Frank and Wong, "Dynamic Political Mobilization," 10, Burt, *The Search for a Civic Voice*, 336–337.

55. Frank and Wong, "Dynamic Political Mobilization," 10.

56. Burt, *The Search for a Civic Voice*, 340.

57. *Los Angeles Times*, May 19, 2005, 1, 18–19; Peter Dreier, Regina Freer, Robert Gottlieb, and Mark Vallianatos, "Movement Mayor: Can Antonio Villaraigosa Change Los Angeles?" *Dissent* (Summer 2006): 21–29.

58. *Los Angeles Times*, May 12, 2005, A14.

59. Quoted in David Bacon and Philip Maldari, "Q&A: Andy Stern," *The Progressive* 69, no. 4 (April 2005): 6. Andy Stern's philosophy of union organizing is outlined in his book *A Country That Works: Getting America Back on Track* (New York: Free Press, 2006).

60. Schiavone, *Unions in Crisis?* 50–51.

61. Quoted in William Johnson, "Staffers Get Squeezed in New SEIU Locals," *Labor Notes*, September 2007, 1–2.

62. Quoted in Local 121, *RN News*, November 2007, 4. See also Schiavone, *Unions in Crisis?* 53–54.

63. Local 121, *RN News*, November 2007, 3–4.

64. SMART (SEIU Member Activists for Reform Today), "The California Alliance Agreement: Lessons Learned in Moving Forward in Organizing California's Nursing Home Industry" (n.p., 2003), 1–12.

65. Quoted in Ellen Dillinger, "Life under SEIU Trusteeship," *Labor Notes*, December 18, 2009, 3.

66. In October 2010, after a bitterly fought election campaign, United Healthcare Workers West defeated the National Union of Healthcare Workers in a union representation election at the California Kaiser Hospital chain, an election the *Los Angeles Times* described as "dishearten[ing]" because it "diverted money and foot soldiers from efforts to organize non-union workers" (*Los Angeles Times*, October 8, 2010, AA3).

67. Schiavone, *Unions in Crisis?* 49–53. See also Marick F. Masters, Ray Gibney,

and Tom Zagenczyk, "The AFL-CIO v. CTW: The Competing Visions, Strategies, and Structures," *Journal of Labor Research* 27, no. 4 (Fall 2006): 473–504.

68. Jennie Gil, "In the House of Labor: A Preliminary Report of the 2005 AFL-CIO Convention," *ATU Local 587 News Review* 28, no. 8 (August 2005): 1.

69. Ibid.

70. Schiavone, *Unions in Crisis?* 51.

71. Gil, "In the House of Labor," 1.

72. For relations between the AFL-CIO, CTW, and the Democratic Party in 2008, see Harold Meyerson, "Labor United and Divided: A Fractured Labor Movement Is Throwing Everything into Its Campaign for Barack Obama," *American Prospect*, August 25, 2008, 14–15.

73. Kim Moody, *U.S. Labor in Trouble and Transition: The Failure of Reform from Above, The Promise of Revival from Below* (New York: Verso, 2007).

74. Harold Meyerson, "Disunite There: Civil War at UNITE-HERE, One of America's Stellar Unions," *American Prospect*, February 26, 2009, 8–9.

75. Quoted in ibid., 9.

76. Harold Meyerson, "The Caesar's Palace Soviet," *American Prospect*, January 15, 2008, 8–10.

77. Janice Fine, *Worker Centers: Organizing Communities on the Edge of the Dream* (Ithaca, N.Y.: ILR/Cornell University Press, 2010). See also Lowell Turner and Daniel B. Cornfield, eds., *Labor in the New Urban Battlegrounds: Local Solidarity in a Global Economy* (Ithaca, N.Y.: ILR/Cornell University Press, 2007).

78. Janet Wasko, "Challenges to Hollywood's Labor Force in the 1990s," in *Global Productions in the Making of the "Information Society,"* ed. Gerald Sussman and John A. Lent (Cresskill, N.J.: Hampton Press, 1998), 173–189.

79. *Los Angeles Times*, May 9, 2010, A8.

80. See, for example, articles in the *Los Angeles Times* (April 15, 2009, A12; September 24, 2010, A9) concerning relations between the city unions and the municipal authorities.

81. J. Gregg Robinson and Judith S. McIlwee, "Obstacles to Unionization in High-Tech Industries," *Work and Occupations* 16, no. 2 (May 1989): 115–136; David Bacon, "Organizing Silicon Valley's High Tech Workers," http://dbacon.igc.org/Unions/04hitec1.htm.

82. Tom Gallagher, "Everybody Loved It, But . . . ," *Z Magazine*, November 1998, 21–28.

83. Héctor L. Delgado, "The Los Angeles Manufacturing Action Project: An Opportunity Squandered?" in Milkman, *Organizing Immigrants*, 235–238.

84. *New York Times*, February 20, 2011, 16, 18; and February 22, 2011, A1, 7; *Los Angeles Times*, February 23, 2011, A3; and February 27, 2011, A21.

CONCLUSION

1. For discussions of Los Angeles exceptionalism, see Carey McWilliams, *California: The Great Exception* (Berkeley: University of California Press, 1999); and Robert A. Schneider, Michael E. Engh, and Catherine Coquery-Vidrovitch, "Historicizing the City of Angels," *American Historical Review* 105, no. 5 (December 2000): 1668–1691.

2. Foster Rhea Dulles and Melvyn Dubofsky, *Labor in America: A History*, 4th ed. (Arlington Heights, Ill.: Harlan Davidson, 1984), 237–238.

3. Edward J. Escobar, *Race, Police, and the Making of a Political Identity: Mexican Americans and the Los Angeles Police Department, 1900–1945* (Berkeley: University of California Press, 1999), chap. 2.

4. Thomas R. Clark, "The Limits of Liberty: Courts, Police, and Labor Unrest in California, 1890–1926" (PhD diss., University of California, Los Angeles, 1994), 375–421.

5. Irving Bernstein, *The Lean Years: A History of the American Worker, 1920–1933* (Baltimore: Penguin Books, 1960), 148.

6. Sidney Fine, *"Without Blare of Trumpets": Walter Drew, the National Erectors' Association, and the Open Shop Movement, 1903–1957* (Ann Arbor: University of Michigan Press, 1995), 208.

7. Larry Ceplair and Steven Englund, *The Inquisition in Hollywood: Politics in the Film Community, 1930–1960* (Berkeley: University of California Press, 1983), 4–5.

8. Ernesto Chávez, *"¡Mi Raza Primero!" (My People First!): Nationalism, Identity, and Insurgency in the Chicano Movement in Los Angeles, 1966–1978* (Berkeley: University of California Press, 2002), 13–14.

9. Ceplair and Englund, *Inquisition in Hollywood*, 143–144.

10. Quoted in Becky Nicolaides, *My Blue Heaven: Life and Politics in the Working-Class Suburbs of Los Angeles, 1920–1965* (Chicago: University of Chicago Press, 2002), 280.

11. David Brion Davis, *The Fear of Conspiracy: Images of Un-American Subversion from the Revolution to the Present* (Ithaca, N.Y.: Cornell University Press, 1971), chaps. 1–2.

12. Sidney Lens, *The Labor Wars: From the Molly Maguires to the Sit-Downs* (Garden City, N.Y.: Anchor Books, 1974), chap. 4; Robert K. Murray, *Red Scare: A Study in National Hysteria, 1919–1920* (Minneapolis: University of Minnesota Press, 1955), chap. 6.

13. Greg Hise, "Industry and Imaginative Geographies," in *Metropolis in the Making: Los Angeles in the 1920s*, ed. Tom Sitton and William Deverell (Berkeley: University of California Press, 2001), 36.

14. Olivier Zunz, *The Changing Face of Inequality: Urbanization, Industrial Development, and Immigrants in Detroit, 1880–1920* (Chicago: University of Chicago Press, 1982), 112–113.

15. Robert Lewis, *Chicago Made: Factory Networks in the Industrial Metropolis* (Chicago: University of Chicago Press, 2008), 24–25.

16. Louis B. Perry and Richard S. Perry, *A History of the Los Angeles Labor Movement, 1911–1941* (Berkeley: University of California Press, 1963), 14.

17. Lynne Pierson Doti and Larry Schweikart, *Banking in the American West: From the Gold Rush to Deregulation* (Norman: University of Oklahoma Press, 1991), 114.

18. E. J. Hobsbawm, *Revolutionaries: Contemporary Essays* (London: Weidenfeld and Nicolson, 1973), 14.

19. David Roediger and Franklin Rosemont, eds., *Haymarket Scrapbook* (Chicago: Charles H. Kerr, 1986), 178.

20. Quoted in ibid., 215.

21. Robert M. Fogelson, *The Fragmented Metropolis: Los Angeles, 1850–1930* (Berkeley: University of California Press, 1967).

22. See the discussion of sunbelt cities in Bernard L. Weinstein and Robert E. Firestine, *Regional Growth and Decline in the United States: The Rise of the Sunbelt and the Decline of the Northeast* (New York: Praeger, 1978).

23. Quoted in Fogelson, *The Fragmented Metropolis*, 195.

24. Ibid., 186.

25. Hise, "Imaginative Geographies," 35.

26. Nicolaides, *My Blue Heaven*, 31–32.

27. Ruth Milkman, *L.A. Story: Immigrant Workers and the Future of the U.S. Labor Movement* (New York: Russell Sage Foundation, 2006), 134.

28. Fred W. Viehe, "Black Gold Suburbs: The Influence of the Extractive Industry on the Suburbanization of Los Angeles, 1890–1930," *Journal of Urban History* 8, no. 1 (November 1981): 3–26.

29. William B. Friedricks, *Henry Huntington and the Creation of Southern California* (Columbus: Ohio State University Press, 1992), chap. 2.

30. Nicolaides, *My Blue Heaven*, 74.

31. Bruce Nelson, *Workers on the Waterfront: Seamen, Longshoremen, and Unionism in the 1930s* (Urbana: University of Illinois Press, 1988), chap. 5. See also Charles P. Larrowe, *Harry Bridges: The Rise and Fall of Radical Labor in the United States* (Westport, Conn.: Lawrence Hill, 1972), chap. 8.

32. Paul Eliel, *The Waterfront and General Strikes, San Francisco, 1934: A Brief History* (San Francisco: Hooper, 1934).

33. Howard Kimeldorf, *Reds or Rackets? The Making of Radical and Conservative Unions on the Waterfront* (Berkeley: University of California Press, 1988), 105–110.

34. Quoted in Executive Minutes, July 28, 1934, folder 4, box 8, ILWU Local 13 Collection, Urban Archives, Oviatt Library, California State University, Northridge.

35. Alvin Averbach, "San Francisco's South of Market District, 1850–1950: The Emergence of a Skid Row," *California Historical Quarterly* 52, no. 3 (Fall 1973): 211.

36. For a discussion of domestic migration that includes material on southwestern-ers migrating both east and west, see James N. Gregory, *The Southern Diaspora: How the Great Migrations of Black and White Southerners Transformed America* (Chapel Hill: University of North Carolina Press, 2005).

37. On black workers in Chicago, see Rick Halpern, *Down on the Killing Floor: Black and White Workers in Chicago's Packinghouses, 1904–1954* (Urbana: University of Illinois Press, 1997). On black workers in Detroit, see August Meier and Elliott Rudwick, *Black Detroit and the Rise of the UAW* (New York: Oxford University Press, 1979).

38. Douglas Flamming, *Bound for Freedom: Black Los Angeles in Jim Crow America* (Berkeley: University of California Press, 2005), chap. 3.

39. Ibid., 170.

40. Gerald Horne, *Fire This Time: The Watts Uprising and the 1960s* (Charlottes-ville: University of Virginia Press, 1995), passim; Thomas J. Sugrue, *The Origins of the Urban Crisis: Race and Inequality in Postwar Detroit* (Princeton, N.J.: Princeton University Press, 1996), chaps. 8–9.

41. Quoted in James A. Geschwender, *Class, Race, and Worker Insurgency: The League of Revolutionary Black Workers* (Cambridge: Cambridge University Press, 1977), 134.

42. Quoted in Ely Chinoy, *Automobile Workers and the American Dream* (Boston: Beacon Press, 1955), 93. See also David Schreiker and Ellen Dolwin, "White Flight and Lost Jobs: Watts Residents Move to the Suburbs," *Journal of Work and Society* 14, no. 2 (Fall 2003): 14–18.

43. In 1930, there were 60,114 immigrants from southern and eastern Europe residing in Los Angeles, who made up 16 percent of the labor force. In Pittsburgh at that time, these immigrant groups constituted 29 percent of the labor force. See Fogel-son, *The Fragmented Metropolis*, 76; and John Bodnar, Roger Simon, and Michael P. Weber, *Lives of Their Own: Blacks, Italians, and Poles in Pittsburgh, 1900–1960* (Urbana: University of Illinois Press, 1982), 187.

44. Kimeldorf, *Reds or Rackets?* 41–42; John Laslett and Mary Tyler, *The ILGWU in Los Angeles, 1907–1988* (Inglewood, Calif.: Ten Star Press, 1989), chaps. 1–2.

45. On Gompers and Strasser, see Nick Salvatore, ed., *Seventy Years of Life and Labor: An Autobiography by Samuel Gompers* (Ithaca, N.Y.: ILR Press, 1984), passim. On Mike Quill, see L. H. Whittemore, *The Man Who Ran the Subways: The Story of Mike Quill* (New York: Holt, Rinehart, and Winston, 1968). On Rose Pesotta, see Elaine J. Leeder, *The Gentle General: Rose Pesotta, Anarchist and Labor Organizer* (Albany, N.Y.: SUNY Press, 1993). On John Brophy, see Brophy, *A Miner's Life: An Autobiography*, ed. John C. P. Hall (Madison: University of Wisconsin Press, 1964), chaps. 1–2.

46. For the Knights of Labor in Los Angeles, see Grace Heilman Stimson, *Rise*

of the Labor Movement in Los Angeles (Berkeley: University of California Press, 1955), chap. 4.

47. For insights into the impact of the Mexican Revolution on immigrants who moved north to Los Angeles, see John Mason Hart, "The Evolution of the Mexican and Mexican-American Working Classes," in *Border Crossings: Mexican and Mexican-American Workers*, ed. John Mason Hart (Wilmington, Del.: Scholarly Resources, 1998), 1–26.

48. Recent research has identified a special L.A. model of unionism characterized by grassroots organizing, immigrant rights, and close links between unions and worker centers. See Ruth Milkman, Joshua Bloom, Victor Narro, eds., *Working for Justice: The L.A. Model of Organizing and Advocacy* (Ithaca, N.Y.: ILR/Cornell University Press, 2010), 7–8.

PRIMARY SOURCES

ARCHIVAL SOURCES

California CIO Council. Register, Union Research and Information Service Records, 1935–1956. Southern California Library for Social Studies and Research, Los Angeles.

Virgil Collins Collection. Walter P. Reuther Library, Wayne State University, Detroit.

Philip Marshall Connelly Papers. Collection of Los Angeles CIO Industrial Union Council Records (Collection 2015). Special Collections, Charles E. Young Research Library, University of California, Los Angeles.

Ephemera, Collection 200. Box 155. Special Collections, Charles E. Young Research Library, University of California, Los Angeles.

Philip J. Ethington. "Segregated Diversity: Race-Ethnicity, Space, and Political Fragmentation in Los Angeles County, 1940–1994." Final Report to John Randolph Haynes and Dora Haynes Foundation, 2000.

Dorothy Healey Papers. Special Collections, Charles E. Young Research Library, University of California, Los Angeles.

Shevy Healey Papers. Southern California Library for Social Studies and Research, Los Angeles.

Henry E. Huntington Collection. Huntington Library, San Marino, Calif.

ILWU Local 13 Collection. Urban Archives, Oviatt Library, California State University, Northridge.

The Life and Times of Rosie the Riveter. Documentary video. Instructional Media Library, University of California, Los Angeles.

Debbie Louis Collection on Civil Rights, 1949–1991. Special Collections, Charles E. Young Research Library, University of California, Los Angeles.

Max Mont Collection, 1941–1980. Urban Archives Center, Oviatt Library, California State University, Northridge.

Oil, Chemical, and Atomic Workers International Union. Local 128 Collection. Western Historical Collections, University of Colorado, Boulder.

Edward Roybal Papers. Special Collections, Charles E. Young Research Library, University of California, Los Angeles.

SEIU Collection. Walter P. Reuther Library, Wayne State University, Detroit.

Tom Thienes. "Contributions toward the History of the City of South Gate." Manuscript written for the Works Progress Administration, 1942. Weaver Library Archives, South Gate, Calif.

UAW Local 216 Collection. Walter P. Reuther Library, Wayne State University, Detroit.

UAW Region 6 Collection. Walter P. Reuther Library, Wayne State University, Detroit.

GOVERNMENT DOCUMENTS

California Bureau of Labor Statistics. *Twelfth Biennial Report, 1905–1906.* Sacramento: State Printing Office, 1907.

———. *Thirty-fourth Annual Report.* Sacramento: State Printing Office, 1924.

California Commission of Immigration and Housing. *First Annual Report of Commission of Immigration and Housing in California.* Sacramento: State Printing Office, 1915.

California State Department of Mines. *Report of Oil and Gas Division.* Sacramento: State Printing Office, 1929.

California State Unemployment Commission. *Abstract of Hearings on Unemployment before the California State Unemployment Commission, April and May 1932.* San Francisco, 1932.

Governor's Commission on the Los Angeles Race Riots. *Violence in the City: An End or a Beginning? A Report.* Los Angeles: Governor's Commission, 1965.

Los Angeles City Council Minutes. Vol. 76. Los Angeles: City Printing Office, 1908. Los Angeles City Hall.

Los Angeles County Commission on Human Relations. *Population and Housing in L.A. County*. Berkeley: Institute of Governmental Studies, 1963.

U.S. Census Bureau. "Wartime Changes in Population and Family Characteristics: Los Angeles Congested Production Area." Series CA-2, no. 5. Washington, D.C.: Government Printing Office, 1944.

U.S. Commission on Civil Rights. *Hearings before United States Commission on Civil Rights, Los Angeles, 1960*. Washington, D.C.: Government Printing Office, 1960.

U.S. Commission on Industrial Relations. *Final Report and Testimony Submitted to the U.S. Commission on Industrial Relations*. 61st Cong., 1st sess. Washington, D.C.: Government Printing Office, 1916.

U.S. Department of Commerce. *Earnings of Factory Workers, 1890–1927*. Washington, D.C.: Government Printing Office, 1929.

U.S. Senate. "Supplementary Exhibits on Los Angeles Chamber of Commerce and Merchants and Manufacturers Association." *Hearings before the Committee on Education and Labor, Subcommittee Investigating Violations of Free Speech and the Rights of Labor*, pt. 63. 76th Cong., 2nd sess. Washington, D.C.: Government Printing Office, 1940.

―――. "The Disadvantaged Status of Unorganized Labor in California's Industrialized Agriculture." *Violations of Free Speech and the Rights of Labor: Report of the Committee on Education and Labor*, pt. 3. 77th Cong., 2nd sess. Washington, D.C.: Government Printing Office, 1942.

―――. "Employers Associations and Collective Bargaining in California." *Violations of Free Speech and the Rights of Labor: Report of the Committee on Education and Labor*, pt. 2. 77th Cong., 2nd sess., no. 1150. Washington, D.C.: Government Printing Office, 1942.

―――. "Employers Associations and Their Labor Policies in California's Industrialized Agriculture." *Violations of Free Speech and the Rights of Labor: Report of the Committee on Education and Labor*, pt. 4. 77th Cong., 2nd sess. Washington, D.C.: Government Printing Office, 1942.

―――. "A Study of Labor Policies of Employers Associations in the Los Angeles Area, 1935–39." *Violations of Free Speech and the Rights of Labor: Report of the Committee on Education and Labor*, pt. 6. 78th Cong., 1st sess. Washington, D.C.: Government Printing Office, 1942.

―――. "Employers Associations and Collective Bargaining in California." *Report of the Committee on Education and Labor, Subcommittee Investigating Violations of Free Speech and the Rights of Labor*. 78th Cong., 2nd sess. Washington, D.C.: Government Printing Office, 1944.

NEWSPAPERS

Labor Herald

Labor Heritage

Los Angeles Citizen

Los Angeles Daily News

Los Angeles Examiner

Los Angeles Times

New York Times

Regeneración

San Francisco Chronicle

San Pedro Pilot

ORAL HISTORIES

Peter ("Pete") Grassi. ILWU Local 13 Oral History Project. Urban Archives Center, Oviatt Library, California State University, Northridge.

Cornelius J. Haggerty. Earl Warren Oral History Project. Bancroft Library, University of California, Berkeley.

The following oral histories are held in the Department of Special Collections (Center for Oral History Research), Charles E. Young Research Library, University of California, Los Angeles:

John Allard

Thomas Bradley

Ben Dobbs

George H. Dunne

Dorothy Healey

Robert W. Kenny

Wyndham Mortimer

Paul Schrade

William Seligman

INDEX

Page numbers in italics indicate figures, maps, and tables.

Estrada, William David, 67

ethno-racial characteristics: Chicago and, 327–28; Detroit and, 327–29; employment and, 245–46, 276–77; high-tech industries and, 319; labor movement's recovery and, 324, 327; minority workers and, *243;* political elections and, 240; racism and, 239–40; separatism and, 256–58, 392n83, 392n85; service industries and, 268, 292; urban renewal projects and, 232; working class and, 8, 14, 37–38, 115–16, 245–46, 327–30. *See also* multiethnic communities; *specific groups*

European immigrants: Americanization movement and, 69; Boyle Heights District and, 225; in Chicago, 329; Democratic Party and, 126; in Detroit, 329; female unionists and, *133,* 133–35; labor movements in East and, 151–52; population statistics and, 17, 410n43; poverty and, 17; racism and, 91. *See also* immigrants; *specific immigrant groups*

"exceptionalism" thesis, 7, 321

Executive Order 8802, 184, 194, 196

Fair Employment Practices Act (1959), 222, 224, 244

Fair Employment Practices Commission (FEPC): 180, 183, 186, 374n18. *See also* California Fair Employment Practices Commission

Fair Labor Standards Act (1938), 173

Faludi, Susan, 272

Federal Emergency Relief Administration, 110, 118

federal government: aircraft industry strike and, 197–99; anti-unionism limitations and, 172–74; civil rights and, 262; labor movement pledge against strikes and, 199; labor policy during World War II and, 196–99, 378n85; power under New Deal for, 140, 143–44. *See also* United States; *specific committees, leaders, and legislation*

Federated Motion Picture Crafts (FMPC), 170

felt industry, 36

female unionists: CIO leadership and, 147; CLC and, 51; consciousness raising and, 260–61; European immigrants as, *133,* 133–35; garment manufacturing industry and, 22–23, 132–35; health care and, 308; ILGWU and, 24, 133, 307–8; labor movement's recovery and, 307–8; LAPD's alliance with anti-union industries and, 44–45; leadership positions and, 308–9; men's ambivalence about, 22–23,

192, 195, 203, 309, 376n64; SEIU and, 308–9; Socialists and, 23, 48. *See also* gender roles and inequality; unions and unionism; women

female workers: AFL and, 194; African Americans and, 185, 195, 204, 377n67; aircraft industry and, 4, 175, 188–89, 190, 196, 204, 370n28; blue-collar, 248; cannery workers strike in Boyle Heights and, 138–40, *139;* consciousness raising and, 132–35, *133,* 139–40, 260–61; dangers in working conditions and, 190; domestic workers and, 189, 204, 244; double standard and, 191; dual labor market and, 376n64; electronics industry and, 268, 279, 280–81, 282; garment manufacturing industry and, 132–35; income for, 23–24, 277; in manufacturing industries, 90; men's ambivalence about, 194, 204, 273, 376n64; minority populations and, 195–96, 204; national loyalty and, 188–89, 196; oil industry and, 97; open shop system criticism by, 22–24; racism against African Americans and, 185; restructuring of labor market and, 268; service industry strikes and, 28, 74; sexual harassment and, 190, 376n54; sexual promiscuity and, 190; shipbuilding industry and, 188, 190, 191; Signal Hill community and, 95; South Gate and, 90; UAW and, 194; unionism and, 194, 300–301; whites and, 188, 192, 194, 195–96, 204; during World War II, 176, 185, 188–93, 194–96, 376n54. *See also* gender roles and inequality; women; *specific ethnic groups and nationalities*

feminism, 204, 240. *See also* gender roles and inequality

FEPC. *See* Fair Employment Practices Commission

Fiesta de Los Angeles, 21, 33

Filipino workers, 15, 111, 185, 279, 282, 304–5, 307, 318, 355n85

finance. *See* economics

"fink hall" (Sea Service Employment Bureau), 81, 140

Firestone Tire and Rubber factory, 90, 144–45, 163

Fitts, Buron, 132, 142, 160, 163

Fix, Michael, 292

Flamming, Douglas, 328

Flint, Michigan, strike in 1936–1937, 129, 153

Flores, Armando, 136–38

Flores Magón, Ricardo and Enrique. *See* Magón brothers and Magonistas

Fogelson, Robert, 325

Long Beach: aircraft industry, 175, 272, 275; automobile industry, 199; conservative workers and, 97, 353n63; demographics, 277; harbor, 94, 176, 178, 183, 271, 287, 327; homeownership, 216; naval shipyard, 183, 271; nonunion workers, 288; oil industry, 94, 97, 98, 99, 128, 163–66, 352n53; shipbuilding industry, 178; union reforms and, 287; white flight to, 329

longshoremen: anarchists and, 72; class consciousness and, 71–72; consciousness raising and, 140–43; CP and, 127; "fink hall" and, 81, 140; immigrants as, 81; industrial unionism and, 145; mechanization and, 290; minority workers and, 247–48; M&M and, 79, 290, 349n81; multiethnic workers and, 72, 81, 141, 365n37; police violence and, 141–42, 325; race relations among, 247; San Francisco and, 79, 141–43, 247; shape-up system and, 71, 79, 326; whites and, 247; Wobblies and, 70–72, 79–82, 349n81. *See also specific unions*

longshoremen in San Pedro, 62–63, 70–72; automated production and, 290–91; CP and, 127; dangers in working conditions and, 290; federal government intervention in strikes in, 140, 143–44; and fragmented character of L.A., effect on strikes, 326–27; racism and, 185, 193–94; San Pedro Harbor and, 5, 5, 45–46, 80; strike in 1916, 79–82, 98, 349n81; strike in 1934, 140–43, 194; UCRA and, 117; Wobblies and, 70–72, 79–82, 349n81. *See also* longshoremen; *specific unions*

López, Frank, 152

Los Angeles: areas of, 3–4, 5; central manufacturing district and, 4–5, 5, 83; dystopian view of, 7–8; fragmented character of, 325–27; industrial geography in, 3–6, 5, 83–84, 234, 279, 326, 327; industrialization and, 8, 324; industrial parks and, 5, 6; industries and locations in, 3–4, 5; multiethnic communities and, 83; population statistics and, 170; San Francisco compared with, 17, 17, 335n20; "sunshine" view of, 7–8; workforce in, 16–17, 17. *See also* myths of Southern California; *specific city departments and organizations*

Los Angeles Alliance for a New Economy (LAANE), 303–4

Los Angeles Board of Education, 252

Los Angeles Building Trades Council, 88, 155, 169, 249. *See also* Building Trades Council

Los Angeles Car Wash Campaign, 318

Los Angeles Central Labor Council (CLC): CIO and, 145–46; CP and, 149; Democratic Party support from, 122, 123; double standard and, 191; education system and, 42; female teachers and, 51; ILGWU and, 156; industrial unionism and, 145; LAPD's alliance with anti-union industries and, 45; leadership and, 22, 58; longshoremen strikes and, 79, 142; *Los Angeles Times* building bombing and, 39–40; membership statistics and, 57, 58; Mexican Americans' relation with whites, 34; minority employment and, 50; NIRA and, 131; printers strike and, 26; Progressive movement and, 47–49; Republican Party support from, 122; Sinclair and, 122. *See also* AFL

Los Angeles Chamber of Commerce (LACC): business' attacks on labor movement and, 284; Cold War's effects on, 228–31; consciousness raising and, 137; criminal syndicalist law and, 78; labor movement's losses and, 47–49; open shop system and, 157, 173–74; propaganda about L.A. and, 7, 14, 104; racism and, 254; strikebreakers and, 44

Los Angeles City Council, 28, 31–32, 41–43, 47–49, 199–200

Los Angeles City Housing Authority (CHA), 178–79, 182, 230, 232–33

Los Angeles Coalition Against Plant Closings (LACAPS), 269

Los Angeles Committee to Protect the Foreign-Born (LACPFB), 223

Los Angeles Country Aerospace Task Force report in 1992, 273

Los Angeles County Board of Supervisors, 112, 142, 305, 307

Los Angeles County Federation of Labor (LACFL): blue-collar workers and, 319; civil rights and, 246; CTW and, 317; interracial political alliance with liberal Jewish community and, 264; labor-Latino alliance and, 309–13, 311, 320; light manufacturing industries and, 319; membership and, 304; racism and, 254; social idealism loss and, 293; UFW and, 259; undocumented immigrant legislation and, 292–93. *See also specific unions*

Los Angeles Examiner, 52, 54, 204

Los Angeles Express, 49

Los Angeles Human Relations Commission in 1979, 292

Los Angeles Manufacturing Action Project (LAMAP), 319

Los Angeles Plaza, 19, 21, 48, 63, 112–13, 114, 124–25, 148, 235

Los Angeles Police Department (LAPD): anti-
immigrant movement and, 69–70; anti-union
industries' alliance with, 44–46, 56, 57, 82,
141, 142, 165; brutality and harassment by,
47–48, 181, 238, 246, 263, 293, 327, 394n109;
corruption and, 64, 111, 115, 123, 142, 165,
322; free speech rights and, 48, 70; minority leaders in, 264, 394n109; PLM protests
and, 69; race riots in 1965 and, 238–39, 238–
40, 239
Los Angeles Railway (LARY), 183, 200
Los Angeles Record, 31–32, 41, 45, 56
Los Angeles River, 4, 59, 124, 225
Los Angeles Times, 23–28, 39, 41, 403, 413, 343, 641.
See also Otis, Harrison Gray
low-wage employment, 268
lumber handlers, 79, 80
Lummis, Charles, 20

M&M. *See* Merchants and Manufacturers
Association
Magón brothers and Magonistas, 62–69, 65, 233,
344nn4,6, 346n34
male unionists: and ambivalence about female
unionists, 22–23, 192, 195, 203, 309, 376n64;
Socialist Party and, 27, 29, 34; white male
leaders and, 135, 147, 150, 248–49, 289. *See
also* gender roles and inequality; men and
male workers; unions and unionism
Mann, Eric, 270–71
manufacturing industries: AFL and CIO rivalry
and, 163; central manufacturing district and,
4–5; the East and, 129; export of, 267–68,
269; female workers and, 90; industrialization and, 8, 65–66, 324; in Midwest, 8;
myths of Southern California and, 16–17, 17,
335n20; plant closings and, 268–71, 275; in
San Francisco, 17, 17, 335n20; service industries as complementary to, 401n96; Watts
and, 91; World War II and, 176, 177, 178. *See
also specific manufacturing industries*
maquiladoras, 4, 280–81. *See also* electronics
industry
Marine Transport Workers Industrial Union
(MTWIU), 80
Martí, José, 325
MASE (Mutual Alliance of Studio Employees), 87
mass production industries, 83, 132, 150–51, 210.
See also specific industries
McAleer, Owen, 28, 32, 41
McDonnell Douglas company, 246, 271–73, 275

McNamara, James B., 39, 40, 52–54, 56–59
McNamara, John J., 39, 40, 52–54, 56–59, 89
McWilliams, Carey, vi, 7, 100, 119, 121, 230,
335n20
Meany, George, 218, 286
Mechanization and Modernization Agreement
(1960), 290
Medina, Eliseo, 311–12
men and male workers: AFL focus on white
craftsmen and, 90, 133–34, 143, 145, 155;
and ambivalence about female workers, 194,
204, 273, 376n64; income and, 275–77, 292;
manhood and, 186–88, 272–73, 274; masculine traditions and, 96, 97; moral reform
movement and, 31–33, 42–43. *See also* gender
roles and inequality; *specific ethnic groups and
nationalities*
Merchants and Manufacturers Association
(M&M), 7, 158; Associated Farmers and, 111;
citrus-growing industry and, 27, 101; civil
rights and, 73; company unions and, 131, 155,
173; construction industries and, 103; criminal syndicalist law and, 78; internal conflicts
in labor movement and, 72; LAPD's alliance
with anti-union industries, 44–46, 79,
349n81; longshoremen and, 79, 290, 349n81;
NAM and, 29; national loyalty and, 103; New
Deal and, 157; NIRA and, 131, 157; NLRB
ruling against, 174; NWLB's civil rights and,
73; open shop system criticism and, 22, 82;
PE freight cars and, 41; printers' strike and,
57; shipping industry and, 72, 140–41
Merriam, Frank, 121, 122
Metal Trades Council of San Francisco, 57
metalworking industry, 22, 56–58, 74
Mexican Communist Party, 223
Mexican Federal Union, 33–35
Mexican Revolution, 15, 24, 62–69, 83, 223, 233,
323, 329–30, 344n4
Mexicans and Mexican Americans: African
Americans' relations with, 254, 256, 290,
312, 313, 400n91; agricultural industry and,
111; Americanization movement and, 42,
69–70; anti-immigration issue and, 296,
402n122; anti-Semitism and, 135; CIO and,
147, 374n18; citrus-growing industry and,
100, 355n85; civil rights and, 138, 148, 217,
241, 256–57, 374n18; class conflicts and,
240; consciousness raising, 132–35, 133, 137,
301–2; CP and, 113; cross-border solidarity and, 35; deportation and, 111–12, 223–24,
357n17; Depression and, 111–12; educa-

and, 124; tracklayers and, 91; during World
War II and, 180–82, 186, 188, 196, 202,
374n18. *See also* racism and race relations
racism and race relations, 2–3; anti-Communism and, 323; Chicago and, 91; civil rights
for African Americans and, 238–41; Cold
War's effects on, 232–34, *233;* employment
and, 240–41; ethno-racial characteristic and,
239–40; homeownership and, 215, 244, 252;
housing and, 240–41, 251, 253–56, *255;* manhood and womanhood as racialized, 186–88;
school segregation and, 240–41, 251–53, 256,
265; undocumented immigrants and, 291–92,
294, 401n100. *See also* racism against African
Americans; racism against Asian Americans;
racism against Mexican Americans
railroad companies, 22, 333n6. *See also specific
companies*
Randolph, A. Philip, 147, 183–84
Reagan, Ronald, 213, 234, 268, 270, 275, 283–
85, 288, 294, 381n17
real estate industry: African American discrimination and, 124, 253–56, *255,* 361n74; Japanese American discrimination case and, 205;
lobbies and, 231. *See also* homeownership;
private housing; public housing
red-baiting and red scare: AFL and, 166, 171,
198, 200, 378n89; Chicago and, 323; CIO
and AFL rivalry and, 166; Cold War's
effects and, 209, 210–14, *213,* 217–21, 318n9,
381n17, 383n40; against Democratic Party,
122; "exceptionalism" thesis and, 323; Hollywood film industry and, 323; labor movement
and, 26–27, 41, 54, 122, 221, 282n50; politics
and, 217–21, 383n40; Socialist Party and, 54.
See also anti-Communism; Cold War
Red Car. *See* Pacific Electric (PE) Railway
Red Cross, 109–10
Reddin, Tom, 246
red scare. *See* red-baiting and red scare
red squad in LAPD, 111, 115, 123, 142, 164–65.
See also Los Angeles Police Department
Regeneración (newspaper), 64, 68, 344n4
relief aid, *109,* 109–10, *112,* 114–16, 118, 276,
*357*n18
Relief Works Protection Association, 115
religious beliefs and religions: clergy alliances
and, 301, 303; immigrants and, 93–94; Prot-
estantism and, 31, 42, 69, 83, 92, 303
rental housing, 102, 181, 224, 228, 238, 240–41,
251, 253–56, *255. See also* homeownership;
housing; private housing

rent control, 224, 228, 230
Republican Party: AFL support for, 122; blue-
collar workers and, 235–36; businesses'
attacks on labor movement and, 285; demographics and, 235; free-market system and,
283; fusion tactic against Socialist Party and,
55, 60; middle class and, 121; Midwest and,
55; presidential elections and, 217, 219; social
and political reform and, 126–27, 361n86;
working class and, 294
Reuther, Walter P., 214, 218–20
Rice, Owen T., 14
right-wing activists, 89, 110–11, 218, 231, 235.
See also left-wing activists; New Right
Rios, Tony, 147, 152, 226, *227*
Rittenhouse, Clay, 160
Rivera, Rosendo, 147, 242–43
Roberts, George B., 144–45
Roche, James, 45
Rodriguez, Gregory, 297
Rogin, Michael, 121, 123
Roosevelt, Franklin D., 116, 118, 126, 184, 196–
97, 201
"Rosie the Riveters," 4, 175, 188–90, *189,* 332n9.
See also aircraft industry
Roybal, Edward, 224–25, *227,* 227–32
rubber industry, 90, 104, 144–45, 151, 163
Rumford Fair Housing Act, 253–56
Russell, Clayton D., 185
Russian Revolution, 77, 323. *See also* Soviet
Union
rust belt, 267–68, 269
Ryan, Joe, 142–43

Sadlowski, Ed, 287, 399n82
Sailors Union of the Pacific, 72, 80
Salvadorans, 15, 277, 281, 302, 308, 309. *See also*
Central Americans
Sánchez, George, 302
San Fernando Valley: anti-Communism and,
323; anti-immigration issue and, 296; high-
tech industries and, 268; Hollywood film
industry and, 84–85; industrial geography
and, 4, *5;* maps and, *278;* minority workers
and, 275; New Right and, 253; Owens River
project and, 16, 29, 51–52; racism in housing and, 256; suburban politics of New Right
and, 234–35; whites and, 253, 263, 296–97,
323
San Francisco: anti-picketing laws and, 157–58;
closed shop and, 79; court's complicity with
open shop and, 322; criminal syndicalist law